Writer's Choice

COMPOSITION AND GRAMMAR

Case Studies: Writers at Work

Laurence Yep
Memoir Writer
Pages 4-9

Indira Freitas Johnson
Artist
Pages 254-259

Arthur Johnson
Historical Actor
Pages 142-147

Bill Kurtis
Television Journalist
Pages 42-47

Gary McLain (Eagle/Walking Turtle)
Travel Writer
Pages 190-195

Julia Alvarez
Novelist
Pages 100-105

Student Advisory Board

Alina Braica

Joshua Zapata

Nitida Wongthipkongka

Eliza Ali

Paul Roustan

Benjamin Rodriguez

Shanna Breckenfeld

Keianna Chatman

Trina Chu

Tashaunda Jackson

Faris Karadsheh

Marinel A. Marty

Writer's Choice

COMPOSITION AND GRAMMAR

Thomas Hart Benton, *Cradling Wheat*, 1938

Consulting Author for Composition
Jacqueline Jones Royster

Grammar Specialist
Mark Lester

Visual-Verbal Learning Specialists
Ligature, Inc.

GLENCOE

Macmillan/McGraw-Hill

New York, New York   Columbus, Ohio   Mission Hills, California   Peoria, Illinois

Front cover includes Alerej von Jawlensky, *Landscape near Oberstdorf.*

Back cover includes *The Greek Child of America* and ticket for a ship.

Send all inquiries to:
GLENCOE DIVISION
Macmillan/McGraw-Hill
15319 Chatsworth Street
P.O. Box 9609
Mission Hills, CA
91346-9609

ISBN 0-02-635759-3
(Student's Edition)
ISBN 0-02-635761-5
(Teacher's Wraparound
Edition)

Printed in the United States of America
2 3 4 5 6 7 8 9 10 AGH 96 95 94 93

Consulting Author for Composition

Jacqueline Jones Royster is Associate Professor of English and Director of the University Writing Center at The Ohio State University. She is also on the faculty at the Bread Loaf School of English, Middlebury, Vermont. Dr. Royster's professional interests, besides improving the teaching of writing, include literacy studies and black feminist literature.

As Consulting Author, Dr. Royster guided the development of focused, modular lessons to engage middle school students in the writing process. She contributed to the articulation of the contents and objectives across all three levels, 6–8. Dr. Royster also prepared extensive critiques of lessons and features from initial outlines through all stages of development. In addition, Dr. Royster advised on elements of the accompanying teaching material, with special attention to assessment.

Grammar Specialist

Mark Lester is Professor of English at Eastern Washington University. He formerly served as Chair of the Department of English as a Second Language, University of Hawaii. He is the author of *Grammar in the Classroom* (Macmillan, 1990) and of numerous professional books and articles.

As Grammar Specialist, Dr. Lester reviewed student's edition material from Part 2: Grammar, Usage, and Mechanics. He wrote the Grammar Hints that appear throughout this section. In addition, Dr. Lester contributed extensively to the *Teacher's Wraparound Edition* for Part 2.

Composition Advisers

Philip M. Anderson is Associate Professor in the Department of Secondary Education and Youth Services at Queens College, City University of New York, where he is also Director of the English Education Program.

Beverly Ann Chin is Professor of English at the University of Montana, where she is Director of Freshman Composition and Co-director of English Teacher Education. She is also Director of the Montana Writing Project.

Charleen Silva Delfino is District English Coordinator for the East Side Union High School District in San Jose, California. She is also Director of the Writing Project at San Jose University.

The advisers helped develop the tables of contents and determine pacing, emphasis, and activities appropriate for middle school students. They reviewed and commented on the manuscript for complete units.

Acknowledgments

Grateful acknowledgment is given authors, publishers, photographers, museums, and agents for permission to reprint the following copyrighted material. Every effort has been made to determine copyright owners. In case of omissions, the Publisher will make acknowledgments in future editions. *Continued on page 694*

Humanities Consultant

Ronne Hartfield is Executive Director of Museum Education at the Art Institute of Chicago. Dr. Hartfield consults widely and is a nationally known expert in the areas of urban arts and multicultural education.

As Humanities Consultant, Dr. Hartfield suggested and critiqued works of fine art and folk art, pointing out esthetic matters (mentioned in the *Teacher's Wraparound Edition*) and suggesting activities for engaging the student's attention.

Visual-Verbal Learning Specialists

Ligature, Inc., is an educational research and development company with offices in Chicago and Boston. Ligature is committed to developing educational materials that bring visual-verbal learning to the tradition of the written word.

As visual-verbal and curriculum specialists, Ligature collaborated on conceiving and implementing the pedagogy of Writer's Choice.

Educational Reviewers

The reviewers read and commented upon manuscripts during the writing process. They also critiqued early drafts of graphic organizers and page layouts.

Toni Elaine Allison
Meridian Middle School
Meridian, Idaho

Amy Burton
Sterling Middle School
Fairfax, Virginia

Mary Ann Evans-Patrick
University of Wisconsin, Oshkosh
Oshkosh, Wisconsin

Marie Hammerle
Oak Creek Elementary School
Cornville, Arizona

Randy Hanson
Mapplewood Middle School
Menasha, Wisconsin

Geraldine Jackson
Mountain Gap Middle School
Huntsville, Alabama

Jeanne Kruger
Blair Middle School
Norfolk, Virginia

Diana McNeil
Pillans Middle School
Mobile, Alabama

Linda Miller
Lake Travis Middle School
Austin, Texas

Nadine Mouser
St. Thomas More School
Houston, Texas

Roslyn Newman
Woodland Middle School
East Meadow, New York

Evelyn Niles
Boys and Girls High School
Brooklyn, New York

Janet E. Ring
Dundee School District 300
Carpentersville, Illinois

Kathleen Oldfield
Main Street School
Waterloo, New York

Student Advisory Board

The Student Advisory Board was formed in an effort to ensure student involvement in the development of *Writer's Choice*. The editors wish to thank members of the board for their enthusiasm and dedication to the project.

The editors also wish to thank the many student writers whose models appear in this book.

Thanks are also due to *Merlyn's Pen* and *Cricket* for cooperation in providing student models.

Writer's Choice

COMPOSITION AND GRAMMAR

Writer's Choice was written for you, the student writer. You're the writer in the title, and real students like you contributed to the materials you'll study. The book is organized into three main parts: (1) Composition; (2) Grammar, Usage, and Mechanics; and (3) Resources and Skills.

Part 1 Composition

The lessons in Composition are designed to give you help with specific writing tasks. You can use the units and lessons in order from beginning to end or select just the ones that help with your own writing needs.

vi

Part 2 Grammar, Usage, and Mechanics

In the unique Troubleshooter you'll learn to identify and correct the most common student writing problems. In later units you'll find plenty of practice to reinforce what you learn. A special unit, entitled Grammar Through Sentence Combining, will help you see the relationship between grammar and your writing.

Part 3 Resources and Skills

You can use these resources and skills not just in English class but wherever you need to communicate effectively. The tone and approach are user-friendly, with many opportunities to practice and apply the skills you learn.

Contents

Previewing Your Book *xviii*

Part 1 Composition

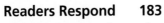
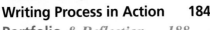

CONTENTS

Part 2 Grammar, Usage, and Mechanics

CONTENTS

CONTENTS

CONTENTS

CONTENTS

Part 3 Resources and Skills

Literature

Each literature selection is an extended example of the mode of writing taught in the unit.

Literature Models

Excerpts from outstanding works of fiction and nonfiction exemplify specific writing skills.

Workshop Literature

Workshops use excerpts to link grammar, usage, or mechanics to literature.

Case Studies

Each case study focuses on a real writer working on a real-life writing project. Come on backstage!

Fine Art •

Fine art—paintings, drawings, photos, and sculpture—is used to teach as well as to inspire.

Writer's Choice

COMPOSITION AND GRAMMAR

Welcome to Writer's Choice! Your writing and your choices are what this book is all about. This book allows you to choose quickly the lesson that will help you with a writing problem or task. You can use any lesson at any time—even if you haven't read earlier lessons. Now, take a few minutes to get to know each of the main parts of the book, which are illustrated on the upcoming pages.

Part 1 Composition

Unit Opener

Case Study

Part 2 Grammar, Usage, and Mechanics

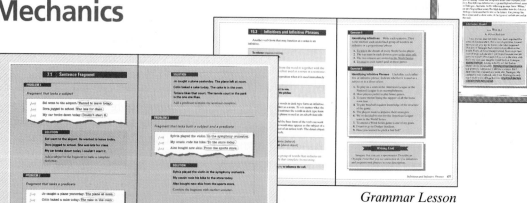

Troubleshooter

Grammar Lesson

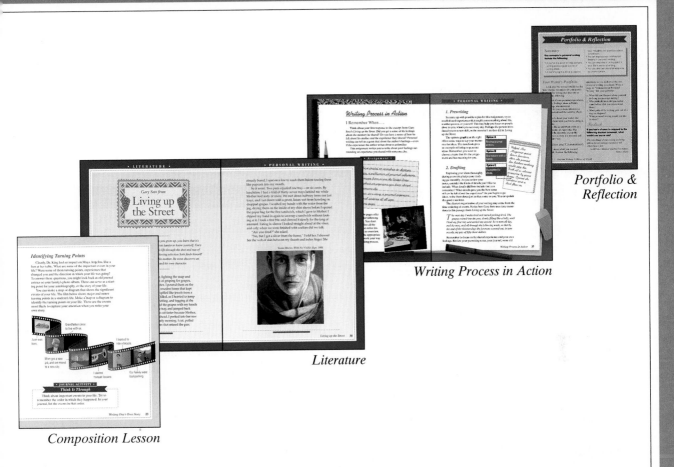

Portfolio & Reflection

Writing Process in Action

Literature

Composition Lesson

Part 3 Resources and Skills

Workshop

Unit Review

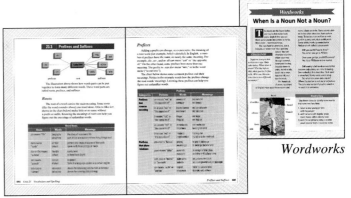

Resources and Skills Lesson

Wordworks

Inside Composition

The basic building block of the Composition units is the four-page lesson. Each lesson clearly focuses on a specific writing problem or task. You will always find clear and specific instruction, models of effective writing, and a variety of writing activities.

Student Models present writing by students like you to help you achieve your own writing goals.

Special Illustrations combine words with images to help you see ideas and master the skills of writing. We call these illustrations visual/verbals.

To Make Yourself Clear

Before you write about a process, gather information through research, observation, or interviews. List the steps of the process in chronological order. Then write your draft. Use transition words, such as *first, next,* and *later,* to connect the steps. The chart shows a plan one student followed to write the explanation that appears below.

Relating a Process	
Organizing Your Writing	**Example**
Topic	How to make a pizza
Audience	Friends
What the audience needs to know	The steps in making the pizza
Gathering information	Watch the video I taped. Read a pizza cookbook.
Listing steps	1. Spread dough. 2. Spread cheese. 3. Add vegetables. 4. Top with fresh tomatoes.

Student Model

The writer lists the four steps in chronological order.

First, spread the dough so that you have an inch-wide rim around the sides. The rim keeps the filling from leaking out while the pizza's cooking. Now it's time to put in the fillings. Place the cheese on the dough to keep it from getting soggy. Then add peppers, onions,

---

5.4   Writing About a Process

Perfect Pizza Dough in Four Easy Steps

How does he do it? He makes it look so easy. The chef whips the ingredients together and kneads the dough. He lets the dough rest so it can rise. Then it's time for the show stopper. He shapes the dough and flings it into the air. Then he catches it without a hitch.

Everyday life is full of processes. Explaining how to do them poses a challenge. Suppose that you want to explain how pizza dough is prepared—the steps leading up to all the flinging and catching. The diagram below breaks down the steps for you.

Making Pizza Dough in Four Steps			
Mix Ingredients	Knead Dough	Let Dough Rise	Shape Dough

To Do and to Understand

Knowing how to do something does not guarantee that you can easily share that knowledge with others. Some people find it more difficult to explain a step-by-step process than to actually do it. Fortunately, you can learn to write about a process so that others can understand. The instructions on the next page explain how to prepare chilies that are almost too hot to handle.

Writer's Choice Pages give you a choice of writing activities to help you apply what you have learned. You'll also find fine art or a special feature on using computers in writing.

• WRITER'S CHOICE •
Activities

Here are some activities to help you apply what you have learned.

1. Guided Assignment

The steps below explain the process for making a leaf print, but the steps are given in the wrong order. Read the steps, and arrange them in chronological order. Then use the steps to write a clear explanation of the process for your science teacher and classmates. Be sure you identify the process in your introduction and include transition words.

1. With the inked side facing up, put the leaf on a clean piece of paper. Tape a piece of rice paper over the leaf.
2. Let the leaf print dry.
3. Select a leaf with distinct veins.
4. Use a clean, dry paint roller to roll over the rice paper from top to bottom.
5. Carefully remove the rice paper from the leaf.
6. Place the leaf, vein side up, on a piece of paper.
7. Put a small amount of printer's ink on a smooth surface, such as glass.

2. Open Assignment

Select one of the following ordinary tasks or one of your own. Write a one-page process explanation for someone who knows little or nothing about the task.

- How to tie your shoes
- How to find a library book on making pizza

3. Cooperative Learning

In a small group brainstorm different kinds of foods you can make or can easily find out how to make. From the list of suggestions, have each member of the group sign up for a food to write a process explanation about. The group leader can record the suggestions and the assignments. Have each member draft a brief but clear step-by-step explanation of how to make the food. Individually read your explanations to the group and discuss how to make the explanations clearer and more informative. Ask a member of the group to assemble the final drafts into a "How to Make It" booklet.

COMPUTER OPTION

Writing About a Process **211**

Literature Models help you learn from the pros. You'll see how published authors have met the writing challenges you face.

Literature Model

Wearing rubber gloves is a wise precaution, especially when you are handling fresh hot chilies. Be careful not to touch your face or eyes while working with them.

To prepare chilies, first rinse them clean in *cold* water. (Hot water may make fumes rise from dried chilies, and even the fumes might irritate your nose and eyes.) Working under cold running water, pull out the stem of each chili and break or cut the chilies in half. Brush out the seeds with your fingers. In most cases the ribs inside are tiny, and can be left intact, but if they seem fleshy, cut them out with a small, sharp knife. Dried chilies should be torn into small pieces, covered with boiling water and soaked for at least 30 minutes before they are used. Fresh chilies may be used at once, or soaked in cold, salted water for an hour to remove some of the hotness.

Recipes: Latin American Cooking

The word "first" helps identify what step to begin with.

What are the steps in preparing fresh chilies?

To explain a process, choose a topic that you understand well and can research if necessary. Then identify your audience and what they may already know. Consider terms they'll understand and those you'll have to explain. You may have either of two purposes in explaining a process. You may be helping readers make or do something themselves, for example, how to make tacos. On the other hand, you may be explaining how something works or happens, such as how a Mexican chef makes tacos.

Writing Process Tips help you connect the skills you're learning to other stages of the writing process.

Grammar
Editing Tip

As you edit your essay, notice that some of your transitions can or do appear in adverb clauses. For information see pages

• JOURNAL ACTIVITY •
Think It Through

In your journal use a cluster map to explore topics for a process explanation. You might choose a hobby or another activity you enjoy. Circle your three best ideas.

Journal Activity, at the bottom of the second page of every lesson, gives you a chance to reflect and respond to the lesson material.

Writing About a Process **209**

Inside Grammar

This grammar handbook works for you, not the other way around. You'll learn how to find and fix errors in your writing. Two special sections—the Troubleshooter and the Workshops—help you expand your grammar skills.

The Troubleshooter presents in one place the solutions to the nine errors most frequently made by student writers. Your teacher may refer you to the Troubleshooter by marking errors in your writing with the abbreviations shown down the far left side of the page.

Unit 7 Troubleshooter

This Troubleshooter is designed to help you correct the common errors that your teacher is likely to mark. Use the Table of Contents below to locate quickly a lesson on a specific error. Your teacher may mark errors with the handwritten code in the left-hand column.

frag	7.1 Sentence Fragment	304
run-on	7.2 Run-on Sentence	306
agr	7.3 Lack of Subject-Verb Agreem	
tense	7.4 Incorrect Verb Tense or Form	
pro	7.5 Incorrect Use of Pronouns	
adj	7.6 Incorrect Use of Adjectives	
com	7.7 Incorrect Use of Commas	
apos	7.8 Incorrect Use of Apostrophe	
cap	7.9 Incorrect Capitalization	

7.1 Sentence Fragment

PROBLEM 1

Fragment that lacks a subject

frag	Sol went to the airport. Wanted to leave today.
frag	Dora jogged to school. Was late for class.
frag	My car broke down today. Couldn't start it.

SOLUTION

Sol went to the airport. He wanted to leave today.
Dora jogged to school. She was late for class.
My car broke down today. I couldn't start it.

Add a subject to the fragment to make a complete sentence.

PROBLEM 2

Fragment that lacks a predicate

frag	Jo caught a plane yesterday. The plane at noon.
frag	Colin baked a cake today. The cake in the oven.
frag	Tatiana likes that court. The tennis court in the park.

SOLUTION

Jo caught a plane yesterday. The plane left at noon.
Colin baked a cake today. The cake is in the oven.
Tatiana likes that court. The tennis court in the park is the one she likes.

Add a predicate to make the sentence complete.

PROBLEM 3

Fragment that lacks both a subject and a predicate

frag	Sylvia played the violin. In the symphony orchestra.
frag	My cousin rode his bike. To the store today.
frag	Alex bought new skis. From the sports store.

SOLUTION

Sylvia played the violin in the symphony orchestra.
My cousin rode his bike to the store today.
Alex bought new skis from the sports store.

Combine the fragment with another sentence.

Need More Help? *If you need more help avoiding sentence fragments, turn to pages 328–329.*

Each of the nine errors is explained in detail in the Troubleshooter.

For each common error, the Troubleshooter shows you the solution. If you need more help, the Troubleshooter also refers you to the appropriate lesson.

Grammar Lessons present instructions on the left-hand page and practical exercises on the right-hand page.

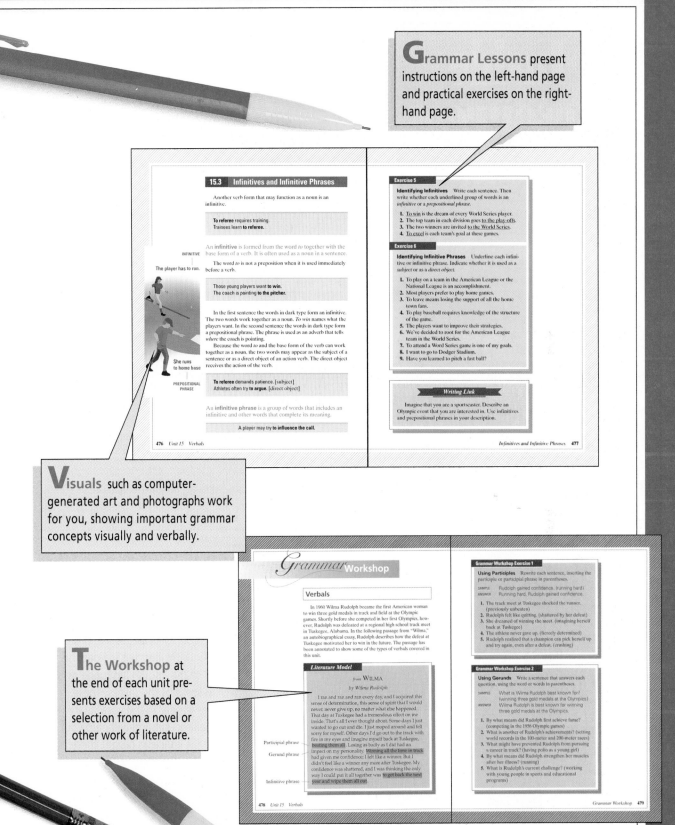

15.3 Infinitives and Infinitive Phrases

Another verb form that may function as a noun is an infinitive.

> To referee requires training.
> Trainees learn to referee.

An **infinitive** is formed from the word *to* together with the base form of a verb. It is often used as a noun in a sentence.

INFINITIVE

The player has to run.

The word *to* is not a preposition when it is used immediately before a verb.

> Those young players want to win.
> The coach is pointing to the pitcher.

She runs to home base

In the first sentence the words in dark type form an infinitive. The two words work together as a noun. *To win* names what the players want. In the second sentence the words in dark type form a prepositional phrase. The phrase is used as an adverb that tells *where* the coach is pointing.

Because the word *to* and the base form of the verb can work together as a noun, the two words may appear as the subject of a sentence or as a direct object of an action verb. The direct object receives the action of the verb.

PREPOSITIONAL PHRASE

> To referee demands patience. [subject]
> Athletes often try to argue. [direct object]

An **infinitive phrase** is a group of words that includes an infinitive and other words that complete its meaning.

> A player may try to influence the call.

476 Unit 15 Verbals

Visuals such as computer-generated art and photographs work for you, showing important grammar concepts visually and verbally.

Exercise 5

Identifying Infinitives Write each sentence. Then write whether each underlined group of words is an *infinitive* or a *prepositional phrase*.

1. <u>To win</u> is the dream of every World Series player.
2. The top team in each division goes <u>to the play-offs</u>.
3. The two winners are invited <u>to the World Series</u>.
4. <u>To excel</u> is each team's goal at these games.

Exercise 6

Identifying Infinitive Phrases Underline each infinitive or infinitive phrase. Indicate whether it is used as a *subject* or as a *direct object*.

1. To play on a team in the American League or the National League is an accomplishment.
2. Most players prefer to play home games.
3. To leave means losing the support of all the home town fans.
4. To play baseball requires knowledge of the structure of the game.
5. The players want to improve their strategies.
6. We've decided to root for the American League team in the World Series.
7. To attend a Word Series game is one of my goals.
8. I want to go to Dodger Stadium.
9. Have you learned to pitch a fast ball?

> #### Writing Link
>
> Imagine that you are a sportscaster. Describe an Olympic event that you are interested in. Use infinitives and prepositional phrases in your description.

Infinitives and Infinitive Phrases **477**

Grammar Workshop

Verbals

In 1960 Wilma Rudolph became the first American woman to win three gold medals in track and field at the Olympic games. Shortly before she competed in her first Olympics, however, Rudolph was defeated at a regional high school track meet in Tuskegee, Alabama. In the following passage from "Wilma," an autobiographical essay, Rudolph describes how the defeat at Tuskegee motivated her to win in the future. The passage has been annotated to show some of the types of verbals covered in this unit.

The Workshop at the end of each unit presents exercises based on a selection from a novel or other work of literature.

Literature Model

from WILMA

by Wilma Rudolph

I ran and ran and ran every day, and I acquired this sense of determination, this sense of spirit that I would never, never give up, no matter what else happened. That day at Tuskegee had a tremendous effect on me inside. That's all I ever thought about. Some days I just wanted to go out and die. I just moped around and felt sorry for myself. Other days I'd go out to the track with fire in my eyes and imagine myself back at Tuskegee, beating them all. Losing as badly as I did had an impact on my personality. Winning all the time in track had given me confidence; I felt like a winner. But I didn't feel like a winner any more after Tuskegee. My confidence was shattered, and I was thinking the only way I could put it all together was to get back the next year and wipe them all out.

Participial phrase

Gerund phrase

Infinitive phrase

478 Unit 15 Verbals

Grammar Workshop Exercise 1

Using Participles Rewrite each sentence, inserting the participle or participial phrase in parentheses.

SAMPLE Rudolph gained confidence. (running hard)
ANSWER Running hard, Rudolph gained confidence.

1. The track meet at Tuskegee shocked the runner. (previously unbeaten)
2. Rudolph felt like quitting. (shattered by her defeat)
3. She dreamed of winning the meet. (imagining herself back at Tuskegee)
4. The athlete never gave up. (fiercely determined)
5. Rudolph realized that a champion can pick herself up and try again, even after a defeat. (crushing)

Grammar Workshop Exercise 2

Using Gerunds Write a sentence that answers each question, using the word or words in parentheses.

SAMPLE What is Wilma Rudolph best known for? (winning three gold medals at the Olympics)
ANSWER Wilma Rudolph is best known for winning three gold medals at the Olympics.

1. By what means did Rudolph first achieve fame? (competing in the 1956 Olympic games)
2. What is another of Rudolph's achievements? (setting world records in the 100-meter and 200-meter races)
3. What might have prevented Rudolph from pursuing a career in track? (having polio as a young girl)
4. By what means did Rudolph strengthen her muscles after her illness? (running)
5. What is Rudolph's current challenge? (working with young people in sports and educational programs)

Grammar Workshop **479**

xxiii

Inside Resources

The lessons in this unit give you the skills necessary to prepare and deliver an oral report, take a test, use a dictionary, and find books in the library. Each lesson is complete, concise, and easy to use.

Graphics help you understand complex information at a glance.

23.3 Prefixes and Suffixes

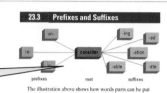

prefixes · root · suffixes

The illustration above shows how words parts can be put together to form many different words. These word parts are called roots, prefixes, and suffixes.

Roots

The root of a word carries the main meaning. Some roots (like the word *consider* above) can stand alone. Others (like *lect*, shown in the chart below) make little or no sense without a prefix or suffix. Knowing the meanings of roots can help you figure out the meanings of unfamiliar words.

Word Roots

Roots	Words	Meanings
bio means "life"	biography biosphere	the story of a person's life part of the atmosphere where living things exist
dent means "tooth"	dentist trident	person who treats diseases of the teeth spear with three prongs, or teeth
flex or *flec* means "to bend"	flexible reflect	easily bent to bend back (light)
lect means "speech"	lecture dialect	a speech form of a language spoken in a certain region
tele means "distant"	television telescope	device for receiving pictures from a distance device for viewing distant things

604 Unit 23 *Vocabulary and Spelling*

Prefixes

Adding a prefix can change, or even reverse, the meaning of a root word (for example, *belief—disbelief*). In English, a number of prefixes have the same, or nearly the same, meaning. For example, *dis-*, *un-*, and *in-* all can mean "not" or "the opposite of." On the other hand, some prefixes have more than one meaning. The prefix *in-*, can also mean "into," as in the word *incise* ("to cut into").

The chart below shows some common prefixes and their meanings. Notice in the example words how the prefixes change the root words' meanings. Learning these prefixes can help you figure out unfamiliar words.

Prefixes

Categories	Prefixes	Words	Meanings
Prefixes that reverse meaning	*un-* means "not" or "the opposite of"	unnatural unhappy	not natural not happy
	in- means "not" or "the opposite of"	inconsiderate intolerant	not considerate not tolerant
	il- means "not" or "the opposite of"	illegal illogical	not legal not logical
	im- means "not" or "the opposite of"	immoderate imbalance	not moderate lacking balance
	ir- means "not" or "the opposite of"	irregular irreplaceable	not regular not able to be replaced
Prefixes that show relations	*pre-* means "before"	prepay prearrange	to pay in advance to arrange beforehand
	post- means "after"	postdate postpone	to assign a later date to delay until a later time
	sub- means "below" or "beneath"	submarine subway	an underwater boat an underground way or passage
	co- means "with" or "partner"	copilot cooperate	relief or second pilot to work with others

Prefixes and Suffixes **605**

Wordworks

When Is a Noun Not a Noun?

The labels on the figure below are nouns that name body parts. English lets you put these same words into action as verbs. Here's how—from head to toe.

You can *head* a committee, *eye* a bargain, or *nose* a car into a parking space. You can *shoulder* a burden, *elbow* your way through a crowd, *hand* over the key, *knuckle* down to work, *thumb* a ride, *back* into a room, *foot* the bill, and *toe* the mark.

For hundreds of years, speakers of English have used these nouns and many others as verbs. Some words shifted in the other direction, from verb to noun. Today you can *walk* on a *walk*, *park* in a *park*, and *pitch* a wild *pitch*. Some shifts involve pronunciation. Notice which syllable you accent:

Will you *perMIT* me to drive?
Yes, when you get a *PERmit.*

Does your garden *proDUCE* carrots?
No, I buy *PROduce* at the market.

Still another shift involves nouns that became adjectives, as in the following: Sara unlocked the *steel* door. Tom wore a *straw* hat. Marty made *onion* soup.

So, when is a noun not a noun? When it's used as a verb or an adjective. The only way to identify such a word is to use it in a sentence.

CHALLENGE

Suppose you got this written message: Ship sails today. What does it mean? Put the before ship; then put the before sails. Why can this sentence have two different meanings?

head
nose
shoulder
hand
elbow
thumb
toe
foot

614

Double Duty

Use these clues to identify some words that have two functions.

1. *noun:* a very young person
   verb: to pamper
2. *verb:* to walk with regular steps
   noun: music with a steady beat
3. *verb:* throw pictures onto a screen
   noun: special work in science class

Wordworks pages like this one provide a light-hearted look at the origins of the English language as well as some of the quirks. These features appear in the vocabulary and spelling unit and will help you master the concepts taught there.

Part 1

Composition

The Morning After the Ice Storm

Outside my frosted window
The ground shines like metal.
Morning sunlight reflects o
The snow-covered rooftops and
Blinds me momentaril
Across the street m
Neighbor's ancient r tree
Glistens in the o bright
Light, its bra hes wearing
Sleeves of ice

The ice fr zes all sounds,
all movements.

Part 1 Composition

A Mirror of Myself

Paul Klee, *Musician*, 1937

Yep PIECES His Past TOGETHER

"I think writers take bits and pieces of the world around them—things they see, things they remember, feelings they felt—and start assembling them in ways to create a world you can walk through and inhabit."

Laurence Yep

Laurence Yep, award-winning writer of fantasies, went in a totally new direction when he decided to write *The Lost Garden*. This personal story, or memoir, of growing up in San Francisco challenged him to piece together his past. He began writing the book shortly after his father's death. "In a way, *The Lost Garden* was therapy," Yep explains. "It was my way to go back to these various places I used to go to with my father, and in some cases I tried to do it physically, but most of the time it was in my imagination and in my memory."

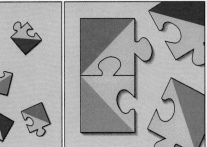

Writing a Memoir

1. Gathering Memories   **2.** Stepping Back   **3.** Assembling the Pieces   **4.** Testing the Fit

FOCUS

The process of writing a memoir can help you look back and rethink your past.

1 Gathering Memories

People make memories by living; writers re-create memories by writing. To write a memoir, a writer must use senses other than sight to evoke, or call up, memories. "The layer of memory that is closest to the brain is not a layer of visual memories; it's the memory of smells. That's why a smell is more evocative than any visual detail," Yep explains.

Yep used memories of smells to help him mentally reconstruct his family's grocery store. The smell of crumbling plaster and wall materials brought back the hot summer afternoons he spent in a place that no longer exists. Smells brought back sights as one memory led to another.

"From there I drew a map of the whole store, as best I could, and as I did that, I started remembering certain corners of the store. I don't know if I put this in the description of the store, but we had three bottles of mango chut-ney that

▼ *Specific details— such as the jars of mango chutney in the Yep family's store— are powerful elements in a memoir.*

Photos of the Pearl Apartments, where Yep lived as a boy, and the family store in San Francisco helped Yep when he was gathering memories.

we had inherited from the former owner, and we never sold them," Yep recalls.

Photographs can also be helpful when gathering memories. During the writing of *The Lost Garden,* Yep kept several photographs of family members in front of him on his desk.

2 Stepping Back

Daily events may seem to be great material for memoir writing. But simply recalling experiences isn't enough. As Yep explains, "Really, the best writing is bringing out the specialness of ordinary things." When writing a memoir, a writer observes his or her own life from a distance. By stepping back, the writer is able to gain a new understanding of past events.

"People think that, because they've lived something, they actually understand it, when that's not true," says Yep. "What they've done is experience it, but understanding is quite another matter—it's the next step."

Yep explains, "What it requires, to understand something, is actually to step away from that experience, so you can look at things more objectively, and that's also one of the steps in writing."

INTERFACE *You are gathering ideas in order to write your memoir. Make a list of your earliest sensory memories. What sounds do you remember? What smells? Sights?*

▲ *Yep's memoir* The Lost Garden *includes many photos from his life.*

3 Assembling the Pieces

Memoir writing can provide a writer with a map of the past. Yep's idea of writing as puzzle solving can help a writer see what to do when the pieces just don't fit. How does a writer solve that problem? Solving problems is the real fun of working puzzles, but it's frustrating when the puzzle pieces don't easily fit together.

In his writing Yep often begins with a memory, such as a scene, or even a name. He makes an inforrnal outline, which he uses as a guide. When problems arise, he accepts the fact that he may have to go back and start again.

As he says, "You realize that you've got to redesign the puzzle, that an outline is only a scaffolding inside of which you've got to build a ship. And sometimes you get the ship almost built, and you realize that this darned thing isn't going to float, and so you have to tear it down, and bring it down to the keel, and begin again."

Whether a writer solves puzzles or builds boats when writing, he or she should not be afraid to try something that might not work.

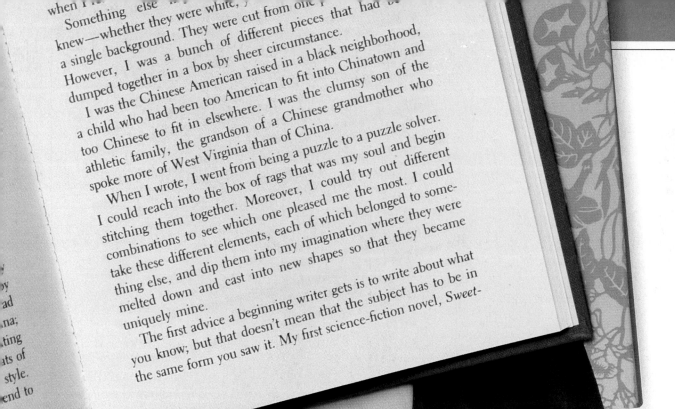

when I...
Something else...
knew—whether they were white, ...
a single background. They were cut from one ...
However, I was a bunch of different pieces that had b...
dumped together in a box by sheer circumstance.

I was the Chinese American raised in a black neighborhood, a child who had been too American to fit into Chinatown and too Chinese to fit in elsewhere. I was the clumsy son of the athletic family, the grandson of a Chinese grandmother who spoke more of West Virginia than of China.

When I wrote, I went from being a puzzle to a puzzle solver. I could reach into the box of rags that was my soul and begin stitching them together. Moreover, I could try out different combinations to see which one pleased me the most. I could take these different elements, each of which belonged to something else, and dip them into my imagination where they were melted down and cast into new shapes so that they became uniquely mine.

The first advice a beginning writer gets is to write about what you know; but that doesn't mean that the subject has to be in the same form you saw it. My first science-fiction novel, Sweet-

4 Testing the Fit

Writing allowed Yep, while growing up, to try out different ideas on paper.

The first question raised about a finished piece of writing is How good is it? What is good writing? Since a memoir reflects a person's own experiences, thoughts, and actions, who is to decide if it's good?

Yep works to achieve certain qualities in his work. One quality is authenticity, the characteristic of being real or true. By asking friends or relatives for their feedback, a writer can see how well his or her point of view has been communicated. But, finally, the writing is whatever the writer wants it to be.

"Writing is sort of a balanced view of things," he explains. Although his concerns for authenticity and balance suggest the writer's responsibilities to others, Yep also writes to please himself. He says, "You have to write for yourself. Writing is a way of exploring other selves and other worlds inside yourself. I think it can be very satisfying, whether you get a good mark on it or not."

ON ASSIGNMENT

1. Nonfiction Writing

Write about someone or something you have lost. It may be a friend who moved away, a relative who died, a place that changed, or a rearrangement of your family structure.

- Use as many senses as possible to open up the memory and your description.

- Try making maps or looking at photographs or other souvenirs of the experience.

- Consider other people who were affected by this loss. How did their reactions compare with your own?

2. About Literature

Write a brief response to an excerpt from Laurence Yep's *The Lost Garden*.

- How does Yep relate his being an outsider to his becoming a writer?

- What do you learn from Yep's experiences?

3. Cooperative Learning

Write a detailed account of something that is part of your everyday experience. The account may be about your way home from school, your lunch, the games you play, your elbows, or whatever. Describe your subject in a way that shows it as an important part of your life.

- Prewrite by listing qualities of the subject (for example, the rough skin on your elbows). Read your list to your group. Use their reactions to decide which details to use in bringing out the "specialness" of this everyday thing.

- Exchange copies of your first draft. Each member should write at least two well-developed comments on each manuscript. The comments might be about details or the overall piece of writing.

- Meet as a group. Each writer reads his or her work aloud. Each member explains his or her written comments to the group.

Case Study: Memoir **9**

Spreading the News

You can't wait to tell them. It's such great news. You grab the phone and call a friend. "I have a brand-new baby sister!" you brag. In a brief note you tell another friend how excited you are about your new sister. These are personal thoughts and feelings, and sometimes you want to share them with friends or family. At other times you may want to keep your thoughts private, but you may still want to write about them.

Getting Personal

Notes to yourself or letters to friends and family are examples of personal writing. A private journal—a book for your most personal thoughts and feelings—is one of the best places for personal writing. What you write is only for you. A classroom journal is another place for personal writing. You can write about private thoughts and feelings, but a classroom journal is also a resource for writing assignments.

When you share personal writing, it is usually with someone you know well—your aunt, your best friend, maybe your classmates. Sometimes you share personal writing with your teachers. And sometimes you write just for yourself. Personal writing is personal because you know your audience so well.

You can include more than just your writing in a journal. You might add photographs, magazine clippings, drawings, or even doodles.

Notice the photograph Lonnel sent with the following letter to his sister.

Dear Tamika,

It's a really nice day here at Bowen Lake. It's almost noon, and the woods and the lake are warm in the sun. I'm sitting on a rock on the top of a kind of hill—as much like a hill as anything they have around here. I haven't seen anyone for over an hour. Earlier two people in a canoe drifted by. They were far away, and I could hardly see them. I could hear their voices, though. It's quiet now. There's a kind of magic in being all alone with nature.

How's the family? Is Jason back from training camp? What's Mom's job like now that she's back at work? Send me news!

Your brother,
Lonnel

• JOURNAL ACTIVITY •
Think It Through

Think about a photo you'd like to include in a letter to a friend. Why would you choose this photo? Why is it important to you?

Jot It Down in a Journal

Your personal thoughts can be recorded in a journal. Writing in a journal can help you explore and remember these thoughts without worrying about what anyone else thinks. The journal excerpt below was written by author Louisa May Alcott as a girl.

Her writing here sounds like a conversation with a close friend.

Do you think this writing could appear in a letter to a friend? Why?

Literature Model

I am in the garret with my papers round me, and a pile of apples to eat while I write my journal, plan stories, and enjoy the patter of rain on the roof, in peace and quiet. . . . Being behind-hand, as usual, I'll make note of the main events up to date, for I don't waste ink in poetry and pages of rubbish now. I've begun to *live*, and have no time for sentimental musing. . . ."

Norma Johnston, *Louisa May:*
The World and Works of Louisa May Alcott

Once you've begun your journal, plan a time for writing in it. Write your plan in your journal. You'll get more out of a journal if you can write in it regularly. You may even enjoy rereading your earlier journal entries. Journal entries will help you remember where you've been and what you might like to share with a friend.

FLORIDA

Dear Wai-Ming,
Florida is great! My cousin David wants to meet you when he visits us in July. The weather's been fine except for Wednesday when it rained. Aunt Sandra drove us into town, though.

Wai-Ming Chou
538 Bedford Ave.
Columbus, Ohio
43212

April 3
I'm really enjoying our visit to Aunt Sandra's. My cousins have all changed — David is almost as tall as I am.
I didn't think it would be so different down here: palm trees, amazing plants and insects, blue-green ocean — and warm sand everywhere!
It's raining today, so Aunt Sandra drove us into town. We had lunch at an old-fashioned diner.

April 4
The sun's out again, and it's warm. Lee says they practically live on the beach when the weather is this nice. The rest of us have to go to school.
We rented bicycles today and rode up the coast. Along one stretch of beach there's a bike path for cyclists and joggers. Dave said he thought he saw dolphins, but no one else saw them.

April 5
Went back to the beach. David's friend Chris came with us, and we

Activities

Artist unknown, Pompeii, *Portrait of a young woman,* first century A.D.

Here are some activities to help you apply what you have learned.

1. Guided Assignment

Write an entry in your journal. You might begin by using the following steps as a guide:

- Write a letter to yourself. Explore what's on your mind. Put your letter in a self-addressed stamped envelope, and mail it to yourself a week later.

- Freewrite about your feelings and thoughts. You might listen to some favorite music while you write.

> **PURPOSE** Self-discovery
> **AUDIENCE** Yourself
> **LENGTH** 1–2 pages

2. Open Assignment

Each example of personal writing in this lesson includes the writer's observations of a setting. Write about a familiar place or one of the settings listed below. Write at least one page describing your ideas and feelings about the setting. If you have a photograph of yourself in the setting, use it to get started. Make a copy of the photograph to keep with this writing.

- the sun setting on a lake
- rain pounding on slick pavement
- trees rippling in a gusty wind
- a rainbow arching above a city skyline

3. Social Studies

The image above is from a wall painting found in the ruins of the ancient city of Pompeii. The city and its people were smothered during the sudden eruption of Mount Vesuvius in A.D. 79. Although thousands died, the city itself was preserved for centuries under layers of volcanic ash.

Write your reactions to the person pictured here.

The Sky's the Limit

Floating in space, you see below you the blue planet, Earth. You can't believe your eyes. You've got to get back to your spaceship and record your observations and questions.

Learning is a kind of exploration, too. Just as astronauts record their observations and findings in space, you can record your explorations as a learner. You can keep a learning log, such as the one below, to help you make sense of your schoolwork. It can contain information on any subject, from the Constitution to constellations.

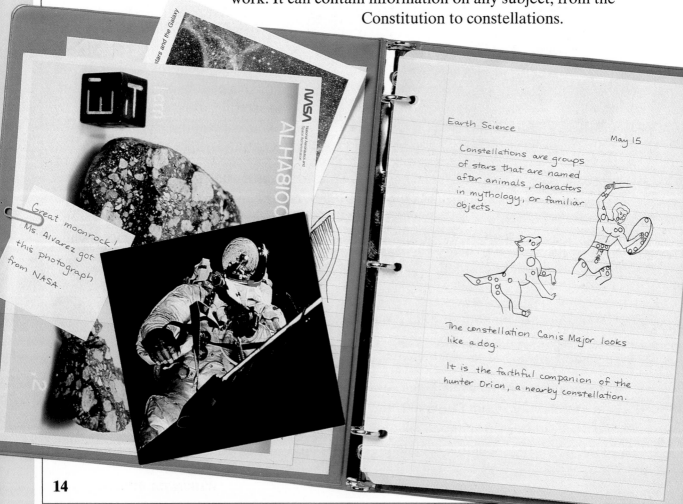

Great moonrock! Ms. Alvarez got this photograph from NASA.

Earth Science   May 15

Constellations are groups of stars that are named after animals, characters in mythology, or familiar objects.

The constellation Canis Major looks like a dog.

It is the faithful companion of the hunter Orion, a nearby constellation.

The Thinking Place

A learning log is a form of personal writing. It's for you. It will help you make your own ideas clearer. Also, you'll become more involved in your learning and more aware of the progress you're making. A learning log isn't simply for notes from your classes. It's a place for you to think about what you're learning in all your classes. After reading a passage in your textbook, for example, you can record your questions and thoughts in your learning log. Perhaps you'll raise these questions during your next class discussion. The chart below shows some kinds of entries you might put in your log. The kind of entry depends on your purpose in writing the entry. The goal is to make the information make sense to *you*.

Keeping a Learning Log	
Purpose	**Entry**
Summarize content.	Very hot stars are blue-white; cooler stars are orange or red.
Identify main ideas.	Sun spots are dark areas on the sun's surface that are cooler than surrounding areas.
Define problems, and ask questions.	I'm still not clear why our sun is called an average star.
Evaluate schoolwork.	The information on planets seemed easier than that on stars (because of the unit review?).

• JOURNAL ACTIVITY •
Try It Out

What questions do you have about something you're learning now? Begin a learning log by writing down one or two of these questions.

Write and Think

Writing about a subject you find difficult can help you get a better grasp of the material. The student who wrote the notes and log below had some questions about a textbook section on the exploration of Mars. After a class discussion of this topic, she reread the textbook passage and looked over her notes. Then she used her learning log to rewrite the passage in her own words.

Scientists are currently developing plans to further explore Mars. Because the distance between Earth and Mars is many millions of kilometers, it could take about three years to get to Mars and back. Because of the long duration of the flight, astronauts would face much more danger than they do in space shuttle missions.

...the near-zero gravity in ou...

How does the question help the student focus on things to learn?

Distance to Mars—
many millions of
kilometers
Length of Mars trip—
maybe three years
Danger—lowered
calcium in bones due
to near-zero gravity;
weak bones might
break once astronauts
land on Mars or
return to Earth

What are some of the problems astronauts will face in exploring Mars?

One of the main problems is the length of the flight. Mars and Earth are many millions of kilometers apart. Traveling to the planet and back could take about three years. On the flight, astronauts' bones will lose calcium because of zero gravity. Once the crew reaches Mars or returns to Earth, their weak bones might fracture easily.

Activities

Here are some activities to help you apply what you have learned.

1. Guided Assignment

Rewrite the paragraph below in your own words. Jot down any additional questions you have about it. Use this assignment as a model to begin your own learning log. Record information that you are studying currently in your classes.

A star begins as a large cloud of gas and dust called a nebula. The particles of gas and dust exert a gravitational force on each other, and the nebula begins to contract. As the particles in the cloud move close together, the temperatures in the nebula increase. When temperatures inside the nebula reach $10,000,000°$ C, fusion begins. The energy released radiates outward through the condensing ball of gas. As the energy radiates into space, a star is born.

PURPOSE To clarify a difficult paragraph in a textbook

AUDIENCE Yourself

LENGTH ½–1 page

2. Open Assignment

Write an entry in your learning log. Use one of the writing ideas below or an idea of your own:

- Write a one-page dialogue between two people, such as scientists who lived at different times but worked on similar problems. For example, you might write a dialogue between Benjamin Franklin and Thomas Edison in which they ask questions about each other's experiments with electricity.
- Create a diagram to explain a process, such as weathering or erosion.
- List five questions about a difficult topic you are studying.

After writing your entry, write a paragraph explaining whether the writing idea you chose helped you with schoolwork.

3. Cooperative Learning

In a small group jot down questions each of you has about the material in a section of your science book. The members should select one or two questions other than their own to answer in their learning logs. Use pictures or diagrams, if necessary, to answer the questions. Then regroup, and discuss the questions and answers in one another's learning logs.

COMPUTER OPTION

You may want to keep your learning log in a computer file. If you have questions or insights about class material, you could record them and answer them later or highlight the main ideas, using the underlining or bold-typeface feature.

Writing About Wishes and Dreams

An Eye on Tomorrow

If I had a photograph of myself ten years from now, this is what I'd see. I am a tall, sleepy-eyed medical student in a white coat. I'm studying to be a heart surgeon. My white coat is rumpled because I slept in it on my break. I'm at a patient's bedside listening to his heart. He had heart surgery yesterday, and I was there in the operating room. During the operation I was

Imagine yourself ten years from now. What do you look like? Are you in school or working for a living? What do you spend most of your time doing? What are your interests? Write your answers in a few sentences. Then read the model at the left to find out what one person imagines about his future.

A journal can help you explore your wishes and dreams about the future. Like the writer imagining the photograph, you can try to put yourself into the world of tomorrow.

Dreaming and Writing

"To slam-dunk ten baskets this season"
"To meet my mother's relatives in Guatemala"
"To work with handicapped children"
"To learn to fly an airplane"

Your wishes tell a great deal about who you are. They help shape who you'll be. Some of your dreams about the future might be noble—for example, to improve the world. Others might be funny, to amuse only yourself. You may realize some wishes tomorrow. To realize others may take the rest of your life .

When you write about the future, you don't have to limit your brainstorming to listing ideas and freewriting paragraphs. You can also use a cluster diagram, like the one below. In your diagram you can record your interests, successes, failures, feelings, and reactions. You can even indicate how they relate to one another. Making connections may help you uncover interests you can combine as you aim to explore your goals.

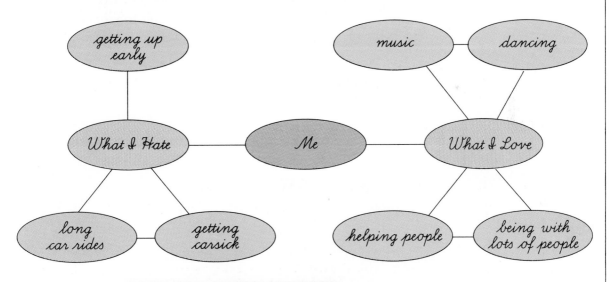

• JOURNAL ACTIVITY •

Try It Out

Make a *me* diagram—a cluster of magazine pictures that illustrates your interests. Write a paragraph in your journal about how the pictures show who you are.

Shaping the Future

You can use your journal to explore your wishes and dreams in several ways. You might freewrite about them in your journal. You might draft a letter to a friend, a relative, or a favorite teacher about a dream for the future. Another possibility is to draw a picture of yourself as you would appear after one of your dreams is fulfilled. Then write two or three sentences describing the person you see in the picture.

In the diary excerpt below, the well-known poet Sylvia Plath reflects, at seventeen, on the future.

Literature Model

What is the best for me? What do I want? I do not know. I love freedom. I deplore constrictions and limitations. . . . I am not as wise as I have thought. I can see, as from a valley, the roads lying open for me, but I cannot see the end—the consequences. . . .

Oh, I love *now,* with all my fears and forebodings, for now I still am not completely molded. My life is still just beginning. I am strong. I long for a cause to devote my energies to. . . .

Sylvia Plath,
Letters Home

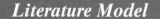

Activities

Here are some activities to help you apply what you have learned.

1. Guided Assignment

In a letter to a friend or family member, write about a goal from your childhood. Choose something that you hoped to achieve, such as learning to swim, which you've now accomplished. The person you write to may have helped or encouraged you to achieve your goal. Write about what you remember thinking and feeling after reaching the goal. Then write about what having achieved it means to you.

Andy Warhol, *Chris Evert,* 1977

PURPOSE	To use writing as a way to think about a childhood dream or goal
AUDIENCE	A friend or a family member who encouraged you
LENGTH	1–2 pages

2. Open Assignment

Follow one of the writing suggestions given on page 20 for exploring your current wishes and dreams. Write at least one page. After you've finished, put your writing away for a few days. Later, at the bottom of the page, jot down your thoughts as you reread the page.

3. Art

The painting above is of American tennis champion Chris Evert Lloyd. The characteristic look of concentration and the tennis racket show who she is. Suppose someone photographs the future you. Your appearance and an object you are holding reflect the career dreams you have achieved. Write one page telling how the picture represents the future you.

A Moment to Remember

As a coordinator of the Southern Christian Leadership Conference (SCLC), Maya Angelou had never met the group's leader, Martin Luther King Jr. She had only heard him speak. When she finally did meet him, she gained a different view. In the model below, read how Angelou, now a well-known writer, describes the moment.

Literature Model

I walked into my office and a man sitting at my desk, with his back turned, spun around, stood up and smiled. Martin King said, "Good afternoon, Miss Angelou. You are right on time."

The surprise was so total that it took me a moment to react to his outstretched hand.

I had worked two months for the SCLC, sent out tens of thousands of letters and invitations signed by Rev. King, made hundreds of statements in his name, but I had never seen him up close. He was shorter than I expected and so young. He had an easy friendliness, which was unsettling. Looking at him in my office, alone, was like seeing a lion sitting down at my dining-room table eating a plate of mustard greens.

Maya Angelou,
The Heart of a Woman

Identifying Turning Points

Clearly, Dr. King had an impact on Maya Angelou, like a lion at her table. What are some of the important events in your life? Were some of them turning points, experiences that changed you and the direction in which your life was going? To answer these questions, you might look back at old journal entries or your family's photo album. These can serve as a starting point for your autobiography, or the story of your life.

You can make a map or diagram that shows the significant events of your life. The film below shows major and minor turning points in a student's life. Make a map or a diagram to identify the turning points in your life. These are the events most likely to capture your attention when you write your own story.

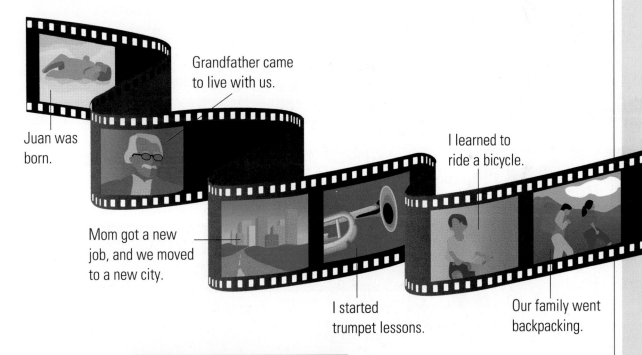

Grandfather came to live with us.

Juan was born.

I learned to ride a bicycle.

Mom got a new job, and we moved to a new city.

I started trumpet lessons.

Our family went backpacking.

• JOURNAL ACTIVITY •

Think It Through

Think about important events in your life. Try to remember the order in which they happened. In your journal, list the events in that order.

Writing About Your Life

After identifying turning points in your life, think about how you felt at those times. Then begin writing. Provide details to bring the event and your feelings to life, as Barry Rosenberg does below.

Student Model

*D*uring cold, snowy days, I love to cuddle up with Shelly. As she lies against me, I feel as though I had just drunk a cup of hot chocolate. Whenever I walk into the room, her eyes light up brighter than the sun as she recognizes me. Then, she smiles her toothless grin and tries to say, "Barrwie." At those times, I love my little Shellster a lot. Since she was born, nothing has been the same; it's been better.

Barry Rosenberg, Southfield, Michigan
First appeared in *Stone Soup*

Which details show that Barry's life has changed for the better?

The chart below shows the steps in writing about a turning point. It includes an event from the map on the last page. Note how the student used details to bring the experience to life.

Writing About Turning Points	
Steps in the Process	**Examples**
Event	start of trumpet lessons
Feelings about event	was happy about taking lessons admired the golden surface of the trumpet loved the bold trumpet sound
Writing about event	*Excited, I lifted the glittering trumpet to my lips. A thundering note marched out. I was sold on the trumpet for life.*

Activities

Miriam Schapiro, *High Steppin' Strutter #1*, 1985

Here are some activities to help you apply what you have learned.

1. Guided Assignment

Use the list in the next column to help you remember significant events or turning points in your life. When you think of one, jot down some of the things you remember most about it. Who was there? What did you see or hear around you? How did you feel? What happened? If you wish, you may use the list you created in the Journal Activity. Then write one page or more in which you explore the event and what it means to you now. Use details that most vividly describe the event.

- first day in school
- learning to ride a bike
- family gatherings

PURPOSE   To explore the effect of significant events, or turning points, in your life

AUDIENCE   Yourself

LENGTH   At least 1 page

2. Open Assignment

Examine the painting on the left. How do you think the dancer feels? Have you ever felt this way? What event caused these feelings? Was this event a turning point? If so, in what way? Write a page or more about the experience for someone you know well.

3. Health

One way to feel good about yourself is to review events in your life that you feel positive about. In your journal complete the following sentence to help you identify these events: "I felt really proud of myself when . . ." Write a one-page description of the incident or event.

I Liked the Part About Lying in Gold

Ray Vinella, *Aspen Grove*, 1960

The clouds pass

The clouds pass in a blue sky
Too white to be true
Before winter sets in
The trees are spending all their money

I lie in gold
Above a green valley
Gold falls on my chest
I am a rich man.

Richard Garcia

Which of the word pictures in the poem lingers in your mind the longest? Which image can you see most clearly in your mind? Record your answer in your journal.

Letting Literature Touch You

Poets pack their writing with vivid pictures created to stir strong feelings, suggest comparisons, and make you think in new and unusual ways. The way you react to a poem can take many different forms. For example, your response may be a quiet smile or a hearty laugh, a flood of memories, or an idea about the future. A poem may inspire a well-thought-out written response. Compare the following journal responses to Richard Garcia's poem.

*I*n the poem "The clouds pass" Richard Garcia explains a great gift of nature. In autumn time nature gives the trees' leaves a beautiful golden color. Now these leaves are the money which the trees are dropping—spending.

Sarah Fisher, Solomon Schechter Day School,
Skokie, Illinois

This reader reacts to Garcia's poem with an explanation and with appreciation.

What aspects of the poem does this reader highlight?

An autumn afternoon. The air is crisp and cool, a hint of the frosty weather to come. But the sun is warm on my skin. Like the trees in Garcia's poem, I want to spend my money before winter arrives and sends me indoors. The warm, gold days of Indian summer make everyone feel rich. Garcia's poem celebrates Indian summer. It makes me feel lucky to be alive to enjoy this glorious time of year.

This reader responds to Garcia's poem with sensory descriptions.

What feelings does Garcia's poem raise for this reader?

• JOURNAL ACTIVITY •

Try It Out

In your journal jot down the name of a poem that you've enjoyed. Close your eyes, and try to remember what you thought and felt as you read the poem. Record your answers in your journal.

Decisions, Decisions . . .

Writing is one way to respond to literature—or to explore your reactions to what you've read. You can express your thoughts and feelings in many ways. You could create an illustration, research a topic based on your reading and write about it, write what one character might say to another, or respond in any number of other ways. Which way is best for you? Begin by asking questions about the literature and how you felt about it. Look at some of the questions below to help you get started.

Questions to Help You Get Started

1. What did the literature make you think about?

2. How did it make you feel?

3. Which words brought pictures to mind?

4. What would you change about it?

Ways to Respond

Write about how the literature makes you feel.

Write a poem expressing your feelings about the work.

Draw a picture of an image from the work.

Write a letter to the author.

Rewrite a passage with your own changes.

Write a poem to the author.

Create a magazine ad for the work.

If the work is a poem, set it to music.

Dramatize a scene from the work.

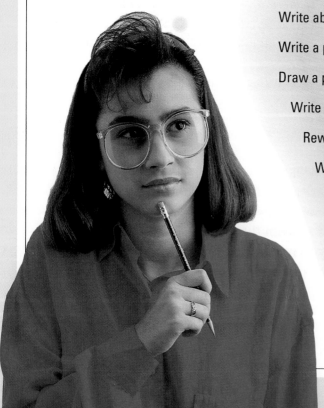

Activities

Here are some activities to help you apply what you have learned.

1. Guided Assignment

Read the following poem, and write an entry in your journal about it. Use the questions below to help you explore your feelings and reactions.

Jukebox Showdown

Two men got into a fight with a jukebox
The air was night and warm
Splattered all over the avenue
Was screws and bolts
Broken 45's all over the place
The police came and arrested all three
The police asked the jukebox questions
Then dropped quarters in

Victor Hernández Cruz

- How did you feel when you finished reading the poem? What in the poem made you feel that way?
- What did you like best about the poem in general? Its subject, its sound, the pictures it created in your mind? Explain.
- Did the poem tell you anything new? Say something you haven't heard before?

PURPOSE   To explore your response to a poem
AUDIENCE   Yourself
LENGTH   1 page or more

2. Open Assignment

Pick four or five poems to read. One of them may be the poem you read for the last Journal Activity. As you read the poems, record your impressions and responses in your journal. From this record write a page about your reactions to the poems, or respond in your own way. Share your response with the class.

3. Cooperative Learning

Each student should find an example of a review of a book, movie, or play. What did the reviewers write about? How did they respond to what they read or saw? Students should write at least one page about the reviews and the reviewers' impressions and responses. Students can share this information and discuss how a review might be different from a personal response in a journal.

COMPUTER OPTION

If you keep your journal on computer, you can use the copy-and-paste option to organize your responses to literature, movies, or plays. You may find that different sections or sentences from your journal are useful. You can copy and paste them to form an outline. You might also copy and paste well-written sentences from your journal to a first draft of a longer paper.

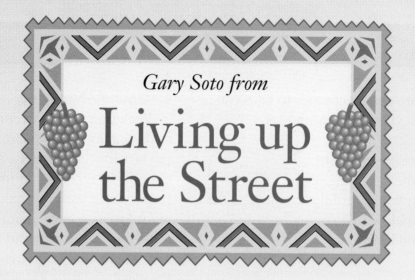

Gary Soto from

Living up the Street

Do you really know your best friend? As you grow up, you learn that it's hard to really know others well. It can be even harder to know yourself. Gary Soto's book Living up the Street *traces his life through the dust and sun of the barrios of Fresno, California. In the following selection Soto finds himself at his first job, picking grapes alongside his mother. He soon discovers an uncomfortable truth about life and his own character.*

I cut another bunch, then another, fighting the snap and whip of vines. After ten minutes of groping for grapes, my first pan brimmed with bunches. I poured them on the paper tray, which was bordered by a wooden frame that kept the grapes from rolling off, and they spilled like jewels from a pirate's chest. The tray was only half filled, so I hurried to jump under the vines and begin groping, cutting, and tugging at the grapes again. I emptied the pan, raked the grapes with my hands to make them look like they filled the tray, and jumped back under the vine on my knees. I tried to cut faster because Mother, in the next row, was slowly moving ahead. I peeked into her row and saw five trays gleaming in the early morning. I cut, pulled hard, and stopped to gather the grapes that missed the pan;

already bored, I spat on a few to wash them before tossing them like popcorn into my mouth.

So it went. Two pans equaled one tray—or six cents. By lunchtime I had a trail of thirty-seven trays behind me while Mother had sixty or more. We met about halfway from our last trays, and I sat down with a grunt, knees wet from kneeling on dropped grapes. I washed my hands with the water from the jug, drying them on the inside of my shirt sleeve before I opened the paper bag for the first sandwich, which I gave to Mother. I dipped my hand in again to unwrap a sandwich without looking at it. I took a first bite and chewed it slowly for the tang of mustard. Eating in silence I looked straight ahead at the vines, and only when we were finished with cookies did we talk.

"Are you tired?" she asked.

"No, but I got a sliver from the frame," I told her. I showed her the web of skin between my thumb and index finger. She

Susan Moore, *With No Visible Sign*, 1988

wrinkled her forehead but said it was nothing.

"How many trays did you do?"

I looked straight ahead, not answering at first. I recounted in my mind the whole morning of bend, cut, pour again and again, before answering a feeble "thirty-seven." No elaboration,[1] no detail. Without looking at me she told me how she had done field work in Texas and Michigan as a child. But I had a difficult time listening to her stories. I played with my grape knife, stabbing it into the ground, but stopped when Mother reminded me that I had better not lose it. I left the knife sticking up like a small, leafless plant. She then talked about school, the junior high I would be going to that fall, and then about Rick and Debra, how sorry they would be that they hadn't come out to pick grapes because they'd have no new clothes for the school year. She stopped talking when she peeked at her watch, a bandless one she kept in her pocket. She got up with an "*Ay, Dios,*" and told me that we'd work until three, leaving me cutting figures in the sand with my knife and dreading the return to work.

Finally I rose and walked slowly back to where I had left off, again kneeling under the vine and fixing the pan under bunches of grapes. By that time, 11:30, the sun was over my shoulder and made me squint and think of the pool at the Y.M.C.A. where I was a summer member. I saw myself diving face first into the water and loving it. I saw myself gleaming like something new, at the edge of the pool. I had to daydream and keep my mind busy because boredom was a terror almost as awful as the work itself. My mind went dumb with stupid things, and I had to keep it moving with dreams of baseball and would-be girlfriends. I even sang, however softly, to keep my mind moving, my hands moving.

I worked less hurriedly and with less vision. I no longer saw that copper pot sitting squat[2] on our stove or Mother waiting for it to whistle. The wardrobe that I imagined, crisp and bright in the closet, numbered only one pair of jeans and two shirts

---

1 **elaboration** (i lab'ə rā'shən) giving more details
2 **squat** (skwot) short and thick; low and broad

Anthony Ortega, *Farmworkers de Califas*, 1990

because, in half a day, six cents times thirty-seven trays was two dollars and twenty-two cents. It became clear to me. If I worked eight hours, I might make four dollars. I'd take this, even gladly, and walk downtown to look into store windows on the mall and long for bright madras [3] shirts from Walter Smith or Coffee's, but settling for two imitation ones from Penney's.

That first day I laid down seventy-three trays while Mother had a hundred and twenty behind her. On the back of an old envelope, she wrote out our numbers and hours. We washed at the pump behind the farm house and walked slowly back to our car for the drive back to town in the afternoon heat. That evening after dinner I sat in a lawn chair listening to music from a transistor radio while Rick and David King played catch. I joined them in a game of pickle, but there was little joy in trying to avoid their tags because I couldn't get the fields out of my mind: I saw

3 madras (mad′rəs) a fine, striped or plaid cotton cloth

myself dropping on my knees under a vine to tug at a branch that wouldn't come off. In bed, when I closed my eyes, I saw the fields, yellow with kicked up dust, and a crooked trail of trays rotting behind me.

The next day I woke tired and started picking tired. The grapes rained into the pan, slowly filling like a belly, until I had my first tray and started my second. So it went all day, and the next, and all through the following week, so that by the end of thirteen days the foreman counted out, in tens mostly, my pay of fifty-three dollars. Mother earned one hundred and forty-eight dollars. She wrote this on her envelope, with a message I didn't bother to ask her about.

The next day I walked with my friend Scott to the downtown mall where we drooled over the clothes behind fancy windows, bought popcorn, and sat at a tier of outside fountains to talk about girls. Finally we went into Penney's for more popcorn, which we ate walking around, before we returned home without buying anything. It wasn't until a few days before school that I let my fifty-three dollars slip quietly from my hands, buying a pair of pants, two shirts, and a maroon T-shirt, the kind that was in style. At home I tried them on while Rick looked on enviously; later, the day before school started, I tried them on again wondering not so much if they were worth it as who would see me first in those clothes.

For Discussion

1. Before he began this job, Gary thought picking grapes would be easy, but it was hard work. Have you ever had a task that seemed easy but turned out to be quite difficult? What did your reaction tell you about yourself?

2. When you get what you wished for, as Gary did when he got to pick grapes, do you ever feel disappointed? Why or why not?

Readers Respond

I clearly remember the scene in which the boy gives up his dreams. He forgets about what he was going to buy, such as a copper teapot for his mother and stylish clothes for himself. He was hit with the reality of hard work. I liked the details about how tired he felt from working

Joshua Zapata

S ince I am Hispanic (Puerto Rican), I put myself in the boy's place. I even enjoy some of the same things that he does. For example, I really like swimming, and I go to the YMCA pool, too.

I remembered well a number of the scenes from the selection. For example, I can still picture the boy's lunch with his mother and the grape picking. I think that, because the author kept my attention by describing these scenes in detail they stayed in my mind.

I would recommend this literature selection to a friend. I think it helps the reader see how some people have to struggle to make a little money.

Paul Roustan

Did You Notice?

1. Did you notice how the author got inside the boy's head? What were his feelings about picking grapes? How did he fight boredom? What dreams did he abandon?

2. What events that you felt strongly about have happened to you lately? Write your reactions in your journal. Indicate whether your feelings about the event have changed.

Writing Process in Action

I Remember When . . .

Think about your first response to the excerpt from Gary Soto's _Living up the Street_. Did you get a sense of his feelings about the memory he shared? Do you have a sense of how he felt about his mother and the experience they shared? Personal writing can tell us a great deal about the author's feelings—even if the experience the author writes about is unfamiliar.

This assignment invites you to write about your feelings surrounding an experience you shared with someone else.

• Assignment •

Context	_You have decided to contribute to America, America, a publication of personal reflections and images from across the United States. Write about an experience you have shared with someone else._
Purpose	_To share, in writing, a personal experience_
Audience	_A general audience of all ages_
Length	_2 or more pages_

The next few pages offer helpful advice for following the assignment. You don't have to remember all the details. Read the entire lesson once to get an overview. Then refer to the appropriate section as you work your way through the writing process.

1. Prewriting

To come up with possible topics for this assignment, try to recall shared experiences that taught you something about life, another person, or yourself. This may help you focus on people close to you, whom you see every day. Perhaps the person introduced you to a new skill, as the narrator's mother did in *Living up the Street.*

The options graphic at the right offers some ways to tap your memories for ideas. The notebook gives an example of listing to generate ideas. Remember, you want to choose a topic that fits the assignment and has meaning for you.

Option A
Review journal entries.

Option B
Brainstorm with a friend.

Option C
Freewrite for ideas.

Helped Mrs. Magnino paint lawn furniture; then she painted her kitchen—nothing could stop her. Both of us almost overcome by paint fumes. Opened the window and a bird flew in.

2. Drafting

Exploring your ideas thoroughly during prewriting helps your drafting go smoothly. As you review your notes, consider the kinds of details you'd like to include. What details did Soto include that you remember? What details gave you the best sense of how he felt about the experience? As you begin to get ideas, write them down just as they come to you. You can polish the good ones later.

The clearest organization of your writing may come from the time-ordering of events. Notice how Gary Soto uses time transitions in this passage from *Living up the Street:*

*T*he next day I woke tired and started picking tired. The grapes rained into the pan, slowly filling like a belly, until I had my first tray and started my second. So it went all day, and the next, and all through the following week, so that by the end of the thirteen days the foreman counted out, in tens mostly, my pay of fifty-three dollars.

Remember to focus on the shared experience and your own feelings. Review your prewriting notes, your journal, some old photos, anything that works. At this stage, don't edit—just write. You may find it helpful to review pages 10–13 and 18–21 for more on personal writing.

3. Revising

When you've completed your draft, take a break. Later, you can return to your work with a critical eye. Then read your draft as though you were hearing about the experience for the first time. Have you made clear to your readers why this experience is important? Is it an experience you shared with someone else, an experience significant to both of you? Questions like these and those below will help you revise your work. Don't worry about spelling and punctuation at this point. You'll have time for that during the editing stage.

Question A

Will my writing capture the reader's interest?

Question B

Have I included interesting details?

Question C

Have I shared my feelings about the experience?

Mrs. Magnino lived down the street from us for as many years as I could remember. Her husband died several years ago. I hardly remember him. ~~her husband passed away.~~ She's been alone ever since, and ~~Now she's~~ has depended on neighbors for favors and help whenever possible. ~~My parents thought it would~~ One day she asked Mom if I could help with a few odd jobs around the yard. ~~be a good idea if I offered to help her around~~ Mom thought it was a good idea. ~~the house.~~

We started by painting her lawn furniture. It hadn't been painted in years, but it was still in decent shape.

Next, read your draft aloud to check the sentence rhythm. Experiment with shortening or combining sentences and varying sentence structure. Take another look at the passage from *Living up the Street.* How does Gary Soto use sentence rhythm to convey the way he feels about his work?

4. Editing

You must complete one more step before you share your writing with others. In the editing stage carefully look over every sentence and word. Don't make your readers struggle through incorrect grammar or misspellings.

Use the checklist on the right to help you edit your writing. If certain grammar or punctuation rules give you problems, add them to the checklist. Then read through your work several times, looking for only one or two kinds of error each time.

Checklist

1. Are there any sentence fragments or run-on sentences?
2. Have I used verb forms and tenses correctly?
3. Have I used standard spelling, capitalization, and punctuation?

5. Presenting

Before you turn in your assignment, think of some suggestions you could give to the editors of *America, America* for the published version of your article. For example, you might suggest some footnotes to help readers with unfamiliar words and for name pronunciations. Maybe you have ideas for illustrations or photographs that could accompany your story. Turn your suggestions in with your writing.

Reflecting

Tap into your experiences and memories for writing ideas. Writing about an experience can reveal more about feelings than simply remembering it can.

Which writing stage gave you the most difficulty in this assignment? Why? What can you do to avoid this problem next time?

Portfolio & Reflection

Summary

Key concepts in personal writing include the following:

- A journal is a place to keep personal writing and is a good source of writing ideas.
- A learning log is a place to explore your thoughts and questions about schoolwork.
- You can explore your wishes and dreams in personal writing.
- You can describe a turning point in your life in personal writing.
- You can also use personal response to create a poem.

Your Writer's Portfolio

Look over the writing you did for this unit. Choose two pieces for your portfolio. Look for writing that does one or more of the following:

- grows out of your personal experiences, thoughts, feelings, ideas, activities, recordings, and memories
- is a way for you to make discoveries about yourself and the world in which you live
- describes in detail your wishes and dreams about what you will be doing in the future
- brings to life an important event or a turning point, an experience that changed the direction of your life
- responds to a poem in a personal and imaginative way

Reflection and Commentary

Think about what you learned in this unit. Answer the following questions as you look over the two pieces of writing you chose. Write a page of "Comments on Personal Writing" for your portfolio.

1. What did you discover about yourself in doing the personal writing?
2. What difficult ideas did you understand better after you wrote about them?
3. What parts of the writing grew out of a map or diagram?
4. What personal writing would you like to share?

Feedback

If you had a chance to respond to the following student comment, what would you say or ask?

The best things about writing are being able to let my feelings out and to tell others how I feel.

Sarah Fisher, Solomon Schechter Day School, Skokie, Illinois

Working Together

Harunobu, *Toi no Tamagawa*, late 1760s

41

KURTIS EXPLORES SCIENCE

"I try to accomplish two things in The New Explorers. *One is to show that scientists are action-oriented, that science is an adventure. I also want to teach scientific ideas in a new way."*

Bill Kurtis

One night back in 1987, TV journalist Bill Kurtis was filming a zoologist who was hunting a new species of bird in Peru. Kurtis said that suddenly "a light went on. In a flash I saw a series of stories following scientists into the field."

Today Kurtis heads Kurtis Productions, and his idea has become a television series called *The New Explorers.* Each program profiles a scientist—a hero to Kurtis—working on science's frontiers or bringing science to nonscientists. Sometimes it features people such as Chris Cheviarina and Jim Hicks—Mr. C and Uncle Jim. They're high school teachers "on a mission to teach physics you can actually understand."

Producing a Documentary

1. Finding the Heroes   2. Gathering Information   3. Creating a Rough Cut   4. Fine-tuning the Show

FOCUS

Like writing, the process of producing a documentary involves research, drafting a script, and editing the film.

▼ *Bill Kurtis often travels when filming* The New Explorers. *His filming location might be the Amazon —or it might even be an amusement park.*

1 Finding the Heroes

Where did Kurtis find Uncle Jim and Mr. C, the heroes for "Rock 'n' Roll Physics"? "A staff member said she knew two teachers who had started an amusement park physics program," said Kurtis.

Kurtis sensed a story. The teachers weren't scientists on the cutting edge. But it sounded as if they were turning physics into a high-voltage adventure. Quickly Kurtis sent his staff into action.

"We have associate producers," he said, "and they make some initial calls. Just like any journalist, we're asking, 'Is this a good story?'"

The teachers were explaining ideas in a fresh way. Kurtis had to figure out how to show that. "I saw this as an opportunity to do some real teaching by using an amusement park," Kurtis said. "I wanted to combine graphics, action, and kids. And I wanted to put these guys on stage and let them do their thing."

2 Gathering Information

▼ For Kurtis and his team, gathering information can mean a library trip just as easily as a field trip.

With this idea in mind, Kurtis's staff went after more information. "We may go to the library," Kurtis said. "We may do interviews. Ultimately, we have to go out and shoot film or video."

In this case, unlike in a feature film, shooting takes place before the script for the show is written. The material gathered from the shoot will help during script-writing.

The first step in shooting "Rock 'n' Roll Physics" was catching the teachers in action. Kurtis sent a camera crew to Barrington High School outside Chicago. "I said, just follow the teachers and shoot everything they do," Kurtis explained. "I wanted to see how good they

were on camera, how good the action was."

At this time, the physics class was wrestling with Newton's first law of motion. It states: An object in motion will remain in motion, and an object at rest will remain at rest, unless external force is applied.

What does Newton's first law of motion mean? In a school hallway the film crew caught Uncle Jim, Mr. C, and the class experimenting with a hovercraft. It was made of a chair, a vacuum cleaner, and a piece of plywood. The hovercraft zoomed down the hall; it became an object in motion! Mr. C yelled for students to grab the hovercraft before it crashed into a wall—in other words, to stop the moving object by applying force. There it was—Newton's first law in action.

INTERFACE *Imagine that you're doing a documentary on this year's science fair. At the fair tomorrow's scientists will demonstrate their ideas. Your audience will include all age groups, scientists and nonscientists. How would you present the science concepts to your audience?*

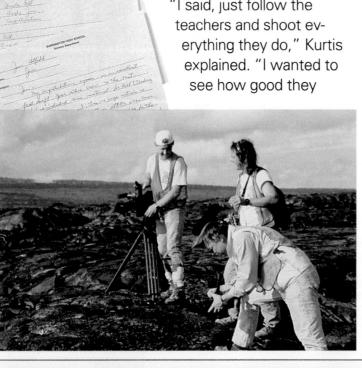

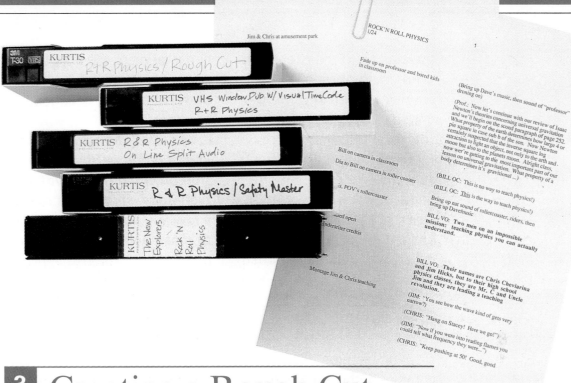

The following text appears on the script papers in the image:

ROCK'N ROLL PHYSICS
1/24

Jim & Chris at amusement park

Fade up on professor and bored kids in classroom

(Bring up Dave's music, then sound of "professor" droning on)

(Prof.: Now let's continue with our review of Isaac Newton's theories concerning universal gravitation and we'll begin on the second paragraph of page 252. What property of the earth determines how large 4 or pie square in case sub b of the son. Now Newton certainly suspected that the inverse square log attraction to light an object, not only to the arth and. moon but also to the planets moon. Alright class, now wer're getting to the most important part of our lesson on universal gravitation. What property of a body determines it's gravitional ...)

(BILL OC: This is no way to teach physics!)

(BILL OC: This is the way to teach physics!)

Bring up nat sound of rollercoaster, riders, then bring up Davemusic

BILL VO: Two men on an impossible mission: teaching physics you can actually understand.

BILL VO: Their names are Chris Cheviarina and Jim Hicks, but to their high school physics classes, they are Mr. C and Uncle Jim and they are leading a teaching revolution.

(JIM: "You see how the wave kind of gets very narrow")

(CHRIS: "Hang on Stacey! Here we go!")

(JIM: "Now if you were into reading flames you could tell what frequency they were...")

(CHRIS: "Keep pushing at 50! Good, good")

Labels on the videotapes:
- KURTIS R+R Physics/Rough Cut
- KURTIS VHS Window Dub W/Visual TimeCode R+R Physics
- KURTIS R&R Physics On Line Split Audio
- KURTIS R&R Physics/Safety Master
- KURTIS The New Explorers Rock N Roll Physics

3 Creating a Rough Cut

With miles of film and heads full of physics, the team met to discuss the show. "We asked, how do we want to tell this story?" Kurtis said.

Kurtis wanted to show the teachers bringing physics to life. So the producer pulled the best moments from the interviews. "These are the most important moments, because they're the ones that really grab you," Kurtis said.

Based on these moments, the script was drafted with a clear opener, a beginning, middle, and end. "You must be able to follow the story," Kurtis said. "You can't lose it along the way."

Next the script called for Kurtis to explain the show's subject and to introduce the heroes—the new explorers. "This is my getting-to-know-you section," Kurtis said. "I want viewers to get to know the heroes and their work. I want people to care about what they're doing."

High-energy scenes would take viewers from class to pool to parking lot to roller coaster. They would teach science, all right, but with color and action. "I like to change the pace often to keep the viewer's attention," Kurtis emphasized.

The ending would show-case students discussing

▲ *The script is used like an outline to guide the production of the documentary.*

the class and their teachers. Who could explain better why Uncle Jim and Mr. C's unusual teaching style works?

Finally, the draft of the script was revised, and fifty hours of video were cut down to four. Kurtis then handed the script to the film editor, who related the best film images to the script. He created a rough cut, or draft, of the show.

INTERFACE *Imagine that you're going to do a television documentary about teen-age fashions. Jot down a few key points you want to make and some ideas for pictures.*

4 Fine-tuning the Show

With pictures and words combined, the show suddenly came to life. What did Kurtis and his team look for now? "Now we're television producers," he said. "Do we have an opening, a beginning, a climax, and a conclusion? Does the story work?"

"I'll tell you," he said, "on 'Rock 'n' Roll Physics' we looked at the rough cut and said, we need to do some work here. Frankly, I wasn't understanding the science."

Kurtis thought bold graphics would help explain more clearly the difficult science concepts. To make better sense of Newton's first law, for instance, Kurtis looked for everyday examples. He wanted to show how objects in motion travel in a straight line unless another force stops them.

Besides adding graphics, the team re-edited the video. They cut some parts and expanded others. After nearly eight weeks of work, "Rock 'n' Roll Physics" was ready to go.

▼ *On location at an amusement park, Uncle Jim and Mr. C. teach physics to their students.*

ON ASSIGNMENT

1. Documentary Writing

Write the opening to a documentary on your favorite sport, music group, or hobby.

- Write one sentence telling the subject of your documentary.
- Think of a funny or exciting way to start the documentary.
- Take one or two minutes to write the opening.

2. About Literature

Brainstorm an idea for a documentary on someone's life.

- Look at some biographies at the library.
- Select one biography for your focus.
- Make a list of ideas for a documentary about some aspect of the person's life, such as a typical day, what he or she does for a living, or an important event.

3. Cooperative Learning

Make your own documentary photo essay.

- With a small group of students, pick a hero in your community or school.
- Choose a job for each person in your group: contact person, interviewer, photographer, and writer.
- Research your hero, and, as a group, decide what to tell and how to tell it.
- Gather pictures, quotes, and other information.
- As a group, discuss ideas and review photographs. Ask the writers to draft an essay.
- Review the draft as a group. Choose photographs to support it, and revise the essay.
- Present your photo essay.

Working Smart

The Camera Club decided to build a darkroom in the basement of their school, Carver Junior High. Do you think they started by taking some boards and nailing them together? Of course not. They thought about a location for their darkroom, how to get a sink, and how to keep the light out. Then they made a few sketches and plans.

A Sensible Process

Just as building doesn't begin with a hammer, writing doesn't begin with a pen. It begins inside your head—with an idea. The first stage of the writing process is an idea stage.

Prewriting The prewriting stage begins with finding and exploring a topic. One useful technique is to search your memory for experiences you'd like to share. Begin by looking at old photos of yourself and your friends, jotting down ideas as you go. Think about which ideas you'd enjoy writing about and

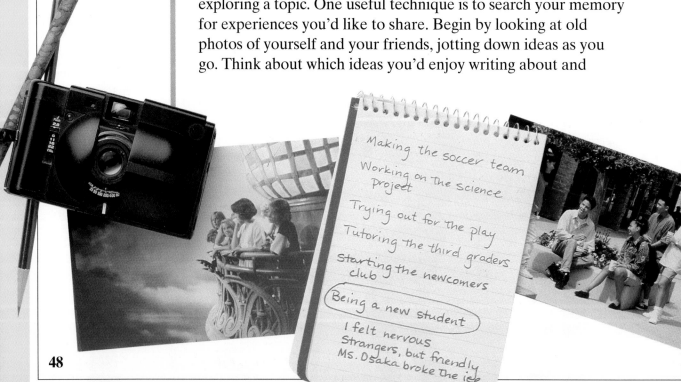

Making the soccer team
Working on the science project
Trying out for the play
Tutoring the third graders
Starting the newcomers club
Being a new student
I felt nervous
Strangers, but friendly
Ms. Osaka broke the ice

which might interest others. Examine the prewriting notes below. Later, also in prewriting, you will decide how to organize the ideas.

Drafting   When you draft, you turn your prewriting notes into sentences and paragraphs. You arrange your ideas in the order you chose in prewriting. New ideas will continue to come. Write them down. Experiment with them. Some will work, and some won't. Your draft may look messy, but don't worry. You can fix it up later.

Revising   Step back and look over what you've written. Read it aloud, and answer questions like the following: Are your ideas clear? Do they fit together? What other details might help your readers understand and enjoy what you've written?

Editing   In the editing stage you examine each word, phrase, and sentence in your writing. It's the time to find and correct any errors in grammar, spelling, and punctuation. Your goal is a neat, error-free copy for others to read and enjoy.

Presenting   The presenting stage means sharing your writing with its audience. You can read a report aloud in class. You can work with others to publish a class poetry book. You can write a letter to the editor of the school newspaper. What other ways can you think of to present your work to readers?

Drafting

I felt nervous walking in that first morning. The halls were crowded. People seemed happy . . . new year. They . . .

Revising

to Carver Junior High School
I felt nervous walking in ∧ that

first morning. The halls were
Friends greeted each other,
crowded. ∧ People seemed happy to
together
be starting a new year ∧. They

didn't seem to need to know a
especially
new person, and one from
faraway Japan○
another country at that.

• JOURNAL ACTIVITY •
Think It Through

Create your own chart to summarize and help you remember the writing process. Refer to it as you complete your writing assignments.

A *Flexible Process*

Novelist James A. Michener once said, "I have never thought of myself as a good writer. Anyone who wants reassurance of that should read one of my first drafts. But I'm one of the world's great rewriters." Most professional writers agree that writing is a messy process. It needs to be messy, because ideas don't often flow in an orderly way. At any stage in the writing process, a writer can have new and better ideas about how to say something, how to get the message across. Don't let those new and better ideas slip away. Write them down.

Think of the writing process as moving forward and backward. For example, if you get stuck while writing your draft because your notes are incomplete, go back to prewriting, and add to your notes. In editing, if a sentence doesn't say enough, rewrite and revise it until you're satisfied. One of this writer's best ideas, about a *small world*, came in a later revision.

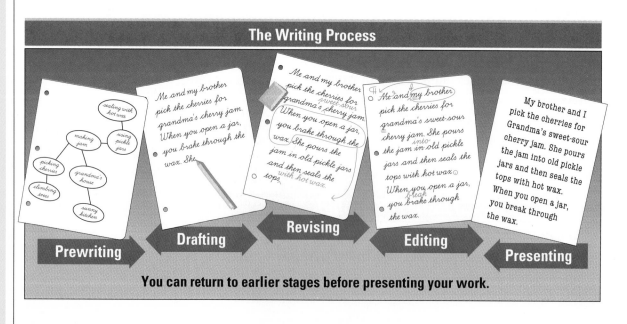

The Writing Process

Prewriting → **Drafting** → **Revising** → **Editing** → **Presenting**

You can return to earlier stages before presenting your work.

Activities

Here are some activities to help you apply what you have learned.

1. Guided Assignment

Study the sketch and the finished sculpture below. Compare the sculpting process with the writing process. Make notes to yourself about some similarities and differences. Use your notes to draft a paragraph in which you address these questions:

- What do you think are the steps in the sculpting process?

- How are they like and unlike the stages of the writing process?

PURPOSE   To compare two creative processes
AUDIENCE   Your English class
LENGTH   ½–1 page

2. Open Assignment

Jot down prewriting notes about one of the events below or another one of your choice. Draft a page or two.

- an event that made you proud
- an event that made you laugh
- an event that taught you something

Claes Oldenburg, *Notebook Page: Cross-section of Toothbrush in Glass, 'sun dial,'* 1980

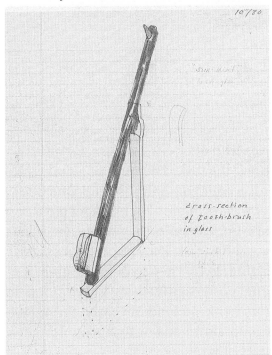

Claes Oldenburg, *Cross-section of a Toothbrush with Paste, in a Cup, on a Sink: Portrait of Coosje's Thinking*, 1983

Working with the Writing Process   **51**

Prewriting: Determining Audience and Purpose

Who and Why?

You wouldn't rake leaves with a fork or eat dinner with a rake. You choose a tool to suit the task. The tools of a writer are words. You must pick words to suit your purpose and your audience. The eighth-graders at Carver Junior High School did a wide variety of writing tasks. For example, they wrote an article about the Foods-of-the-World Festival. They wrote post cards during their trip to Washington, D.C. They wrote a program for the talent show. They created posters advertising the craft fair. Finally, they made a memory book—a kind of yearbook—about their eighth-grade activities. Jot down one or two possible audiences for each of these pieces of writing.

Think: Who Will Read It?

Writers benefit from knowing who their readers are. With this knowledge, writers can tailor what they write to their readers' ability to understand and enjoy it. How does the writer of the first article below signal that he's writing for young readers?

Literature Model

Hollis Conway has always had long, skinny legs. When he was growing up in Shreveport, Louisiana, his minister called him Linky Legs.

Little did anyone know that those slender legs would one day launch Hollis over a high-jump bar set nearly eight feet off the ground! Hollis, now 24, is one of the best high jumpers in history.

Sports Illustrated for Kids

What words and ideas make this opening right for young readers?

Literature Model

Low, smoky clouds rolled in off the Wasatch Mountains above Provo, Utah, last Saturday night as high jumper Hollis Conway prepared for his second attempt at an American record 7′ 9¾″.

Merrell Noden, *Sports Illustrated*

What audience do you think this writer had in mind?

• JOURNAL ACTIVITY •

Think It Through

Find two magazines, one for teen-agers and one for adults. Examine some articles, and make notes about how the words and ideas reflect each audience.

Think: What Is Your Purpose?

The purpose of both passages about high jumping is to inform. The selection below has a different purpose—to narrate, or tell a story. Read this narrative about an exciting event in the writer's life. To consider two more purposes for writing, consult the chart below.

What purpose and audience do you think Ken had in mind? How does his writing reflect both?

Student Model

*F*inally, it was my turn. . . . I ran as fast as I could, and approaching the first hurdle, I made it over but bumped my toe slightly. I was embarrassed. I ran on, afraid that I would repeat my error on the next hurdle. Perspiration rolled down my face.

I leaped over the second hurdle with the grace of an antelope; I felt as if my feet had wings. My classmates cheered. I heard comments like "Boy, that kid's good!" and "Wow, look at him go!"

I then flew over the third hurdle like an eagle and raced to the finish line. The gym teacher looked at his stopwatch in disbelief. "You got the highest score in the class, Ken!" he said. I felt good that I had done something better than everybody else.

Ken Priebe, Grosse Pointe Woods, Michigan
First appeared in *Cricket*

Purposes for Writing	
To describe	Although short and thin, Ken was a fast runner.
To narrate	Finally, Ken leaped over the last hurdle.
To inform	Ken finished in first place because of his great efforts.
To persuade	Your contribution will help support the track team.

Here are some activities to help you apply what you have learned.

1. Guided Assignment

Study the painting below, and plan a personal response. First, select an audience:

- a young child
- your teacher
- a friend
- a local art-museum director

Then select a purpose:

- to describe the painting
- to narrate the story the painting tells
- to explain what the painting is like
- to persuade a museum director to buy it

Make some prewriting notes about the painting. Select words and ideas that seem to fit the audience and purpose you chose.

PURPOSE	Your choice
AUDIENCE	Your choice
LENGTH	1 page

2. Open Assignment

Select a TV program you enjoy that a young child might also like. Jot down some notes about the program. Draft a half-page review recommending the program to a child and a second review recommending the program to the child's parents.

3. Mathematics

Think of a problem-solving strategy you learned recently in a math assignment. Then imagine that a classmate has been ill and you have been asked to write an explanation to send home with the assignment. Make notes about the steps involved in the strategy. Then draft your explanation.

Elizabeth Nourse, *Humble Ménage*, 1897

Time to Brainstorm

The eighth-graders had decided to make a memory book about their last year at Carver Junior High. Which activities would they include? Miguel said, "Let's brainstorm."

"What's brainstorming?" asked Lee. "It sounds dangerous."

"It's not rain in the brain," said Miguel, "but it can be as exciting as a storm. It's tossing ideas back and forth to come up with new ideas. I'll start. Let's include the opening football game. I have a great photo we can use."

Todd jotted down each idea. "The skit we put on in the after-school program," Ayako said. "That was fun!" In brainstorming, one idea sparked others, so the class listed all of them. Later they decided which ideas to include in their memory book.

Opening football game
Skit for after-school program
Art museum trip

Exploring Your Topic

Once you have a topic for any creative project, you can explore it by freewriting, clustering, or listing. To freewrite, set a time limit—say, ten minutes—and write everything that comes to mind about the topic. When the time's up, read your freewriting. Often your best ideas—or at least the seeds of them—will have popped out. Two other helpful techniques are clustering and listing. Some students used clustering to explore ideas for the memory book. Kelly listed details about the class mural project. Each idea was judged important. Deciding what's in and what's out comes later.

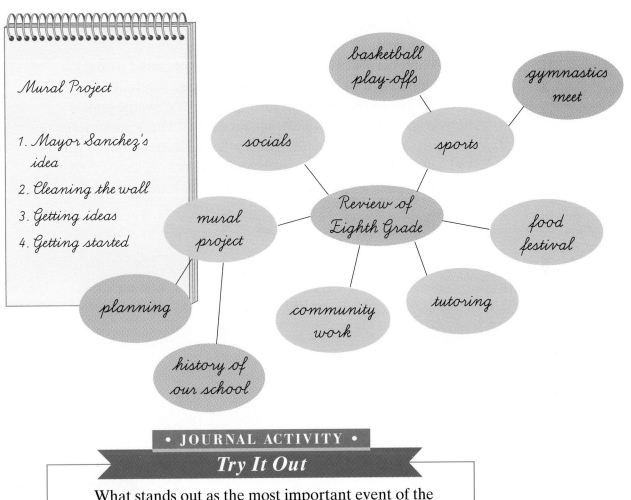

Mural Project

1. Mayor Sanchez's idea
2. Cleaning the wall
3. Getting ideas
4. Getting started

• JOURNAL ACTIVITY •

Try It Out

What stands out as the most important event of the past school year? Set a timer for ten minutes. In your journal freewrite about why the event was important.

Gathering Facts and Details

Writers start with what they know, but they often need more information to help them shape their ideas. To find it, they tap a wide range of sources, such as books, magazines, and newspapers. Sometimes the best sources are people with special knowledge of the topic. For example, Ayako wondered, "What did the audience in the after-school program think of our skit?" To find out, she interviewed some children who'd seen the skit.

Before you conduct an interview, make up a list of questions, such as those Ayako listed below. At the interview take notes. With the interviewee's permission you can use a tape recorder as well. After the interview reread your notes, and jot down what you've learned.

To conduct a successful interview, come prepared with good questions. Listen well. Record the information carefully. Don't interrupt or rush ahead to the next question. Allow the person time to answer, and ask follow-up questions: "That's interesting. Can you say more about it?" The firsthand information you get will help make your writing lively and realistic.

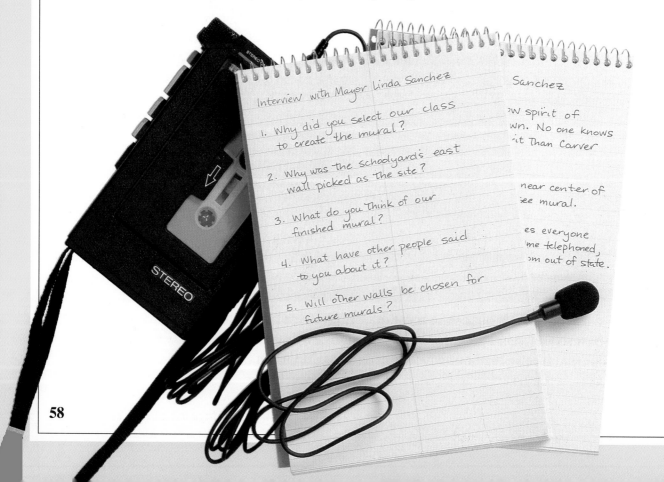

Interview with Mayor Linda Sanchez

1. Why did you select our class to create the mural?

2. Why was the schoolyard's east wall picked as the site?

3. What do you think of our finished mural?

4. What have other people said to you about it?

5. Will other walls be chosen for future murals?

Sanchez

ow spirit of
wn. No one knows
it than Carver

near center of
ee mural.

es everyone
me telephoned,
om out of state.

Activities

Here are some activities to help you apply what you have learned.

1. Guided Assignment

Recall a personal experience that meant something special to you. For example, think of experiences you had in the past school year: at home, with your friends, on a family or school outing, or on a vacation trip. Examine the freewriting you did for the Journal Activity in this lesson. Once you have a topic, use prewriting techniques to explore it and gather details. Using your prewriting notes, draft a letter to a friend or relative explaining what the experience was and what made it special. Afterward, if you wish, make a neat final copy, and mail the letter.

PURPOSE	To share a personal experience
AUDIENCE	A friend or family member
LENGTH	1–2 pages

2. Open Assignment

Select a person to interview about a specific topic. For example, you might interview a teacher or coach to find out how the person chose his or her career. You might interview a neighbor or even a family member about a historic event that happened before you were born, such as a war or an important election.

- Prepare your questions in advance.
- Take a notebook, a pencil, and, if the interviewee gives you permission, a tape recorder.
- Listen carefully, do not interrupt, and ask follow-up questions.

Write up the interview, based on the notes you took.

3. Cooperative Learning

In a small group brainstorm to create a list of public figures that you consider important. You might list entertainers, athletes, writers, and political leaders. Gather names from each group member.

Working individually, choose one public figure as your topic for a free writing session. Explore reasons why you think the person is important. Finally, work together to create a group list of ideas for an essay titled "What Makes an Important Person Important?" Using the list, have each member individually write a one- to two-page paper. Share the papers with the group.

COMPUTER OPTION

A computer allows you to do "invisible writing," which is an excellent freewriting technique. Choose a topic, and set a timer for ten minutes. Dim the screen, and begin to freewrite about your topic. Since you cannot see what you are writing, you will be able to let your ideas flow without interrupting your thoughts to make corrections.

Prewriting: Organizing Ideas

Thanks for the Memories

Imagine that you have a garden that contains both beautiful flowers and scraggly weeds. You must dig up and throw away the weeds so that the flowers can thrive. The writing process is similar. Rafael got ready to "weed" his ideas for the introduction to the class memory book. He gathered his notes about the year's events. He found some resources, such as back issues of the school newspaper, to help him fill in missing details. What, for example, was the date of the craft fair? Who planned the mural project? What activities were more special than others? Why?

Time to Weed

Not all the ideas you gather on a topic belong in your writing. You have to decide what to keep and what to take out. Here's how to do it. First, decide what you want to say about your topic, and express your idea in one sentence. Then list the details, and cross out any that don't belong. Rafael asked himself which activities really helped to support his idea about "the activities our class did together." Notice how he weeded his list.

Listing ideas

The activities our class did together made eighth grade a year to remember.

talent show–April

mural project–October

tutoring   not a group activity

craft fair–May

Olympic Day–June

parent's night   more for the parents

Foods-of-the-World Festival–December

class trip–March

visiting author   she talked, we listened

• JOURNAL ACTIVITY •
Try It Out

Write a sentence expressing your opinion about a school activity, either positive or negative. List details about the activity. Then think: Which details support my main idea? Which do not? Cross out the "weeds."

Time to Organize

Now you need to organize your ideas in a way that makes sense. How you do that depends on your purpose: to describe, to narrate, to inform, or to persuade.

To describe something, you sometimes arrange the details in order of location, or spatial order. You might start by describing what you see first; then move from left to right or from near to far. To narrate a story, you'd usually arrange the events in the order they happened, or chronological order. If you plan to give reasons for an opinion, you might choose order of importance. You'd begin with your most important reason and then work toward your least important. Or you might do the opposite, putting your most important reason last. Examine Rafael's prewriting notes. Which order did he choose? Why?

Could Rafael have chosen another order for these details? Explain your answer.

Organizing ideas

The activities our class did together made eighth grade a year to remember.

(4) talent show—April

(1) mural project—October

tutoring

(5) craft fair—May

(6) Olympic Day—June

parent's night

(2) Foods-of-the-World Festival—December

(3) class trip—March

visiting author

Activities

Here are some activities to help you apply what you have learned.

1. Guided Assignment

Select one of the following topics that interests you:

- a place where I can be alone
- a game or contest I always remember
- a rule or law that should change

Jot down some notes, using freewriting, listing, or clustering. If necessary, investigate your topic by interviewing or reading. Then follow these steps:

- Write a sentence expressing your main idea, and list details below it.
- Weed your list, keeping only those details that support your main idea.
- Arrange the ideas in a logical order, and number them.
- If you wish, use your prewriting notes to draft a page or two about the topic.

PURPOSE   To use prewriting techniques to generate and organize ideas
AUDIENCE   Your English class
LENGTH   1–2 pages

2. Open Assignment

Recall the three methods of organization discussed in this unit. Examine each of the following topics, and indicate which method you would choose to organize a paper. Explain your reasons for making each choice.

- the view from my homeroom window
- why I like . . . (a sport, a type of music, a particular hobby or game)
- a trip to the moon

3. Cooperative Learning

In a small group students should brainstorm to create a list of jobs they might like to have someday. Each group member should copy the completed list. Individually each member should cross out the jobs that seem less attractive and number the remaining jobs in order of importance with number one as the favorite. The group should then brainstorm about reasons for their choices. Working individually, each member should list reasons for choosing his or her favorite job, numbering them in order of importance.

COMPUTER OPTION

If your word-processing program includes an outlining feature, try using it to organize your ideas about the jobs you find appealing. Write down a main idea, using the three or four jobs that seem attractive to you. Order these jobs by importance, putting your favorite job last. Develop your outline by listing each job and then the reasons for each choice. The jobs will be major headings on your outline, and the reasons will be subheads.

Filling Up the White Space

Before painting a mural, an artist makes sketches on paper, sometimes on the wall itself. The artist may change the sketches many times, deciding what to include and how to arrange and rearrange it all. These steps could be called prepainting, since they're similar to prewriting. This mural artist is painting images on the wall. Rafael is at a similar point in the writing process. His next step is drafting. He'll turn his prewriting notes into the sentences and paragraphs that will work together to introduce the class memory book.

Starting, Stopping, Starting Again

First, Rafael rereads his prewriting notes, thinking about his purpose, audience, and list of ideas. He's ready to draft. One place to begin is at the beginning, with an introduction. Keep in mind that leads, or openings, are important. A writer must create interest and make readers want to keep reading. Try out some techniques that professionals use in writing leads. For example, ask a question, present an unusual detail, or use a dramatic quotation. Be sure to state the main idea clearly and explain what will follow. Here's a first draft of the memory-book introduction.

Was it worth the wait? Turn the pages to see for yourself. Remember how hard it was to decide what to include in our memory book? We finally picked the great activities our eighth-grade class did together. Join us as we relive the mural project, the Foods-of-the-World Festival, the D.C. trip, the talent show, the craft fair, and the Olympic Day.

What does Rafael accomplish in his first and last sentences?

Not all writers begin at the beginning. Some start in the middle, on a part that seems easier to write. Others tackle their conclusion first. Drafting means trying options and taking chances. You may get stuck. To get unstuck, try one of these strategies.

Ways of Getting Unstuck

Draw a picture about your topic.	Have a healthful snack.	Freewrite in your journal.	Take a walk, or ride your bike.

• JOURNAL ACTIVITY •

Think It Through

What strategies have helped you start drafting or get unstuck? What new strategies could you try? In your journal make a list to use when you're stuck.

Letting It Flow

As you draft, use your prewriting notes. They'll remind you of your purpose, audience, and plan of organization. Let your ideas flow freely. Don't interrupt the flow of ideas by thinking about grammar or spelling or even about writing in paragraphs. Remember, you'll have a chance to make changes later.

Later, the writer will correct spelling errors in this line. When the ideas are flowing, keep going!

How can we forget The mural project began the year. The idea was to capture the spirit of our school and community in paint strokes. Barb and Deji led us in forming comitees, and then we all got into the act. Four paint-soaked months later our beautiful mural was done, ready for all to see.

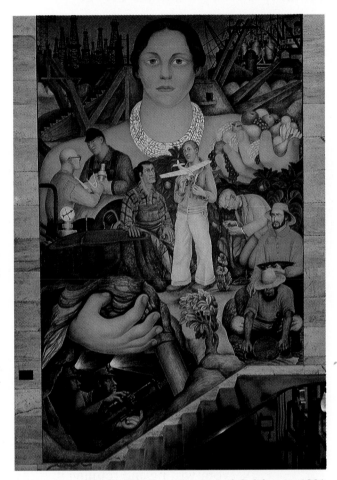

Diego Rivera, *Allegory of California*, 1931

Here are some activities to help you apply what you have learned.

1. Guided Assignment

Study the mural above. Then write a description of it, following these steps:

- **Prewriting** Look closely at each part of the mural, and jot down what you notice. Think about what message it seems to express. What is the mural about? What does it say to you? Write in one sentence what you think the mural says, and then brainstorm about what makes you think so. Select a method of organization, and number your ideas using that order.

- **Drafting** Reread your prewriting notes. Then draft your description using the organizational method you chose above. Let your ideas flow freely.

PURPOSE   To plan and draft a description of the mural

AUDIENCE   Your classmates

LENGTH   1–2 pages

2. Open Assignment

Imagine that you are a professional artist. Think of a mural, a sculpture, or another work of art you could create for your school or city. Jot down a description of the work and some reasons why you think the school or city should display it. Finally, draft a letter to the principal or mayor requesting permission to present your finished work of art.

3. Music

Choose one of your favorite songs. Write down some of the lyrics. Imagine that the songwriter has asked you to write another verse. Make a list of first thoughts. Select one idea that seems promising, and draft a verse.

Revising: Taking a Fresh Look

Changing the Recipe

Ben took stuffed grape leaves to the Foods-of-the-World Festival. He'd used his mom's Lebanese recipe. His family tasted it. They told him, "Add pine nuts," and, "You need more raisins," until finally they said, "It's just right!"

No one expects to prepare a new recipe perfectly the first time, without even a taste test. Similarly, no one should expect to create perfect writing without revising. The word *revise* means "taking a fresh look" at your writing and refining it.

Revising for Clarity and Sense

After you've finished your first draft, put it aside for a time—at least a day, if possible. When you see it again, you can tell better how it will sound to readers. Read it aloud, asking yourself, Is this clear? Does it make sense? Have I chosen the right words? The revising stage is a good time to consider whether you've used the best words. You might use a thesaurus to help you find words that say exactly what you mean. Examine the suggested revisions on the facing page. Then study the following chart to help you revise.

Eighth-grade eating habits may have been changed forever by this event. Foods from places like Puerto Rico, India, and China expanded our taste experiences. *Spicy dishes* ~~Food,~~ such as tacos and curries made peanut butter sandwiches seem like kids' stuff. Who can forget the parade of taste sensations that marched across our tongues at the Foods-of-the-World Festival? ~~Jenny Diaz covered the tables with blue and white tablecoths and put a colorful bouquet on each one.~~

How did the writer improve the paragraph by changing "food" to "spicy dishes"?

Moving this topic sentence to the beginning will help the writer focus on the main idea.

Questions for Revising

1. Is my writing clear? Does it make sense?
2. What is my purpose, and do I accomplish it?
3. Do I consider my audience?
4. Have I chosen the best, most precise words?
5. Do I stay on the topic? Do I say enough about it?

• JOURNAL ACTIVITY •
Try It Out

Review your journal for accounts of recent events in your life, or recall events from the past. List some you'd like to write about. Circle those you could combine.

Peer Reviewing

One way to identify trouble spots in your work is to ask other writers to read and comment on it. These peer reviewers will see your writing with a fresh eye. You can return the favor by looking over their work. As a peer reviewer, comment first on what is successful about the piece—in other words, say what works well for you. Then suggest any changes you think would help readers understand better. Read the paragraph below, comparing the peer reviewer's comments with the writer's revisions.

You made the food festival sound like fun.

Maybe you should list the ingredients.

Does the sentence about learning to cook belong?

I am confused by the last sentence.

We sampled delicious treats from several countries, but among the highlights *of the festival* were the pot stickers from the kitchen of Ms. Yu, our teacher. Ms. Yu used *an old family recipe* a way that had been passed down to her from her mother. Her mother taught her how to cook. Ms. Yu offered everyone a fortune cookie. Reading our fortunes aloud added a touch of humor to the event. Our greatest fortune came *when Ms. Yu gave us* with the recipe for those yummy pot stickers.

You can follow all or some or none of your peer reviewer's suggestions. Notice that the writer of the paragraph above made two of the three suggested changes. A peer reviewer's comments can help you decide what changes to make, but as the writer you're in charge.

Activities

Here are some activities to help you apply what you have learned.

1. Guided Assignment

The painting below will be exhibited in a gallery near your school. Imagine that you have been asked to write an article about it for your school newspaper. Explain what you see in the painting. Describe how the painting makes you feel. When you've completed your first draft, review it for clarity, and revise it as needed.

- Ask yourself the revision questions presented in this lesson.
- Ask a peer reviewer to read your draft and make comments.

Jacob Lawrence, *Village Quartet,* 1954

- Consider your peer reviewer's comments, and revise your writing.

PURPOSE   To use your ideas and a peer reviewer's ideas in revising an article

AUDIENCE   Teachers and students

LENGTH   1–2 pages

2. Open Assignment

Think of a person who has been important in your life, and explain why to your classmates. For example, a coach has helped you overcome shyness, a teacher has encouraged your interest in science, or an aunt or uncle shares your interest in your family's roots. Take prewriting notes, and draft one to two pages about how the person has been important to you. Revise your writing for clarity and sense, keeping your audience and purpose in mind.

3. Music

Jacob Lawrence's painting depicts four musicians playing jazz. Listen to a piece of jazz, and take notes about how the music makes you feel. Then draft a page describing the music and its effect on you. Ask a peer reviewer to comment on your draft. Then revise it for clarity.

Revising: Writing Unified Paragraphs

Not Every Picture Tells a Story

Alicia looked for photos taken on the class trip. She found two that portrayed the same area, but one of them caught her eye because it focused attention on the Washington Monument. This dramatic photo would help her tell the story of an exciting day.

As a writer you want to make sure each paragraph has a single, clear focus. Jot down some ways of doing so.

Checking for Unity

A paragraph is unified if all its sentences work together to express one main idea. That main idea is often expressed in a topic sentence, which may appear at the beginning or the end or even in the middle. In revising, decide whether the main idea would be clearer if you added or revised a topic sentence. Make sure all the details support the main idea. What unifies the paragraphs below?

Literature Model

There are two levels on which to enjoy a tour through black history in the nation's capital: Visit those neighborhoods that stand now and those monuments erected in memory of past struggles and accomplishments. Then, as you drive or walk around the city, try to imagine what once was.

Since 1790, when Congress ordered that a federal city be built on the Potomac River, blacks have made rich and varied contributions. Benjamin Banneker, a black surveyor, assisted Pierre L'Enfant, the city's designer, in laying out the new capital. When the temperamental L'Enfant was dismissed, taking his design notes with him, Banneker's memory was invaluable.

Patrice Gaines-Carter,
"Washington as a Mecca of Black History"

The details explain the "two levels" introduced in the topic sentence.

Why does the writer begin a new paragraph here?

• JOURNAL ACTIVITY •
Try It Out

List ten or more random ideas about your town or city. Review your list, and write topic sentences for paragraphs that could include two or more of the ideas.

Holding Ideas Together

The ideas in a paragraph must relate in clearly understandable ways. Writers connect their ideas, using words and phrases called transitions. Notice the transitions in the following memory-book passage.

Transitions

Time

after	before	finally
first	next	at once

Place

above	across	beside
below	next to	near

Cause and Effect

as a result	because
since	therefore

Using Transition Words

After our long bus ride, we were glad to reach our hotel in downtown Washington, D.C. The next morning found us revived and ready for our tour. The first stop was the Washington Monument. After waiting in line for an hour, we took the minute-long elevator ride to the top. When we got there, we looked out across the city. How awesome it was!

Our next stop was the Lincoln Memorial. Since Lincoln is one of my heroes, I took some photos of the seated statue. The statue's huge size reminded me of what a great president Lincoln was.

You don't think about transitions as you draft. When you revise, however, you should see that you've made smooth connections between ideas. In descriptive writing you may use spatial transitions, such as *nearby* and *on one side*. In narrative writing you may arrange ideas chronologically and use time transitions, such as *first* and *then*. When writing to explain, you can use cause-and-effect transitions, such as *therefore* and *as a result*.

Here are some activities to help you apply what you have learned.

1. Guided Assignment

You have been asked to write a column for a travel magazine for young teens. You are to describe something memorable you saw on your trip to a city or town in the United States. When you have completed your first draft, revise each paragraph for unity, answering these questions:

- What is my single main idea?
- Which sentence clearly states the main idea?
- Do my ideas flow smoothly? Do I need to add transitions?

PURPOSE To consider audience in revising for unity
AUDIENCE Young teens
LENGTH 1–2 pages

2. Open Assignment

In a letter to a friend, write a one-page account of one of the following events or an event of your choice. Using what you have learned in this lesson, revise your writing for unity. Add transitions to make time order clear.

- the final moments of a close race
- the conclusion of a mystery story
- the end of a great (or terrible) day

3. Art

Examine the painting below. Notice how the artist draws the viewer in through a series of doorways and windows. Draft a paragraph that describes the painting. In revising, make sure that you have used transitions to help your reader understand.

Monika Steinhoff, *La Plazuela, La Fonda (Hotel)— Santa Fe, New Mexico*, 1984

Revising: Writing Unified Paragraphs **75**

Revising: Writing Varied Sentences

Tonight's Attractions

Kim and Emily were arranging the program for the class talent show. Above all, they wanted the show to entertain and please the audience. Originally they decided to open with three vocal solos in a row, but during the first rehearsal they saw that this arrangement didn't work. They rearranged the program. The show would open with a vocal solo, followed by a stand-up comedy act and a modern-dance routine before the next vocal solo. The variety would keep the show flowing and would give it a pleasing rhythm.

In much the same way, a writer strives to produce a pleasing rhythm in his or her sentences. When you revise, read your sentences aloud, and listen to them. What will they sound like to your readers? Do they seem to plod along like three vocal solos in a row? Or do they flow smoothly with the rhythm of a well-planned talent show?

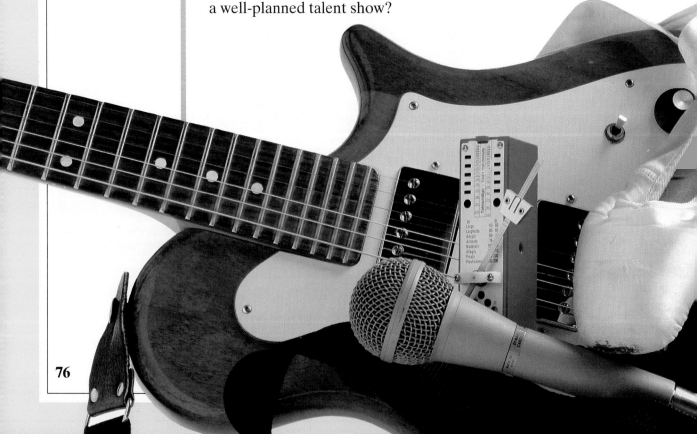

Varying Sentence Structure

One way to give your writing a pleasing rhythm is to vary your sentence structure. Instead of always beginning with a subject, start some sentences with an adverb, a prepositional phrase, a participial phrase, or a subordinate clause. Rafael noticed that he'd used the same basic pattern—a subject followed by a predicate—over and over again. Notice how he achieved a better rhythm by varying his sentence beginnings.

> *To open the show,*
> ~~The opening act was~~ Maria. ~~She~~ sang the song "Memory" from the musical *Cats*. Everyone was surprised at the emotion Maria put into her song. *Since* She's usually so quiet. Raoul performed next. His comedy act drew peals of laughter from the audience. ~~We weren't surprised by that.~~ Raoul is funny *even when he's not on stage.*
> *and Kim*
> For the next act Shanti performed a dance routine to rap music. ~~Kim danced with her.~~

How did Rafael begin his first sentence?

What else did Rafael do to vary his sentences?

• JOURNAL ACTIVITY •

Think It Through

Read at least one page of your writing aloud. How does it sound? Examine the sentence patterns. Look especially at your sentence beginnings. Jot down different ways to vary the structure and patterns of sentences.

Varying Sentence Length

Good writers avoid the monotony of many long sentences in a row and the choppiness of many short ones. The narrator of the selection below is a young boy traveling by train from Mexico to California. Notice the sentence rhythm. Then study the graphic to see how you can "cut and paste" to revise your sentences for length.

> **Literature Model**
>
> **D**uring the afternoon dark clouds had piled up over us, rolling over the desert from the mountains. At sunset the first drops fell on our canvas roof. The rain picked up and the train slowed down. It was pouring when we began to pass the adobe huts of a town. We passed another train standing on a siding, the deck of our flatcar flooded and the awnings above us sagging with rainwater and leaking. It was night.
>
> Ernesto Galarza, *Barrio Boy*

Which sentences vary widely in length, and how does this kind of variety affect the writing?

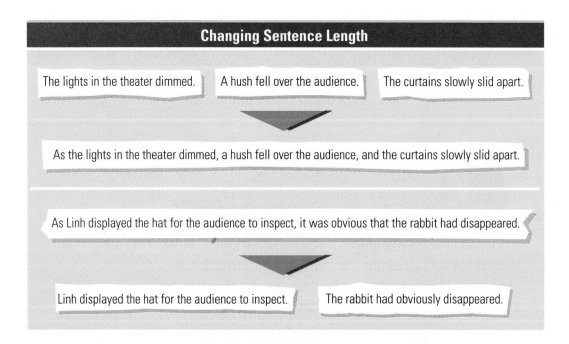

Changing Sentence Length

The lights in the theater dimmed.   A hush fell over the audience.   The curtains slowly slid apart.

As the lights in the theater dimmed, a hush fell over the audience, and the curtains slowly slid apart.

As Linh displayed the hat for the audience to inspect, it was obvious that the rabbit had disappeared.

Linh displayed the hat for the audience to inspect.   The rabbit had obviously disappeared.

Activities

Here are some activities to help you apply what you have learned.

1. Guided Assignment

Think of an unusual occupation, and imagine that you want to pursue it as your career. Write to a friend describing your feelings about what you want to do. Read your writing aloud, listening to the sentences. Do they all sound alike? If so, revise your letter to vary its rhythm and pace. Begin your sentences in different ways. "Cut and paste" to vary your sentence length.

PURPOSE	To revise your writing to give it liveliness and variety
AUDIENCE	A friend
LENGTH	1 page

2. Open Assignment

Choose one of the topics below or another topic related to the entertainment business. Use a prewriting technique to begin. Then draft a paragraph about the topic. Before revising, read your draft aloud, or ask a classmate to read it. Pay attention to the individual sentences. Then, using what you have learned in this lesson, vary your sentence structure and length. Read your revised paragraph, listening for a smooth flow and a pleasing rhythm.

- music video
- the influence of the media (radio, television, newspapers, movies) on young teens

- an entertainer you admire and would like to know

3. Cooperative Learning

With a small group, practice revising your sentences for variety and rhythm. Select a movie or a television program that all members of the group have seen. Together discuss the plot and characters. Each member of the group should choose a different aspect of the movie or program and write a paragraph about it. One member should record the assignments.

When everyone has finished writing, work together to suggest ways of revising to vary your sentences. Look over your work for the Journal Activity to recall ways of varying sentence beginnings.

Finally, assemble your paragraphs into a small booklet. Individuals can copy the paragraphs neatly, incorporating the suggested revisions, and prepare a final copy with a cover and title.

COMPUTER OPTION

All word-processing programs include an editing feature that allows you to cut and paste easily. Using this feature, you can delete sentence parts or move them. This is especially useful when combining two or three short sentences into one long one or when breaking a long sentence into two or three shorter ones.

Revising: Writing Varied Sentences　**79**

Editing: Fine-tuning Your Work

Showing Off Your Best

The long-awaited memory book is just about finished. After all that hard work, the first thing people see shouldn't be a misspelled word on the cover. Correcting the spelling may seem a little thing, but it's important to do before the book reaches its audience.

Taking time to edit your own writing is just as important. During the editing stage your goal is to get your writing ready to share with others. You want to make it as nearly perfect as possible. Ask a peer reviewer to look it over. A fresh pair of eyes will often catch mistakes you have overlooked.

Checking Your Sentences

The first step is editing your sentences. Read them over carefully to check word choice and to identify any sentence fragments or run-on sentences. Examine the following edited paragraph. The writer has identified errors and marked them with proofreading symbols.

Proofreading			
Symbol	**Meaning**	**Symbol**	**Meaning**
∧	Insert	⊙	Period
⌒	Delete	⌄	Comma
⌒	Reverse	≡	Capital letter
¶	New paragraph	/	Lower-case letter

Lydia displayed
At the craft fair∧ Several items of jewelry made from ordinary office supplies. One of the most beautiful pieces was a pin in the shape of a skyscraper⊙ it was made out of neon-colored paper clips, gold staples, and the cap from a portable pencil sharpener.

The writer has broken the sentence into two shorter ones. Is there another way to correct this run-on sentence?

• JOURNAL ACTIVITY •
Try It Out

In your journal freewrite about the spirit of the group activities at Carver Junior High or at your own school. What words capture that spirit?

Proofreading for Mechanics

Some writers proofread as they draft and revise. Most writers, however, concentrate on getting their ideas down. Then, after editing for sentence structure, they proofread for errors in mechanics—spelling, capitalization, punctuation. What is the meaning of each proofreading mark used in this paragraph?

Why did the writer circle "staggerd" and "principle"?

¶ After the minimarathon had ended and the last few runners had (staggerd) into the schoolyard, the closing ceremonies for Olympic Day began. Justin, our star musician, had composed a song just for this day. The words reflected the spirit of the events. With the winning athletes leading the parade, we marched into the School auditorium, singing Justin's song. Ms. tsao, our (principle), handed out ribbons as we all cheered.

© Chronicle Features, 1981 Larson 11-2

"Mind if we check the ears?"

You edit your work because you want to make your ideas clear. Once you've proofread your draft, prepare a clean final copy. Read your work over one more time. If you still find a small mistake, correct it neatly.

Activities

Here are some activities to help you apply what you have learned.

1. Guided Assignment

Imagine your class has created a memory book. You've decided to sell copies to parents and friends to raise money for extracurricular programs. You've written the following draft of an ad to promote sales. Copy it, and use the proofreading symbols to edit it. Then prepare a neat final copy.

What an eventful year for the eighth grade at Carver Junior High School! Now you can share our wonderful memorys by purchasing a copy of the class memory book, called <u>this unforgettable year</u>, for just $3.95, the book is availible in the social center at the School, or you can order a copy by calling 555–1234. Don't delay, the number of copies is limited.

PURPOSE   To practice using proofreading symbols in editing
AUDIENCE   Parents and friends
LENGTH   1 paragraph

2. Open Assignment

Select a paragraph you have written for a subject other than English. Correct any fragments or run-on sentences you find. Then proofread for errors in spelling, capitalization, and punctuation, using the chart on page 81. Prepare a clean final copy that includes the corrections.

3. Cooperative Learning

In a small group brainstorm ideas about the spirit of the Olympic Games. Mention specific events you remember. Then, on your own, look through newspapers, magazines, and books to find information on the most recent Olympics. What were the most exciting moments? Write a paragraph summarizing a story you believe captures the spirit of the Olympics.

Next, in a small group read your papers aloud. Pass them around, and have each member check for clarity and sense, varied sentence structure, or varied sentence length. Pass them around again, and have each member look for fragments and run-ons, misspelled words, incorrect or missing capitalization, or faulty punctuation. Write your peer-review comments on a separate sheet of paper. Finally, make a clean final copy.

COMPUTER OPTION

The ability of your word-processing program to check spelling can be useful, but do not leave it all up to the computer. Your program probably won't alert you if you've written *form* instead of *from* or *their* instead of *there*. After using your computer to find obvious misspellings, proofread for errors only humans can identify.

Presenting: Sharing What You've Written

Going Public

What did the eighth-graders—Todd, Rafael, Ben, Kara, Deji, and the others—do with their completed memory book? What would you do with something in which you'd invested so much time, energy, and talent? You'd probably be proud, excited, and eager to share it. The eighth-graders were.

Look at the picture pages below. Then read the revised and edited paragraphs on page 85 about the Foods-of-the-World Festival. Who in Carver Junior High School will probably want a copy of *This Unforgettable Year*? What audience might the memory book have outside the school?

This Unforgettable Year in Pictures

Mrs. Talerico waited with us patiently to visit the United States Capitol.

Everybody helped us with the Foods-of-the-World Festival. The result was a feast fit for a king or queen of any nation.

The talent show gave everyone a chance to perform. Sylvia Lin practiced her solo for hours before going on stage.

Presenting to School Friends

At school you can present your writing to one of the best audiences you'll ever find, your own peers. Here are some ideas. Submit your writing to the school newspaper. Write the text for a bulletin-board display for science class, or create a poster to promote an activity. Some classes exchange letters with students in other states or countries. Some publish an anthology of poems and stories. Some publish a memory book or yearbook. Here is one page from *This Unforgettable Year.*

Who can forget the parade of taste sensations that marched across our tongues at the Foods-of-the-World Festival? This event may have changed eighth-grade eating habits forever. Foods from places such as Puerto Rico, India, and China expanded our taste experiences. Spicy dishes such as tacos and curries made peanut butter sandwiches seem like kids' stuff.

Among the highlights of the festival were the pot stickers from the kitchen of Ms. Yu, our teacher. Ms. Yu used an old family recipe passed down to her from her mother. These traditional treats tickled our taste buds and made us all want to travel to China. To add to our pleasure, Ms. Yu offered everyone a fortune cookie. Reading our fortunes aloud added a touch of humor. Our greatest fortune came when Ms. Yu gave us the recipe for those yummy pot stickers.

• JOURNAL ACTIVITY •
Think It Through

In your journal, list opportunities for presenting your writing in your school. Choose two you would like to try, and find out where and how to submit your work.

Presenting to Others

How can you "publish" your writing outside school? One of the best ways is to write letters to friends and family members. If you have ideas about a local problem, write a letter to the editor of your local newspaper. If you have an interest in a hobby or sport, you can probably find at least one specialty magazine about it, and you can exchange ideas with fellow enthusiasts through the letters-to-the-editor column. Two excellent magazines, *Merlyn's Pen* and *Stone Soup*, consist entirely of stories, poems, and other writing by students your age.

Contests offer still another opportunity for presenting your writing. The National Council of Teachers of English and other local and national organizations sponsor writing contests for young people. Your teacher or librarian may know about local groups, such as civic and veterans organizations, that sponsor essay contests. Can you find other ideas in the collage below?

Activities

Here are some activities to help you apply what you have learned.

1. Guided Assignment

Find three pieces of your writing that you have handed to a teacher for an assignment in either English or another subject. Think about how you could present each of these pieces to a larger audience, either in school or outside school. Be sure to refer to the list you prepared for the last Journal Activity. Choose the piece you like best, prepare it for the chosen audience, and present it.

PURPOSE   To go public with your writing
AUDIENCE   Your choice
LENGTH   Your choice

2. Open Assignment

Write a letter to a friend or relative about one of the topics listed below or about another topic of your choice. Think about your audience as you draft the letter. Make sure you have stated your ideas clearly. Carefully revise and proofread. Correct any mistakes in grammar, spelling, punctuation, or capitalization. Then make a clean copy, and submit your work to a local newspaper or national magazine. If you can't locate the address of the publication, ask your teacher or librarian for help.

- athletics and competition at the grade-school level
- the positive or negative influence of television on young people
- effective ways to overcome stage fright

3. Cooperative Learning

In a small group, plan a class newsletter. Brainstorm possible ideas for articles and stories related to school activities and events. One member of the group should record the ideas as they are suggested. Once the group has decided what activities and events to include in the newsletter, each member should choose a writing assignment. When all members have completed their writing, come together to revise and edit each piece. Then work together to lay out the newsletter. If possible, duplicate a copy for each class member. Or present your completed newsletter as part of a classroom bulletin-board display.

COMPUTER OPTION

To give your newsletter a professional look, use your computer and a desk-top publishing program to design it and lay it out. You can use a graphics program to create a logo—a special design that identifies the publication—and illustrations. For a clean, crisp appearance, use a laser printer if one is available.

WALTER DEAN MYERS

THE GAME

Growing up in Harlem and playing basketball prepared Walter Dean Myers
to write the book Fast Sam, Cool Clyde, and Stuff. *With New York City's*
116th Street as the setting, Myers tells how Stuff and his friends learn
to rely on each other during good times and bad. In this chapter
Stuff reports the play-by-play action at the year's most important
neighborhood basketball game.

We had practiced and practiced until it ran out of our ears. Every guy on the team knew every play. We were ready. It meant the championship. Everybody was there. I never saw so many people at the center at one time. We had never seen the other team play but Sam said that he knew some of the players and that they were good. Mr. Reese told us to go out and play as hard as we could every moment we were on the floor. We all shook hands in the locker room and then went out. Mostly we tried to ignore them warming up at the other end of the court but we couldn't help but look a few times. They were doing exactly what we were doing, just shooting a few lay-ups and waiting for the game to begin.

They got the first tap and started passing the ball around. I mean they really started passing the ball around faster than anything I had ever seen. Zip! Zip! Zip! Two points! I didn't even know how they could *see* the ball, let alone get it inside to their big man. We brought the ball down and one of their players stole the ball from Sam. We got back on defense but they weren't in a hurry. The same old thing. Zip! Zip! Zip! Two points! They could pass the ball better than anybody I ever saw. Then we brought the ball down again and Chalky missed a jump shot. He missed the backboard, the rim, everything. One of their players caught the ball and then brought it down and a few seconds later the score was 6–0. We couldn't even get close enough to foul them. Chalky brought the ball down again, passed to Sam cutting across the lane, and then walked. They brought the ball down and it was 8–0.

They were really enjoying the game. You could see. Every time they scored they'd slap hands and carry on. Also, they had some cheerleaders. They had about five girls with little pink skirts on and white sweaters cheering for them.

Clyde brought the ball down this time, passed into our center, a guy named Leon, and Leon turned and missed a hook. They got the rebound and came down, and Chalky missed a steal and fouled his man. That's when Mr. Reese called time out.

"Okay, now, just trade basket for basket. They make a basket, you take your time and you make a basket—don't rush it." Mr. Reese looked at his starting five. "Okay, now, every once in a while take a look over at me and I'll let you know when I want you to make your move. If I put my hands palm down, just keep on playing cool. If I stand up and put my hands up like this"—he put both hands up near his face—"that means to make your move. You understand that?"

Everyone said that they understood. When the ball was back in play Chalky and Sam and Leon started setting picks from the outside and then passed to Clyde for our first two points. They got the ball and started passing around again. Zip! Zip! Zip! But this time we were just waiting for that pass underneath and they knew it. Finally they tried a shot from outside and Chalky slapped it away to Sam on the break. We came down real quick and scored. On the way back Mr. Reese showed everybody that his palms were down. To keep playing cool.

They missed their next shot and fouled Chalky. They called time

Red Grooms, *Fast Break*, 1983–1984

out and, much to my surprise, Mr. Reese put me in. My heart was beating so fast I thought I was going to have a heart attack. Chalky missed the foul shot but Leon slapped the ball out to Clyde, who passed it to me. I dribbled about two steps and threw it back to Leon in the bucket. Then I didn't know what to do so I did what Mr. Reese always told us. If you don't know what to do then, just move around. I started moving toward the corner and then I ran quickly toward the basket. I saw Sam coming at me from the other direction and it was a play. Two guards cutting past and one of the defensive men gets picked off. I ran as close as I could to Sam, and his man got picked off. Chalky threw the ball into him for an easy lay-up. They came down and missed again but one of their men got the rebound in. We brought the ball down and Sam went along the base line for a jump shot, but their center knocked the ball away. I caught it just before it went out at the corner and shot the ball. I remembered what Mr. Reese had said about following your shot in, and I started in after the ball but it went right in. It didn't touch the rim or anything. Swish!

One of their players said to watch out for 17—that was me. I played about two minutes more, then Mr. Reese took me out. But I had scored another basket on a lay-up. We were coming back. Chalky and Sam were knocking away just about anything their guards were throwing up, and Leon, Chalky, and Sam controlled the defensive backboard. Mr. Reese brought in Cap, and Cap got fouled two times in two plays. At the end of the half, when I thought we were doing pretty well, I found out the score was 36–29. They were beating us by seven points. Mr. Reese didn't seem worried, though.

"Okay, everybody, stay cool. No sweat. Just keep it nice and easy."

We came out in the second half and played it pretty cool. Once we came within one point, but then they ran it up to five again. We kept looking over to Mr. Reese to see what he wanted us to do and he would just put his palms down and nod his head for us to play cool. There were six minutes to go when Mr. Reese put me and another guy named Turk in. Now I didn't really understand why he did this because I know I'm not the best basketball player in the world, although I'm not bad, and I know Turk is worse than me. Also, he took out both Sam and Chalky, our two best players. We were still losing by five points, too. And they weren't doing anything wrong. There was a jump ball between Leon and their center when all of a sudden this big cheer goes up and everybody looks over to the side-lines. Well, there was Gloria, BB, Maria, Sharon, Kitty, and about four other girls, all dressed in white blouses and black skirts and with big T's on their blouses and they were our cheerleaders. One of their players said something stupid about them but I liked them. They looked real good to me. We controlled the jump and Turk drove right down the lane and made a lay-up. Turk actually made the lay-up. Turk once missed seven lay-ups in a row in practice and no one was even guarding him. But this one he made. Then one of their men double-dribbled and we got the ball and I passed it to Leon, who threw up a shot and got fouled. The shot went in and when he made the foul shot it added up to a three-point play. They started down court and Mr. Reese started yelling for us to give a foul.

"Foul him! Foul him!" he yelled from the sidelines.

Now this was something we had worked on in practice and that Mr. Reese had told us would only work once in a game. Anybody who plays basketball knows that if you're fouled while shooting the ball you get two foul shots and if you're fouled while not shooting the ball you only get one. So when a guy knows you're going to foul him he'll try to get off a quick shot. At least that's what we hoped. When their guard came across the mid-court line, I ran at him as if I was going to foul him. Then, just as I was going to touch him, I stopped short and moved around him without touching him. Sure enough, he threw the ball wildly toward the basket. It went over the base line and it was our ball. Mr. Reese took me out and Turk and put Sam and Chalky back in. And the game was just about over.

We hadn't realized it but in the two minutes that me and Turk played the score had been tied. When Sam and Chalky came back in they outscored the other team by four points in the last four minutes. We were the champs. We got the first-place trophies and we were so happy we were all jumping around and slapping each other on the back. Gloria and the other girls were just as happy as we were, and when we found that we had an extra trophy we gave it to them. Then Mr. Reese took us all in the locker room and shook each guy's hand and then went out and invited the parents and the girls in. He made a little speech about how he was proud of us and all, and not just because we won tonight but because we had worked so hard to win. When he finished everybody started clapping for us and, as usual, I started boo-hooing. But it wasn't so bad this time because Leon starting boo-hooing worse than me.

You know what high is? We felt so good the next couple of days that it was ridiculous. We'd see someone in the street and we'd just walk up and be happy. Really.

For Discussion

1. When you are part of a dedicated group, like Stuff's team, how do you react to winning? How do you react to losing?

2. Imagine how you would feel if the coach made you sit on the bench at a crucial point in the game. What effect might your reaction have on the outcome of the game?

Readers Respond

The story made me feel as if I was part of the game. The coach, Mr. Reese, was my favorite character. When the team was losing by several points, he told them to keep cool, and he kept them steady. He also kept them together. Without teamwork, a team would have nothing.

Benjamin Rodriguez

This story is about winning a basketball game. The players were not the best, but they had spirit and hope, and that helped them through a very tough game.

My favorite character was Mr. Reese, the coach. He trusted his players, and he gave playing time to them all. He didn't show favoritism. I remember the scene in which he let some less able players get on the court. I was surprised because the team was behind, but their coach had confidence in them. The writer made Mr. Reese seem real by showing how happy he was and how proud of his players. It was his spirit that the players drew upon.

Keianna Chatman

Do You Agree?

1. Do you agree that Mr. Reese had a great deal to do with the team's success? If so, write in your journal about what qualities made him an excellent coach. Then compare him with a coach or a teacher you've known and liked.

2. How does Walter Dean Myers build suspense in this story? What details about the other team create suspense at the beginning? When did you suspect or realize that Stuff's team was going to win?

Writing Process in Action

Play by Play

Action-packed writing like "The Game" is exciting to read. You get caught up in the action, and you read quickly, eager to know what will happen next and how it will all turn out. Writing an action scene can be even more fun than reading one. When you write, you get to relive every exciting moment of the event that you're relating. The following assignment invites you to write an account of an exciting event you've experienced.

• Assignment •

Context	This year, the theme of your school newspaper's annual writing contest is "And You Were There." Entries must portray an exciting event experienced by the writer.
Purpose	To involve readers with your account of an exciting event
Audience	Readers of your school newspaper
Length	2 or more pages

The following pages offer step-by-step advice on how to approach this assignment. Don't feel that you have to remember everything you read. You can always refer back for help as needed.

1. Prewriting

What have you done recently that was exciting? Did you compete in a race or a chess match? Did you attend a concert or a pep rally? Did you have your artwork shown at an exhibit? Have you performed as a singer, an actor, or a dancer?

Use one of the options at the right, or an idea of your own, to begin thinking about a topic. Once you've decided what you'd like to write about, develop your ideas by listing, brainstorming, or interviewing.

Look at pages 56–59 for suggestions on using brainstorming to develop a topic. Pages 60–63 tell you how to use lists to make sure your supporting details fit your main idea.

Option A

Brainstorm ideas.

Option B

Read through your journal.

Option C

Look at old programs and photos.

Person skiing through very heavy snow. Brother Michael's wedding. Big snowstorm night before. Cars snowed in, buses late. People got to Village Hall any way they could.

2. Drafting

You can make an account of an event exciting by creating suspense. One way to create suspense is to emphasize time pressures. For example, in the brainstorming example above, the writer has focused on guests fighting the snow to get to a wedding on time.

Walter Dean Myers uses time pressures to create suspense throughout his account of the basketball game in the excerpt from "The Game." Look at this example:

> We came out in the second half and played it pretty cool. Once we came within one point, but then they ran it up to five again. We kept looking over to Mr. Reese to see what he wanted us to do and he would just put his palms down and nod his head for us to play cool. There were six minutes to go when Mr. Reese put me and another guy named Turk in.

As you write your draft, think about ways to emphasize the time element to create suspense. One way is to keep your readers aware of how much time is left to finish a task. For example, in movies or on television, a hero needs to defuse a bomb before it explodes. Suspense is created by repeatedly showing the bomb's timer slowly ticking away the minutes and seconds.

Remember, in the drafting stage you need to express your ideas by using sentences and paragraphs. You can make changes later. See page 64 for more help with drafting.

3. Revising

Review the assignment to make sure that what you've written satisfies the assignment's requirements. Make sure you haven't strayed from your topic.

Sometimes it's a good idea to set your writing aside for a day. Then read over your work as if you were seeing it for the first time. The questions below can help you think about revising.

Question A

Is my account clear?

Question B

Have I built suspense?

Question C

Have I used vivid details to involve the reader?

"I can't imagine where she is," Michael said counted the eighth ring of his call to Anika's. into the receiver as he paced back and forth. and the wedding was scheduled for noon. Eleven thirty, I wanted to ask if they'd had a knowing that she was probably stuck in the snow, fight, but I kept my mouth shut. from the front door of the Village Hall. Just then I heard Kenny yell, "Hey, everyone, As I reached the door, you've got to see this!" I couldn't believe my eyes.

It was Anika in her wedding dress, skiing down the street to the hall. It was 11:45. The guests who had made it to the hall applauded when Anika came inside, shaking the snow from her dress.

4. *Editing*

You've worked hard to decide what you want to say and how to say it well. As you prepare your article to send to "And You Were There," be sure to get rid of any errors. A careful editing job shows your readers that you care about your work and you don't want errors to distract them from your ideas.

The checklist at the right will help you catch errors you might otherwise overlook. Usually writers edit for only one kind of error at a time. Of course you always want to be on the watch for all errors, but if you do look for one kind at a time, you will probably do a better job of finding them. Use a dictionary and the Grammar, Usage, and Mechanics part of this book to help you with your editing.

Checklist

1. Have I used transitions well?
2. Is every word spelled correctly?
3. Have I used sentence variety?
4. Have I used standard spelling, grammar, capitalization, and punctuation?

5. *Presenting*

Make sure your account of an exciting event is neatly written or typed on clean white paper before you submit it to "And You Were There."

As an alternative way of presenting your writing, you might like to give an oral presentation. Let the excitement of the event come through in your voice, facial expressions, and gestures. You might want to include recorded background noise or music for your presentation. For example, you might want to record the sound of a crowd cheering or booing if your account is of a sports event.

Reflecting

Consider the experience you wrote about for this assignment. Has writing about it led you to view the experience in a different way? Did you find yourself forming a conclusion about your experience that hadn't occurred to you before you began to write?

Portfolio & Reflection

Summary

Key concepts in the writing process include the following:

- The writing process consists of sensible, specific stages.
- It is a flexible process, allowing writers to move back and forth.
- Prewriting means finding and exploring a topic, choosing a purpose and audience, and organizing ideas.
- Drafting means turning prewriting notes into sentences and paragraphs.
- Revising involves checking writing for clarity and sense and for varied sentence structure and length.
- Editing means correcting errors in sentence structure and mechanics.
- Presenting means sharing your writing with readers.

Your Writer's Portfolio

Look over the writing you did for this unit. Choose your two favorite pieces for your portfolio. Look for writing that does the following:

- grows out of ideas found and explored in prewriting
- contains words and ideas that reflect a specific audience and purpose
- opens in a way that interests readers and explains what will follow
- reflects revisions you made after you and a peer reviewed it
- reflects careful editing for sentence structure and mechanics

Reflection and Commentary

Think about what you learned in this unit. Answer the following questions as you look over the two pieces of writing you chose. Write a page of "Comments on the Writing Process" for your portfolio.

1. Which prewriting techniques will you probably use in other writing? Why?
2. What stage of the writing process do you need to work on the most?
3. What piece of your writing reflects the benefits of peer reviewing?
4. If your best writing for this unit were considered for publication in a class magazine, how would you prepare it?

Feedback

If you had a chance to respond to the following student comment, what would you say or ask?

I think that the hardest thing about writing is finding a topic.

Melissa Best, Canyon Park Junior High School, Bothell, Washington

Writing to Describe

A Closer Look

Marc Chagall, *Landscape at Peira-cava: the cloud*, 1930

A Novel

Alvarez Describes Home

"I began to write because it was a way to master words. It was also a way to make a home in words, in language. And you know, I always say that I left the Dominican Republic, and I landed not in the United States, but in the English language."

Julia Alvarez

Writer Julia Alvarez was ten years old when her family moved from the Dominican Republic to the United States. Her first language was Spanish. While learning English, she found out that words often have meanings that are more complex and more descriptive than their dictionary definitions.

Julia Alvarez grew up to write *How the Garcia Girls Lost Their Accents*, an award-winning novel about immigrant experiences similar to her own. Writing allows

Writing a Description

sheep... grazing... powder puffs... cumulus... clouds... looking at a sheep farm

1. Playing with Words   **2.** Discovering Details   **3.** Revising for the Reader

FOCUS

Writing description helps to recall memories and to share and clarify experiences.

Alvarez to bring back memories and to describe what makes her feel at home. As she explains, "Entering the world of the imagination, that's a portable homeland. You don't lose that. You take that anywhere you go. And you know, I can take out my pad of paper in the Dominican Republic, here in Vermont, in California, in Turkey—and it's the same blank page. It's the same sense of creating a world, of making meaning, wherever you go."

▼ *Alvarez says that "writing became my new place" when she moved from the Dominican Republic.*

1   Playing with Words

"Much of writing is playfulness with words. It's trying things out," Alvarez says. "You're not probably going to get it right the first time. So just let yourself get *some* of it right."

Learning to create vivid description takes time and practice for every writer. The writer must learn to notice the things of the world and to describe those things in fresh

ways. To help herself do this, Alvarez plays a word game. In her journal she'll describe what she sees in daily life. She might look at the sheep grazing near her house and think of different images to describe them, such as powder puffs and cumulus clouds. As she explains, "What's great is that maybe two weeks down the line— maybe two years down the line—wouldn't you know it, but I'll have a character looking at a sheep farm!"

2 Discovering Details

People often say that something important is "beyond words." Yet Julia Alvarez finds the words to describe complicated experiences of feelings and memories. "I think when somebody says that they can't describe something, they're trying for the big thing, instead of the little details that, of course, they can describe," she says.

Alvarez creates large effects with small details. She notices the intimate details that bring a reader close to a character or experience. The detail might be the feel of sun shining on top of a character's head. Or it might be the look of Mrs. Garcia's neck while she is combing her hair. When writing

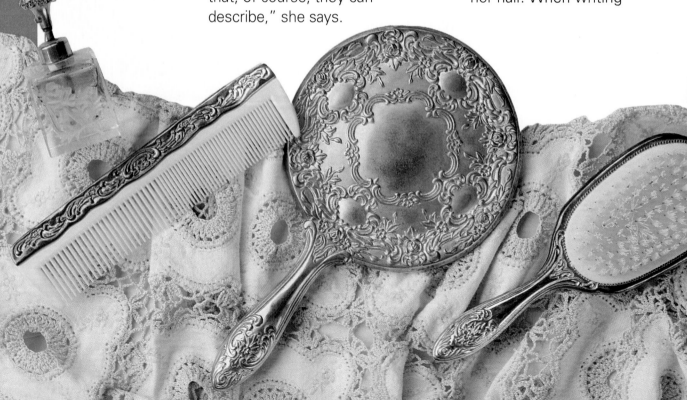

> Sandi leaned her elbows on the vanity and watched her mother comb her dark hair in the mirror. Tonight Mami was turning back into the beauty she had been back home. Her face was pale and tragic in the lamplight; her bright eyes shone like amber held up to the light. She wore a black dress with a scoop back and wide shoulders so her long neck had the appearance of a swan gliding on a lake. Around her neck sparkled her good necklace that had real diamonds.

the description of Mrs. Garcia in the chapter "Floor Show," Alvarez wanted to give a picture of what the mother looked like. Alvarez says, "I was trying to get a sense of the glamour and beauty of the mother, as seen from a little girl's eyes. I wanted to show that there was something beautiful and mysterious about the mother."

INTERFACE **Think about a childhood experience that you remember as being beautiful or mysterious. Try to remember specific details.**

▲ *In this passage from* How the Garcia Girls Lost Their Accents, *Alvarez describes the mother through the eyes of young Sandi.*

3 Revising for the Reader

Playing with words and finding details in memories and observations can be fun. Revising those early notes and journal entries can also be exciting and satisfying. As Alvarez explains,

"That's part of the fun—when it all falls into place. You know, I'll discover something, and then all of a sudden, I'll have to go back and redo the beginning."

Alvarez sometimes reads her work out loud after she writes a few sentences. In this way, she does some revising as she goes along. Still, details sometimes surprise her, and the direction a description takes may differ from what she imagined when she started writing. Alvarez says, "As you revise and revise, you happen upon things that you see are working. Then you polish them, or bring in new things to enhance them."

Having someone else read a description out loud can also help a writer to hear what needs revising. "What you write gets coated with your voice," Alvarez explains. "Having somebody else read out loud to you, you hear all the places that it's really off, in a way you can't hear it when you're writing."

Revision also demands that a writer think of her or his readers. The writer must revise and revise until the description fully brings an outsider into the private world of memories. As Alvarez says, "I know it's a process! And that certain things that get you started in a description later have to go."

ON ASSIGNMENT

1. Creative Writing

Describe a personal memory for an audience of eighth-graders living one hundred years from now.

- Think of a childhood memory—playing with friends, going to the dentist, raking leaves.

- Many aspects of daily life will probably change in the future, so choose clear descriptive details to describe your experience.

- Use details to show how you felt about this experience.

2. Descriptive Writing

Write a descriptive portrait of someone you know.

- Choose someone you know to describe.

- Make a list of details you notice about the person. Perhaps she wears a particular pair of earrings. Perhaps he walks a certain way.

- What kind of feelings do you want to convey about the person to your future readers?

3. Cooperative Learning

Julia Alvarez does word-play exercises to develop her abilities to observe and describe the world around her. Here's a chance to play the description game.

- Meet with a small group. Each member writes down one thing in the room.

- Go around the circle.

After someone reads an item, stop, and write down at least one image that describes that thing. Read your images out loud to one another.

- Choose one of your images to develop into a one-paragraph description.

- Exchange manuscripts with a partner, and read each other's work out loud. Discuss how the description works and how it could be improved.

- Revise your description.

Steamy Summer Evenings

How would you describe summertime? What comes to mind when you hear the word? Do you hear a summer storm rumbling in the distance? Do you feel the sticky air on your skin as you sit on a crowded bus? Can you hear the shouting and cheering at a softball game? A good description will re-create sights, sounds, and other impressions. Like writer Lorraine Hansberry's recollection of summer in Chicago, it will make the writer's memory come to life for you.

Literature Model

*E*venings were spent mainly on the back porches where screen doors slammed in the darkness with those really very special summertime sounds. And, sometimes, when Chicago nights got too steamy, the whole family got into the car and went to the park and slept out in the open on blankets. Those were, of course, the best times of all because the grownups were invariably reminded of having been children in rural parts of the country and told the best stories then. And it was also cool and sweet to be on the grass and there was usually the scent of freshly cut lemons or melons in the air. And Daddy would lie on his back, as fathers must, and explain about how men thought the stars above us came to be and how far away they were.

Lorraine Hansberry, "On Summer"

You Are There

Descriptive writing often starts with a memory or an observation—something that caught your attention. The details that made someone or something stay in your mind become the raw material for creating a description. Notice how writer Nicholasa Mohr brings to life details about Puerto Rico through the observation of one of her characters.

*S*he saw the morning mist settling like puffs of smoke scattered over the range of mountains that surrounded the entire country-side. Sharp mountainous peaks and curves covered with many shades of green foliage that changed constantly from light to dark, intense or soft tones, depending on the time of day and the direction of the rays of the brilliant tropical sun. Ah, the path, she smiled, following the road that led to her village. Lali inhaled the sweet and spicy fragrance of the flower gardens that sprinkled the countryside in abundance.

Nicholasa Mohr, *In Nueva York*

What words does the writer use to help you see the changing mountains?

Mohr draws you into her memories with a walk along the path.

• JOURNAL ACTIVITY •
Think It Through

Think about how Nicholasa Mohr brings her village to life. List at least five words that the author uses to describe it. If you wish, write each word in a sentence that describes something familiar to you.

When you edit, use verb tenses consistently. For more information see pages 370–379.

Wherever You Look

You probably read descriptions more often than you realize. Good descriptive writing involves using your senses to observe, selecting precise details, and organizing your ideas. The chart below shows some examples of descriptive writing. In the model that follows the chart, Michael Lim describes a very unusual fish.

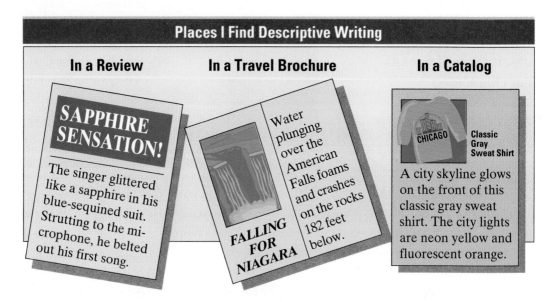

Places I Find Descriptive Writing

In a Review

SAPPHIRE SENSATION!

The singer glittered like a sapphire in his blue-sequined suit. Strutting to the microphone, he belted out his first song.

In a Travel Brochure

Water plunging over the American Falls foams and crashes on the rocks 182 feet below.

FALLING FOR NIAGARA

In a Catalog

CHICAGO

Classic Gray Sweat Shirt

A city skyline glows on the front of this classic gray sweat shirt. The city lights are neon yellow and fluorescent orange.

Student Model

The writer includes details such as the color and shape of the fish to help the reader see it.

*A*t the bottom of the pool, in the very center, was a fish, lying quietly. . . . The fish was a blazing yellow with streaks of almost metallic blue running down its sides, resembling a slender torpedo in shape. It was at least several feet long, streamlined, its head and tail tapered down from its thicker body. The fish's fins and tail were the same blue as its streaks, only translucent.

Michael Lim,
The American International School, Vienna, Austria
First appeared in *Merlyn's Pen*

Artist unknown, Mughal, *Fantastic Birds,* c. 1590

Here are some activities to help you apply what you have learned.

1. Guided Assignment

Picture in your mind a person you enjoy spending time with. List words or phrases that capture the person's appearance and personality, such as *laughing eyes, muscular,* or *ready for anything.* Then read your list and mark the items that best describe the person. Use these details in a written description. Show your writing to someone else who knows the person. Discuss other details you could include to complete your description. Then revise your writing.

PURPOSE To describe someone you like by reconstructing details from memory

AUDIENCE Yourself and someone who knows the person you are describing

LENGTH 1–2 pages

2. Open Assignment

Look at the words you chose for your Journal Activity. What other words could you use to describe something familiar to you? Write words that tell how it looks, sounds, smells, tastes, and feels. Then use these words to write a one-page description.

3. Art

You think that one of the birds in the painting above would look great on a T-shirt. Write to a friend who is a designer and ask him or her if your idea is a good one. Describe the bird carefully, including as many physical details as possible—its color, the shape of the feathers and beak, the position of its body. Look for other details to describe, such as what it is doing.

Making an Impression

Imagine that you've stepped into the painting below. What do you see, hear, feel, smell, and taste? Write a brief description of your surroundings.

Thomas Hart Benton, *Cradling Wheat*, 1938

Using Your Senses

You perceive the world through your senses. If you were in a kitchen, you might smell bread baking, hear pans clattering, see a floury counter, feel the hard crust of freshly baked bread, or taste a hearty slice. Writers provide details that appeal to different senses to depict a scene effectively. Beverly Cleary uses details like these to share childhood walks in the country.

As you prewrite, closing your eyes and concentrating on the senses of taste, touch, hearing, and smell will help you take notes for descriptions.

*T*hese walks, with the sound of cowbells tinkling in the woods by the river, and bobwhites, like fat little hens, calling their names, filled me with joy as I searched for flowers whose names Mother taught me: shy kitten's ears with grayish white, soft-haired pointed petals which grew flat to the ground and which I stroked, pretending they really were kitten's ears; buttercups and Johnny-jump-ups to be gathered by the handful; stalks of foxgloves with pink bell-shaped flowers which I picked and fitted over my fingers, pretending I was a fox wearing gloves; robin's eggs, speckled and shaped like a broken eggshell, which had such a strong odor Mother tactfully placed my bouquet in a mason jar on the back porch "so they will look pretty when Daddy comes in."

Beverly Cleary, *A Girl from Yamhill*

What words does Cleary use to appeal to different senses?

Cleary, like all good writers, tries to engage her reader's senses when she writes a description. Even if you've never set foot on a farm, you can imagine yourself there as you read the model. You can hear the tinkling cowbells and see grayish white kitten's ears. You can feel the velvet touch of petals and smell the nasty odor of robin's-eggs flowers. The writer takes you with her by telling exactly what she experienced. Think about a place you know well. What words could you use to take your audience there?

• JOURNAL ACTIVITY •
Try It Out

In your journal, list words and phrases describing a meal you remember: where it took place, the food you ate, the people you were with. Think of all five senses when selecting the words and phrases.

Appealing to the Senses

The process of writing a good description begins with careful observation. This first step may be difficult, though, if you are not used to looking at things closely. Without looking, write a description of something behind you. Then check to see if you got the details right. The chart shows how you can move from observing details to writing descriptions. In the model, Jessica Griffiths uses details she observed to describe a familiar day.

From Observing to Writing	
Impressions	**Description**
New (short) haircut Relaxed smile	Mr. Marshall greets students with a relaxed smile. His thick black hair, which was rather long last year, is clipped neatly above his ears.
Slamming lockers Squeaky new shoes	As the hallways fill with students, locker doors slam with a staccato beat. New shoes squeak in a skid across the freshly polished floor.
Shiny pencil sharpener Smelly pencil shavings	On the first day of school, the shiny pencil sharpener doesn't get a rest. It grinds pencils to a sharp point. The strong smell of shavings fills the air.

Student Model

What sounds of the first day of school does the writer describe?

The writer combines sounds and scents to create this description.

The first day of school is always exciting and a bit scary. Students greet old friends, and teachers chat in the hallways. The squeak of new shoes and the scuffling of sneakers on the linoleum floor mingle with the girls' giggling. Slamming lockers echo in the long corridors. The scent of bubble gum contrasts with the sharp smell of erasers and lead shavings. Pencil sharpeners grinding are a reminder that class has started. Late students hurry to their classrooms. A new school year has begun.

Jessica Griffiths, Springman Junior High School, Glenview, Illinois

Activities

Here are some activities to help you apply what you have learned.

1. Guided Assignment

For three days, practice being a good observer. On the first day, observe a person. Use as many senses as possible, and record your impressions. Follow the same procedure on the second day, observing a place; and on the third day, a thing.

A week later, without checking your notes, list the details you remember about the person, place, and thing you observed. Compare the details you listed with the notes you took as you observed. How much did you remember? What kinds of details did you forget? Now use your notes to write one paragraph each about the person, the place, and the thing. Have a friend read each of your paragraphs. Ask the person to tell you if your descriptions are vivid. Taking into account your friend's suggestions, revise your writing so that it comes to life.

PURPOSE   To improve sensory observation in writing description
AUDIENCE   A friend
LENGTH   1–2 pages

2. Open Assignment

Think of a place you remember well, such as one listed in the next column. When you think of this place, what do you see? Hear? Taste? Smell? Touch? Record the details that come to mind. Using the details, write a one-page description of the place to share with a friend who has never been there.

- the cafeteria of a school you used to attend
- a park you went to when you were younger
- a street in the neighborhood where you used to live

COMPUTER OPTION

If you use a computer to write the Open Assignment, you may want to triple-space a printout of your first draft. Use the extra space between the lines to write comments or corrections as you revise your draft.

3. Cooperative Learning

In a group, list names of characters from television or books. Select characters familiar to everyone in the group. Write the characters' names on slips of paper, and take turns drawing a name. Working independently, list details that describe the character whose name you've drawn. Then write a description of the character. Share your description, and challenge the group to guess the character you described. Discuss additional details that could bring the character into sharper focus, and rewrite.

Lost: Beagle with Bent Tail

LOST
During Storm

Small dog, smooth coat.
Some black marks.
Funny-looking tail.
Please call 555-3454
if you see our dog.

Harry the beagle is
LOST
Mixed brown, black,
and white coat.
Pink nose
with small black marks.
All-black ears.
Tail bent slightly.
Please call 555-3454.

Lost dogs are not always easy to find. But a precise description can help people identify a dog and return it safely to its owner. Which of the posters above do you think would be more helpful in identifying Harry? Why?

Choosing Precise Nouns and Adjectives

A good description includes specific nouns and exact adjectives. A precise noun, *beagle* or *Harry*, is more informative than a general noun, *dog*. The adjectives *brown, black*, and *white* describe the dog's coat more precisely than the vague adjective *smooth* does. The difference between a general and a precise description is like the difference between the dogs in the pictures. Notice the precise words Sarah Burch used on the next page.

From General to Specific		
Dog	Golden Retriever	Jake

A s the sound of thunder rumbles through the foggy November rain, you sit next to the roaring fire in your cozy living room. Waiting patiently for the wicked storm to pass, you notice clouds of varying shapes and textures highlighted by zig-zags of lightning. Branches plunge to the ground as winds gust violently. Rain forms muddy puddles along the rutty driveway. The crackling birch in the fireplace and the constant glow of the embers comfort you throughout the ferocious storm.

Sarah Burch, Springman Junior High School, Glenview, Illinois

What adjectives does the writer use to contrast the scenes inside and outside the house?

• JOURNAL ACTIVITY •

Try It Out

Think of an object that is important to you, and imagine that you have lost it. Make a list of words that describe the lost object. Then use the words to write a notice asking for help in locating the object.

Choosing Precise Verbs and Adverbs

Just as precise nouns and adjectives help create a vivid description, precise verbs and adverbs energize descriptive writing. Your choice of words will depend on the impression you want to make. For example, you might decide on the verb *devour* or *gobble*, rather than *eat*, to describe the action of eating hungrily. You might choose the adverb *fiercely*, rather than *angrily*, to communicate reacting furiously.

Notice how the writer concentrated on finding more precise verbs and more vivid adverbs as she revised her description of her guinea pig.

Find examples of precise, well-chosen adverbs.

Why does "whirls" create a clearer picture of Attila than "circles"?

"Stalks" is more exact than "walks."

Attila is a guinea pig with an attitude. From his tiny white ears to his short black legs, Attila wages war mercilessly. Mealtime is his battlefield. At dinner time he fixes his beady eyes on me as he ~~eats~~ *devours* his well-prepared guinea pig salad. Then his plump, black-and-white body tenses. He waits impatiently for the main course. Attila ~~scratches~~ *claws* ~~angrily~~ *fiercely* at the cage. He ~~circles~~ *whirls* around the cage. All night long Attila ~~walks~~ *stalks* restlessly near his plate. The next morning the battle begins again.

Here are some activities to help you apply what you have learned.

1. Guided Assignment

Write a description of an animal you have seen. The animal may be a pet, a zoo animal, or a wild animal. Follow these steps to write a vivid description:

- If possible, observe the animal first-hand and jot down your observations. Include notes on the animal's physical characteristics, actions, and personality. If you can't observe the animal directly, use a photograph or drawing, or view a television nature program.
- Read your notes and pick out the details you want to include in your description. Then write a draft.
- Revise your draft, replacing general words with more precise ones. If you need help, look in a thesaurus.

PURPOSE   To use precise words to create vivid and energetic descriptions
AUDIENCE   People who like animals
LENGTH   1–2 pages

2. Open Assignment

Imagine that you have the power to observe things from an animal's point of view. Using precise words, write a one-page description of an object for a humorous magazine. You may choose your own topic or one of these:

- a canoe as it might seem to a whale
- a pizza slice as it appears to an ant
- a ball of yarn from the point of view of a cat playing with it

3. Cooperative Learning

A small group can revise the following piece of writing. One person in the group should list more precise nouns. The second should list more vivid adjectives. The third should list stronger verbs. The fourth should list more intense adverbs. The group should then decide which suggestions to use in the revision. Finally, one member of the group can make a copy that includes all the changes.

The football players ran quickly onto the wet field for their first game of the season. Their uniforms were bright yellow. Every player's jaw tensed with determination. Each pair of eyes looked eager to begin the game. At kickoff the team yelled loudly and started to play.

COMPUTER OPTION

Many word-processing programs have an electronic thesaurus to help you find synonyms. You highlight the term you want to replace, and the thesaurus will list different options. You can use the thesaurus to add precise words to your writing.

Shh! Artist at Work

Jan Vermeer, *Allegory of the Art of Painting*, c. 1665–1670

Don't disturb him. You quietly pull back the curtain to get a better view. There he is, just beyond the wooden-backed chair and the fabric-draped table. You see him lost in concentration, his easel in front of him. What is he painting? You gaze in the direction the artist is looking and find out. He is painting the model, with her large book and crowning wreath of leaves. The Flemish painter Jan Vermeer arranged the details in this image so that the viewer's eye moves from behind the artist to the scene he is painting. Writers, like painters, arrange the details of a scene in a certain order and for a particular reason.

Creating Order in Space

Writers can order details in several ways, depending on the point in space that seems a logical starting place. When looking at a building, for example, you might first see a nearby detail, such as the decorative door frame. Then, farther up the front of the building, you notice decorative stone faces above the windows. To describe this building, you could order these details from near to far.

Three Kinds of Spatial Order		
Top to Bottom	**Near to Far**	**Left to Right**

Prewriting Tip

If you write a description using spatial order, you may wish to draw a picture to help you collect and organize the details you want to include.

Sometimes a scene lends itself to a particular kind of spatial order. Note how Laurence Yep uses top-to-bottom spatial order to describe a Chinese playground.

Literature Model

In those days, it consisted of levels. The first level near the alley that became known as Hang Ah Alley was a volleyball and a tennis court. Down the steps was the next level with a sandbox (which was usually full of fleas), a small director's building, a Ping-Pong table, an area covered by tan bark that housed a slide, a set of bars, and a set of swings and other simple equipment.

Laurence Yep, *The Lost Garden*

Which words in the description identify the spatial order as top to bottom?

• JOURNAL ACTIVITY •
Think It Through

Imagine that you are at a place you remember well. Choose a spatial order to observe details about the place. In your journal, list the details in that order.

Orienting the Reader

When you use spatial order, you must give your audience a way to picture the scene as you move from one detail to the next. Transition words, such as *under, to the right,* and *behind,* help to link details in order. As your readers read, they follow the path you've created. Notice how transition words act as directional signposts in Sarah Fisher's description of a room and in the diagram based on her description.

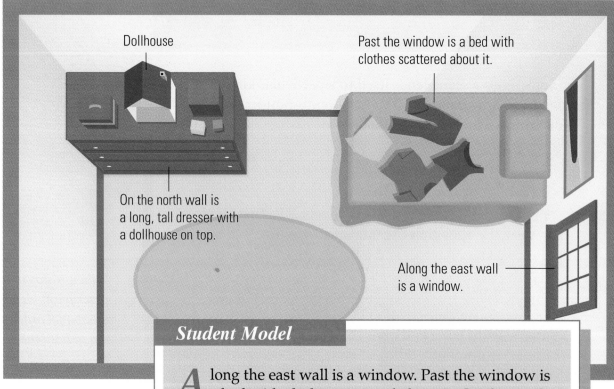

Dollhouse

Past the window is a bed with clothes scattered about it.

On the north wall is a long, tall dresser with a dollhouse on top.

Along the east wall is a window.

Student Model

*A*long the east wall is a window. Past the window is a bed with clothes scattered about it. On the north wall is a long, tall dresser with a dollhouse on top. To the right of the dollhouse are three jewelry boxes, one big and two small. To the left of the dollhouse is a purple box with a pink handle. This box holds my hair accessories and small gift boxes.

Sarah Fisher, Solomon Schechter Day School, Skokie, Illinois

Notice how Sarah uses phrases like "on the north wall" to help you find your way around the room.

Activities

Carolyn Brady, *Sky Blue and Peach*, 1989

Here are some activities to help you apply what you have learned.

1. Guided Assignment

Follow the steps below in writing a description of a classroom you were in last year. Write it for someone who has never seen the room.

- Decide which spatial order is the most natural way to arrange details.

- List details in the order that you will include them. Select transition words to link details.
- Use your list to write a rough draft of your description. As you revise, make sure your use of spatial order is logical and easy to follow.
- Give your description to a person who hasn't seen the place you are describing. Ask the person to use your description to draw a picture of the place.

PURPOSE   To use spatial order in a description
AUDIENCE   A friend
LENGTH   1 page

2. Open Assignment

In one or more pages write a description of a person, place, or thing, using a spatial order you wouldn't normally use. Choose one of the ideas suggested below or an idea of your own:

- a park, from top to bottom
- a person's head, from back to front
- a ballpark, described outward from the pitcher's mound

3. Art

Look closely at Carolyn Brady's painting *Sky Blue and Peach*. Write a one-page description of the painting, using one kind of spatial order. Show your description to a friend and ask if he or she can identify the type of spatial order you've used.

Using Spatial Order **121**

Packed with Memories

Your packed suitcase bulges before you. You're in a new apartment halfway across the country from your old home, about to unpack and start a new life. Suddenly your thoughts turn to the things you couldn't bring with you. You couldn't pack the bustle of the city outside your kitchen window. The basketball backboard that shook with the fury of your slam-dunks was left to rust in the rain. You decide to write to one of your old friends. In the letter you describe the things you brought with you and the treasures you left behind.

How can you describe something that is important to you? Notice how Amanda Morgan describes something that is important to her.

Student Model

T eddy is no placid-looking bear. He is stubborn looking. He is very well loved (as bears often get), and he is beginning to come apart at the seams. Mom tried to fix this tragic problem by sewing him up with bright red-and-blue yarn. The yarn is faded and looking a bit tattered itself, for the surgery was done about nine years ago.

Amanda Morgan, Neskowin, Oregon
First appeared in *Treasures: Stories and Art
by Students in Oregon*

Minding the Details

The process of writing a good description often begins with choosing an object or event that has meaning for you. It may be right in front of your eyes, or it may be stored in your memory. Once you decide on your subject, take notes on details that will help you describe it. If you're looking at the object or event, you might jot down the details you observe. If you're remembering something, list details that make it meaningful to you.

Asking yourself questions can help you choose details. For example, you might ask how something appears at different times of the day. You might ask what senses you use to observe an event or what you might compare the event to. The questions below may help you choose descriptive details.

1. How old is my bike?

   My brother bought it new three years ago.

2. What condition is it in?

   worn but well cared for; cracked seat

3. What color is my bike?

   mostly metallic blue with gray tires

4. What memories about my bike come to mind?

   the first time I rode it down our street after
   moving here; riding in the rain with Chris

• JOURNAL ACTIVITY •

Think It Through

Write three or four questions about something that is important to you. Draw a picture of the object, filling in details that answer some of your questions.

Pulling a Description Together

As you list the important details that describe a thing, you can also think about ways to group these details. The thing itself may suggest a certain kind of grouping. For example, you might organize the details of a flower by shape or color. The chart below shows three principles you can use to group details.

Grouping Details by Different Principles	
Principle	**Examples**
Shape/Color	Baggy blue-gray sweater, ankle-length denim skirt
Appearance/Function	Porch chair, rusted and bent, but still comfortable
Whole/Parts	Broken checkerboard, a bag of dominoes

Revising Tip

As you revise a description, be sure the details you have included help the reader follow the order you are using.

As you draft your description, use sensory details to bring your subject to life. Remember to use precise language, follow spatial order, and include transitions. Notice how Leslie Marmon Silko describes sandstone. Here she uses a *simile*—a comparison between two dissimilar things linked by the word *like* or *as*.

What precise adjectives does the writer use?

Literature Model

But this time there was something about the colors of the sandstone. The reddish pink and orange yellow looked as if they had been taken from the center of the sky as the sun went down. She had never seen such intense color in sandstone. She had always remembered it being shades of pale yellow or peppered white—colors for walls and fences. But these rocks looked as if rain had just fallen on them.

Leslie Marmon Silko, "Private Property"

Activities

Here are some activities to help you apply what you have learned.

1. Guided Assignment

You are a writer working on clothing advertisements. Find photographs of three eye-catching items. Then write a description of each. Make the description brief but chock-full of details. Include the following information:

- some clever words to attract the audience's attention
- identification of the clothing item
- the kind of material it is made of
- significant features, such as design and construction
- colors, patterns, and sizes
- place it is made and its price

When you have finished writing your descriptions, show them to a friend. Ask the friend to comment on how well the descriptions match the photographs and how appealing you have made the items.

PURPOSE   To use precise details in writing an effective description

AUDIENCE   Readers of a clothing ad and a friend

LENGTH   1–2 pages

2. Open Assignment

Think of something that was important to you in your childhood, such as a book or stuffed animal. Write a description of it to share with a friend. Pick out the details you will include in your description. Then group the details according to one of the principles listed on page 124. Before you revise the rough draft of your description, ask your friend to read and comment on the draft.

3. Cooperative Learning

In a small group have each member select something that has special meaning for him or her. You might choose the thing you sketched in the Journal Activity. Write a one-page description of it. The description should provide plenty of details. Then group members should exchange papers. Each person may read the description carefully and sketch the thing described. Afterward, take turns sharing descriptions and sketches. Discuss ways in which details in the descriptions helped to make the sketches.

COMPUTER OPTION

Before working on any of the assignments on this page, you may want to create two computer vocabulary files. One lists words that describe or name sensory details. The other lists transition words. In your file of sensory details, you might list adjectives that describe colors, shapes, textures, and sizes. Refer to the lists as you draft a description.

Writing About Literature
Describing the Subject of a Biography

Real People

You know yourself best. But your family and friends also have a strong sense of who you are. In the following passage Lisa Aldred uses the words of a family friend, Odell Payne, to describe a boy who would later become Supreme Court Justice Thurgood Marshall.

Literature Model

H e "was a jolly boy who always had something to say." But, she added, Thurgood showed a serious side as well. "I can still see him coming down Division Street every Sunday afternoon about one o'clock," she said. "He'd be wearing knee pants with both hands dug way into his pockets and be kicking a stone in front of him as he crossed over to Dolphin Street to visit his grandparents at their big grocery store on the corner. He was in a deep study, that boy, and it was plain something was going on inside him."

Lisa Aldred, *Thurgood Marshall*

Lisa Aldred gives a verbal snapshot of young Thurgood Marshall walking down the street kicking a stone. She illustrates the future judge's serious side by showing him deep in thought. With his hands in his pockets, he concentrates on the stone in front of him. He seems to block out all else.

Forming Strong Impressions

A biography tells the story of a real person's life. By telling what the person did and said, a biography can bring the person on the page to life. Usually a biography describes a person's physical appearance and personality. Such descriptions help the reader form impressions of the person. Here are some students' reactions to young Thurgood Marshall.

The description of the boy reminds me of my cousin Wilma. She used to spend hours skipping stones at the pond. I once crept up behind her. She didn't even notice me. Like Thurgood, Wilma was always "in a deep study." Sometimes that annoyed me, though!

In what way does Thurgood remind this student of his cousin Wilma?

I just read a book my grandfather should read. It tells about the early life of Thurgood Marshall, who was a Supreme Court justice. Grandfather's always telling me to pay attention. If he reads the book, he'll know I'm just "in a deep study."

This student has a good impression of Thurgood because he sees some of his own traits in the famous man.

• JOURNAL ACTIVITY •
Try It Out

Describe someone you know well doing something he or she does often. Be sure to consider how this action illustrates your subject's personality.

Focusing on the Subject

A good description of a person allows the reader to visualize the person. But appearances tell only a small part of the story. Often a person's thoughts and actions reveal far more about the person than what's on the surface. A good biography paints a portrait of the person, including his or her personality and attitudes. With precise language, sensory details, clear organization, and strong transitions, the subject of a biography comes into sharp focus. After reading Jean Fritz's *The Great Little Madison,* Andrea Gaines wrote the imaginary letter below. Notice how she used details that paint the young Madison's portrait.

Student Model

What details of Madison's appearance does Andrea provide?

What details of Madison's personality does Andrea point out?

Eighteenth-century Princeton University

October 16, 1769

Dear Aunt Winnefred,

How are you?

Sorry I haven't written you lately, but I've been busy here at Princeton. This is only my first year here, but I feel as though I have a number of friends already. One of them is a quiet sophomore, James Madison. He's kind of short and thin, and has a very low voice. His handsome face glows with energy. He throws himself into everything he does, whether it's reading books, protesting British taxes, or joining student fun.

I must run to class. I'll write to you later about my other friends.

Your loving niece,
Susan

Andrea Gaines,
Martha M. Ruggles
Elementary School,
Chicago, Illinois

Joan Brown, *The Night Before the Alcatraz Swim,* 1975

- What is the woman wearing? List colors and other details.
- What event does the title of the painting predict will happen?
- Note the woman's face and posture. What might be on her mind? What kind of person might she be?

Draft your description. Then check to see if you have used details that tell who the person is.

PURPOSE To write a description of the subject of the painting
AUDIENCE Readers of the biography
LENGTH 1–2 pages

2. Open Assignment

Write a one-page biography about a favorite fictional character of your choice. Select important details about the character from the story. You may make up information about the character if it fits with what you know about him or her.

Here are some activities to help you apply what you have learned.

1. Guided Assignment

Suppose you were going to write a biography of the woman in the painting above. Write a description of the woman for the biography. The following questions about the painting may help you plan:

3. Social Studies

Write a description of a historical figure whom you admire. Read a biographical account to gather information about the person. Then write a one-page description of the person at your age. Include information about the person's appearance, personality, and ideas.

David Weitzman
from
Thrashin' Time

In Thrashin' Time: Harvest Days in the Dakotas *David Weitzman describes
farm life in 1912 North Dakota as a boy might remember it. The book
recounts young Peter Anders's memories of the days when machines began to
relieve the tiring manual labor of farm workers. In the following passage
Peter recalls an extraordinary autumn day when the whole neighborhood
gathers to see a steam traction engine for the first time.*

Anna and I began pestering Pa to take us over to see the
new engine. But it didn't take much doing. I could tell
he wanted to go as much as we did. Pa glanced again
at the smoke billowing into the sky. "Ya, sure, we can go. I'll
finish up a bit here. Peter, you go hitch the horses up to the
wagon. Maggie, if you and Anna put up a picnic, we'll go have
us a look at that steam engine."

We got there to find that a lot of folks had come in wagons
and buggies to gather 'round and watch the thrashin'.[1] Steam
engines were still new in these parts. And there it was, the

---

1 thrashin' (thrash' in) [or threshing (thresh'ing)] separating grain or seeds
from a plant

engine with its dark blue boiler, shiny brass whistle, red wheels all decorated with yellow stripes, gears spinning and rods going back and forth, rocking gently in time to the puffs of smoke from the stack—*tucka-tucka-tucka-tucka-tucka*. The sounds, that's what I liked. *Tucka-tucka-tucka-tucka* and the little steam engine going *ss—ss—ss—ss—ss—ss—ss*. The engine was quieter than I thought it would be. It was almost alive like the horses working everywhere 'round it. And the horses. Why, I'll betcha there were sixty head, big horses—Belgians and Percherons [2]—coming and going that afternoon. Teams pulled bundle wagons heaped tall with sheaves of wheat in from the fields, pulled wagons of yellow grain away from the separator to the silo. Another team hauled the water wagon, and another wagon brought loads of cord wood to keep the engine running sunup to sundown.

David Weitzman, from *Thrashin' Time*, 1991

It was like the Fourth of July. Kids clambered up and slid down the hay stacks, played tag and skip-to-my-lou. Some of the men were pitching horseshoes and you could hear the thump of shoes fallen too short and the solid clank of a ringer. The women looked after all the little kids and put out lunches on big tables—heaps of potato salad, sandwiches, cakes and cookies and frosty pitchers of iced tea. Dogs napped in the dark cool under the wagons, not paying any mind to the puppies tumbling all over them. The older boys

2 **Belgians** (Bel′ jənz) **and Percherons** (Pur′ chə ronz′) large, powerful horses used to drag heavy loads

stood around together, pretending they were chewing plugs of tobacco, hawking and spitting, like the thrashermen, only theirs wouldn't come brown. The men stood around the engine and the separator, puffing on their pipes, thumbs hooked under their suspenders. They inspected every part of that machine, pointing to this and that, looked up and down the belt stretching between the engine and the separator in a long figure eight. Most of them had never seen a steam traction engine before.

Some of the older folks didn't like the new machine. "The old ways is the best ways," one of them said, tugging on his whiskers. "All this talk about steam engines is just a bunch of gibble-gabble," agreed another, "I'll stick to my oxen and horses." Others told of hearing all about engines exploding, killing and maiming[3] the thrashin' crews, of careless engineers starting fires that burned up the farmer's whole crop and his barn besides. "Horses live off the land, " Mr. Bauer said, "and don't need wood or coal. No, nothin' but some hay and oats and we don't have to buy that! What's more they give you foals." He reached over and rubbed his hand down the neck of a stout gray Percheron mare hitched to a grain wagon. "All you get from steam engines is debt." Mr. Bjork agreed, "and what would we do for fertilizer? Steam engines don't make much manure, you know." Everyone laughed. "More trouble than they're worth. Why last year Silas McGregor had to come borrow my oxen to pull his engine out of the mud. Wouldn't have one of those smoke-snortin' strawburners on my place," old Mr. Erstad scoffed, turning and waving away the scene.

But Mr. Torgrimson, now I could tell he was enjoying it. We were looking at the steam engine there up on the boiler, the connecting rod whizzing back and forth and the flywheel spinning so that the spokes were just a red blur. He was smiling and his eyes just twinkled. Then he pointed the stem of his pipe at the engine, squinted in a thoughtful way and rocked back

---

3 maiming (māmʹ ing) causing an injury so as to cripple or cause the loss of some necessary part of the body

and forth on his heels. "You know, Peter, that's a wonderful thing, the steam engine. You're witnessin' the beginnin's of real scientific farmin'." He couldn't take his eyes off that engine. "I read about a steam outfit— over Casselton way it was— that thrashed more than six thousand bushels in one day! Imagine that, six thousand bushels in just one day! Why you and your Ma and Pa all workin' together couldn't do more'n twenty or thirty in the same time."

Mr. Torgrimson was the one who told me all about bonanza farming, where a bunch of engines would start out together, side-by-side, before daybreak, each pulling a fourteen-bottom plow almost as wide as our house. "They go all day, Peter,

Thomas Hart Benton, *July Hay*, 1943

breakin' up thousands of acres of prairie grasslands before they rest at night—some even have head lamps so they can just keep going all night. The holdin's are so big, young fellow, that they go on 'n on for days like that 'fore they reach their line and turn 'round and plow back to where they started. Day after day, week after week they go up and back. Then they sowed all that land to wheat and thrashed one hundred and sixty-two thousand—here, I'll just write that number in the dust so you can see how big it is—162,000 bushels of wheat that season."

I could tell Pa liked the engine too. He got up on the wagon and pitched bundles for a while, and then stood on the engine platform talking to the engineer, Mr. Parker. When he got down, he came over and put his hand on my shoulder, all the time looking at the engine, shaking his head like he couldn't believe his eyes. "Parker's got some machine there, by jippers, quite an outfit. What do you think about all this, Peter, steam power instead of horse power?"

I wasn't sure. "If the engine took the place of the horses, I think I'd miss Annie and Lulu and Quinn. Wouldn't you, Pa?"

"I would, but, you know, horse-power thrashin' is awful hard on them, son. Sure, I'd miss them, but we work them hard all year plowin' and diskin',[4] and seedin' and mowin'. Then just when they're so tuckered out, about to drop and needin' a good rest, we put them to thrashin'. You and I both have seen too many good horses broken, seen them drop, die of the heat and tiredness right there in the traces. And for all their work we might get a hundred bushels, maybe two in a day. I don't know, Peter, maybe steam power is a better thing. I just don't know." Pa chuckled and his eyes got all crinkled and wrinkled with laugh lines the way they do. "I do know one thing though. If you asked the horses, I betcha they wouldn't be against this new steam power the way some folks 'round here are."

4 diskin' (disk′ in) breaking up soil with a disk-shaped tool

For Discussion

1. Has there been a day as memorable to you as this day seems to be to Peter? Why was the day you remember so important?

2. How do you react when you hear sayings like "The old ways is the best ways"? Now imagine you are sixty-five years old. In what ways might your reaction be different than it is at your present age?

Readers Respond

The beginning of the story captured my attention. The author gave a good, detailed look at the steam engine. Then the story really got rolling.

I enjoyed reading different points of view about the steam engine. I also liked reading the thoughts and feelings of the narrator. It made the story more real.

I recommend this story. It is a good description of America's past.

Nitida Wongthipkongka

I liked the scene in which the older people argued about the steam engine. They talked about the disadvantages of modern technology. Mr. Torgrimson was different, though. The invention thrilled him, and he thought about all the advantages of the invention.

I remember most clearly Mr. Torgrimson's talking with Peter about bonanza farming. He went on and on about how all that work could be done. He was my favorite character because he knew more about modern technology than the others and seemed more thoughtful.

I would end the story differently. I would have the father choose whether he wanted the steam engine or horses.

Marinel A. Marty

Did You Notice?

1. Did you notice how the author described the steam engine? How did it sound? What did it look like? What could it do?

2. Have you ever seen an amazing invention at a museum or at any other public place? Have you looked at one in a book? Write a paragraph describing the invention. Include sensory details to bring the invention to life.

Writing Process in Action

Harvesting Details

Harvesting crops—it's something farmers know all about. But many city people can't quite picture it. Through his descriptions in *Thrashin' Time,* though, David Weitzman enables even city dwellers to imagine the scene of an old-time harvest. Weitzman lets you use your senses to bring his descriptions to life. The following assignment invites you to describe something you know all about—the people, places, and things that are part of your favorite hobby.

• Assignment •

Context	You are writing an article for the magazine *Popular Hobbies.* This magazine contains descriptions of the people, places, and things associated with various student hobbies.
Purpose	To describe people, places, and things related to your favorite hobby
Audience	Student readers of *Popular Hobbies*
Length	2 or more pages

For advice on how to approach this assignment, read the next few pages. Don't feel that you have to remember everything. You can always come back to these pages during the writing process.

1. Prewriting

Start by thinking about the people, places, and things that go with your favorite hobby. Ask yourself, "What place or places does my hobby take me to?" "What types of people do I usually meet?" "What things do I use with my hobby?" To explore your answers, you might use one or all the options at the right. Perhaps you'll observe and take notes, as pages 106–117 discussed. Maybe you'll use your journal to recall details. You might also freewrite, as in the example.

Option A
Observe and take notes on details.

Option B
Review your journal.

Option C
Explore your ideas through freewriting.

I zoom along the smooth path by the park. People picnic, play radios, and eat things like fried chicken. I remember my bike rides by the songs I hear and food that I smell.

2. Drafting

Look over your prewriting and think about ways of organizing your material into clear images. You might start with the most important details and move to the least important. Or you might start with the details closest to you and move toward those farther away. There are many possibilities. Just use the one that makes the most sense to you. Remember, you're trying to paint a clear picture that grabs and holds your reader's attention with sensory language. You're trying to set the scene for your hobby. Notice how Weitzman sets the scene at the harvest:

> *It was like the Fourth of July. Kids clambered up and slid down the hay stacks, played tag and skip-to-my-lou. Some of the men were pitching horseshoes and you could hear the thump of shoes fallen too short and the solid clank of a ringer. The women looked after all the little kids and put out lunches on big tables—heaps of potato salad, sandwiches, cakes and cookies, and frosty pitchers of iced tea.*

A description rich in detail and sensory language can put your readers in the scene. It can give them a clear picture of the world your hobby takes you to.

3. Revising

Begin by rereading the assignment. Have you written what's been asked for? As soon as you're satisfied that you have, you can move on.

Now it's time to look at your draft and make it better. But first put your draft aside for a day, if possible. During this time, you might go back and review pages 68–79. Then reread your draft. Watch for vague images, details that seem out of order, and weak transitions. Ask yourself if your description paints a clear picture of the people and places you want to describe.

At this point, you may want to show your draft to a peer reviewer. Show what you've written, and tell him or her what you're trying to accomplish. You can decide whether or not you can use your peer reviewer's comments.

Take a look at the revision below. Notice the questions this writer asked. You'll probably want to use questions like these to guide your own revisions. Remember, revising is where many great writers do their best work, so work with care.

Question A

Have I used all my senses?

Question B

Are my images crisp and clear?

Question C

Are my details specific and linked with transitions?

> Biking by the park is a great hobby because
> of all the picnics you wiz past. On weekends you
> zoom blasting and smell the barbecues
> can go by and hear radios. You pass by all the
> on soft blankets
> people sitting or throwing Frisbees. And
> see
> sometimes when you sea people you know, you
> can stop and talk to them or share a glass of
> sweet pink
> lemonade. Alongside you all the sights, sounds,
> and smells blur together.

4. Editing

By editing, you can polish your description and take out any mistakes. Read your description several times, using the checklist at the right. Ask a different question each time through. You should read for other errors as well. For example, you might check your punctuation on your first pass and check spelling on your second pass. Afterward, have someone else review your work. Often other people can see your mistakes better than you can. They can also tell you if your description makes sense. If it does, then congratulate yourself. You're ready to present your writing.

Checklist

1. *Have I described important details?*
2. *Will my introduction grab attention?*
3. *Have I used standard spelling, capitalization, and punctuation?*

5. Presenting

Now you're ready to send your description to the magazine. You may want to draw a picture of what you've described and include it with your description. Even without the drawing, readers should be able to get a clear picture simply from what you've described. They should be able to imagine the people, places, and things you notice while you enjoy your hobby.

Reflecting

You've presented your work. Now think about your description from a reader's point of view. Ask yourself, "What about this description would someone want to read?" Find at least two parts that capture your attention. Then think about the power descriptive writing has to call up images for a reader.

Portfolio & Reflection

Summary

Key concepts in writing a description include the following:

- Descriptive writing begins with a memory or an observation.
- Sensory details in descriptive writing create vivid word pictures.
- Describing an object involves choosing and arranging details.
- Good descriptions use precise language—nouns, adjectives, verbs, and adverbs.
- Clear spatial order in a place description helps the audience picture the scene.
- A description of the subject of a biography includes details about the person's appearance, actions, and attitudes.

Your Writer's Portfolio

Look over the writing you did for this unit. Choose two pieces for your portfolio. Look for writing that does one or more of the following:

- grows out of personal memories or observations
- creates vivid word pictures
- includes sensory details that appeal to more than one of the five senses
- uses precise language
- arranges details in a clear spatial order
- demonstrates an effective choice and arrangement of details
- describes the appearance and attitudes of a biographical subject

Reflection and Commentary

Think about what you learned in this unit. Answer the following questions as you look over the two pieces of writing you chose. Write a page of "Comments on Writing a Description" for your portfolio.

1. With what memory or observation does each description start?
2. Which details create a vivid picture? What senses do they appeal to?
3. What precise words bring each description to life?
4. How does the organization pull each piece together?

Feedback

If you had a chance to respond to the following student comment, what would you say or ask?

I approached my descriptive writing assignment by brainstorming descriptive words and then putting them into sentences.

Sarah Burch, Springman Junior High School,
Glenview, Illinois

Writing to Tell a Story

Bringing History to Life

Jacob Kass, *The Saw Mill*, 1980

JOHNSON

INTERPRETS

Ashby

"I think a lot of people who come to Williamsburg don't understand that Williamsburg represents more than the lives of the rich and famous. . . . I like talking about the fact that ordinary people sustained, survived, and moved on."

Arthur Johnson

A s an interpreter of African-American history for Colonial Williamsburg, Arthur Johnson draws twentieth-century visitors into the 1700s. As carriages slowly creak past the old brick buildings, visitors come upon Johnson in costume, as he spins the story of Matthew Ashby. The six-foot five-inch bearded giant in colonial work clothes begins by explaining what he's up to. "I'm getting some runners and putting them up and getting these barrels on the cart here," Ashby grins. "You see, Mr. Prentis has given me some credit for taking these barrels and boxes down to Queen Anne's Port. That's what I do. I'm a carter, a carter by trade. I take anything, anywhere, anytime."

Creating a Narrative

1. Researching Ashby

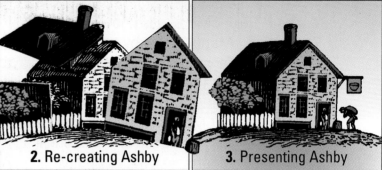

2. Re-creating Ashby

3. Presenting Ashby

FOCUS

Characters in a narrative are believable when placed in a realistic setting and presented with personal challenges.

1 Researching Ashby

At Williamsburg every restored building and costumed character is based on historical fact. Matthew Ashby was one of many African Americans who made up 50 percent of Williamsburg's population in the 1700s. "He was born free sometime in the 1720s," Johnson says. "As a teenager, he worked with a slave by the name of Joe who took care of horses and carted his master's property. Ashby learned his work from Joe."

Ashby met his wife, Ann, when she was a slave and married her in 1762. During this time Ashby worked hard as a carter and earned a good reputation in Williamsburg and won freedom for Ann and their two children in 1769.

Johnson learned these facts from a report based on documents that survived the Revolutionary War. Ashby's will, for example, listed his belongings. Among them were carpenter's tools and a harness for two horses and a cart.

2 Re-creating Ashby

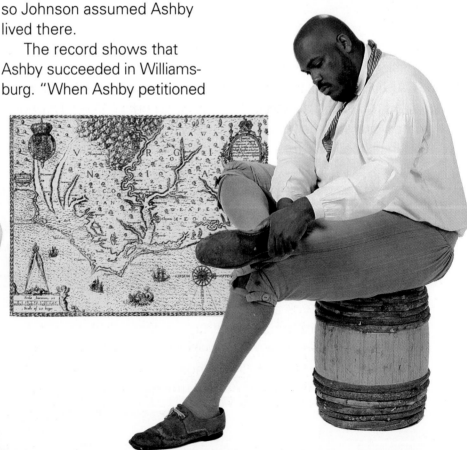

▼ Arthur Johnson prepares for his role as Matthew Ashby.

More was known about Matthew Ashby than about most free blacks of the 1700s, yet the historical record was thin. How did Johnson flesh out Matthew Ashby's character? He began with historical reports, as well as original records and documents.

"With a skeleton of facts, we can add meat to a character, based on what we know about the period," Johnson explains. Historians know a free-black community once existed outside Williamsburg, so Johnson assumed Ashby lived there.

The record shows that Ashby succeeded in Williamsburg. "When Ashby petitioned for his family's freedom, the council said . . . we're going to free his wife and children," Johnson says.

Day by day Johnson reviewed these facts. He tried to see the world as Ashby did. Then, in front of a mirror, Johnson practiced speaking as Ashby may have spoken. Later, he practiced in front of his wife. She listened, commented, and encouraged Johnson.

All this work enabled Johnson to become Matthew

Ashby, to tell stories about this eighteenth-century man's life. For example, Johnson—in character as Ashby—recalls the day he "jumped the broom," or got married.

"I'll never forget when I got married," Ashby said. "For me it was a great, great day. You see, that night the preacher had come around. His name was Gowan. It seemed like all of my friends were around, such as Adam, who gave me a bucket.

"Gowan said a few words to Ann and me. And it seemed like when he told us to jump over that broom—and we jumped—Ann let me jump the farthest, to let me know that she would be with me no matter what."

While practicing to be Ashby, Johnson had to remember to stay in character.

"Matthew wouldn't say a word like *cool*," Johnson says. Nor would he recognize modern things like video-cams. What would Ashby do if a visitor asked to take his picture? "In the eighteenth century there were no cameras," Johnson explains. "So Matthew would say, 'Sir, I don't know what you're talking about. And whatever that is you're holding up to your eye, please, you might want to take it down.'"

▼ *In character as Ashby, Johnson performs Ashby's daily tasks as a carter.*

INTERFACE

Suppose you're going to write a narrative about one of your relatives. What documents could you use as a factual basis for your story?

3 Presenting Ashby

Once Johnson felt sure of his character, he took Ashby and his narratives public. Ashby works at Prentis & Company on Duke of Gloucester Street, Williamsburg's main thoroughfare. There he loads and unloads goods for Mr. Prentis.

To draw out an audience, Ashby calls to visitors strolling by. "Good day," Ashby hollers. "Do you mind if we borrow your children? We need some help on the wagon."

Through his work he shows how eighteenth-century people used their minds to lift and carry loads. Johnson explains, "You had to know physics in the sense that you had to use levers and fulcrums. You had to know how to move a barrel that weighed half a ton."

When everything is loaded, Ashby relaxes and answers questions. "How long have you been doing this?" "When do you get up?" "Where do you live?"

From Ashby's answers, visitors learn about him and the lives of free blacks. Visitors learn what it took to survive in eighteenth-century Williamsburg. "I feel I can relate to Matthew Ashby because Ashby would be a survivor whether he was in the eighteenth century or the twentieth century."

▼ *As Ashby, Johnson involves Williamsburg visitors in his work. A visitor strolling by might be tossed a bundle and told to take it to Mr. Prentis.*

ON ASSIGNMENT

1. Creative Writing

Gather ideas for a story about a historical character.

- Think of a historical character you'd like to write a narrative about. You can choose someone famous, like Clara Barton, or someone unknown, like a woman who traveled the Oregon Trail.

- Jot down questions about the person's character, the time and place he or she lived, and the short experience you want to re-create.

- Next to each question, write down sources where you may find the answers.

2. About Literature

Write a narrative based on a fictional encounter between two historical characters.

- Choose a history book from the library.

- Write down notes about two historical characters.

What are their names? What jobs do they perform? Where are they from? What makes each of them interesting?

- Develop a fictional dialogue between the characters you've selected. If the two characters met, what questions do you think they might ask one another?

3. Cooperative Learning

Create a story about teen-agers at another time in history.

- Meet as a small group. Choose a period in American history.

- Assign a topic to each person to research. For example, find out what girls in the country generally did. What did boys in cities do?

- Meet as a group and share what you've learned.

- Brainstorm ideas for a narrative about one teen-ager.

- As a group write a short story about your character.

- As a group edit the story and share it with the class.

Case Study: Narrative **147**

Writing the Stories of History

True Tales of the Past

Jacob Lawrence, *Frederick Douglass Series, No. 21, The Fugitive,* 1938-1939

History is more than just names and dates you learn for a test. Choose any time period, and you'll find exciting stories of real people who changed the world. The 1800s, for example, gave us the great anti-slavery fighter Frederick Douglass. Notice how artist Jacob Lawrence has brought one part of Douglass's story to life in a work of art. Like a story, this painting presents one event in Douglass's life. A person, a place, an event—the basic elements of a story are here.

Finding Your Inspiration

Remember that *narrative* is another word for *story*. A historical narrative is a story about events in history. Some writers get their ideas for historical narrative from an event; others, from a person.

Like Jacob Lawrence, writer Victoria Ortiz was inspired by an 1800s activist. Ortiz was a civil rights worker in Mississippi when she became interested in Sojourner Truth. The biography she wrote tells how Sojourner spoke strongly for the abolition of slavery and for women's rights. A former slave, Sojourner was uneducated, but she lectured with wit and power. As the account on the next page shows, Sojourner was ahead of her time in her views on women's rights.

*O*ne of the first times Sojourner was present at a Woman's Rights Convention was in October, 1850, in Worcester, Massachusetts. As she later retold the experience to Harriet Beecher Stowe, Sojourner sat for a long time listening to Frederick Douglass, Lucy Stone, Wendell Phillips, William Lloyd Garrison, and Ernestine Rose speak about women's rights. She soon became intrigued, and when called upon to speak she presented her position quite concisely: "Sisters, I aren't clear what you be after. If women want any rights more than they got, why don't they just take them and not be talking about it?" For Sojourner, it was obvious that action was more effective than words.

Victoria Ortiz, *Sojourner Truth: A Self-Made Woman*

Note that Sojourner Truth was a real person involved in a real event in history.

Why do you think some of the same people were advocates of both abolition and women's rights?

To find a topic for a historical narrative, think about people, places, times, and events in history that interest you. A person, a setting, an event—any one of these can spark an idea for a historical narrative.

Once you have found an idea, your next prewriting step is exploring the idea and narrowing it. For example, if you decide to write about a person, you can narrow your topic by focusing on a single event in the person's life. With only one event to work on, you can explore the details in depth. After all, it's the details, such as Sojourner's statement on women's rights, that bring history to life.

• JOURNAL ACTIVITY •
Think It Through

Create a chart entitled Story Ideas from History. Make three columns, headed Person, Event, and Setting. Skim your history textbook for ideas for historical narratives. List each under the appropriate heading.

Drawing Your Readers In

Suppose you have a topic, some notes, and a list of supporting details. Realistic details are especially important in telling about a historical event. Most writers uncover valuable details through research. Sometimes, however, a writer also needs to imagine likely details to keep a narrative realistic and exciting. When you're ready to draft your historical narrative, you can use realistic details in your introduction to hook your reader immediately.

A good introduction sets the scene. Often it presents a person, a setting, and an event. It may introduce a problem the main character faces, making readers want to find out what will happen next. What problem does this paragraph introduce?

What question does this introduction raise? How does this question make readers want to keep on reading?

It's a bright August morning in 1962. Many of the major grape growers of southern California have come to Delano City Hall to hear a man named César Chávez. He has come to talk with the people who have the power to improve the lives of his followers. The outcome will have a serious effect on the farm workers' future.

Introducing a Historical Narrative	
Persons	César Chávez, the grape growers
Event	A meeting to discuss the problems of farm workers
Setting	A bright August morning in 1962 at the City Hall in Delano, California

Activities

Here are some activities to help you apply what you have learned.

1. Guided Assignment

Fifth-graders study American history, and they enjoy stories. Think of an event, a person, and a setting you could use in a narrative for fifth-graders. Consult the chart Story Ideas from History in your journal, and plan a historical narrative for younger students to read. Here are some ideas:

- A young girl begins the long journey west on a wagon train.
- A young boy returns home after fighting in the Battle of Gettysburg.

Make prewriting notes, and draft your introduction. Set the scene by introducing one or more persons, a setting, and an event. You might also introduce a problem, so readers will want to read on to discover how it is solved.

PURPOSE   To introduce a historical narrative
AUDIENCE   Fifth-grade students
LENGTH   ½–1 page

COMPUTER OPTION

Use your computer and printer to prepare scripts. Your word-processing program allows you to indent actors' parts so that each character's name is clearly visible in the left margin.

2. Open Assignment

Imagine you're a news writer at some time and place in American history. (For ideas, refer to the lists you made for the Journal Activity.) You've been assigned a fast-breaking story. You don't know most details yet, but the news is important enough to get into the next edition. Write a scene-setting paragraph, including these elements:

- the person chiefly involved in the event
- the event, including a problem
- the time and place of the event

3. Cooperative Learning

In a group, brainstorm for historical periods that have many exciting stories, such as the California Gold Rush. Pick a period, and brainstorm for story ideas. Each member should list persons, settings, and events, including problems the persons faced.

Next, work individually to write a narrative introduction. Read your introductions as a group. Then assemble them in a booklet named for your general topic. Assign each member one task: duplicating the introductions, illustrating the booklet, binding the booklet, or providing a cover and title. Later, read the introductions, choose one you like (your own or another), and complete the narrative.

Using Chronological Order

What Time Is It, Please?

"Hey, did you see that great story on TV last night?"

People didn't always *see* stories. They heard them, or they read them. Today, movies, television, and videotapes allow us to tell stories in words and images. Think of a time when you used pictures alone, or pictures with words, to tell a story—in a comic strip, a slide series, a videotape, or even a photo album. Make notes in your journal about how you arranged your pictures to tell a story.

Choosing a Time Frame

Any story, whether in words, images, or both, is likely to make better sense if the writer thinks about time order, or chronology. When you write a narrative, you have to decide on a time frame—when your story will begin and end. As the chart on the next page suggests, time spans for narratives vary widely. Some narratives cover decades, even centuries. A short narrative may cover days, hours, or even minutes.

Homesick: My Own Story is a narrative about Jean Fritz's childhood in China and her teen years in the United States. Fritz presents realistic pictures of life in China and small-town America in the early 1900s. The following selection tells about a time just before she began eighth grade in her first American school. Notice how she relates some of one day's events in the order in which they happened, or chronological order. What details suggest that the time is long ago?

*T*he next day Aunt Margaret took me to Caldwell's store on Main Street and bought me a red-and-black-plaid gingham [cotton] dress with a white collar and narrow black patent leather belt that went around my hips. She took me to a beauty parlor and I had my hair shingled [a close-cut style].

When I got home, I tried on my dress. "How do I look?" I asked my grandmother.

"As if you'd just stepped out of a bandbox [a box for hats and collars; means 'perfectly groomed']."

I wasn't sure that was the look I was aiming for. "But do I look like a regular eighth grader?"

"As regular as they come," she assured me.

Jean Fritz, *Homesick: My Own Story*

What words used here would not be used in describing a well-dressed eighth-grader today?

Time Spans for Historical Narratives

A Day				
A Lifetime				
Two Centuries				

• JOURNAL ACTIVITY •
Think It Through

Draw timelines for two narratives you've read, a novel and a short story. How do you think the time frame of a novel often differs from that of a short story?

Making Time Order Clear

Editing Tip

When you edit your historical narrative, check your facts carefully to make sure they are accurate. Give special attention to dates and names.

Ben Aylesworth researched the history of Wheaton, Illinois, a city near his home. He visited the Wheaton History Center and the Wheaton Public Library, where he read about his topic. He also interviewed his grandmother. Finally, Ben decided to focus on one event in the city's history. He related the stages of the event in chronological order.

As he drafted, Ben used good transitions. Transitions are words such as *later* and *afterward* that make the order of events clearer. In writing a narrative, think about transitions. Be as specific as possible. If you always use *first, next,* and *finally,* your writing may sound dull.

Student Model

Lester Schrader, *Theft of the Records,* mid- to late nineteenth century

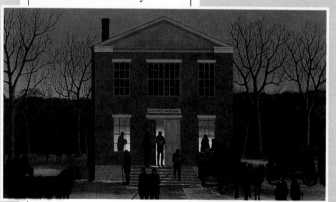

H ow would you feel if citizens of a rival town stole your town's records, forever changing its history? In 1838 Naperville held the county records of the new DuPage County. Naperville and nearby Wheaton were fierce rivals. Both wanted the county seat. In an 1867 referendum Wheaton narrowly won the county seat, but the records stayed in Naperville.

Late one night that year, some young Wheaton men broke into the Naperville courthouse and stole the county records. An alarm sounded, and they dropped some of the papers. Later, fearing another raid, Naperville officials moved the remaining records to Chicago for safekeeping. But these were destroyed in the Great Chicago Fire of 1871. Wheaton has been the county seat ever since that famous midnight raid.

Ben Aylesworth, Hadley Junior High School,
Glen Ellyn, Illinois

What transitions does Ben use to make the chronological order clear?

Activities

Here are some activities to help you apply what you have learned.

1. Guided Assignment

By the mid-2000s today's events will be part of the history that children study in school. Write a narrative to help future historians. Remember that holidays and other special events reveal a great deal about people. Therefore, a future historian will want to know about special events in your school and community. Plan and write a narrative about an annual event. Here are some examples:

- a concert
- a game or tournament
- a holiday parade and picnic

Choose an event, and list its stages. Remember, by the 2000s the event may be long forgotten, so details are important. Arrange the stages in chronological order. In drafting and revising, use appropriate transitions.

PURPOSE   To narrate the story of a school or community event
AUDIENCE People of the mid-2000s
LENGTH   1–2 pages

2. Open Assignment

Using your school or public library, research the history of a city or town that you have visited or would like to visit. Then write a narrative in chronological order. Here are possible topics:

- a battle fought in the town
- the birth or death of a great citizen
- the beginning of a business or industry
- an event for which the town is famous

COMPUTER OPTION

Historical writing often involves research. Your PC can help you record and store the facts as you uncover them. Type each piece of information, give it a heading, and box it so it looks like a note card. In drafting and revising, you can use your computer's cut-and-paste feature to move information from your notes to your draft.

3. Cooperative Learning

In a small group, plan and write a historical narrative about your town or city. Your audience will be your community's citizens.

Divide the research among group members. Start by interviewing people and, if possible, by visiting a local museum, library, or city hall. Pool the results of your research. Then work individually to write a narrative about your community's history. Focus on one incident, and arrange the details, or stages of the event, in chronological order. Include transitions to make the order of the events clear. Review one another's narratives, and revise your own as needed. Finally, read the narratives aloud in class.

Establishing Point of View

Viewing the Past from the Future

What will you be telling your grandchildren in the year 2040 about your life now? Don't laugh. The next century isn't that far away! When you begin a narrative, it makes good sense to tell your story in a fresh, new way. Justin Hoest did just that in the story below. Justin speaks in the voice of a fictional grandfather in the early 2000s, telling his grandson about the 1960s civil rights movement.

Student Model

*L*et me start in the beginning. I was born in Birmingham, Alabama, in 1952. Back then, in southern states, it was segregated. There were separate water fountains, waiting rooms, stores, schools. Everywhere, some people were trying to keep segregation, and others were trying to stop it. The times were troubled.

"Martin Luther King Jr. came to Birmingham when I was ten. I met him some years later during the Selma marches. He helped organize demonstrations. There were sit-ins like in Nashville, and adults would picket up and down the streets. We'd go to the meeting house in the evening. We would sing all night, or so it seemed. Everyone would dress in nice clothes, and the church smelled so good with the fresh candles burning. ➡

Note that although the story is fiction, it is set in a real time and place.

Song filled the place:

> I'm so glad; I'm fightin' for my rights;
> I'm so glad; I'm fightin' for my rights;
> Glory, Hallelujah!

"Finally my day came. We were clapping and singing. Some of us were carrying signs. The day was bright, but there was a menacing dark cloud lingering in the sky. We weren't scared, only nervous. Our feet on the hard pavement made a sound that represented the whole movement."

Justin Hoest, Maplewood Middle School,
Menasha, Wisconsin

Why do you think Justin chose to have the grandfather tell his own story?

In the First Person

In telling his story, Justin has chosen a first-person point of view. That is, he lets the grandfather tell the story using the pronouns *I* and *me*. First-person narratives describe just what the narrator witnesses and thinks. You as the reader see all the events through the narrator's eyes and view them as the narrator views them. In this photo a reporter is getting a first-person account of the game.

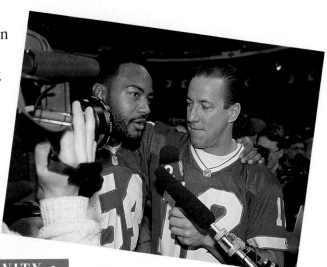

• JOURNAL ACTIVITY •
Try It Out

Make column headings that name three important events in American history. In ten minutes create as many fictional characters as you can think of under each heading. They may be participants, like the grandfather, or just observers.

Grammar
Editing Tip

In editing your narrative, check to make sure you've used subject and object pronouns correctly. For more on using pronouns, see pages 396–397.

In the Third Person

Many short stories and other narratives are told from a third-person point of view, using the pronouns *he, she, it,* and *they.* The following narrative poem uses the pronoun *she,* since the main characters are the Island Queen and her daughter. Who are these characters? If you know something about the history of the American Revolution, you might be able to figure it out.

Literature Model

Т here was an old lady lived over the sea
　　And she was an Island Queen.
Her daughter lived off in a new country,
With an ocean of water between;
The old lady's pockets were full of gold
But never contented was she,
So she called on her daughter to pay her a tax
Of three pence a pound on her tea.

The tea was conveyed to the daughter's door,
All down by the ocean's side;
And the bouncing girl pour'd out every pound
In the dark and boiling tide;
And then she called out to the Island Queen,
"O mother, dear mother," quoth she,
"Your tea you may have when 'tis steep'd enough
But never a tax from me."

Traditional

Formats

Journal

Ballad

Letters

What point of view will you choose for your narrative? A short story, an imaginary journal or letter, a song, or a narrative poem can have a first-person point of view. The main character is then the *I* of the story. Or you can tell your story in the third person. The main character is *he* or *she.* Decide on your point of view in prewriting. Then use your imagination to bring a little history to life.

Activities

Janet Fish, *Charles, Drummer, Lorna, Roxanne and Jonathan,* 1986

Here are some activities to help you apply what you have learned.

1. Guided Assignment

What part of your average school day do you like best? Think of something you'd like to remember about school for many years to come, long after the event is part of history. It could be your favorite class, an athletic event, a club, a computer lab, or another activity. Write in the first person to tell about it. Try to show not only what the event or activity was like but also how you thought about it at the time.

PURPOSE   To use the first-person point of view in a personal narrative
AUDIENCE   An older friend or relative
LENGTH   1–2 pages

2. Open Assignment

Imagine what's happening in the painting above. Write a page about what's going on as told by one of the people in the painting, using a first-person point of view. Don't identify yourself in the writing—see if a friend reading it can guess who you are.

3. Music

Narrative poems called ballads often tell the stories of those who participate in major events of their time. These events might be earthquakes, wars, space flights, building projects, even World Series victories. Choose a simple, familiar melody, and create new words for it. Retell the story of one or more people involved in a major event. Write your story in the first or third person.

4.4 | Writing Realistic Dialogue

He Said, She Said

Anthony Ortega, *Two Little Old Men,* 1984

Study the picture above. What do you think the two figures might be saying? How do you think they might be saying it? Jot down your ideas.

Next, read two different openers that were written for the same story. Which of these openers would be more likely to keep you reading? Why?

Jenny said she saw Joseph walking home.

Jenny burst in, shouting, "Hey, everybody, Joseph's come home!"

Letting Them Speak for Themselves

Dialogue—direct quotations of spoken words or conversations—is a way of revealing character. What does the following conversation reveal about Hideyo and his mother?

Mother opened her mouth and could not close it for several seconds.

"Most of my classmates have enlisted," said Hideyo, serious for once. "I have decided to go to help our country."

"You cannot go, Hideyo!" Mother told him. "You must talk with Father. You just cannot make such a decision alone."

"Mother, I have already sent in my application," said Hideyo. "I will take the written and physical examinations!"

"How could you?" Mother moaned. "Why didn't you tell me?"

"I am eighteen. Big enough to make my own decision."

Yoko Kawashima Watkins, *So Far from the Bamboo Grove*

> *The mother's words tell you she loves her son and fears for his life.*

> *What does the dialogue reveal about Hideyo?*

Getting your characters to speak for themselves is easier when you write about someone you know well. Just ask yourself, "What would this person say here?" After you start drafting dialogue, put it aside for a day or so. Does it sound authentic when you reread it? If not, how could you improve it?

Grammar
Editing Tip

As you edit your dialogue, check your punctuation, capitalization, and paragraphing. For more about writing dialogue, see pages 548–549.

• JOURNAL ACTIVITY •
Try It Out

Listen to the speech of others, and jot down bits of conversation you hear. Next to each quotation identify the speaker—a bus driver, for instance, or a relative.

Making Conversation

Your dialogue will sound natural if your characters talk the way real people do. Read a natural-sounding dialogue between a brother and sister. What did the writer do to make this conversation sound realistic?

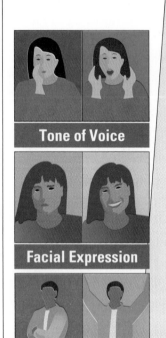

Tone of Voice

Facial Expression

Body Language

"I can too run!" Antonio glared at her, arms locked stubbornly over his chest.

"I didn't say you can't run, 'Tonio," Gina retorted. "I just said I can run faster than you!"

"Yeah, well, I can run farther!"

Gina rolled her eyes. "In your dreams, <u>fratello</u>!" she crowed. "You can't even run without tripping on something!"

"Can too!"

"Think about it, 'Tonio! Remember last year's Fourth of July picnic? Who wanted to run barefoot and then stepped on a wasp four seconds into the race? Not me!" Gina roared.

Notice the slang, the sentence fragments, the contractions, and the descriptions of facial expressions and body language. Without these, the conversation would sound stiff and unnatural. For example, suppose the writer had Gina say this: "I am sorry, but you are badly mistaken, brother. You cannot run without falling down." Even Gina's use of the Italian term *fratello*, which means "brother," adds interest.

Activities

Here are some activities to help you apply what you have learned.

1. Guided Assignment

You and a friend disagree about what entertainment to watch tonight (will it be a movie, a video, or a concert). Write a dialogue in which you discuss, perhaps heatedly, the reasons for your choices. Begin by jotting down specific examples of entertainment that you'd pick and some that you wouldn't pick. You might include some you don't like at all. Jot down words and phrases that you and your friend would be likely to use in conversation.

PURPOSE To create realistic dialogue about a disagreement
AUDIENCE Your teacher and classmates
LENGTH 2–3 pages

2. Open Assignment

Your family's history can suggest topics for dialogue. Interview older relatives to learn about important events in the lives of your grandparents and great-grandparents. Such events could include the birth of their first child, moving to a new town, the end of a war, or their first telephone or television set. Then write an imaginary conversation they might have had at such a time.

Hughie Lee-Smith, *Man Standing on His Head,* 1969

3. Art

What are the men in this painting saying to each other, or are they silent? What are they doing in this open space? How does this painting make you feel? Write a dialogue between two students who are viewing the painting at an exhibition.

Relating a Historical Event

Her Own Story in Her Own Voice

How would it feel to be in a new country, far from all that was once sweet and familiar? Hannah Wilson captures some of those feelings in her narrative about a Japanese immigrant of the 1920s. Is her story true? Yes and no. Before she wrote, Hannah read widely about the immigration of Japanese Americans. Then she created a fictional character, confronted her with a problem, and let her tell her own story in her own voice.

Andō Hiroshige, *The Wave*, c. 1850

Student Model

Mamma—I wish she were here now. I still miss her so much. I wish with all my heart she could be here to see this baby born. I remember how comforting she always was. I need that comfort now. Every day seems the same to me. Up at dawn, fix breakfast for Seiji and myself, off to work in the fields all day while Seiji goes fishing, hardly stopping to eat. The lonely nights when Seiji must stay on the fishing boats all night.

I love America and Seiji, and I want a baby so much, but I miss Mamma and Papa and Sachiko and Akiko.

Hannah Wilson, Newton Elementary School,
Strafford, Vermont

What can you tell about the person whose voice you hear in this narrative?

Creating a Character

Suppose that, like Hannah Wilson, you've chosen immigration as the subject for your narrative. Your next step is investigation. You might begin by reading immigration stories, jotting down details about ordinary people's lives. Then you could think of a character and imagine problems the character might face at any point in the experience. Can you see the germ of one or more story ideas in these prewriting notes?

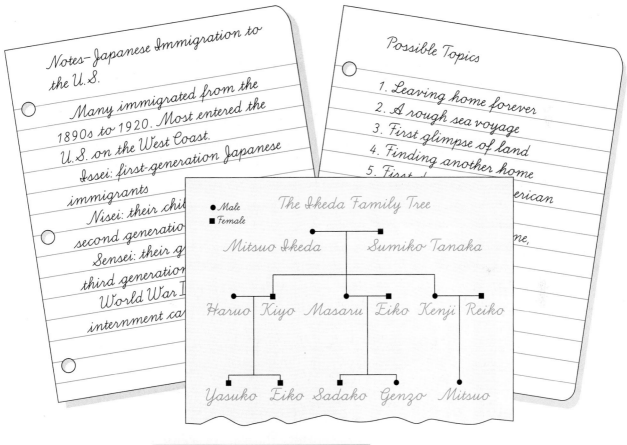

Notes—Japanese Immigration to the U.S.

Many immigrated from the 1890s to 1920. Most entered the U.S. on the West Coast.
Issei: first-generation Japanese immigrants
Nisei: their chil... second generatio...
Sensei: their g... third generation...
World War I...
internment ca...

Possible Topics
1. Leaving home forever
2. A rough sea voyage
3. First glimpse of land
4. Finding another home
5. First ...
...erican
...ne,

The Ikeda Family Tree
● Male
■ Female

Mitsuo Ikeda   Sumiko Tanaka

Haruo Kiyo Masaru Eiko Kenji Reiko

Yasuko Eiko Sadako Genzo Mitsuo

· JOURNAL ACTIVITY ·
Try It Out

Talk to a friend or family member about the person's immigration experience. Create a fictional character in the same time and place, and freewrite about problems your character might face.

Choosing Your Approach

Prewriting Tip

In prewriting, look for details about the setting. You can use these later to enrich your narrative with strong, colorful descriptions.

After giving your character a problem, or conflict, you should decide on an approach. For example, you could write a short story, a series of journal entries, or some letters home. Formats such as these allow you to show a character's feelings as well as his or her actions.

Like Hannah, Philip Garran wrote an immigration story. In his prewriting investigation, he researched the sad story of the Irish potato crop failures. These led to famine and caused many to leave their homeland. Unlike Hannah, Philip focused on the early part of the experience, before his main character left home. He, too, wrote a fictional journal entry. Notice, however, that Philip's story takes place before, not after, the voyage to the United States.

Contract Ticket No. 32893
INSPECTION CARD.
(Immigrants and Steerage Passengers.)
Port of Departure, LIVERPOOL.
Name of Ship MEGANTIC
Date of Departure, Jan. 8th, 1921.
Delaney Lillie
Name
Last

Using sensory language, Philip paints a vivid word picture of the Irish countryside and conveys the narrator's feelings for his homeland.

What possible conflict is the writer setting up in these sentences?

Student Model

July 30, 1849

At last my father has found a ship. We have packed all of our belongings, and Dad has sold the cottage for a very small sum of money. However, it was almost enough to pay for the tickets, and we borrowed the rest from my Uncle Paul.

We will be leaving in three days. I will miss the green fields, the blue sky, and the sparkly rivers and lakes. But I will not miss the misery that has descended on us like fog. I hear that America is a land of amazing wealth, and the land there is incredibly cheap. I can't wait to see America.

Philip Garran, Newton Elementary School,
Strafford, Vermont

Activities

Here are some activities to help you apply what you have learned.

1. Guided Assignment

Pick a country that has become dangerous to live in. Imagine that you're fleeing from it, hoping to find peace and safety in the United States. You're now on board the boat or ship in which you are making your escape. Write the entry you'll add to your personal journal tonight. Focus on your flight from home, the voyage itself, or your future in the United States. Try to convey your feelings as well as the facts and events.

PURPOSE	To identify with an immigrant's experiences and to create details that reflect them
AUDIENCE	Yourself
LENGTH	1–2 pages

2. Open Assignment

Select one of the following ideas or an idea of your own, and write the beginning of a short story. Include a character, a setting, and a suggestion for a problem your character will have to face.

- You are part of a host family helping to settle an immigrant family in the United States.
- You are a member of a once-wealthy immigrant family. All your riches were left behind, and now you must get used to a completely new way of life.

3. Art

Write the next letter that the young woman in the painting will send home. Include a narrative that tells what she is looking at and what she feels.

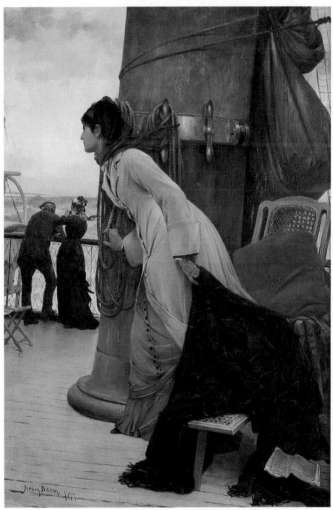

Henry Bacon, *First Sight of Land*, 1877

Writing a News Story

Today's News, Tomorrow's History

Collaborating on Computers

Computer Museum consults Martin Luther King Jr. Middle School students in developing new exhibit

By Teresa A. Martin
SPECIAL TO THE GLOBE

When the Computer Museum designed its new 3,600-square-foot, $1 million personal computer exhibit, it looked for inspiration in many places, including an eighth-grade class at the Martin Luther King Jr. Middle School in Dorchester, Massachusetts.

The collaboration was so successful that the

museum is making such arrangements part of the development of all future exhibits.

"One of the things you often see is lip service to consulting with schools," said Greg Welch, director of exhibits at the museum. "But for us this was a concerted effort to find out their needs."

The exhibit in question, which opened last month and will be permanent, is called "Tools and Toys: The Amazing Personal Computer."

News stories record history as it happens and can become a resource for future historians. Read the news story above, and jot down answers to these questions: What happened? When? Where? Who was involved? How did it happen? Why was the event important?

Telling the Five Ws and an H

News writers try to answer all or most of these questions—
who? what? when? where? why? and *how?*—in their lead, or
opening. Often the writers start by presenting the basic facts at
the beginning of the story. Then they add the details. How many
of the basic questions—five Ws and an H—are answered in each
lead below?

FLORIDA BRACES FOR HURRICANE ANDREW
Associated Press

MIAMI–Hurricane Andrew
surged relentlessly toward
southern Florida Sunday,
and forecasters warned it
would be the most powerful
storm to hit the United
States in decades. More than
1 million residents were told
to flee.

A SUMMER SEARCH
BY MARK FERENCHIK
Repository staff writer

LAKE TWP.–What did
teacher Pete Esterle do for
his summer vacation? He
went slogging through a
south Florida swamp, in
search of an airplane wreck
apparently undisturbed for
about 50 years. Esterle, an
art teacher at Lake High
School, and his brother
found it earlier this month.

RUNAWAY CHIMP FINDS UNWILLING PLAYMATE
New York Times News Service

INMAN, S.C.–A 78-year-old
woman hanging sheets on a
clothesline Monday became
the unsuspecting playmate
of a rambunctious chimpan-
zee that, along with two
companions, escaped from
nearby Hollywild Animal
Park.

Some leads present only the basic facts; the details come
later in the story. Other leads open with a question or an
intriguing detail designed to get their readers' attention and
draw them into the piece. Which one of the leads above opens
with an attention grabber?

> ### Drafting Tip
>
> When you draft,
> include precise
> nouns and power-
> ful verbs. These will
> help you to say
> more using fewer
> words.

• JOURNAL ACTIVITY •
Think It Through

Many things happen in a school day. Think about
what happened yesterday, and choose one newsworthy
event. Write answers to the five Ws and H.

Going into Detail

As you investigate a topic for a news story, gather all the information you can. After writing the lead, news writers bring their story to life with details. Read the opening section of this news story.

Literature Model

*T*he national anthems played most often four years ago in Seoul—those of the USSR and the German Democratic Republic (GDR)—will be noticeably missing during the 25th Olympic Games that begin today. Now, the USSR and GDR no longer exist, and neither does the intense East-West rivalry that has marked the Games during the Cold War era.

This will be the first Olympics in decades with no "good guys" or "bad guys," and that could make these Games the most refreshing in recent memory— approaching the Olympic ideal of spectators cheering for the best athletes regardless of the country they represent.

Bud Greenspan, *Parade*

According to Bud Greenspan, why are there no "good guys" or "bad guys" in this Olympics?

As you write your news story, remember to include information that will add authority and interest. Try to cover all sides of the story. Be fair, and save your own opinions for a letter to the editor. Finally, be sure your facts are accurate and names are spelled correctly.

If you were in this audience, how could you exemplify the "Olympic ideal"?

Activities

Here are some activities to help you apply what you have learned.

1. Guided Assignment

You have one of the best seats at an important athletic contest in your school. Your school newspaper editor has asked you to cover the event and to write a news story about it. Create a lead and two detail paragraphs for the story.

Begin by making a cluster diagram with the name of the event in the center. Add details around it for the five Ws and H to help you with the lead. Add further details to bring your story to life.

PURPOSE   To create a lead and add details to bring a news story to life
AUDIENCE   Readers of your school newspaper
LENGTH   1–2 pages

COMPUTER OPTION

Most word-processing software allows you to print text in parallel columns as in a newspaper. Find out how to set up the format line for this option, and print out your story in newspaper format.

2. Open Assignment

What's the most exciting recent happening in your life? Imagine that the event is going to become a news story in your local paper and you've been chosen to write it. What will you say? Use an idea that you listed for the Journal Activity or another idea of your choice. Then follow these steps:

- List everything that happened. Then go back and cross out the least important and least colorful details.
- Choose and expand on the highlight of the event. Explain its importance.
- Tell what made the event exciting.

3. Cooperative Learning

In a group of three, decide on a news story to write for your local newspaper. Think about events such as the following:

- the opening of a new store or restaurant in your neighborhood
- the involvement of eighth-graders in a tutoring program for younger children
- a friend's success in a state music competition

After group members have agreed on a topic, research the details. Each member should be responsible for two of the five Ws and H. Take prewriting notes on these details. Individually each member should use them in writing a draft. Finally, regroup to do the following:

- Read, review, and revise your drafts. Each lead should draw readers in and include most of the five Ws and H.
- Think of a strong headline.
- Edit your news stories, and prepare a neat final copy of each.

Ordinary Players with Extraordinary Roles

Wednesday, 29 March, 1944

Dear Kitty,

Bolkestein, an M.P. [Member of Parliament], was speaking on the Dutch News from London, and he said that they ought to make a collection of diaries and letters after the war. Of course, they all [Anne's family and the others in hiding with them] made a rush at my diary immediately. Just imagine how interesting it would be if I were to publish a romance of the "Secret Annexe." The title alone would be enough to make people think it was a detective story.

But, seriously, it would seem quite funny ten years after the war if we Jews were to tell how we lived and what we ate and talked about here. Although I tell you a lot, still, even so, you only know very little of our lives.

Anne Frank: *The Diary of a Young Girl*

You may have heard or read about Anne Frank. She was a Jewish girl, born in Germany in 1929, ten years before World War II began. Her family moved to the Netherlands to escape the Nazis. Later, when Anne was thirteen, her family had to live in hiding in a secret room of an Amsterdam building. There she kept a diary, which she addressed as Kitty and wrote as a series of letters. After more than three years, the family was discovered and taken to a concentration camp, where Anne died.

Responding to Historical Events

As a firsthand account, *The Diary of a Young Girl* offers glimpses of the reality of war. Johanna Yngvason responded to Anne's diary by describing the terror of living in hiding. She focuses on historic events as they affected ordinary people such as Anne and her family.

Student Model

"Hide! Hide! The Nazis are invading!" This was a terrifying sound heard by many Jews, many times, and caused them to go into hiding. A small closet became a bedroom, an attic became a home. . . . The Jews were rounded up like cattle and shipped off to concentration camps such as Auschwitz and Bergen-Belsen, where the majority of them died.

Such a fate befell young Anne Frank. . . . The only surviving member of the party, Anne's beloved father, returned to the dusty attic after the war. There in the rubble was the diary, which he later published. . . . Although Anne didn't survive the Holocaust, her thoughts and memories live on.

Johanna Yngvason, Canyon Park Junior High School, Bothell, Washington

Johanna reflects Anne's dread when she uses the word "terrifying" in her response.

What does this sentence reveal about Johanna's own feelings?

When you respond in writing to a nonfiction narrative, be sure to follow Johanna's example. Tell what happened, but add your own thoughts and feelings as well.

• JOURNAL ACTIVITY •
Think It Through

Take a few moments to reflect on a nonfiction narrative that moved you. How did you feel? Write some words and phrases that best express your feelings.

Revising Tip

As you revise, a thesaurus can help you locate just the right words to express your thoughts and feelings about a nonfiction historical narrative.

Responding to People Behind the Events

Amy Groat read and wrote about *Farewell to Manzanar*. This nonfiction narrative tells the story of Jeanne Wakatsuki, interned with her family in a wartime relocation camp for Asian Americans. Notice how Amy sympathizes with Jeanne.

Student Model

*F*arewell to Manzanar deals with a mixture of problems that bombarded the internees in the camp Manzanar. The minorities of today deal with the same discrimination but in a subtler form. By reading and discussing this book, eighth-graders in our district will have a better understanding of the events and traumas that rocked Japanese Americans during World War II. . . .

When the Wakatsuki family reentered the "real world," Jeanne faced a cultural gap between herself and her classmates. She wanted desperately to fit in but was discriminated against because of her ethnic background. She eventually was able to blend in with her classmates by joining after-school activities, but she was never able to deal with the generation gap in her family.

Amy Groat, Oak Creek Ranch School,
Cornville, Arizona

Amy shows how important the book was to her by suggesting that everyone in the district should read it.

Which words and expressions reveal Amy's sympathy for Jeanne Wakatsuki?

Did you ever wonder why you like some books more than others? One reason may be that the characters are something like you; in them you see yourself. A way of responding to a historical narrative—fiction or nonfiction—is to show how a character is like you. In reading *Farewell to Manzanar*, Amy learned about another time and place and discovered that the people were like her.

Activities

Here are some activities to help you apply what you have learned.

1. Guided Assignment

Choose a historical narrative you have read, and write a response. Refer to your Journal Activity notes. Your response should have two goals:

- Provide a brief summary of what the book is about.

Diego Rivera, *Flower Vendor*, 1949

- Respond personally to the story, focusing on events or people. Explain how you felt about the book and why.

PURPOSE To explore your personal feelings about a nonfiction historical narrative
AUDIENCE Your teacher and classmates
LENGTH 2–3 pages

2. Open Assignment

Suppose you lived during World War II and became one of its victims on or off the battlefield. Explain what you want readers to know about you and your experiences. Take one of the following approaches, or find one of your own:

- Explain how you feel about being a victim of circumstances.
- Describe what you did to continue your daily routine despite wartime events going on around you.
- Tell how you feel about the way the situation affected another person.

3. Social Studies

This painting shows women gathering flowers in Mexico. Peasants who gathered flowers often worked long hours in difficult conditions. Jot down some ideas for a historical narrative you might write about these workers. Then write a page or two of the narrative.

Katherine Paterson
from

LYDDIE

In the mid-1800s long workdays in a factory could exhaust the mind and body. Yet the hope for a better life prompted many to join the ranks of factory laborers. Katherine Paterson's historical narrative relates how thirteen-year-old Lydia Worthen travels to Lowell, Massachusetts, seeking mill work and the chance for a new life. Beginning at 4:30 A.M., Lyddie's tough, first full day ends with relief that comes from an unexpected source.

The four-thirty bell clanged the house awake. From every direction, Lyddie could hear the shrill voices of girls calling to one another, even singing. Someone on another floor was imitating a rooster. From the other side of the bed Betsy groaned and turned over, but Lyddie was up, dressing quickly in the dark as she had always done in the windowless attic of the inn.

Her stomach rumbled, but she ignored it. There would be no breakfast until seven, and that was two and a half hours away. By five the girls had crowded through the main gate, jostled their way up the outside staircase on the far end of the mill, cleaned their machines, and stood waiting for the workday to begin.

"Not too tired this morning?" Diana asked by way of greeting.

Lyddie shook her head. Her feet were sore, but she'd felt tireder after a day behind the plow.

"Good. Today will be something more strenuous, I fear. We'll work all three looms together, all right? Until you feel quite sure of everything."

Lyddie felt a bit as though the older girls were whispering in church. It seemed almost that quiet in the great loom room. The only real noise was the creaking from the ceiling of the leather belts that connected the wheels in the weaving room to the gigantic waterwheel in the basement.

The overseer came in, nodded good morning, and pushed a low wooden stool under a cord dangling from the assembly of wheels and belts above his head. His little red mouth pursed, he stepped up on the stool and pulled out his pocket watch. At the

Constantin Meunier, *In the Black Country*, c. 1860–80

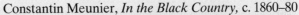

same moment, the bell in the tower above the roof began to ring. He yanked the cord, the wide leather belt above him shifted from a loose to a tight pulley, and suddenly all the hundred or so silent looms, in raucous[1] concert, shuddered and groaned into fearsome life. Lyddie's first full day as a factory girl had begun.

Within five minutes, her head felt like a log being split to splinters. She kept shaking it, as though she could rid it of the noise, or at least the pain, but both only seemed to grow more intense. If that weren't trial enough, a few hours of standing in her proud new boots and her feet had swollen so that the laces cut into her flesh. She bent down quickly to loosen them, and when she found the right lace was knotted, she burst into tears. Or perhaps the tears were caused by the swirling dust and lint.

Now that she thought of it, she could hardly breathe, the air was so laden with moisture and debris.[2] She snatched a moment to run to the window. She had to get air, but the window was nailed shut against the April morning. She leaned her forehead against it; even the glass seemed hot. Her apron brushed the pots of red geraniums crowding the wide sill. They were flourishing in this hot house. She coughed, trying to free her throat and lungs for breath.

Then she felt, rather than saw, Diana. "Mr. Marsden has his eye on you," the older girl said gently, and put her arm on Lyddie's shoulder to turn her back toward the looms. She pointed to the stalled loom and the broken warp[3] thread that must be tied. Even though Diana had stopped the loom, Lyddie stood rubbing the powder into her fingertips, hesitating to plunge her hands into the bowels of the machine. Diana urged her with a light touch.

I stared down a black bear, Lyddie reminded herself. She took a deep breath, fished out the broken ends, and began to tie the weaver's knot that Diana had shown her over and over again the afternoon before. Finally, Lyddie managed to make a

1 raucous (rô′kəs) hoarse; rough-sounding
2 debris (də brē′) bits of rubbish; litter
3 warp (wôrp) threads running lengthwise in a loom

Eyre Crowe, *The Dinner Hour, Wigan*, 1874

clumsy knot, and Diana pulled the lever, and the loom shuddered to life once more.

How could she ever get accustomed to this inferno?[4] Even when the girls were set free at 7:00, it was to push and shove their way across the bridge and down the street to their boardinghouses, bolt down their hearty breakfast, and rush back, stomachs still churning, for "ring in" at 7:35. Nearly half the mealtime was spent simply going up and down the staircase, across the mill yard and bridge, down the row of houses—just getting to and from the meal. And the din[5] in the dining room was nearly as loud as the racket in the mill—thirty young women chewing and calling at the same time, reaching for the platters of flapjacks and pitchers of syrup, ignoring cries from the other end of the table to pass anything.

4 **inferno** (in fur′nō) hell or any place suggesting hell
5 **din** (din) a loud, continuous noise

Philip Evergood, *Lily and the Sparrows*, 1939

Her quiet meals in the corner of the kitchen with Triphena, even her meager bowls of bark soup in the cabin with the seldom talkative Charlie, seemed like feasts compared to the huge, rushed, noisy affairs in Mrs. Bedlow's house. The half hour at noonday dinner with more food than she had ever had set before her at one time was worse than breakfast.

At last the evening bell rang, and Mr. Marsden pulled the cord to end the day. Diana walked with her to the place by the door where the girls hung their bonnets and shawls, and handed Lyddie hers. "Let's forget about studying those regulations tonight," she said. "It's been too long a day already."

Lyddie nodded. Yesterday seemed years in the past. She couldn't even remember why she'd thought the regulations important enough to bother with.

She had lost all appetite. The very smell of supper made her nauseous [6]—beans heavy with pork fat and brown injun bread with orange cheese, fried potatoes, of course, and flapjacks with apple sauce, baked Indian pudding with cream and plum cake for dessert. Lyddie nibbled at the brown bread and washed it down with a little scalding tea. How could the others eat so heartily and with such a clatter of dishes and shrieks of conversation? She longed only to get to the room, take off her boots, massage her abused feet, and lay down her aching head. While the other girls pulled their chairs from the table and scraped

---

6 nauseous (nô′shəs) feeling sickness in the stomach

them about to form little circles in the parlor area, Lyddie dragged herself from the table and up the stairs.

Betsy was already there before her, her current novel in her hand. She laughed at the sight of Lyddie. "The first full day! And up to now you thought yourself a strapping country farm girl who could do anything, didn't you?"

Lyddie did not try to answer back. She simply sank to her side of the double bed and took off the offending shoes and began to rub her swollen feet.

"If you've got an older pair"—Betsy's voice was almost gentle—"more stretched and softer . . ."

Lyddie nodded. Tomorrow she'd wear Triphena's without the stuffing. They were still stiff from the trip and she'd be awkward rushing back and forth to meals, but at least there'd be room for her feet to swell.

She undressed, slipped on her shabby night shift, and slid under the quilt. Betsy glanced over at her. "To bed so soon?"

Lyddie could only nod again. It was as though she could not possibly squeeze a word through her lips. Betsy smiled again. She ain't laughing at me, Lyddie realized. She's remembering how it was.

"Shall I read to you?" Betsy asked.

Lyddie nodded gratefully and closed her eyes and turned her back against the candlelight.

Betsy did not give any explanation of the novel she was reading, simply commenced to read aloud where she had broken off reading to herself. Even though Lyddie's head was still choked with lint and battered with noise, she struggled to get the sense of the story.

The child was in some kind of poorhouse, it seemed, and he was hungry. Lyddie knew about hungry children. Rachel, Agnes, Charlie—they had all been hungry that winter of the bear. The hungry little boy in the story had held up his bowl to the poorhouse overseer and said:

"Please sir, I want some more."

And for this the overseer—she could see his little rosebud mouth rounded in horror—for this the overseer had screamed out at the child. In her mind's eye little Oliver Twist looked exactly like a younger Charlie. The cruel overseer had screamed and hauled the boy before a sort of agent. And for what crime? For the monstrous crime of wanting more to eat.

"That boy will be hung," the agent had prophesied. "I know that boy will be hung."

She fought sleep, ravenous[7] for every word. She had not had any appetite for the bountiful meal downstairs, but now she was feeling a hunger she knew nothing about. She had to know what would happen to little Oliver. Would he indeed be hanged just because he wanted more gruel?

She opened her eyes and turned to watch Betsy, who was absorbed in her reading. Then Betsy sensed her watching, and looked up from the book. "It's a marvelous story, isn't it? I saw the author once—Mr. Charles Dickens. He visited our factory. Let me see—I was already in the spinning room—it must have been in—"

But Lyddie cared nothing for authors or dates. "Don't stop reading the story, please, " she croaked out.

"Never fear, little Lyddie. No more interruptions," Betsy promised, and read on, though her voice grew raspy with fatigue, until the bell rang for curfew. She stuck a hair ribbon in the place. "Till tomorrow night," she whispered as the feet of an army of girls could be heard thundering up the staircase.

7 ravenous (rav′ə nəs) greedy

For Discussion

1. Lyddie chose to work in the mills. What serious choices have you had to make? How have they affected your life?

2. Reading can be a way to find enjoyment even when life itself isn't so pleasant. If you were Lyddie, why would you be eager to hear the rest of Oliver's story?

Readers Respond

Lyddie was my favorite character because what she did was adventurous and courageous at the same time. It was adventurous because Lyddie was living and working on her own. It was courageous because her job in the mill was hard. I liked the fact that Lyddie got to feel what it was like to be an adult.

Trina Chu

This story is about a thirteen-year-old girl, Lyddie, who lived the life of an adult. After her first full day working in the mill, she was so exhausted that she didn't have enough energy to speak. She was my favorite character because of her courage to work in a mill at her age.

I would recommend this story to a friend. I enjoyed it and was curious to know what would happen next. I would ask my friend to read the story and discuss her opinions with me.

Eliza Ali

Do You Agree?

1. Do you agree that books can make a difference in a person's life? How did Lyddie respond when Betsy read to her from *Oliver Twist*? What books can you name that have made a difference in your life, and how have they done so?

2. Have you ever felt as tired as Lyddie, too tired even to eat or talk? In your journal make notes about a time when you felt very tired. List several details about how tiredness affected your thoughts and feelings as well as your body.

Writing Process in Action

A Day in the Life

Who says you can't travel back in time? Some of the best books do just that—taking their readers along for the ride. Think of a book you've enjoyed that was set in the past. Chances are the book told a fascinating story, perhaps one like Katherine Paterson told in *Lyddie,* on page 176. Historical narrative offers a glimpse of the past as it was viewed—and lived—by a particular person, character, or group. You're invited to write a historical narrative about one of your relatives or someone else who interests you.

• Assignment •

Context	You are going to write a historical narrative about an ancestor or someone else whose life is important to you. Although you may find facts about this person, you'll have to invent some likely–and lively–details about speech, actions, and attitudes.
Purpose	To make the past come alive in a historical narrative.
Audience	Your family or friends
Length	2 or more pages

For advice on how to approach this assignment, read the next few pages. You don't have to remember everything. Just remember to reread these pages during the writing process.

1. Prewriting

Is there a person in history whose life fascinates you? Would you like to know more about how an ancestor came to this country? You can begin exploring ideas about your subject's life by interviewing relatives or acquaintances who might know the most about that person. You can look at old photo albums for pictures of where people lived, played, and worked in those days. Letters, diaries, and family records are other sources of information. Read stories about the period in which your subject lived, and notice details about how people worked, dressed, ate, and entertained. Jot down notes and story ideas in your journal or on note cards. Begin thinking about where you might begin and end your narrative. You can list a rough chronology of events, or simply begin writing where it feels right to begin.

Option A

Interview people, look at photos, read letters.

Option B

Read about the period.

Option C

Jot down notes about a turning point in the story.

Krista given money on her eighteenth birthday. Not much—the farm in Denmark was too poor. Older children used money to move to the city to find work. Krista wanted to go to America.

2. Drafting

As you draft your historical narrative, try to include sensory details that will make the life of your subject real for your readers. Put your readers in the subject's shoes. Let your readers experience the events and surroundings of the past as your subject might have experienced them. Notice the way Katherine Paterson portrays the factory where Lyddie works. Instead of simply saying "the factory was noisy," or "Lyddie's feet hurt," Paterson takes her readers back to the mill to see Lyddie and to feel her pain:

W*ithin five minutes, her head felt like a log being split to splinters. She kept shaking it, as though she could rid it of the noise, or at least the pain, but both only seemed to grow* *more intense. If that weren't trial enough, a few hours of standing in her proud new boots and her feet had swollen so that the laces cut into her flesh.*

If you get stuck while drafting, look again at your prewriting notes for fresh ideas. Your writing may flow more easily if you try to keep in mind the order in which events took place. Review pages 152–155 if you need a reminder about chronological order.

3. Revising

Look back at the original assignment when you are ready to revise. Have you fulfilled the assignment? As you read what you've written, ask yourself whether every detail, sentence, and paragraph adds something to your historical narrative.

Sometimes, asking a teacher or friend to read your draft can help you make revisions. Reading your draft out loud can also help you decide what kinds of changes to make. Think about questions, such as those below, as you revise your work.

Question A

Does every sentence contribute to my narrative?

Question B

Does the action of my story flow logically?

Question C

Have I established a clear point of view?

Krista's feet were bleeding by the time she walked the nine miles from the station to the farm where she was to work. She wished she had heavy boots, instead of her Sunday brought old shoes instead of her best shoes, with to America. her This farm was bigger than the one she had left behind in Denmark. As she thought of the scrubbing, mending, and cooking hours of hard work that faced her, she became her heart sank. sat.

4. Editing

You've worked hard to figure out what you want to say and how to say it well. Since you'll be sharing this with your family or friends, you'll want them to pay attention to the story you're going to tell them, not to any errors you might have made. During the editing stage eliminate mistakes that might detract from the ideas and feelings you want to share.

This checklist will help you catch errors you might otherwise overlook. You'll want your historical narrative to reflect your hard work, so read and reread your work with care.

Checklist

1. *Do my details create a setting?*
2. *Is the order of the events clear?*
3. *Do I use a consistent point of view?*
4. *Have I used standard spelling, capitalization, and punctuation?*

5. Presenting

As you prepare your historical narrative, think about photographs and drawings that you could include with your writing. Include a portrait of your subject if you have a photograph, or consider drawing one of your own. Pictures of a house or city your subject lived in and of clothing or vehicles from your subject's era will also add to your narrative. A computer may help you with some old-fashioned type styles and designs.

Reflecting

Writing about someone for a historical narrative may have taught you a lot about him or her, your family, and a specific time and place in history. How was this person's life like or unlike yours? What in your life would your subject have had difficulty understanding? What aspects of your life would this person have envied or enjoyed?

Portfolio & Reflection

Summary

Key concepts in narrative writing include the following:

- Narratives are stories. Ideas for historical narratives come from events, persons, times, and places of history.
- Arranging events in chronological order helps readers follow the action.
- A narrative is told from a first-person or a third-person point of view.
- Dialogue enlivens narrative and shows how the characters think and feel.
- News stories focus on the facts: *who, what, when, where, why,* and *how.*
- A review of a historical narrative summarizes and evaluates the book.

Your Writer's Portfolio

Look over the writing you did for this unit. Choose two pieces for your portfolio. Look for writing that does the following:

- grows out of your prewriting ideas
- portrays realistically a person, event, and setting from history
- has an opening that introduces a person, event, and setting and draws readers into the story
- uses lively dialogue that shows what the characters are like
- uses fictional but true-to-life characters to portray a historical era or event
- opens with a lead that tells most or all of the five Ws and an H

Reflection and Commentary

Think about what you learned in this unit. Answer the following questions as you look over the two pieces of writing you chose. Write a page of "Comments on Writing a Story" for your portfolio.

1. What prewriting steps gave you the best ideas for historical narratives?
2. Where did you use actual persons, events, and settings of history?
3. Where did you put fictional characters and events in a historical setting?
4. Which elements of narrative writing did you handle best?

Feedback

If you had a chance to respond to the following student comment, what would you say or ask?

Sometimes when I hear other kids my age read their stories, I can tell what I should have done, or what they could have done to improve their papers.

Anana Intini, Herrick Junior High School,
Downers Grove, Illinois

Writing to Inform and Explain

Finding Meaning

Ernie Pepion, *Artist and Assistants*, 1990

McLAIN GUIDES TRAVELERS

"We as Americans say that America is the melting pot of the world. Yet there are huge holes between cultures. We don't understand, or we aren't even interested in, each other at times. So I think we need to exchange ideas and information, take the best of all and . . . put it together—and maybe that will become what America is."

Gary McLain (Eagle/Walking Turtle)

On crisp winter days in 1989, Gary McLain walked for hours along the wooded banks of the Blue River in Kansas. McLain, a Choctaw-Irish author and artist, was writing *Indian America,* a traveler's guide to Native American tribes in the continental United States. Long walks helped him think about the book.

McLain hoped his guide would invite non-Indian travelers into his world. "Most non-Indian people probably don't understand what it means to be Indian," he says. "So that's what I tried to do—explain what it means to be an Indian."

Writing a Guidebook

| 1. Collecting the Facts | 2. Writing the Book | 3. Revising for Publication |

FOCUS

Keeping in mind what the reader needs to know is important when writing explanations.

1 Collecting the Facts

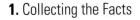

When McLain decided to write *Indian America,* he already knew a great deal about many Native American tribes. Even so, he needed to gather much more information.

Using his knowledge and a list from the Bureau of Indian Affairs, McLain mailed 500 letters to tribal offices around the country. Of the 500 letters sent, three hundred tribal offices responded with information that travelers would need. Information included the tribe's name, address, tribal office phone number, and location; and its public ceremonies and art forms. Some tribes even responded with histories written by tribal historians. McLain also did library research. Before long he had a stack of material three feet tall.

With the facts in hand, McLain next decided on the parts and organization of his guide. He says, "I divided the country into nine regions based mostly on how Indian people live."

McLain planned to open the guidebook with information on Indian beliefs. The guide to the tribes would follow, organized region by region. To help travelers picture these locations, McLain decided to include regional maps.

INTERFACE *You've been asked to write an article on big cultural celebrations in the United States, such as Chinese New Year, Cinco de Mayo, and Thanksgiving. Decide which events to cover. List the sources where you would look for information.*

▼ *In the Great Plains section of* Indian America, *McLain includes information about the traditions of the people—how the young and old cared for and taught one another.*

2 Writing the Book

With his book plan in mind, McLain started writing, a job that would take him three months. For days at a time, he wrote from sunup to mid-morning, from mid-afternoon until 10:00 P.M.

As McLain worked with his material, he used two writing styles to present information. In the introduction to each region, he wrote in a conversational manner. For example, in his introduction to the Great Plains, McLain explained how people

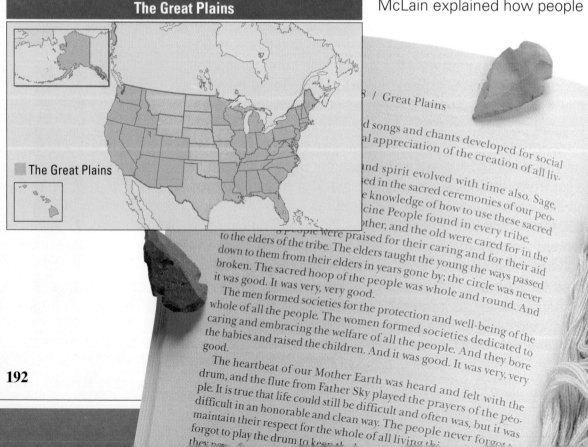

The Great Plains

The Great Plains

8 / Great Plains

d songs and chants developed for social al appreciation of the creation of all liv.

nd spirit evolved with time also. Sage, ed in the sacred ceremonies of our peo- e knowledge of how to use these sacred cine People found in every tribe.

to the elders of the tribe. The elders taught the young the ways passed down to them from their elders in years gone by; the circle was never broken. The sacred hoop of the people was whole and round. And it was good. It was very, very good.

The men formed societies for the protection and well-being of the whole of all the people. The women formed societies dedicated to caring and embracing the welfare of all the people. And they bore the babies and raised the children. And it was good. It was very, very good.

The heartbeat of our Mother Earth was heard and felt with the drum, and the flute from Father Sky played the prayers of the peo- ple. It is true that life could still be difficult and often was, but it was difficult in an honorable and clean way. The people never forgot maintain their respect for the whole of all living th forgot to play the drum to keep

were bound together in a great sacred hoop.

McLain used a much different writing style for his guide to each tribe. Here, he wrote in short sentences for travelers on the go. Then he organized the chunks of copy just as he had organized his letter: name, tribal office address, and phone number; details on ceremonies and art forms; and, finally, visitor information.

In the visitor-information section, McLain provided travelers with useful and intriguing facts. For the Taos Pueblo in New Mexico, he focused on photography rules for visitors. For the Cherokee in North Carolina, he described a restored Cherokee village, a museum, and various tourist activities. By contrast, his section on the Comanches in Oklahoma discussed the tribe's history, not its modern life. The reason?

"There are no more reservations in Oklahoma," McLain explains. "The Comanches live in white frame houses that don't look much different from those in Ohio or Indiana. Yet the Comanches were hunters who lived up and down the central plains. They were

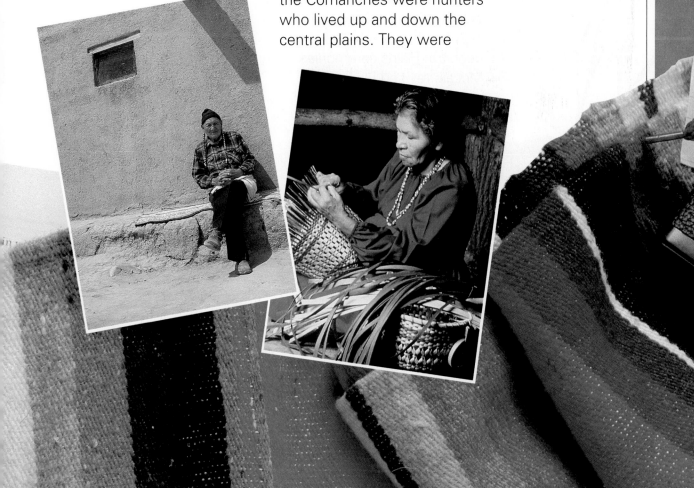

great horsemen and great warriors and had much ceremony in their lives. I thought a little more attention to the history of the tribe could help visitors feel connected to these people."

INTERFACE **Imagine you're going to write a guide to places like the Alamo and the Lincoln Memorial—places that help explain North American culture. Write down a list of ideas for your guide.**

▼ *In* Indian America *Gary McLain explains the use of sweetgrass and sage.*

3 Revising for Publication

Once McLain had his book on paper, he revised sections to make them clearer and more engaging. In some instances, he took his editor's advice and clarified cloudy explanations. McLain's editor also asked him to expand his section on sweetgrass and sage, healing plants used by Medicine People in Plains ceremonies. McLain revised his brief comment to read: "The Medicine People use sage, cedar, and sweetgrass, and the sweet smell carries the healing forward from the past into the future . . . in the sacred dances of our people across the land."

INDIAN AMERICA

A Traveler's Companion

SECOND EDITION

/WALKING TURTLE

er of 1st Annual Denali Press Award

ON ASSIGNMENT

1. Expository Writing

Brainstorm an explanation of a North American place, culture, or historical event that interests you.

- Choose a subject to explain. Consider topics such as how the railroads were built or what life on the prairie was like.

- Make a list of three or four key points that interest you.

2. About Literature

Write a poem or story explaining one of your family's customs.

- Choose a family custom that has meaning for you. Consider the way your family observes special occasions.

- Jot down all the details of this custom that you can think of. Also jot down how this family tradition makes you feel.

- Draft a short poem or story that explains this

important family custom and what it means to you.

3. Cooperative Learning

Develop a travel poster explaining your community to visitors.

- In a small group, pick an audience for your poster,. such as business people or students traveling with their families.

- Identify one or more jobs for each person in your group. You'll need

researchers, writers, editors, and illustrators.

- As a group, decide who will do which task and begin researching and drafting.

- Review the drafts as a group. Decide what maps and illustrations you need for your poster.

- Meet to revise the copy and review the art. Write a title for your poster.

- Assemble your poster and present it to the class.

Springing into Summer

The long, dark Alaskan winter is over at last. It's summer—time for outdoor fun. The Inuits, natives of the Far North, know just what to do. Below, Kevin Osborne explains a traditional game they still play, a blanket toss with an animal skin.

Literature Model

Members of the community grabbed hold of the edge of an animal skin. When everyone pulled at once, the center snapped up, propelling the person who sat or stood in the center of the skin into the air, just as if he or she were on a trampoline. The leader of the most successful whaling crew was often rewarded with the place on the skin; it was then a matter of pride to remain standing throughout the vigorous tossing.

Kevin Osborn, *The Peoples of the Arctic*

Writing to Inform

Osborn explains an Inuit blanket toss. He tells the steps in the process in the order they occur. His explanation is an example of expository writing—writing that explains and informs.

The most familiar form of expository writing is the essay. An essay consists of an introduction, a body, and a conclusion. The introduction usually contains a thesis statement, which is a sentence that states the main idea of the essay. The body, made up of one or more paragraphs, includes details that support the thesis statement. The conclusion draws the essay to a close. It may restate what has been said or suggest a different way of looking at the material. Notice in the introduction below how Michele Casey begins her essay on sharks.

Student Model

Although shark attacks do occur, they are not so frequent that swimmers must arm themselves with shark repellents. Survivors of airplane or ship disasters, though, need an effective shark repellent, since they have practically no defenses. The most promising advances are sound/electronic barriers. All other methods have major drawbacks.

Michele Casey, Glen Crest Junior High School,
Glen Ellyn, Illinois

What is the thesis statement in Michele's essay?

The body of her essay discusses various shark repellents. Her conclusion states, "Shark repellents of today and the future will help prevent further disaster for survivors at sea."

• JOURNAL ACTIVITY •
Try It Out

Imagine that a friend has asked you to write directions for a game you know well. In your journal write a thesis statement explaining the main goal of the game.

Choosing a Type That Works

You may never write a definition of a shark repellent or an explanation of a blanket toss. You may, however, define a hobby term or write directions for a friend. For each of these explanations, you use one type of expository writing. The chart below shows four types. To write about dolphins, the writer of the model below chose cause and effect.

Prewriting Tip

While prewriting, brainstorm a list of questions your essay should answer. Then answer the questions in your draft.

Types of Expository Writing	
Type	**Sample Writing**
Definition	*Sivuquad,* a name for St. Lawrence Island, means squeezed dry. The islanders believed that a giant had made the island from dried mud.
Process	To breathe, a whale surfaces in a forward rolling motion. For two seconds, it blows out and breathes in as much as 2,100 quarts of air.
Compare-Contrast	The boats in a coastal fishing fleet often stay at sea for days or weeks. Long-range fishing fleet vessels can remain at sea for months.
Cause-Effect	The discovery of oil and gas in Alaska in 1968 led to widespread development in that region of the world.

According to the writer, why has the dolphin been protected?

For centuries dolphins have fascinated people. Stories about dolphins that guided ships and rescued swimmers have led some people to idealize these creatures. Further, traditional respect and increasing public concern have resulted in measures intended to protect the dolphin.

Activities

Here are some activities to help you apply what you have learned.

1. Guided Assignment

You live near the Arctic Circle, and you are writing your first letter to a pen pal in North America. In the letter explain these aspects of your life:

- The average winter temperature is –30° F, or –34° C.
- In much of the Arctic Circle, the sun does not shine during the winter.
- Under the low, swampy land lies permanently frozen soil.

PURPOSE   To help your pen pal picture where you live

AUDIENCE   A pen pal your age who lives in North America

LENGTH   1 page

2. Open Assignment

Suppose that a television program called *What in the World?* is one of your favorites. During each show viewers are challenged to send an answer to a question. Choose one of the following questions or one you feel sure you can answer. Write an essay that answers it.

- What is a solar eclipse?
- How are a whale and a dolphin alike?

3. Social Studies

Like writing, some images also inform and explain. The Japanese print below reflects the influence of Western trade with Japan, beginning about the middle of the nineteenth century. Write at least one page describing influences of the Western world that you notice in the print. If you wish, consult an encyclopedia to verify your examples.

Hiroshige III, *Bank of Japan at Eitai Bridge,* 1884

5.2 | Structuring an Explanation

The Heart of a Computer Beats Silently

It's like magic. In a flash computers can tackle mountains of information. How do they do it? You can't tell just by glancing at their glass faces. Silent, invisible electrical pulses flow inside them, as Carol W. Brown explains in the model below.

Literature Model

P rinted circuit boards are the heart of the computer. On them are mounted the transistors, capacitors, chips, and other electrical marvels that create a computer. Their undersides have ribbons of solder, through which electricity flows. It is not necessary for you to have the foggiest idea how all this works. But do consider how small, lightweight, and portable the printed circuit boards are. Each board has a special function: some provide memory for the computer; others provide the processing and arithmetic logic functions; still others convert the power supply to and from the required voltages.

Carol W. Brown, *The Minicomputer Simplified*

Selecting the Details

Supporting details are the heart of your writing. They support the thesis statement in the introduction of your essay. The details you select for an essay will depend on the type of expository writing you're doing. For example, if you're writing a cause-and-effect essay, you might use reasons as supporting details. Carol W. Brown uses facts to define circuit boards. You can also use statistics, examples, or incidents to support what you say. Note the examples of the types of details listed in the chart below.

Details in Expository Writing	
Type	**Example**
Facts	Momenta International of California introduced a computer that can recognize and interpret printed handwriting.
Statistics	The processor inside a typical computer can carry out one million additions in only a second.
Examples/ Incidents	The optical processor is an example of a computer that uses light beams to process information.
Reasons	Computer manufacturers are developing smaller computers because businesspeople demand them for use when they travel.

• JOURNAL ACTIVITY •
Try It Out

Read an article in a newspaper or magazine. Look for the thesis statement, and identify in your journal the different types of supporting details.

Arranging the Details

Once you've selected supporting details for your explanation, you're ready to organize them. Consider your purpose. Ask yourself what you're trying to do in your essay. For example, are you going to show the cause and effect of a tidal wave? Are you going to point out in a comparison-contrast essay the similarities and differences between two comedians? Questions such as these can help you organize your ideas—the supporting details—logically.

You might choose any number of ways to arrange information and supporting details. If, for example, you're defining something, you might arrange features from most to least significant. If you're writing about a process, then chronological order, or time order, might be more useful. Notice the kinds of details and their arrangement that Emilie Baltz uses in the model below.

Student Model

What types of details are in the writing?

What kind of organization does the writer use?

T homas Edison's invention of the electric light bulb in 1879 came about only after a long, hard process. Finding the right material for the tiny filament inside the light bulb had been difficult. Edison tested 1,600 materials before finally using a piece of burned thread. Because it contained no air, the thread did not burn quickly inside the bulb. This invention would eventually bring light into the world.

Emilie Baltz, Hufford Junior High School, Joliet, Illinois

Activities

Here are some activities to help you apply what you have learned.

1. Guided Assignment

You have invented an inexpensive pocket computer. You have to explain to the head of a computer sales firm what your computer does. Use the following details to write your explanation. Write them in your own words. Feel free to be creative and to add ideas of your own.

- The price for this computer will be under one hundred dollars. Other personal computers cost thousands.
- The computer is smaller than a paperback book. It weighs less than a pound, and it runs on batteries. A student could carry it in a pocket.
- You can write on the screen with a penlike tool. The computer translates and remembers what you write so that you can look it up later.
- Students can use the computer to take notes at the library and in the classroom. Adults can use it to jot down grocery lists, appointments, telephone numbers, and more.
- It can be hooked up to a telephone in order to send and to receive data.

PURPOSE   To use supporting details effectively to explain the features of a new computer
AUDIENCE   The head of a computer firm
LENGTH   ½–1 page

COMPUTER OPTION

You can use a computer to illustrate your explanation with pictures, graphs, charts, and diagrams. Some word-processing programs have graphic functions. Some programs can change statistics to graphs. Clip art—pictures you can copy and paste into your document—is also available.

2. Open Assignment

Imagine that you are writing the "Tell me why…" column in the science section of a student magazine. Choose one of the topics below or one of your own, and explain it in a page or two.

- Why volcanoes erupt
- Why and how spiders make webs
- What a galaxy is

3. Cooperative Learning

In a small group take turns explaining the same historical event. Focus on its causes. Choose an event that occurred during your lifetime. Include as many details as possible in your explanations. As other group members speak, jot down details included in their explanations that you did not include in yours. When everyone has had a turn, compare lists, and together decide on the most important details. Then individually write a draft that explains the event and its causes.

5.3 | Writing to Compare and Contrast

My Kind of Music

    The concert crowd cheers wildly. Tanya claps along in time to the rhythms of Latin music. At another concert across town, Ben gets caught up in the wail of the country sound. Tanya and Ben enjoy two kinds of music that are different in some ways and alike in others. Think about two kinds of music. Jot down two or three things about them that are similar and two or three things that are different.

Identifying Similarities and Differences

When you compare two things, you explain how they're similar. When you contrast two things, you explain how they're different. For example, you might compare the American origins of two kinds of music. You might contrast the slow beat of one of these with the lively beat of the other. Comparing and contrasting two items can be a useful way of explaining them.

Before you write a compare-and-contrast essay, you might identify similarities and differences. A Venn diagram, such as the one below, may help you. Be sure that your subjects are related, as two kinds of music are. Also, compare and contrast the same set of features, such as cultural sources and sound, that relate to the subjects.

Drafting Tip

When drafting an opening sentence for a compare-and-contrast essay, choose words that will grab your reader's attention.

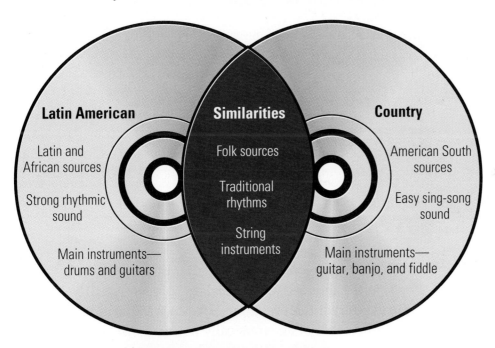

Latin American

Latin and African sources

Strong rhythmic sound

Main instruments— drums and guitars

Similarities

Folk sources

Traditional rhythms

String instruments

Country

American South sources

Easy sing-song sound

Main instruments— guitar, banjo, and fiddle

• JOURNAL ACTIVITY •
Think It Through

Think of two musical artists or groups that are related in some way. In your journal make a Venn diagram. Use the diagram to compare and contrast the musicians in terms of the same features.

Organizing Compare-and-Contrast Writing

You can organize compare-and-contrast writing by subject or by feature. In organizing by subject, you discuss the features of one subject and then the features of the other. For example, you might explain the sources and sound of Latin music and then discuss the contrasting sources and sound of country music. When organizing by feature, you discuss one feature at a time for both subjects. For example, you might examine the sources of both Latin music and country music before discussing their sound. How did Michael Shapiro organize the paragraph below on classical musicians Yo-Yo Ma and Emanuel Ax?

Organizing by Subject or Feature

Subject ▶ Latin music sources are Latin American and African. The beat of the music is strong and rhythmic. Country music, on the other hand, comes from the American South.

Feature ▶ Latin music comes from Latin America and Africa, while country music grew out of America's South. The sound of the two kinds of music is also different. Latin is rhythmic and country music is sing-songy.

Literature Model

Does the writer organize his contrast by feature or by subject?

How are Yo-Yo Ma and Emanuel Ax different?

They seem, on the surface, an unlikely pair, as is often the case with friends who never seem to lose the rhythm of their relationship. Ma was the child wonder who came of age musically in the warm embrace of such mentors as Isaac Stern and Leonard Rose. Ax grew up never knowing whether he would be able to become a concert pianist. For Ma playing the cello has always come easily. For Ax the musician's life is one for which he feels forever grateful.

Michael Shapiro, "Yo-Yo and Manny"

John Biggers, *Jubilee—Ghana Harvest Festival*, 1959

Here are some activities to help you apply what you have learned.

1. Guided Assignment

Suppose that you are testing two competing brands of athletic shoes for the manufacturer of one of the brands. You are to prepare a written explanation comparing and contrasting the two brands. Create a Venn diagram to help you identify similarities and differences between the two shoes. Shoe A is white with orange and purple racing stripes. It is leather with a suede toe. It cannot be washed because of the leather trim. Shoe B is white with dark blue stitching. It is canvas and can be machine washed.

PURPOSE	To compare and contrast two athletic shoes
AUDIENCE	Shoe manufacturer
LENGTH	1 page

2. Open Assignment

You are studying for a test that may ask you to compare and contrast some people, places, or things. Choose two items from the list below or two items related to a subject you are studying in school. Prepare for the test by writing a one- or two-page essay comparing and contrasting the items.

- two characters from a book
- two cities in your state
- hurricanes and tornadoes

3. Art

Study the painting above. Then look at the painting *Bank of Japan at Eitai Bridge* on page 199. Imagine that these two paintings appear in an exhibit. Write at least one page comparing and contrasting the subjects of the paintings.

Writing to Compare and Contrast **207**

Writing About a Process

Perfect Pizza Dough in Four Easy Steps

How does he do it? He makes it look so easy. The chef whips the ingredients together and kneads the dough. He lets the dough rest so it can rise. Then it's time for the show stopper. He shapes the dough and flings it into the air. Then he catches it without a hitch.

Everyday life is full of processes. Explaining how to do them poses a challenge. Suppose that you want to explain how pizza dough is prepared—the steps leading up to all the flinging and catching. The diagram below breaks down the steps for you.

Making Pizza Dough in Four Steps

| Mix Ingrediants | Knead Dough | Let Dough Rise | Shape Dough |

To Do and to Understand

Knowing how to do something does not guarantee that you can easily share that knowledge with others. Some people find it more difficult to explain a step-by-step process than to actually do it. Fortunately, you can learn to write about a process so that others can understand. The instructions on the next page explain how to prepare chilies that are almost too hot to handle.

W earing rubber gloves is a wise precaution, especially when you are handling fresh hot chilies. Be careful not to touch your face or eyes while working with them.

To prepare chilies, first rinse them clean in *cold* water. (Hot water may make fumes rise from dried chilies, and even the fumes might irritate your nose and eyes.) Working under cold running water, pull out the stem of each chili and break or cut the chilies in half. Brush out the seeds with your fingers. In most cases the ribs inside are tiny, and can be left intact, but if they seem fleshy, cut them out with a small, sharp knife. Dried chilies should be torn into small pieces, covered with boiling water and soaked for at least 30 minutes before they are used. Fresh chilies may be used at once, or soaked in cold, salted water for an hour to remove some of the hotness.

Recipes: Latin American Cooking

The word "first" helps identify what step to begin with.

What are the steps in preparing fresh chilies?

To explain a process, choose a topic that you understand well and can research if necessary. Then identify your audience and what they may already know. Consider terms they'll understand and those you'll have to explain. You may have either of two purposes in explaining a process. You may be helping readers make or do something themselves, for example, how to make tacos. On the other hand, you may be explaining how something works or happens, such as how a Mexican chef makes tacos.

Grammar
Editing Tip

As you edit your essay, notice that some of your transitions can or do appear in adverb clauses. For information see pages 462–463.

• JOURNAL ACTIVITY •
Think It Through

In your journal use a cluster map to explore topics for a process explanation. You might choose a hobby or another activity you enjoy. Circle your three best ideas.

To Make Yourself Clear

Before you write about a process, gather information through research, observation, or interviews. List the steps of the process in chronological order. Then write your draft. Use transition words, such as *first, next,* and *later,* to connect the steps. The chart shows a plan one student followed to write the explanation that appears below.

Relating a Process	
Organizing Your Writing	**Example**
Topic	How to make a pizza
Audience	Friends
What the audience needs to know	The steps in making the pizza
Gathering information	Watch the video I taped. Read a pizza cookbook.
Listing steps	1. Spread dough. 2. Spread cheese. 3. Add vegetables. 4. Top with fresh tomatoes.

Student Model

The writer lists the four steps in chronological order.

What transition words does the writer use in the explanation?

First, spread the dough so that you have an inch-wide rim around the sides. The rim keeps the filling from leaking out while the pizza's cooking. Now it's time to put in the fillings. Place the cheese on the dough to keep it from getting soggy. Then add peppers, onions, or other vegetables that could burn if they were on top. Place fresh chopped tomatoes over the vegetables. Your pizza's oven-ready.

Luke Lapenta Proskine, Wilmette Junior High School, Wilmette, Illinois

Activities

Here are some activities to help you apply what you have learned.

1. Guided Assignment

The steps below explain the process for making a leaf print, but the steps are given in the wrong order. Read the steps, and arrange them in chronological order. Then use the steps to write a clear explanation of the process for your science teacher and classmates. Be sure you identify the process in your introduction and include transition words.

1. With the inked side facing up, put the leaf on a clean piece of paper. Tape a piece of rice paper over the leaf.
2. Let the leaf print dry.
3. Select a leaf with distinct veins.
4. Use a clean, dry paint roller to roll over the rice paper from top to bottom.
5. Carefully remove the rice paper from the leaf.
6. Place the leaf, vein side up, on a piece of paper.
7. Put a small amount of printer's ink on a smooth surface, such as glass. Coat a paint roller with the ink, and spread the ink to cover the leaf completely.

PURPOSE To organize details effectively
AUDIENCE Teacher and classmates in science class
LENGTH 1 page

2. Open Assignment

Select one of the following ordinary tasks or one of your own. Write a one-page process explanation for someone who knows little or nothing about the task.

- How to tie your shoes
- How to find a library book on making pizza

3. Cooperative Learning

In a small group brainstorm different kinds of foods you can make or can easily find out how to make. From the list of suggestions, have each member of the group sign up for a food to write a process explanation about. The group leader can record the suggestions and the assignments. Have each member draft a brief but clear step-by-step explanation of how to make the food. Individually read your explanations to the group and discuss how to make the explanations clearer and more informative. Ask a member of the group to assemble the final drafts into a "How to Make It" booklet.

COMPUTER OPTION

You might make your "How to Make It" booklet livelier by using diagrams and illustrations. If you have a drawing software program, you can use your computer to create illustrated charts.

Explaining Connections Between Events

The Sky in a Skyscraper

The skyscraper reflects billowing clouds. You ask yourself, Why are some skyscrapers' windows like mirrors? Notice how James Cross Giblin answers this question.

Literature Model

The energy crisis of the 1970s presented yet another threat to the windows in homes, schools, and office buildings. The all-glass architectural styles of the postwar years had depended on a steady supply of inexpensive fuel for heating and air-conditioning. Now there was a danger that that supply might be cut off, or drastically reduced.

To conserve energy and meet the demand for even better climate control in buildings, manufacturers developed an improved window covering—reflective glass. Reflective glass was coated with a thin, transparent metallic film. This mirrorlike coating reflected the sun's rays away from the glass and lowered heat gain within the building much more than mere tinted glass could.

James Cross Giblin, *Let There Be Light*

What Cause and Effect Is

Giblin uses cause and effect to explain the origins of mirror-like skyscraper windows. The cause (the energy crisis) led to an effect (the development of reflective-glass windows). A cause-and-effect explanation may show one cause and one effect. Or it may explain a series of effects resulting from a single cause. It can also present multiple causes and multiple effects.

You should make sure your topic describes true cause and effect. Because one event follows another doesn't mean that the first caused the second. Suppose you close a window, and then the phone rings. Shutting the window didn't make the phone ring. Notice how Nick Poole used cause and effect in this paragraph.

TERRITORIAL GROWTH OF THE UNITED STATES.

Student Model

During the nineteenth century, Americans were part of a tremendous expansion westward. These pioneering Americans left their homes back east for at least three reasons. Some were seeking fertile soil for farming. Many were looking for economic development. Trade was one way of making money. The pioneers traded with Native Americans, especially for furs. Various goods were also available from Mexicans. Finally, other Americans just went west for the adventure.

Nick Poole, Wilmette Junior High School, Wilmette, Illinois

What three causes of westward expansion does Nick identify?

• JOURNAL ACTIVITY •
Try It Out

Select a recent event that held some particular meaning for you. Identify the cause or effect of the event. In your journal, list each cause or effect.

How Cause and Effect Works

Drafting Tip

When drafting, use transitions such as the following to help you make cause-and-effect relationships clear: *so, if, then, since, because, therefore, as a result.*

The chart below shows the steps you can take to organize a cause-and-effect essay. First, select a topic, and ask yourself if a clear cause-and-effect relationship exists. Next, explore the types of cause-and-effect relationships present. Is there one cause for several effects? Are there several causes leading to a single effect? Or are there multiple causes with multiple effects?

Finally, choose a pattern of organization for your writing. You can organize your cause-and-effect draft in one of two ways. One method involves identifying a cause and then explaining its effects. The other method involves stating an effect and then discussing its cause or causes. After you've completed your draft, review it to be sure the cause-and-effect relationships are clear.

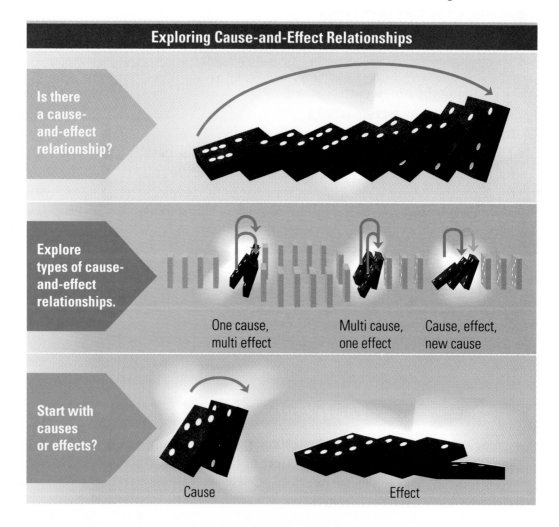

Exploring Cause-and-Effect Relationships

Is there a cause-and-effect relationship?

Explore types of cause-and-effect relationships.

One cause, multi effect

Multi cause, one effect

Cause, effect, new cause

Start with causes or effects?

Cause

Effect

Activities

Here are some activities to help you apply what you have learned.

1. Guided Assignment

You have been asked to give a talk to a group of concerned citizens. The topic is the causes behind the destruction of the world's rain forests. Write a one-page essay to present to the group. In your explanation use the following facts and others you find on your own.

- People have cleared from 14 to 55 million acres every year for farms, cities, mines, and timber projects.

David Hockney, *A Bigger Splash*, 1967

- Scientists fear that hundreds of thousands of plants and animals will die out because of the destruction.

PURPOSE To alert people to the causes and effects of the rain forests' destruction

AUDIENCE A group of citizens concerned about the rain forests

LENGTH 1 page

2. Open Assignment

Find some information about one of the topics below or one of your own choosing. Write a one-page cause-and-effect explanation.

- How did Rosa Parks cause changes in civil rights legislation?
- How has the Americans with Disabilities Act opened up opportunities for disabled people in our community?

3. Science

The painting on the left offers an artistic version of a cause-and-effect relationship that involves water. You might write about the cause and effect depicted in the painting. Alternatively, you might write a cause-and-effect essay that scientifically explores the behavior of water.

Explaining Connections Between Events **215**

Answering an Essay Question

America on Wheels

How did the invention of the automobile change daily life in the United States?

You read the question and eye the clock. You have half an hour to write your answer. Where do you start? This lesson will help you to plan answers to essay test questions.

Planning Your Answer

Writing a good answer to an essay question takes some planning. First, read the question carefully. Then decide roughly how many minutes you'll spend on each of the following tasks. Your first tasks include underlining key words and jotting down key ideas to include in the answer. You'll then develop a thesis statement, a brief outline, and a draft. Finally, you'll revise as time permits.

Begin planning your answer. Look at the question for clue words that can help you compose your answer. Then identify key ideas you'll want to discuss. You might explore them by using a cluster diagram or organize them by renumbering. The facing page shows how a student organized some key ideas to answer the test question. The chart below gives examples of clue words.

Revising Tip

When you revise your answer, cross out any unnecessary details. Insert details that will make your answer more complete.

People → Farmers are no longer isolated. Places

Places like motels, drive-ins, and large shopping malls are a part of daily life.

People within cities can travel to jobs many miles from their homes.

People can drive many miles on short or long vacations.

> *The items in the list have been grouped as they will be discussed in the draft.*

Clue Words in Essay Questions

Clue Word	Action to take	Example
Describe	Use precise details to paint a picture of something.	Describe the appearance of the first Ford Model T.
Explain	Use facts, examples, or reasons to tell why or how.	Explain how the car was developed.
Compare	Tell how two or more subjects are alike.	Compare the steam car and the electric car.
Contrast	Tell how two or more subjects are different.	Contrast the Model T with a car of today.
Summarize	State main points in brief form.	Summarize how a four-cycle engine works.

• JOURNAL ACTIVITY •
Try It Out

In your journal use one clue word from the chart to write a question. Choose a topic that intrigues you. Take notes you would need to answer it.

Writing Your Answer

Your answer should be a well-organized essay. The introduction to your essay should contain a statement identifying the main ideas in your answer. An effective way to begin is by restating the question.

Follow your introductory statement with the body of your answer. Include information from your notes as you write your supporting details. Then write a conclusion that restates your beginning statement and summarizes your answer. When you've finished your draft, see whether your content words match the content words of the question. These are the key words that relate to the subject matter. Finally, revise and edit your draft. Notice how one writer drafted an answer to the question on page 216.

> The first sentence of the answer restates the question.

> What details does the writer use in the body to show the change in Americans' daily life?

> The conclusion restates the introductory statement.

The invention of the automobile has changed daily life in the United States in two important ways. First, Americans are constantly on the move. City people can drive to jobs far from their homes. Farmers can travel to stores and offices miles away. Vacationers can drive to faraway places. Second, American businesses now provide services to go. Motels, drive-ins, and malls suit the needs of Americans on the run. Automobiles have changed America into a nation on wheels.

Activities

Artist unknown, Eagle carved from one piece of pine, Salem, Massachusetts, c.1900

Here are some activities to help you apply what you have learned.

1. Guided Assignment

Write an essay question dealing with the image above. This particular eagle symbolizes the United States and was carved in the early 1800s. Keep these ideas in mind as you organize your answer:

- Congress selected the eagle as the national bird and symbol of the American spirit.
- The Latin words on the carving mean "Out of many, one."

PURPOSE To practice writing effective answers to essay questions

AUDIENCE Your American History teacher

LENGTH ½ page

2. Open Assignment

Use the plan in this lesson to answer an essay question, using one of the following ideas or one of your own:

- Answer the question for which you wrote notes in the Journal Activity.
- Explain how a bill becomes a law.

3. Literature

Look through your literature textbook for an essay question related to literature you have read and enjoyed. Select a question you would like to answer. Assume that you have forty-five minutes to compose an answer. Write the question, and then answer it. Apply the procedure you have learned in this lesson.

Flight School for Geese

You flip the channel and stare at the television screen. You can't believe your eyes. A man is flying an airplane, leading a flock of Canada geese. It turns out that the man has raised these geese, which were orphaned. Because they can't learn to fly on their own, the pilot decided to teach them to fly, using his airplane. Your mind spins with questions. When are geese ready to learn to fly? Where do they fly in the winter? How do they know when to leave?

Finding a Research Topic

You can explore the answers to intriguing questions by writing about them. When you prepare to write a research report, think about things you'd like to know more about. Read your journal for thoughts, questions, and possible topics. Brainstorm a list of questions that you'd like to explore.

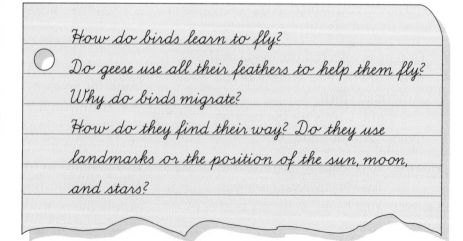

How do birds learn to fly?

Do geese use all their feathers to help them fly?

Why do birds migrate?

How do they find their way? Do they use landmarks or the position of the sun, moon, and stars?

Sometimes it's difficult to know whether your questions pertain to one topic or to several. How do you decide? Start by considering the length of your report. Is your goal a two-page report or a twelve-page report? In the amount of space you have, you should be able to present your topic to your readers' satisfaction. The list of questions on page 220, for example, is about birds. The general topic of birds is too large for one report. The topic of Canada goose feathers is probably too narrow. The topic of Canada goose migration is probably just the right size for a report.

Now consider your purpose and your audience. What do you want to explain? What information do you want to share? Decide who your readers will be and how much they already know about your topic. Will you be able to provide all the necessary background information and facts?

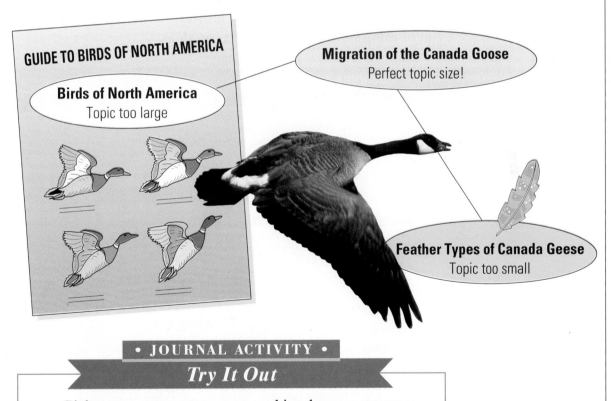

GUIDE TO BIRDS OF NORTH AMERICA

Birds of North America
Topic too large

Migration of the Canada Goose
Perfect topic size!

Feather Types of Canada Geese
Topic too small

• JOURNAL ACTIVITY •

Try It Out

Pick a news or sports event, and jot down some questions about it. Is there a report topic here? If so, write about what you might include in the report.

Getting the Facts

Grammar
Editing Tip

When editing, check the spelling and capitalization of proper nouns. For more information see pages 526–531.

Now it's time to gather the facts you'll need to begin drafting your report. Don't rely on one source. Try to find as many sources as you can. The chart below lists the kinds of sources available in the library and gives an example of each. It also shows the form in which you identify, or cite, your sources in your notes. You'll use the same form in your final paper. Pages 575–596 offer more information on using the library.

Many report writers use index cards to record notes from sources. Use one card for each note, and include your source. Read the source carefully so that you can summarize the information in your own words. You may also quote directly. When you do, you must copy word for word the information you want to quote. Use quotation marks in your notes. Later you'll know which information you summarized and which you quoted directly. In your report you must let your readers know when you're using someone else's words or ideas.

Sources and Identification

Source	Examples	How to Identify Sources
Books	*Birds* *A Field Guide to the Birds* *Bird Migration*	Mead, Chris. Bird Migration. New York: Facts on File Publications, 1983.
Magazines & Newspapers	*Audubon* *Discover* *Houston Chronicle*	Warden, J.W. "Migration! The Great Spring Event." Petersen's Photographic Magazine, April 1992:22–25.
Encyclopedias	*The World Book Encyclopedia* *The Illustrated Encyclopedia of the Animal Kingdom*	"Canada Goose." The World Book Encyclopedia. 1978 ed., 3:124.
Video materials	*Audubon Society's Video Guide to the Birds of North America: Volume 1*	Audubon Society's Video Guide to Birds of North America: 1. Godfrey-Stadin Productions, 1985.

Here are some activities to help you apply what you have learned.

1. Guided Assignment

The small figure of a dog below was created by an Aztec artist hundreds of years ago. The Aztec civilization flourished in what is now Mexico. What do you think this sculpture tells us about the way the Aztecs felt about dogs? If you could travel back in time, what questions would you ask the sculptor? Jot down some questions as you study the sculpture. One or more of your questions should suggest a report topic.

PURPOSE   To select an appropriate research topic and write questions about it
AUDIENCE   Yourself
LENGTH   3 or 4 note cards or 1 page of notes

2. Open Assignment

Select a current news or sports event that interests you, and research it. Reread the questions you jotted down about current events in your journal. You may use newspapers, magazines, and television news broadcasts. Take notes from each source. How does their presentation of the facts differ? Did one source give more information than another? Did any source present opinions on the event? In one or two pages explain how your knowledge of the event might have been different had you consulted only one source.

3. Science

Did Benjamin Franklin really fly a kite during a thunderstorm and discover electricity? At the library, research this question or another science question that interests you. List the question you researched, and summarize your findings.

Stone dog, Aztec artifact, Mexico, c. 1250–1519

A *Letter That Means Business*

The library isn't the only source of information on a topic. You can write a business letter to request information or to ask someone for an interview. Writing a business letter can help you get answers to questions that other sources can't answer.

1565 Shadyside Road
Dover, DE 19809
January 10, 19--

Ms. Maria Washington, Director
Sellar's Island
National Wildlife Refuge
Route 3
Tyler, DE 19968

Dear Ms. Washington:

I am an eighth-grade student at Dover Junior High School in Dover, Delaware, and I am working on a report on the migration of the Canada goose. I am writing to you to ask for information on the Canada geese that spend the winter at Sellar's Island. I'd appreciate it very much if you would answer these questions for me.

1. What features at Sellar's Island attract the large flock of geese?

2. What is the estimate for the actual number of geese that pass through each winter?

3. Have you done any leg banding to try to find out whether the same geese return each year?

The answers to these questions, and any other information that you can provide, will be very helpful to me in my report.

I live only about thirty miles from Sellar's Island. Would it be convenient for me to visit you for a brief interview and a tour of the refuge? I could arrange to come any weekday after school in the next two weeks.

Thank you for your help. I look forward to hearing from you and learning more about the Canada goose.

Yours truly,

Roberto Estevado

Roberto Estevado

The Business of a Business Letter

When you write a business letter, you should have a clear reason for writing. If you're writing a business letter to request information, state your questions clearly. Make your request specific and reasonable, and make sure you're asking for information you can't get anywhere else. If you're requesting an interview, tell what you want to discuss. Suggest some dates and times. Business letters have other uses, such as placing an order or lodging a complaint. A letter to the editor is a business letter written to express an opinion.

Grammar
Editing Tip

When editing, check your use of pronouns and antecedents. For more information see pages 394–395.

Guidelines for Writing Business Letters

1. Use correct business-letter form. Some dictionaries and typing manuals outline different forms of business letters.

2. Be courteous, and use standard English.

3. Be brief and to the point. Explain why you need the information.

4. Use clean, white or off-white paper. Make a neat presentation.

5. Be considerate. Request only information you can't get another way. If unsure where to find information, ask your librarian.

6. When requesting an interview, make it easy for the interviewee to meet with you. Suggest a few dates.

Don't be shy about writing a business letter to request information. Many people will be pleased that you're interested in their field and will be happy to tell you what they know.

• JOURNAL ACTIVITY •
Think It Through

Look in your journal for a possible report topic. What information about it couldn't you find at the library? Brainstorm other possible sources for this information and how you would get it.

Getting Down to Business

Readers expect business letters to be clear and to follow certain rules. At the beginning of your letter introduce yourself and your purpose for writing. Use the paragraphs that follow to support your purpose with details. Then make it clear exactly what you want from the reader. Are you requesting an interview? Are you asking for answers to specific questions? Show your draft to a peer reviewer, and ask whether your message is clear. Use the sample business letter in this lesson as a guide. Your readers will notice the care you took in writing to them. They are then more likely to respond to you.

The heading gives the writer's address and the date on separate lines.

Sellar's Island
National Wildlife Refuge
Route 3
Tyler, DE 19968
January 15, 19—

Mr. Roberto Estevado
1565 Shadyside Road
Dover, DE 19809

Dear Mr. Estevado:

The inside address gives the name, title, and address of the person to whom the letter is being sent.

I was pleased to receive your letter of January 10 regarding the annual Canada goose migration to Sellar's Island. Here are the answers to your questions.

The introductory paragraph states the purpose for writing.

1. Located on a flat coastal plain, only about ten feet above sea level, Sellar's Island offers an ideal environment for Canada geese. It has large marshy areas, brushy woodlands, and vast expanses of fresh water. We have also "improved" the environment by planting more than fifteen acres of grain.

2. Our studies indicate that approximately twenty thousand Canada geese winter at Sellar's Island.

3. We have done many studies on the goose population, including leg banding. I have enclosed a copy of our latest report. As it indicates, large numbers of the same geese do tend to return to us each year.

The body presents supporting details— reasons and facts.

I would be happy to meet with you for an interview and a tour of the refuge facilities. Would 4:00 P.M. on Tuesday, January 23, be convenient? I've enclosed a brochure describing the facilities at Sellar's Island, which also provides directions here.

Sincerely,

Maria Washington

Maria Washington
Director

Use Sincerely *or* Yours truly, *followed by a comma, for the closing.*

Activities

Here are some activities to help you apply what you have learned.

1. Guided Assignment

Suppose that your favorite musician, artist, or professional athlete is coming to your city. Two weeks ago you wrote to this person to request an interview. The person agreed! You will have only thirty minutes for the interview, and your subject wants to know what you will be discussing.

Interviews run more smoothly when the person holding the interview plans the questions ahead of time. Write a draft of your questions. Then number the questions to show the order in which you will present them. You might show your questions to a peer reviewer or share them with a friend. Would either of them make any changes that you would agree with?

Now draft a second letter to the interviewee. Reintroduce yourself and your purpose for writing. Summarize the questions you are planning to ask during the interview.

PURPOSE   To draft a letter containing well-thought-out questions for a proposed interview
AUDIENCE   The subject of your interview
LENGTH   1–2 pages

2. Open Assignment

Select one of the following situations for writing a business letter, or make up a situation of your own. Then write an appropriate letter.

- to order tickets for a concert
- to request an interview with a local artist
- to request information about joining a club

3. Cooperative Learning

In a small group, practice writing business letters that ask experts for information for research paper topics. Follow these steps:

- Take turns describing your topics. As a group, brainstorm which experts might provide each group member with important source materials.
- Work independently to locate the name and address of one expert on your topic. Then draft a business letter to that person.
- Meet as a group to go over everyone's letter. Discuss possible revisions.

COMPUTER OPTION

Perhaps someone in your group will find that you have misspelled a word or name in your business letter. Check whether your word-processing program has a search (or find) and replace feature. Using this feature, you can tell your computer to find every use of the misspelled word or name.

Reports: Planning and Drafting

Whatever Works!

© Watterson 1992. Universal Press Syndicate

Like Calvin, you've decided on a topic for your report. Unlike Calvin, however, you've done your research. Now that you've collected so much valuable information on your topic, you may be unsure where to go from here. Fortunately, there are a few strategies to help you begin.

Developing a Plan of Action

Now you can use your research notes to begin planning and drafting your report. Make sure you have a clear idea of your purpose for writing and of your audience. For example, the purpose of Roberto's report is to explain the migration of the Canada goose. His audience includes his teacher and classmates. Knowing your purpose and audience will help focus your planning and drafting.

Review your notes, looking for a focus or a main idea that you can express in a sentence or two. This main idea is the angle or question that guided your research. Try drafting a thesis statement based on this main idea. Although your thesis statement may change, it can guide you as you write your outline.

An outline and thesis statement cover the main points of a report. Group your notes according to subtopic. Although all Roberto's notes are about goose migration, he could group them into subtopics. These appear on his outline as major headings. Here Roberto's thesis statement appears at the top, followed by his outline.

The thesis statement tells what the topic is and what the main idea of the report is.

The Canada goose's migration pattern has dramatically changed in recent years.

I. Characteristics of the Canada goose

A. What the Canada goose looks and sounds like as it flies overhead

B. What its traditional migration pattern used to be

C. How the pattern has changed

II. Basic needs of the Canada goose

A. Food

B. Water

C. Protection

III. Why and where the Canada goose used to migrate

The major outline heads state the main ideas of the paragraphs. Subheads note supporting facts and details.

Like all wildlife, Canada geese have a few basic requirements for ⸺ and their

Source: John Terborgh, Where Have All the Birds Gone? Princeton

⸺re World War I, corn harveste⸺ ⸺d. Later harvested by machine-⸺ ⸺0 percent of crop in field. This ⸺ ⸺ions of birds. Therefore "the win⸺ ⸺ carrying capacity for Canada geese ⸺ has probably been raised many fol⸺

Putting the Plan into Action

Revising Tip

When revising, refer to your outline and thesis statement to make sure you have included all your main ideas in your draft.

You've worked hard to get your ideas organized. Now use your notes and outline to draft the three main parts of your report. The introduction presents your topic and thesis statement. It offers a chance to engage your readers. It should grab their attention. Consider including a thought-provoking quotation, fact, statement, eyewitness account, or anecdote. The body supports your thesis statement with reasons and facts. The conclusion may reflect your thesis statement by summarizing main points. It should bring the report to a logical and graceful end. Does your paper raise any new issues or questions? Try including them in the conclusion.

Notice the process followed below in drafting a report from notes and an outline. Grammar and spelling errors will be corrected later.

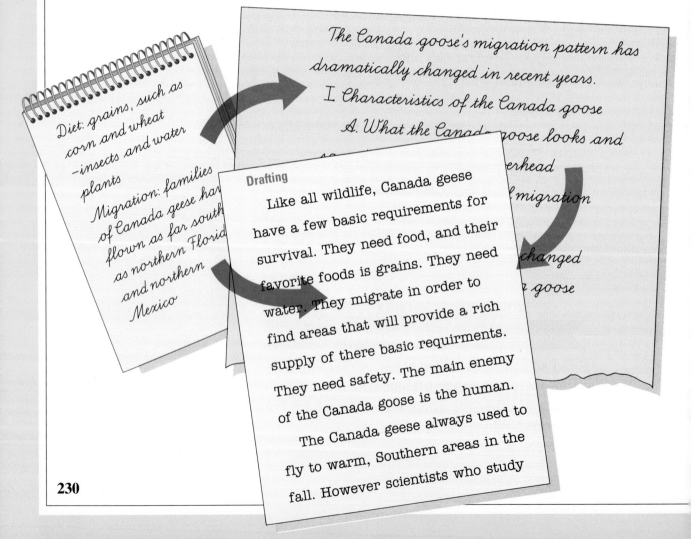

Diet: grains, such as corn and wheat
—insects and water plants

Migration: families of Canada geese ha[ve] flown as far south as northern Florid[a] and northern Mexico

The Canada goose's migration pattern has dramatically changed in recent years.
I Characteristics of the Canada goose
A. What the Cana[da g]oose looks and
[...]erhead
[...] migration
[...]changed
[...] goose

Drafting

Like all wildlife, Canada geese have a few basic requirements for survival. They need food, and their favorite foods is grains. They need water. They migrate in order to find areas that will provide a rich supply of there basic requirments. They need safety. The main enemy of the Canada goose is the human.

The Canada geese always used to fly to warm, Southern areas in the fall. However scientists who study

Activities

Here are some activities to help you apply what you have learned.

1. Guided Assignment

The following is part of an outline and notes that a student wrote for a report on the life of John Muir, a famous naturalist. Based on the following, write a page on Muir's childhood and youth.

II. Muir's early life
   A. Born in Dunbar, Scotland, on April 21, 1838
   B. Started school when he was three
   C. Liked to explore fields and meadows and to go rock climbing
   D. Moved to America when he was ten years old
   E. Grew up on a farm in Wisconsin

Youth

Muir was known for his inventions; grew to love nature; entered University of Wisconsin at 22; became interested in botany.

PURPOSE   To use an outline as a springboard for a first draft
AUDIENCE Yourself
LENGTH   1 page

2. Open Assignment

Select one of the following research topics or one of your own. Then write an introductory paragraph including a thesis statement that clearly and briefly states your approach to the topic.

- the importance of a school athletic program
- the history of jazz
- advances in treating the common cold

3. Cooperative Learning

Get together with a partner to review outlines and thesis statements you are writing. Follow these steps:

- Take turns describing what your paper is about and what you plan to say about your topic.
- Serve as each other's peer reviewer. Discuss whether the thesis statement is clear and to the point. How might it be strengthened? Then examine each other's outline. Does it represent a clear plan to follow? Does it include all the points the writer wants to make? Do the points appear in the correct order?
- Working independently, decide how you might revise your thesis statement and outline, based on your peer editor's suggestions.

COMPUTER OPTION

Check to see whether your word-processing program has an Outlining feature. If so, it might prove to be a useful aid as you plan and organize the structure of your report.

Getting the Big Picture

Sometimes you can become so involved in something that you can no longer judge it for what it is. Writing your report can place you too close to it to evaluate it objectively. You need to read your report as if for the first time.

Reading Between the Lines

After you've finished the first draft of your report, put it aside for a while so you can return to it with a fresh eye. Now you can begin revising. Start by reading for sense. Does each sentence fit with the sentences around it? Have you used transitions to help your readers get from one main idea to the next? Are your main ideas clear? Try to put yourself in your readers' place. If they know little or nothing about the topic, imagine that you don't either. Read carefully. The hints in the following chart may help you.

Revising Checklist

Question	Example
Do the main ideas in the paper support the thesis statement?	Summarize the main idea of each paragraph in the paper's body. Be sure that each main idea supports the thesis statement.
Do the main ideas appear in a logical sequence that builds to the conclusion?	List the main ideas in the order they appear. Can you think of a better order?
Does the conclusion sum up the main ideas and reflect the report's purpose?	Summarize the conclusion, and compare it with the thesis statement. The thesis statement should lead to the conclusion.

Like all wildlife, Canada geese have a few basic requirements for survival. They need food, an ample supply of and their favorite foods is grains. They need water. They migrate to find areas that will provide a rich supply of there basic requirments. also They need safety. protection from their predators The main enemy of the Canada predator goose is the human.

The Canada geese always used to fly to warm, Southern areas in the fall. However scientists who study these birds have discovered a change.

Moving this sentence connects two important thoughts.

• JOURNAL ACTIVITY •

Try It Out

In your journal, review some of your earliest writing. How would you revise your writing now? Jot down some notes, or revise a passage. Notice the difference a fresh eye can make.

Crossing the t's and Dotting the i's

When you edit your report, you proofread for any errors in grammar, spelling, punctuation, and word use. For more information, review pages 80–83. For help with a particular problem, see the Grammar, Usage, and Mechanics Table of Contents on page 302. You may find it easier to proofread for one type of error at a time. Some word-processing programs will help you check for spelling errors. Remember, however, to read your draft for missing words and words that are easily confused, such as *their* and *there.* If you add a bibliography—a listing of your sources—follow the examples given on page 222. Don't forget to attach a clean cover sheet to your report, giving your name, the title of your report, and the date.

A spelling error is corrected.

Two nouns are changed to correct an error in subject-verb agreement.

> Like all wildlife, Canada geese have a few basic requirements for survival. They migrate to find areas that will provide a rich suply of there basic requirments. They need an ample supply of food. Their favorite foods is grains. They need water. They also need protection from their predators. The main predator of the Canada goose is the human.
>
> Canada geese always used to fly to warm, Southern areas in the fall. However, scientists who study these birds have discovered a change. Over the past few years, more and more Canada geese have remained in northern areas during the winter.

Migration Habits of Canada Geese

Activities

Here are some activities to help you apply what you have learned.

1. Guided Assignment

The sentences below come from an early draft of Roberto's report on the migration of Canada geese. Each may be improved by revision; some contain errors that should be corrected through proofreading. Rework each sentence, revising and editing as needed.

1. According to Maria Washington of the Sellar's Island National Wildlife Refuge, each year more than twenty thousand Canada Geese spend the winter their annually.
2. A flock of gooses often contains up to three generations, for a mail and a female usually mate for life and often the pair they stay with their parents.
3. During the interview, Ms. Washington states that "three acers planted with corn was enough to suply food to a flock of three thousand."

PURPOSE To gain practice in editing and revising skills

AUDIENCE Yourself

LENGTH 3 revised and edited sentences

2. Open Assignment

Describe how one of the following graphic aids or a graphic aid of your choice might be used to illustrate a report. Choose a topic for the report, and explain what the graphic contributes to readers' understanding of the topic.

- a map
- a bar graph
- a diagram or line drawing

3. Cooperative Learning

Work in a small group to practice your revising and editing skills. Follow these steps:

- With other group members, choose a draft you have recently written.
- Take turns reading your drafts aloud.
- Exchange papers with a partner in the group. Write revision suggestions for each other.
- With your partner discuss each other's suggested changes. Make only the changes that you agree with. (Remember, it is your paper, and all final decisions are yours.)
- Exchange papers; edit for errors in spelling and sentence structure.
- Talk about specific ways in which it helped to have a fresh eye read your draft.

COMPUTER OPTION

Proofread your report carefully—even after your computer checks for spelling errors. Most spelling-checker programs cannot catch errors caused by homonyms.

A Whisper of Ice

In the northern city, frost glazes the cars. Your breath is fog. The trees in the park are orange and scarlet red. Their leaves rustle and tumble in the bitter wind. Cries of migrating birds shatter the stillness. Fall is here. The two poems below describe one part of fall—migration. As you read them, jot down some of your reactions.

Fall

The geese flying south
In a row long and V-shaped
Pulling in winter.

Sally Andresen

Something Told the Wild Geese

Something told the wild geese
   It was time to go.
Though the fields lay golden
   Something whispered,—"Snow."
Leaves were green and stirring,
   Berries luster-glossed,
But beneath warm feathers
   Something cautioned,—"Frost."
All the sagging orchards
   Steamed with amber spice,
But each wild breast stiffened
   At remembered ice.
Something told the wild geese
   It was time to fly,—
Summer sun was on their wings,
   Winter in their cry.

Rachel Field

A Personal Reaction

Reading a poem is like listening to a song. It may create a picture in your mind, stir feelings, or bring back a memory. Think about the pictures you saw in your mind as you read the two poems on the previous page. Did they bring back memories? Jot down your responses to the following questions. One student's answer to the second question follows.

Questions About the Poems

1. In which poem do you see the geese from a distance? In which close up? Compare and contrast these views.

2. What sensory details does each poet use to describe the change of seasons from fall to winter?

3. How would you summarize the poems?

4. How would you compare their forms?

> In "Fall" I look at a <u>V</u> of geese straining in the sky. They seem to be pulling in winter. In "Something Told the Wild Geese" I see the geese with summer sun on their wings. Below them I notice golden fields, shiny, sparkling berries, and orchards full of ripened fruit.

• JOURNAL ACTIVITY •
Think It Through

Find two poems about the same topic. In your journal, note any details that interest you. Which poem do you like better? Why? Jot down your impressions.

An Essay That Compares and Contrasts

To begin a comparison-contrast essay, you might use a diagram such as the one below. Decide how to structure your essay. You can write about the features of one poem and then write about the same kind of features in another. Or you can compare and contrast the poems one feature at a time.

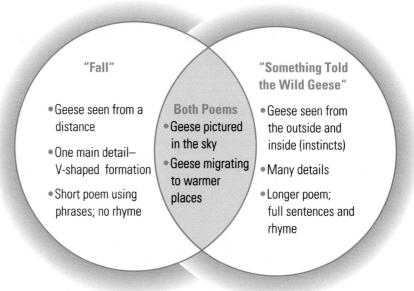

"Fall"
- Geese seen from a distance
- One main detail— V-shaped formation
- Short poem using phrases; no rhyme

Both Poems
- Geese pictured in the sky
- Geese migrating to warmer places

"Something Told the Wild Geese"
- Geese seen from the outside and inside (instincts)
- Many details
- Longer poem; full sentences and rhyme

Student Model

The introduction identifies the two poems and states the thesis.

What method of organization did this student use to compare and contrast the two poems?

"Fall" and "Something Told the Wild Geese" are two very different poems about geese. "Something Told the Wild Geese" is a sixteen-line poem that rhymes. Using descriptive words, the poet paints pictures of geese, fields, and orchards. "Fall," however, is a short poem that does not rhyme. This poem shows geese flying, pulling in a different season. Reading the two poems is like looking at two different snapshots of geese.

John Moore, Wilmette Junior High School,
Wilmettte, Illinois

Activities

Here are some activities to help you apply what you have learned.

1. Guided Assignment

The poem below is about a sunset. Create a diagram in which you compare and contrast the features of this poem with another poem about the sun. Then write an essay telling how the two poems are alike and different.

Sunset

The sun spun like
a tossed coin.
It whirled on the azure sky,
it clattered into the horizon,
it clicked in the slot,
and neon-lights popped
and blinked "Time expired,"
as on a parking meter.

Oswald Mbuyiseni Mtshali

PURPOSE To explore the ways that two poems are different and the same

AUDIENCE Yourself

LENGTH 1 page

2. Open Assignment

Select two of something that you can compare and contrast, such as two poems about rivers. Write at least a page organizing your comparison-and-contrast essay either by subject or by feature.

3. Social Studies

Study the image of the dog below. Then turn back to the figure of a dog on page 223. The photograph shown here was taken by a contemporary artist. Study both images for similarities and differences. In a page or two compare and contrast the images and what they might say about each culture.

William Wegman, *Blue Period*, 1981

BRENT ASHABRANNER

from

Always to Remember

The United States's involvement in the Vietnam War ended in 1973. It remained a social issue because so many Americans had never agreed with the reasons for the conflict. In 1980 Vietnam veteran Jan Scruggs and lawyers Robert Doubek and John Wheeler persuaded Congress to approve the building of a Vietnam War memorial in Washington, D.C. In the following essay Brent Ashabranner examines the resolution of this issue by focusing on the memorial's young designer, Maya Ying Lin.

The memorial had been authorized by Congress "in honor and recognition of the men and women of the Armed Forces of the United States who served in the Vietnam War." The law, however, said not a word about what the memorial should be or what it should look like. That was left up to the Vietnam Veterans Memorial Fund, but the law did state that the memorial design and plans would have to be approved by the Secretary of the Interior, the Commission of Fine Arts, and the National Capital Planning Commission.

What would the memorial be? What should it look like? Who would design it? Scruggs, Doubek, and Wheeler didn't

A section of the Vietnam Veterans Memorial

know, but they were determined that the memorial should help bring closer together a nation still bitterly divided by the Vietnam War. It couldn't be something like the Marine Corps Memorial showing American troops planting a flag on enemy soil at Iwo Jima. It couldn't be a giant dove with an olive branch of peace in its beak. It had to soothe passions, not stir them up. But there was one thing Jan Scruggs insisted on: the memorial, whatever it turned out to be, would have to show the name of every man and woman killed or missing in the war.

The answer, they decided, was to hold a national design competition open to all Americans. The winning design would receive a prize of $20,000, but the real prize would be the winner's knowledge that the memorial would become a part of American history on the Mall in Washington, D.C. Although fund raising was only well started at this point, the choosing of a memorial design could not be delayed if the memorial was to be built by Veteran's Day, 1982. H. Ross Perot contributed the $160,000 necessary to hold the competition, and a panel of distinguished architects, landscape architects, sculptors, and design specialists was chosen to decide the winner.

Announcement of the competition in October, 1980, brought an astonishing response. The Vietnam Veterans Memorial Fund received over five thousand inquiries. They came from every state in the nation and from every field of design; as expected, architects and sculptors were particularly interested. Everyone who inquired received a booklet explaining the criteria.[1] Among the most important: the memorial could not make a political statement about the war; it must contain the names of all persons killed or missing in action in the war; it must be in harmony with its location on the Mall.

A total of 2,573 individuals and teams registered for the competition. They were sent photographs of the memorial site, maps of the area around the site and of the entire Mall, and other technical design information. The competitors had three months to prepare their designs, which had to be received by March 31, 1981.

Of the 2,573 registrants, 1,421 submitted designs, a record number for such a design competition. When the designs were spread out for jury selection, they filled a large airplane hangar.[2] The jury's task was to select the design which, in their judgment, was the best in meeting these criteria:

- a design that honored the memory of those Americans who served and died in the Vietnam War.
- a design of high artistic merit.
- a design which would be harmonious with its site, including visual harmony with the Lincoln Memorial and the Washington Monument.
- a design that could take its place in the "historic continuity" of America's national art.
- a design that would be buildable, durable, and not too hard to maintain.

---

1 criteria (krī tir′ē ə) standards, rules or tests by which something is judged

2 hangar (hang′ər) a building or shed to keep airplanes in

The designs were displayed without any indication of the designer's name so that they could be judged anonymously, on their design merits alone. The jury spent one week reviewing all the designs in the airplane hangar. On May 1 it made its report to the Vietnam Veterans Memorial Fund; the experts declared Entry Number 1,026 the winner. The report called it "the finest and most appropriate" of all submitted and said it was "superbly harmonious" with the site on the Mall. Remarking upon the "simple and forthright" materials needed to build the winning entry, the report concludes:

> This memorial with its wall of names, becomes a place of quiet reflection, and a tribute to those who served their nation in difficult times. All who come here can find it a place of healing. This will be a quiet memorial, one that achieves an excellent relationship with both the Lincoln Memorial or Washington Monument, and relates the visitor to them. It is uniquely horizontal, entering the earth rather than piercing the sky.
>
> This is very much a memorial of our own times, one that could not have been achieved in another time and place. The designer has created an eloquent[3] place where the simple meeting of earth, sky and remembered names contain messages for all who will know this place.

The eight jurors signed their names to the report, a unanimous decision.

When the name of the winner was revealed, the art and architecture worlds were stunned. It was not the name of a nationally famous architect or sculptor, as most people had been sure it would be. The creator of Entry Number 1,026 was a twenty-one-year-old student at Yale University. Her name—unknown as yet in any field of art or architecture—was Maya Ying Lin.

How could this be? How could an undergraduate student win one of the most important design competitions ever held? How could she beat out some of the top names in American art and architecture? Who was Maya Ying Lin?

---

3 eloquent (el'ə kwənt) showing an ability to use words well

The answer to that question provided some of the other answers, at least in part. Maya Lin, reporters soon discovered, was a Chinese-American girl who had been born and raised in the small midwestern city of Athens, Ohio. Her father, Henry Huan Lin, was a ceramicist[4] of considerable reputation and dean of fine arts at Ohio University in Athens. Her mother, Julia C. Lin, was a poet and professor of Oriental and English literature. Maya Lin's parents were born to culturally prominent families in China. When the Communists came to power in China in the 1940s, Henry and Julia Lin left the country and in time made their way to the United States.

Maya Lin grew up in an environment of art and literature. She was interested in sculpture and made both small and large sculptural figures, one cast in bronze. She learned silversmithing and made jewelry. She was surrounded by books and read a great deal, especially fantasies such as *The Hobbit* and *Lord of the Rings*.

But she also found time to work at McDonald's. "It was about the only way to make money in the summer," she said.

A covaledictorian[5] at high school graduation, Maya Lin went to Yale without a clear notion of what she wanted to study and eventually decided to major in Yale's undergraduate program in architecture. During her junior year she studied in Europe and found herself increasingly interested in cemetery architecture. "In Europe there's very little space, so graveyards are used as parks," she said. "Cemeteries are cities of the dead in European countries, but they are also living gardens."

In France, Maya Lin was deeply moved by the war memorial to those who died in the Somme offensive in 1916 during World War I. The great arch by architect Sir Edwin Lutyens is considered one of the world's most outstanding war memorials.

---

4 **ceramicist** (sə ram′ə sist) an expert in making pottery
5 **covaledictorian** (cō′ val ə dik tôr′ ē ən) one who shares the position of the highest-ranking student in a class, who delivers the farewell address at graduation.

The Vietnam Veterans Memorial in Constitution Gardens, Washington, D.C.

Back at Yale for her senior year, Maya Lin enrolled in Professor Andrus Burr's course in funerary (burial) architecture. The Vietnam Veterans Memorial competition had recently been announced, and although the memorial would be a cenotaph— a monument in honor of persons buried someplace else—Professor Burr thought that having his students prepare a design of the memorial would be a worthwhile course assignment.

Surely, no classroom exercise ever had such spectacular results.

After receiving the assignment, Maya Lin and two of her classmates decided to make the day's journey from New Haven, Connecticut, to Washington to look at the site where the memorial would be built. On the day of their visit, Maya Lin remembers, Constitution Gardens was awash with a late November sun; the park was full of light, alive with joggers and people walking beside the lake.

"It was while I was at the site that I designed it," Maya Lin said later in an interview about the memorial with *Washington Post* writer Phil McCombs. "I just sort of visualized it. It just popped into my head. Some people were playing Frisbee. It was a beautiful park. I didn't want to destroy a living park. You use the landscape. You don't fight with it. You absorb the landscape. . . . When I looked at the site I just knew I wanted something horizontal that took you in, that made you feel safe within the park, yet at the same time reminding you of the dead. So I just imagined opening up the earth. . . ."

When Maya Lin returned to Yale, she made a clay model of the vision that had come to her in Constitution Gardens. She showed it to Professor Burr; he liked her conception and encouraged her to enter the memorial competition. She put her design on paper, a task that took six weeks, and mailed it to Washington barely in time to meet the March 31 deadline.

A month and a day later, Maya Lin was attending class. Her roommate slipped into the classroom and handed her a note. Washington was calling and would call back in fifteen minutes. Maya Lin hurried to her room. The call came. She had won the memorial competition.

For Discussion

1. What do you think it would feel like to be Lin's age and to have created a monument that will become part of history? If you were Lin, what would you want to do next?

2. Lin was deeply affected by a World War I memorial. Do you think that memorials are an appropriate way to remember those who died in a war? Why or why not?

Readers Respond

"Always to Remember" was a good selection. I was so surprised when I found out that a twenty-year-old unknown artist from Yale won an important competition.

Since I'm a history buff, I enjoyed reading everything about the memorial wall and what it took to make it.

I would recommend this selection, especially to friends who like history or need more information about the memorial competition.

Shanna Breckenfeld

I enjoyed reading about the competition to choose the memorial for the soldiers who served in Vietnam. I had never heard about it before. I was very surprised when I read that a student attending Yale won. I had predicted that one of the architects would win.

If I had written this selection, I would provide more details about the competition. I would write some background information about Maya Ying Lin.

I would recommend this selection to a friend. I think that they too would be surprised to hear who won the competition.

Faris Karadsheh

Did You Notice?

1. Did you notice how the author introduces the competition? What details does he give in the body about the competition? How does he organize them? How does he conclude the essay?

2. What competition are you familiar with? A sports competition? A science competition? Write an essay about the competition. Be sure you have a good introduction, body, and conclusion.

Writing Process in Action

Unforgettable Facts

In *Always to Remember,* on pages 240–246, Brent Ashabranner explains how the Vietnam Veterans Memorial came to be built, beginning years ago with an idea. Although he uses many facts and statistics, his writing reads like a fascinating story as well as an informative account.

Your expository writing might teach your readers something. Think of it! Consider, though, that your readers will want to read what you've written only if it attracts their interest and holds it.

• Assignment •

Context	You have been asked to write about how a certain statue, memorial, or commemorative building came to be built in your neighborhood, city, or state. Your writing will be published in a guidebook for travelers.
Purpose	To inform travelers about the development and construction of a landmark
Audience	Visitors to your neighborhood, city, or state
Length	2 or more pages

For advice on doing this assignment, read the next few pages. Also, turn back to the lessons in this unit as needed. If you have questions during any stage of the writing process, don't hesitate to refer again to a lesson that will help you.

1. Prewriting

You might begin your prewriting by listing your own first impressions of various landmarks in your city. When did you first see them? With your parents? On a school field trip? Had you heard about these landmarks before you visited them? What particulars about the landmarks especially interested you?

Another approach is to think about where you'd take friends or relatives from out of town. What places and details would most fascinate them?

The options at the right and the suggestions on pages 56–59 can be helpful, too. As you prewrite, you may not come up with all the answers, but you'll be giving yourself a number of different choices.

Option A

Make a cluster diagram of local places of interest.

Option B

List five or six of your favorite places.

Option C

Do some small-group brain-storming.

Freedom House, on Hamilton Pike—historic home, Underground Railroad, museum about slavery in America. Just celebrated its twentieth anniversary as official landmark. Others in area: Strauss Hall?

2. Drafting

You've finished the prewriting phase and you're ready to draft. Of all you've written, what do you like the best? Which subject appeals most to you? Which would provide the best details for forming a piece of expository writing?

As you begin the drafting process, you may find it helpful to refer back to the section on handling details on pages 200–203. Think of the different ways you might organize your writing. Even if you aren't using step-by-step order, you'll want to show a clear-cut progression of ideas. Recall how the literature selection followed the steps in the plan for choosing a monument design:

A total of 2,573 individuals and teams registered for the competition. They were sent photographs of the memorial site and of the entire Mall, and other technical design information. The competitors had three months to prepare their designs, which had to be received by March 31, 1981.

Of the 2,573 registrants, 1,421 submitted designs, a record number for such a design competition. When the designs were spread out for jury selection, they filled a large airplane hangar.

The purpose of drafting is to get your words onto paper. It's important, therefore, to keep moving. If your writing contains many statistics, as the passage above does, you probably shouldn't stop to check every fact at this point. You can do that later as part of the revising process.

3. Revising

As you reread your draft, imagine yourself as a tour guide giving an oral presentation. You're speaking to visitors at the site you've chosen to write about. What questions do they have? How can you help them understand the importance of this place? How can you keep them from wandering off?

Checking your facts is important at this point. For help with other specific changes, review pages 232–235.

Question A

Will my introduction command attention?

Question B

Are my details organized clearly?

Question C

Does my conclusion reflect the main idea?

You can explore our history at
Freedom House, is half a mile west of town
one-
on Hamilton Pike. It once was the home of

Jeremiah and Abigail Hamilton, the young
from Boston 1843
couple who moved here in 1842. As tensions

over slavery grew, the Hamiltons stood with the

abolitionists. They learned about people who

opened their homes to escaping slaves as part

of the Underground Railroad.

4. Editing

At this point, you've put a lot of time and effort into the assignment. Don't let a few editing mistakes spoil the effect of an otherwise good piece of writing. When you read over your revised draft, ask yourself questions like those listed on the right. If any part of the draft doesn't sound quite right, you may want to get additional advice from a teacher or friend.

Checklist

1. Do all the subjects and verbs agree?
2. Is my use of pronouns correct?
3. Are all sentences complete?
4. Have I used standard spelling, capitalization, and punctuation?

5. Presenting

Before you present your finished work, consider having someone at your chamber of commerce or local historical society read it. That person might be able to give you some little-known details that you could add to the paper. Also, you might consider attaching copies of authentic photos (people who inspired the memorial, a building being renovated, a statue being installed).

Reflecting

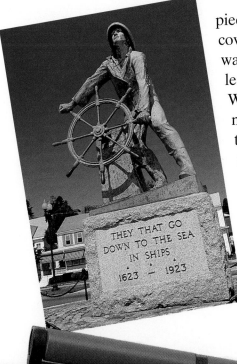

While writing this expository piece, you may have made discoveries about yourself and the way you think. What did you learn about how you get ideas? What did you learn about your methods of organizing your thoughts? Did you discover techniques that help you write more easily and accurately? How can you apply what you learned to your next experience with expository writing? Can you think of other subjects for expository writing?

Writing Process in Action **251**

Portfolio & Reflection

Summary

Key concepts in expository writing include the following:

- An essay includes an introduction, a body, and a conclusion.
- Four types of expository writing are definition, process, compare-and-contrast, and cause-and-effect.
- Choosing and organizing details well gets your message across clearly.
- An answer to an essay question should be a well-organized essay.
- Report writing includes researching a topic; gathering information; planning and drafting; revising, editing, and presenting.
- One way to respond to poetry is to write a compare-and-contrast essay.

Your Writer's Portfolio

Look over the writing you did for this unit. Choose two pieces for your portfolio. Look for writing that does one or more of the following:

- grows out of such prewriting techniques as charts, lists, and diagrams
- has a clear introduction, body, and conclusion
- contains facts, statistics, examples or incidents, or reasons
- demonstrates strong organization and smooth transition

Reflection and Commentary

Think about what you learned in this unit. Answer the following questions as you look over the two pieces of writing you chose. Write a page of "Comments on Writing a Story" for your portfolio.

1. What prewriting steps did you try, and how did they help you?
2. What types of expository writing did you use? What kinds of supporting details?
3. What steps did you go through in writing your report?
4. What other responses did you have to the two poems you wrote about?

Feedback

If you had a chance to respond to the following student comment, what would you say or ask?

I usually approach writing assignments by first talking to friends. If I like their ideas, I'll work with them in my own writing.

John Moore, Wilmette Junior High School, Wilmette, Illinois

Writing to Persuade

Making a Difference

John Ahearn, *Back to School*, 1985–1986

Proposal

Johnson Persuades with Proposals

"Sometimes I think things click very quickly. And sometimes you really have to struggle with them. Certain parts don't say exactly what you want them to say, and it's hard to figure out why they're not saying that. So you have to keep working."

Indira Freitas Johnson

Struggle is central to artist Indira Freitas Johnson's work. In her drawings and sculptures she often creates images of hands, eyes, feet, and wheels to show the personal and physical challenges of going through life. In her current project, *Double Vision,* Johnson combines the artistic themes of struggle and action.

She also combines the roles of visual artist and writer. Johnson's drawings will be used by SHARE, a group in Bombay, India, to fashion into quilts. She now writes proposals to obtain funding support for *Double Vision.*

254

Writing a Proposal

1. Getting Started   **2.** Writing to the Audience   **3.** Revising to Persuade

FOCUS

When writing a persuasive proposal, you need to present your ideas and goals to a specific audience.

1 Getting Started

Johnson says, "I sometimes think that getting started is very difficult. You have all these ideas. I think that's when you just need to start." At this early stage, when she is trying to describe her ideas for a project, she simply gets words down onto paper. She tries to explain her project ideas as clearly as possible. But she doesn't worry that her prose isn't perfect or that her ideas aren't yet totally coherent. "I think from that initial writing you can say, 'This part is good' or 'This part needs reworking' or 'Juggle it around.'"

Research also helps Johnson to develop her ideas. "Very often," she says, "I'll go to the library and just read up on

◄ Indira Johnson uses images of hands in a great deal of her work. This piece is titled Charged Movement *(1990).*

▲ *The ideas that Johnson generates in her drawings eventually appear in details of the quilts made by SHARE.*

various aspects of a particular project that I want to do. For example, I'll ask myself, 'Has it been done before?'" Research helps Johnson find out if ideas that are similar to her own have worked in other places. Sometimes her research even involves traveling to the site of the project.

2 Writing to the Audience

A successful proposal adapts to the concerns and interests of the audience. Adapting to the audience involves adjusting the language and information of the proposal. Audiences made up of general readers have needs different from an audience of experts.

Johnson's art brings her into contact with many individuals and organizations, both in the United States and in India. "Who am I asking for support?" she asks herself as she writes. She then adapts her approach to persuade that audience. She matches the features of her project to the benefits her audience can expect. If her readers are an arts-related group, Johnson stresses the artistic aspects of the project. If the audience is interested in social service or cultural issues, she emphasizes those points in the proposal.

Adapting to an audience also means that the writer pays attention to subtle suggestions of language. Often the writer must adapt the style of writing to commu-nicate exactly what the project is about. In her proposal for *Double Vision,* Johnson avoided the pronoun *I.* She referred to herself as Indira because she wanted to stress that she was a member of a group effort and that this was not just her personal project.

INTERFACE *What are the most important things you need to know about an audience?*

▼ *In her proposal for* Double Vision, *Johnson emphasized the group effort for the project.*

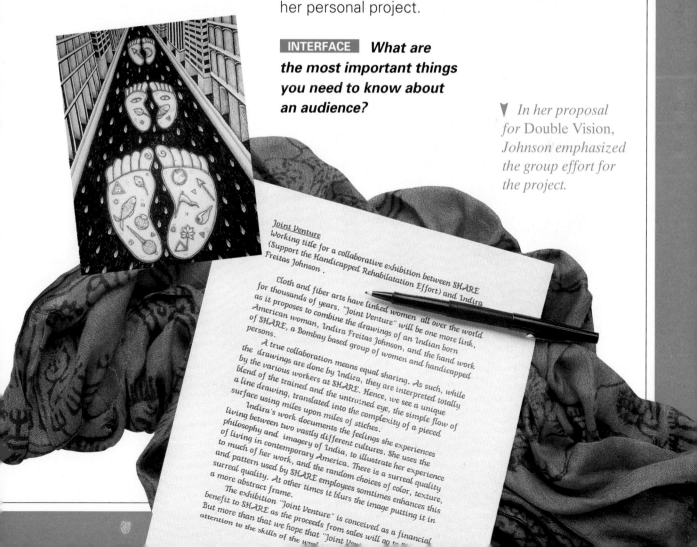

Joint Venture
Working title for a collaborative exhibition between SHARE (Support the Handicapped Rehabilatation Effort) and Indira Freitas Johnson.

Cloth and fiber arts have linked women all over the world for thousands of years. "Joint Venture" will be one more link, as it proposes to combine the drawings of an Indian born American woman, Indira Freitas Johnson, and the hand work of SHARE, a Bombay based group of women and handicapped persons.

A true collaboration means equal sharing. As such, while the drawings are done by Indira, they are interpreted totally by the various workers at SHARE. Hence, we see a unique blend of the trained and the untrained eye, the simple flow of a line drawing, translated into the complexity of a pieced surface using miles upon miles of stiches.

Indira's work documents the feelings she experiences living between two vastly different cultures. She uses the philosophy and imagery of India, to illustrate her experience of living in contemporary America. There is a surreal quality to much of her work, and the random choices of color, texture, and pattern used by SHARE employees somtimes enhances this surreal quality. At other times it blurs the image putting it in a more abstract frame.

The exhibition "Joint Venture" is conceived as a financial benefit to SHARE as the proceeds from sales will go to SHARE. But more than that we hope that "Joint Ven... attention to the skills of the wor...

3 Revising to Persuade

Johnson knows the stage of revising well. "When I was writing in school, my father always said that there was no way to write a good paper the first time. You have to rewrite," she recalls.

For Johnson rewriting sometimes means reseeing. As Johnson explains, "What happens very often is you become too close to a particular subject. You may have the sense that you're explaining it very clearly. But, because you know all the details, you could be skipping over important facts." Johnson likes to ask someone outside the project, often her son or the owner of the gallery that shows her work, to read her proposal in order to see if it makes sense.

Response from a reader helps Johnson avoid problems she knows that she sometimes has with her writing. "I have a tendency to write something that has beautiful words and sounds really nice, but is it really pinpointing the meaning?" After getting reader response, Johnson revises one more time.

▼ *When revising, Johnson felt that she must write as precisely as possible, especially since she was trying to persuade people to donate money. Support for the project depended on her ability to persuade.*

ON ASSIGNMENT

1. Persuasive Writing

Write a short proposal to gain support for a project that, like *Double Vision,* would have both artistic and social benefits in your area.

- Prewrite to explore ideas. Who has special needs in your area? Who has special talents? How can you put them together? Specify your purpose. What will you propose?

- Research to gather ideas and evidence.

- Write a proposal to the audience of your choice.

- Ask a few friends to read and comment.

- Revise your draft, considering your friends' comments.

2. About Literature

Imagine that one of your favorite books has gone out of print. Write a persuasive letter to the publisher proposing its republication.

- Prewrite by making a list of reasons why this is one of your favorite books.

- Expand your list to include ways the publisher might benefit from re-publishing the book.

- Draft the letter.

- Ask someone to read your letter and to comment.

- Revise the letter.

3. Cooperative Learning

Write a one-page proposal, directed to your school administration, inviting an artist, musi-cian, writer, actor, or dancer to discuss his or her art.

- Meet as a group to decide which artist to invite. Brainstorm strategies for your approach. Use the group notes as you prewrite on your own.

- Research and write your own proposal.

- Meet again as a group to assess proposals.

- Write a proposal as a group. Carefully revise and proofread your work before submitting it.

Case Study: Proposal **259**

Words for a Change

In April 1917, when President Woodrow Wilson asked Congress to declare war against Germany, he said that "the world must be made safe for democracy." He also spoke of a "war to end wars." Wilson's words became popular wartime slogans, changing the way many Americans thought about the war. His words also affected people's actions, helping to gain support for the war in the form of money, work, and troops. The poster on this page, which was displayed all over the country, used a few words along with a powerful visual image to carry its persuasive message. Many who saw the poster enlisted.

Here's My Opinion

Words can have awesome power, as history has demonstrated again and again. You can plug into that power source by learning to write persuasively. The purpose of persuasive writing is to affect the thoughts and actions of others, usually to bring about change. Persuasion can be slippery, however, and difficult to recognize. Facts are sometimes used to persuade readers to agree with an opinion. Stories, fables, and anecdotes are often used in the same way. Notice that in the student model April Barnes expresses her concern about an environmental issue by asking and answering questions.

One of the most disturbing trends I see is the drain-ing of wetlands. Thousand-year-old swamps are being destroyed in just days to build skyscrapers and shopping malls or to plant crops. Where are ducks, geese, and other wildfowl going to raise their families or find food and rest when migrating? The answer is simple: each species will slowly die. These animals' habitats are being taken from *all* of us. It is sad, it truly is, to know the birds I love are moving closer to extinction.

April Barnes, Decatur, Alabama
First appeared in *Merlyn's Pen*

April wants her readers to take the problem personally, as she does. How does she appeal to their emotions?

Your world is full of topics for persuasive writing. What changes would you like to see in your school and community and in the larger world? By exploring the following sources, you can discover some issues on which to express your opinion.

Look for Issues in Your Reading

Look for Issues in the Media

Look for Issues in Conversation

• JOURNAL ACTIVITY •
Try It Out

List some changes you'd like to see, making one list from each source above. As you study this unit, add to your lists, and use the ideas in your persuasive writing.

Here's Why

Research is an important step in persuasive writing. Your opinions will carry weight only if you can back them up. To gather support, you must investigate your topic by reading, observing, and discussing, and sometimes by interviewing experts—those with special knowledge about the issue. Patrick MacRoy felt strongly about a local issue, an electric company's plan to run wires along a popular nature trail. He wrote the following article for his school paper.

What information does Patrick include to show the usefulness of the path?

Notice that Patrick supports his opinion by referring to expert sources.

Student Model

The Prairie Path is one of the last areas around here in which to enjoy nature. It is used by cyclists, hikers, horseback riders, and even schools as a site for nature classes. It was even recognized by the U.S. government as a national recreation trail. Groups like Friends of the Illinois Prairie Path are working hard [to save] the trail by circulating petitions and holding public meetings. Citizen groups say there are alternate routes for the power lines, if [the electric company] is willing to find them.

If you want to help save the path, there will be a petition to sign in the lunchroom for the next few days. Thanks for your help.

Patrick MacRoy, Glen Ellyn, Illinois
First appeared in *Call of the Wildcat*

Activities

Here are some activities to help you apply what you have learned.

1. Guided Assignment

Your city council is debating whether to install the sculpture shown below in a park near your home. Consider the issue, and write a statement of your opinion. You might begin by listing details about your own tastes and the tastes of other citizens, other sculptures already in the area, and any maintenance the sculpture might require. Base your opinion mainly on close observation of the sculpture.

PURPOSE To persuade the city council to install (or not to install) the sculpture
AUDIENCE City council members
LENGTH 1–2 pages

2. Open Assignment

Think of an environmental issue that affects your school or community. You might see an appropriate issue on the list you created for this lesson's Journal Activity. Read about it, and discuss it with others. Make prewriting notes, and write a statement about a change you'd like to see. Explain and support your statement in one or two pages.

3. Social Studies

In 1939 and 1940, while World War II raged in Europe, Americans debated whether to enter the conflict. Some believed that the United States should fight Nazi Germany. Others took an "America First" stand, saying that the United States should stay out of European wars. Create an imaginary character who has come out strongly on one side of the issue, and write a short speech for him or her to deliver.

Miriam Schapiro, *Anna and David,* 1987

Pro and Con

If you've visited a zoo, you've seen people of all ages looking at and learning about animals from around the world. However, what was once a place for fun and education has become a subject of controversy. Some people, called animal-rights advocates, claim that animals belong only in the wild and not in captivity. Other people defend zoos as humane, well-designed environments that preserve endangered species and educate people of all ages. Should zoos exist?

What Is Your Position?

Persuasive writing often grows out of a disagreement on an issue that has at least two sides. Taking a position means standing up for one side. Whatever your opinion, it's a good idea to explore the issue thoroughly, creating pro and con lists like those in the following prewriting notes on zoos. Read the notes. Then read the final, summary paragraph of one student's persuasive essay. What stand has she taken? Do you agree or disagree?

Pro
1. Zoos protect endangered species.
2. Modern zoo environments resemble habitats.
3. Zoos educate public about conservation.
4. Zoos are run by professionals.

Con
1. Zoos are animal prisons.
2. Captivity changes animals' behavior.
3. Animals should not be entertainment.
4. Capture/confinement can hurt animals.

Student Model

Zoos today are important to the survival of many species. They do not abuse the animals, but instead they offer a safe and healthy environment. At the same time they provide an enjoyable viewing experience for people of all ages. This gives us an opportunity to better appreciate animals and learn more about their preservation. As stated in the *Utne Reader* [a general-interest magazine about ideas and issues], zoos are "institutions we should see not as abusers of the world's animals, but as vital forces saving animals from extinction."

Jacqueline Parks, Springman Junior High School, Glenview, Illinois

According to Jacqueline, how do zoos benefit both animals and people?

Grammar Editing Tip

In editing, use a comma before the conjunction *and, but, or,* or *nor* when it joins the two main clauses of a compound sentence. For more on compound sentences, turn to page 542.

• JOURNAL ACTIVITY •
Try It Out

Think of an issue on which people have opposing views, and create pro and con lists like the ones above. Try to include strong points on both sides.

Who Are Your Readers?

Your audience is always important in writing but especially so in persuasive writing. When your goal is to influence opinions, you need to know your readers—who they are and how they think. The first model, from the foreword of a book for children, is written to their parents. The second one speaks to educators.

What criticism of video games is Berry answering?

Literature Model

*I*t isn't that video games in and of themselves are harmful. Problems arise instead when the attitudes, priorities, or habits of their users are out of line. That's why children must be encouraged to view video games in a balanced, reasonable way and to take responsibility for their proper use.

Joy Wilt Berry, *What to Do When Your Mom or Dad Says . . ."Don't Overdo with Video Games!"*

What criticism of video games is Turkle answering?

Literature Model

*T*here is nothing mindless about mastering a video game. The game demands skills that are complex and differentiated . . . and when one game is mastered, there is thinking about how to generalize strategies to other games. There is learning how to learn.

Dr. Sherry Turkle,
The Second Self: Computers and Human Spirit

Both writers defend video games but for different readers. Berry reassures worried parents, explaining that attitudes and not video games are the problem. Turkle speaks about thinking skills, which educators seek to develop.

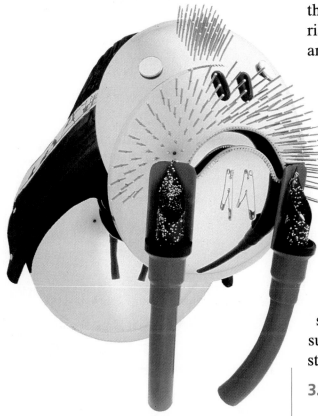

Larry Beck, *Punk Walrus Inua,* 1986

Here are some writing activities to help you apply what you have learned.

1. Guided Assignment

As the interior designer for a major hotel chain, you find yourself having to defend a work you've hung in the lobby of a new hotel in Alaska. The hotel owner says that the work—*Punk Walrus Inua,* a mask made by an Inuit artist—is not art. "How can something made of junk be art?" the owner wrote in a letter.

Study the image closely, noting how the artist has made use of "found materials" to create a combination of shapes and textures. Write a letter to the owner defending your purchase of the work.

PURPOSE	To persuade someone of the value of an unusual art work
AUDIENCE	Someone who has paid for the work but dislikes it
LENGTH	1–2 pages

2. Open Assignment

Think of a controversial issue on which you have not yet formed an opinion. Develop a list of supporting details for each side. Decide which side is stronger, and defend it in a persuasive piece directed at others who are still undecided.

3. Health and Safety

You've traveled back in time to the 1800s. You're aboard an English sailing ship docked in a Caribbean harbor. The sailors tell you that for months they've eaten nothing but hard biscuits and salt pork, with no fresh fruits or vegetables. Now their gums are bleeding. They've heard from other sailors that oranges will help the condition, but they can't find any on this island. Instead, they find limes, which they don't like. Using evidence that is easy to understand, write a conversation between yourself and one of the sailors. Try to persuade the sailor to eat the limes.

To Buy or Not to Buy?

Nutrition information per one-ounce serving:

Calories	90
Protein	4 g
Carbohydrates	20 g
Fat	0 g
Cholesterol	0 mg
Sodium	0 mg
Potassium	105 mg

YOUR GOOD-HEALTH GAME PLAN

SUPER BOWL

"DELICIOUS"

FITNESS FLAKES

Imagine that you're in a grocery store. Your shopping list says "healthful cereal," so you hurry past Sugary Chunks and Sweet Treats. You spot an unfamiliar brand, Super Bowl Fitness Flakes. Read the labels on the box. Do you notice any difference in the kinds of information they give? When it's time to make your choice, which information will be more helpful? Why?

Identifying Your Evidence

To persuade others, you must present support, or evidence, for your position. The cereal box illustrates two kinds of evidence, facts and opinions. Facts can be proved—the cereal could be tested for the number of calories per one-ounce serving. Opinions are personal judgments, such as "delicious." They can't be proved. The following paragraph includes facts, opinions, and some other kinds of evidence, as detailed in the chart below it.

Many Americans hate their bodies. "We have declared war on our bodies," charges Andrew Kimbrell, the author of <u>The Human Body Shop</u>. This war includes 34 percent of all men and 38 percent of all women. They spent $33 billion on diets in 1990. A preteen boy guzzles protein drinks, hoping to increase his size and strength, while a fifty-five-year-old woman gets a face-lift. Technology and social pressure are causing us to make extreme changes.

Evidence in Persuasive Writing	
Kinds	**Examples**
Fact	Americans spent $33 billion on the diet industry in 1990.
Opinion	"We have declared war on our bodies."
Statistic	Thirty-four percent of men and 38 percent of women spent $33 billion on diets in 1990.
Example	A fifty-five-year-old woman gets a face-lift.
Reason	Technology and social pressure cause us to make extreme changes.

• JOURNAL ACTIVITY •

Think It Through

Jot down the evidence that persuaded you to change your mind about something or someone. Label it as one or more of the five kinds shown above.

Selecting Your Evidence

Presenting Tip

When you present your persuasive writing, remember that charts, graphs, and other images can make your evidence clear and bring it to life.

Not all pieces of evidence are equally strong. Statements can sound like facts but be untrue. Some "facts" are really opinions in disguise. Also, some people who offer opinions are experts on the issue, while others are not. Some evidence isn't relevant; it doesn't prove what the writer says it proves, or it has no bearing on the issue. As you read, examine the evidence in this paragraph.

Literature Model

No beverage in America gives water greater competition than flavored soft drinks. And probably no other choice presents a more serious threat to good nutritional health. Soft drinks are the epitome [ideal example] of empty calories. They contain water (with or without carbon dioxide), artificial colorings and flavorings, and sugar—as many as *6 teaspoons of sugar in one 8-ounce serving!* Nothing else. Some noncarbonated drinks add vitamin C, and "fruit" or "fruit-flavored" drinks may even contain some real fruit juice. But for the most part, they are just wet, sweet calories.

Jane Brody, *Jane Brody's Nutrition Book*

What kind of evidence does this sentence contain, facts or opinions?

Brody says that Americans choose soft drinks over water, and "no other choice presents a more serious threat to good nutritional health." Does she persuade you? Why or why not?

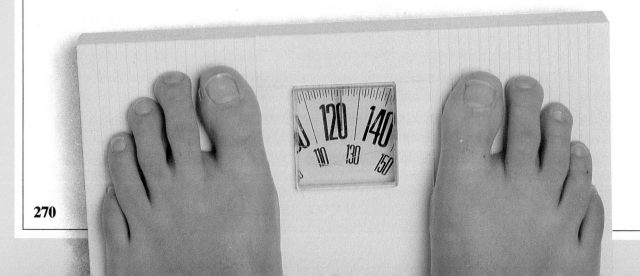

Here are some writing activities to help you apply what you have learned.

1. Guided Assignment

Imagine that you are planning to look for a part-time job. You realize that interviews can be difficult, especially if you don't have much work experience. Since you're nervous about having to answer questions on the spot, you decide to organize your thoughts in writing, preparing to answer questions such as, Why should I hire you?

Think about your experiences at home, in school, and in your community. What evidence can you use to show that you are responsible, hard working, good with people, and equipped with whatever other traits you think will persuade the interviewer? What facts, opinions, statistics, examples, and reasons will help you persuade your way to a job?

PURPOSE   To persuade an employer to hire you
AUDIENCE   Yourself and your prospective employer
LENGTH   1–2 pages

COMPUTER OPTION

Create a list of questions that an interviewer might ask a job seeker. Store these in a computer file that others will be able to use later as they practice interviewing techniques.

2. Open Assignment

Usually you look for evidence supporting a position you already hold. Sometimes, however, the reverse happens. A fact "grabs" you, and you want to learn enough to develop a position on the issue. Find a piece of evidence, such as the fact that some fast-food chains have switched from polystyrene containers to paper.

Brainstorm about what the evidence tells you. What questions does it raise? Try to connect this piece of evidence with what you already know. From this brainstorming, develop a persuasive piece of one to two pages for an audience of your choice.

3. Cooperative Learning

Has the world become warmer because of excess carbon dioxide and other gases? Are recent extreme temperatures simply normal climatic variations? Controversy over the greenhouse effect heated up during the drought summer of 1988, and the questions remain unanswered.

With two or three classmates, research the existence and possible causes of the greenhouse effect. Prepare a short panel discussion for the class. Group members will use some current opinions to try to persuade the class to take a particular stand on the greenhouse effect. Afterwards, the class may discuss the presentation and its strengths and weaknesses.

Writing for Results

© Watterson 1992. Universal Press Syndicate

As Calvin shows in the cartoon, even a reluctant audience can be reached with the right attention-grabbing strategy. Even the most brilliant ideas achieve nothing unless they reach an audience. So first you must find a way to get your audience's attention.

Getting Attention

Every day, newspapers and magazines, television and radio compete for your attention. You've probably learned how to tune out many of the thousands of words and images that bombard you. When you write persuasively, remember that it's the same for your readers. Whenever you want their attention, you must compete with all the noise and clutter that surrounds them.

How can you make your message stand out from all the rest? As many writers have discovered, a playful imagination can work wonders. The following student model brings an everyday object to life in a humorous, imaginative way, drawing attention to an important issue.

*A*s one of the many cheap, unreliable, plastic department store bags, I'd like to speak out. Even though humans think of us as worthless, I wish they wouldn't throw us out their car windows, leaving us to fight for our lives on busy, treacherous highways. Wind gusts from cars going sixty miles an hour blow our flimsy bodies everywhere. Sometimes we land on windshields and cause accidents. Even worse, humans often leave us to baby-sit their small children. Don't get me wrong—we like kids, but not when they put us over their heads or in their mouths and begin to choke, turn blue, and die. . . .

So please, be careful when you dispose of us. Don't throw us out car windows or give us to babies. We like humans and definitely would not want to have them angry at us for wrecking their cars and killing their kids.

Dina Morrison, Pittsburgh, Pennsylvania
First appeared in *Merlyn's Pen*

The surprise of a talking plastic bag attracts the reader's attention and arouses interest.

What problems does the writer identify, and how does she suggest that people solve them?

Some lively formats you could try for persuasive writing include real-life stories, fables, parables, ballads, and letters to people from the past or future. You might consider using visuals, such as pictures, charts, and graphs, to call attention to the issue.

• JOURNAL ACTIVITY •
Try It Out

Poet Robert Frost said that if there is no surprise for the writer, there will be no surprise for the reader. List some surprising images, characters, and stories that have attracted your attention to persuasive messages.

Making Your Case

Your case, or argument, consists of a statement of your position and supporting evidence arranged in an orderly manner. Notice how this writer includes an answer to an opposing idea.

This is the topic sentence, since it expresses the main idea. What is the main idea?

> On quiet nights the sound of a distant train reminds me of a time when railroads provided our most reliable passenger transportation. Rail passenger service, vital to America's past, can be even more important to its future. But, you say, trains are slower. True, but with today's crowded airports and new "bullet-train" technology rail service can compete with the airlines in speed as well as cost. Trains use less fuel per passenger-mile than planes, cars, or buses. Most important, their fuel efficiency conserves oil and decreases air pollution.

The writer says this idea is the most important. Do you agree? Why might the writer have saved it for last?

First, the paragraph grabs attention with a nostalgic image of trains. Then it presents its main point, answers an opposing idea, and provides supporting evidence. The following chart summarizes what you should include in almost any argument.

Editing Tip

In editing, make sure your verb tenses are consistent. For more information on verb tense, see page 370.

How to Build Your Case
1. State your position clearly.
2. Present sound, relevant evidence.
3. Answer the opposition.
4. Begin or end with your strongest point.

Here are some writing activities to help you apply what you have learned.

1. Guided Assignment

Your school decides that warnings for various kinds of safety measures have failed to gain students' attention and interest. You are appointed to a student committee whose job is to develop a strategy for reaching young teen-agers. You decide to create a comic character whose carelessness often leads to minor accidents.

Write a series of three safety bulletins that use your character to draw teen-agers' attention to safety concerns. They might address such issues as traffic safety or fire safety. Consider how you'll use a comic character to explore serious issues about safety. If you wish, create illustrations for your bulletins.

PURPOSE To persuade readers to pay greater attention to safety
AUDIENCE Students at your school
LENGTH ½–1 page each

COMPUTER OPTION

If your school has computers linked in a local network, you might have a message function or bulletin board feature. Consider ways you might adapt the safety bulletins of the Guided Assignment to present them as on-screen bulletins.

2. Open Assignment

Your school system is considering ending athletic contests among schools in your district. Supporters of this view argue that the athletic program wastes money and takes time away from education. Write a letter to your local school board making a case for continued support of interscholastic athletics. Choose a strategy to gain attention and interest. What evidence will persuade your audience? How will you build your argument?

3. Cooperative Learning

Your class has decided to raise money for band uniforms, new books for the school library, meals for homeless families, or another project of your choice. As a class decide what the money is to be used for. Meet in small groups, and decide on a fund-raiser, such as a carwash, a special athletic event, or a bake sale. Then plan and write an information sheet to be sent home. Your purpose will be to persuade families to support the fund-raiser. One group member should take prewriting notes as you brainstorm about the kind of fund-raiser and why people should support it. Assign individual group members to prepare a draft, review and edit the draft, and prepare a neat final copy on a typewriter or computer. The class may choose the information sheet they find the most persuasive.

Balancing Act

Writing persuasively is not easy. Just as the acrobats at the left must have sturdy equipment, your position must have strong support. And just as the acrobats have to synchronize their movements, you must organize your ideas so that they all work together to make your point.

Taking Another Look

The word *revising* means "seeing again." To revise persuasive writing, set it aside for a time, and return to it later. You often have assignments that are due on a certain date, so you can't wait days or weeks to finish a piece of writing. However, professional writers agree that setting your work aside, even if only for a day, will give you a fresh, new perspective. You may find, as many writers have, that your best ideas will come during revision.

Peer reviewing is another helpful technique. Before you revise, ask a classmate to read your draft to help you identify any problems. To see how peer reviewing works, read the following draft. Then read the peer reviewer's comments, and decide whether you agree with them.

Paragraph 1:
I like your opening paragraph. It grabs my attention. Are the slang words OK here?

Paragraph 2:
Good ideas, but you provide little evidence. Do you have any facts and examples?

Paragraph 3:
Is summer employment a reason why you don't want year-round school? Can you make this paragraph clearer?

I have something to say to those adults who want to keep schools open all year long. Give me a break! Please don't do anything so drastic! Eliminating summer vacation will cause enormous stress for everyone. Teachers will burn out faster. Nobody will pay attention in class in the middle of July, and the air-conditioning bills will be enormous. Also, additional salaries for teachers and janitors will be astronomical!

Year-round school will not help education, but it may reduce learning because many students take summer jobs to save for college tuition.

Notice that this peer review contains questions and suggestions but not commands. As a writer, you should read over the comments, decide which ones you agree with, and make those changes. In the end you have to do your own evaluating. After all, you're the only one who knows exactly what you want to persuade your readers to believe or to do.

Drafting Tip

When drafting, remember that slang is inappropriate for any but the most informal writing, such as a personal note or friendly letter.

• JOURNAL ACTIVITY •
Think It Through

List specific ways in which you've used a peer reviewer in the past. List other uses you might make of a peer reviewer in the future. In your opinion what are the characteristics of a good peer reviewer?

Filling In the Gaps

A frequent problem with persuasive writing is holes, or gaps, in the argument. The writer states a position but fails to support it. These questions will help you revise your persuasive writing.

Revising Persuasive Writing
1. Do I make my position clear?
2. Do I present enough evidence?
3. Is the evidence strong? Is it relevant?
4. Do I keep my audience in mind?
5. Do I achieve my purpose?

Revision is far more than simply changing a word here and there. You may need to add, delete, or move whole sentences and paragraphs. During the revising stage you must read, ask yourself questions, experiment, and revise some more. It's your job to make your work persuasive. The paragraph below works well because David Levine supports his point with strong evidence.

What position does Levine state in the first sentence?

Levine's evidence is powerful, reliable, and relevant to his audience.

Literature Model

Staying in school and graduating extends the range of options of what you can do with your life. It's also a fact that the consequences of dropping out are severe and the prospects for dropouts are bleak. According to the National Dropout Prevention Center, less than 50 percent of dropouts find jobs when they leave school. When they do, they earn 60 percent less than high school graduates (over a lifetime that adds up to $250,000).

David Levine, "I'm Outta Here"
First appeared in *Seventeen*

Activities

Here are some writing activities to help you apply what you have learned.

1. Guided Assignment

Take another look at a writing assignment that you completed earlier in this unit or a persuasive piece that you wrote for a different class. Consider the five questions on the chart on the preceding page. Then revise the piece.

PURPOSE   To review and revise an earlier piece of persuasive writing

AUDIENCE   Yourself

LENGTH   1–2 pages

2. Open Assignment

Take another look at a persuasive piece you've written. Choose a different audience, and try prewriting again to generate additional ideas for persuading this new audience. How will you need to adapt your word choice and sentence structure? What changes will you have to make in the kind of evidence you choose and in the way you present it?

Rewrite the piece for the new audience. You'll find it helpful to think about the chart on page 278. Add a short note in which you identify your new audience and describe the changes you made in revising for a different reader.

3. Cooperative Learning

Form a group of three including yourself. Each group member should choose a piece of his or her persuasive writing that could be improved by revision. Make copies of it for the rest of the group.

Group members should read carefully each copy they receive. They should write their questions and comments on the copies. They should start by commenting on something that they think is effective or deserving of praise. Then they should ask a question or make a suggestion about how the writer could improve the piece and make it more persuasive.

Each member should bring the comments to a workshop session. There, members should reread and discuss each piece, compare the comments, and answer any questions the writer may still have about what works and what doesn't. After the workshop session, each writer should study the notes and suggestions, evaluate them, and revise the piece.

COMPUTER OPTION

Sometimes writers prefer to revise at their computer terminals. Having a revision checklist right on the screen, along with the piece of writing you want to revise, is helpful. Develop a list of ten or twelve items for the checklist.

And Now a Word from Our Persuasive Writer

Isn't it time you set
your kids straight on tomato frogs?

Visit Brookfield Zoo, and your kids can see how nature's creatures *really* look, instead of jumping to conclusions. To find out more, call us at 708-485-0263. We're closer than you think.
BROOKFIELD ZOO
Where Imagination Runs Wild

Advertising is almost everywhere you look, and it uses many approaches to persuade you. Advertisements sell products, places, candidates, ideas—all kinds of things. This billboard promotes a zoo by using an unusual image. Does the ad make you want to visit Brookfield Zoo? Jot down your reaction and some reasons for it. Consider why the ad works or doesn't work for you.

Persuasive Writing That Sells

All those catchy commercial slogans that pop up in ads—and in your memory—come from the minds, pens, and computers of ad writers. Persuasive writing is their business. Ad writers present the product (candidate, idea, place) in ways that will appeal to targeted audiences. Since ads aim at certain markets, ad writers must understand their audiences very well. They learn who the possible buyers are. They know about the buyers' hopes and dreams and how they are likely to spend their money. Market research draws detailed profiles of consumers. Ad writers use these as their starting point.

Writing an ad demands imagination and a lively sense of language. Also, and very important, writing an ad demands economy of words. If people have too much to read, they won't read anything.

Advertisers have summarized four basic goals as AIDA. That is, ads should attract Attention, arouse Interest, create Desire, and cause Action. The chart below, which contains typical responses to the zoo ad, shows how AIDA works.

Prewriting Tip

You can create memorable ads by playing with words. For example, use figures of speech such as personification ("make your carpet happy").

AIDA in Action

Attention	"Tomato frogs! What an unusual name for an animal!"
Interest	"*Where imagination runs wild.* I certainly want to help my kids to develop their imaginations."
Desire	"I want my kids to learn about many things, including tomato frogs. Let's visit the zoo."
Action	"I'll call this number to find out what the zoo's hours are and what's the best way to get there."

• JOURNAL ACTIVITY •
Think It Through

Find a magazine or newspaper ad that you think is persuasive. Paste it into your journal. Identify its audience, and make an AIDA chart like the one above.

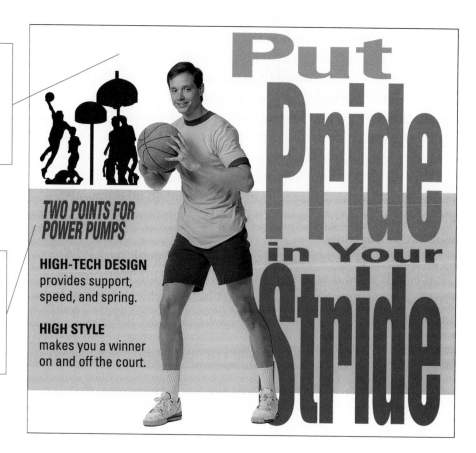

The slogan appeals to the consumer's desire for athletic and personal confidence.

How do words and images work in this ad to persuade consumers to buy Power Pumps?

TWO POINTS FOR POWER PUMPS

HIGH-TECH DESIGN provides support, speed, and spring.

HIGH STYLE makes you a winner on and off the court.

The Tricky Business of Truth

Advertising is tricky. As the AIDA chart shows, an ad can turn facts into feelings. The fact is that children can see tomato frogs at the zoo, but the ad appeals to feelings of curiosity and parental concern. Ad writers know that consumers base decisions about what to buy on feelings more than on facts. It's important to remember that ads appeal to both positive feelings (hope, love, duty) and negative feelings (guilt, fear, envy).

Sometimes ads use language primarily for the way it sounds rather than for what it means. Words may sound scientific, for example, but actually say nothing except "buy this product." What does "high-tech design" mean? Advertisers must maintain certain standards of truth, but communicating "truth" is a complicated task.

Now look at the Power Pumps ad again. What are some techniques it uses to persuade its audience to buy? What are some reasons why this ad might or might not work?

Activities

Here are some writing activities to help you apply what you have learned.

1. Guided Assignment

Imagine you've succeeded in bringing some of Faith Ringgold's works to your own community. Your job now is to write a half-page newspaper ad for the exhibit. You decide to focus on this "story quilt," which is your favorite. You notice how Ringgold combines quilting and painting. You examine the face of Martin Luther King, the figures behind him, and the slogans that inspired these and others during the civil rights movement. Remember, in an ad your goals are attention, interest, desire, and action.

PURPOSE To persuade someone to visit an exhibit

AUDIENCE Citizens in your community

LENGTH ½ page

Faith Ringgold, *Dream Two: King and the Sisterhood*, 1988

2. Open Assignment

Pizza, bagels, tacos, and egg rolls were not always widely available in the United States. In the last forty years mass marketing has made these foods part of many Americans' diets. Choose a food associated with another country, or one that is local or regional in your own area. Write an ad of one-half to one page introducing the dish and persuading people to try it.

3. Social Studies

Advertising is part of the American way of life, including our politics. Choose someone you think should be elected to Congress. He or she might be a neighbor, teacher, relative, or friend. Write a one-page ad introducing the candidate to voters, ages eighteen to thirty years, and persuading them to support the person.

Creating an Ad **283**

Exercise Your Right to Write

The fact that you can't vote yet doesn't mean you can't have a voice in public decision making. One of the most influential public arenas is the editorial page, and it's open to everyone, including you. Most newspapers and magazines invite letters from their readers. The following letter appeared in a popular magazine for young readers. Read the letter. Recall that the main idea is often at or near the beginning. This letter writer, however, has saved his main idea, the point he wants to make, for the end. Why do you think he did that?

Dear Editor:

In the fall of 1989, I fractured one of my vertebrae playing football. I remained inactive for several months, wearing a full-body plastic jacket. The injury means no more football, no more soccer, no more baseball, or anything! As you may have noticed, my injury has a big effect on my life. Now I just go and watch my friends play.

I am not telling everybody to stop playing football. I'm just telling them to wear the right equipment.

Jon Good, Summit, New Jersey

First appeared in <u>Sports Illustrated for Kids</u>

Dear Editor (And All Other Readers)

A letter to the editor is really a letter to the readers of the newspaper or magazine. Some letters persuade us by including evidence, or support, for the writers' opinions. Jon uses his own experience as support for his main idea, the need for football players to use the right equipment. In the letter below, Philip takes a stand on an issue you may have thought about—whether certain sports are for girls only or for boys only. Do you agree with him about gymnastics? What about other sports?

Dear Editor:

I would like to tell readers that gymnastics is not only a sport for girls, but that it's also a sport for boys! Many people make fun of boys in this sport, but gymnastics is hard work, and all that hard work pays off when you get older. If you look at the men in the Olympics, you will see that they are fairly strong. So all you boys out there, don't tease us. Try gymnastics and see for yourselves: It's fun!

Philip Trevino, Gilroy, California

First appeared in <u>Sports Illustrated for Kids</u>

What is the writer's opinion, and what evidence does he use to support it?

• JOURNAL ACTIVITY •
Think It Through

In a newspaper or magazine find a letter to the editor that changes your mind, and paste it into your journal. Make notes about what makes it persuasive.

Sincerely (and Persuasively) Yours

Presenting Tip

When you write a letter to the editor, you are far more likely to see it in print if you use the correct business-letter form. For example, see pages 224–226.

Frustration and anger have inspired many a letter to the editor. To make your letter persuasive, however, you should try to keep uncontrolled emotion from weakening your message. Editors reject angry outbursts. Notice that the following letter expresses strong emotions but supports the writer's point in a calm, controlled way. Remember that there are usually at least two sides to an issue. You should express *your* viewpoint reasonably; if you do, your letter will be much more persuasive.

How might referring to the magazine's purpose make Kelinda's letter more persuasive?

Student Model

Dear Editor,

I am a thirteen-year-old native St. Louisan who lives in North County. I was extremely hurt when an article appeared in your April issue about plush and desirable places to live. To my surprise North County never appeared in the article. Why? North County is a beautiful place to live, filled with friendly faces. This to me, and probably many people, is extremely desirable.

The homes and subdivisions of this area are just as nice as the [ones] in the counties you featured. If you are *St. Louis Magazine*, then you should make a conscientious effort to represent *all* of the Metropolitan St. Louis area.

Kelinda Peaples, Florissant, Missouri
First appeared in *St. Louis Magazine*

Activities

Here are some writing activities to help you apply what you have learned.

1. Guided Assignment

Recently a local newspaper ran a five-part series on teen-agers who have been in trouble with the law. The paper also featured a story on teen-age spendthrifts—teens who spend excessive amounts of money. This week an editorial criticized teens, stating, "Teen-agers today are lazy, and they have bad manners. All they seem to care about is entertainment, food, and fancy clothes."

You decide it's time to set the record straight. Write a letter to the editor in which you defend your generation and point out the newspaper's inaccurate portrayal of young people. Use strong, specific evidence, and make your case in a calm, reasonable way. Remember that your purpose is to persuade adult readers that today's young people are not lazy or bad mannered.

PURPOSE   To change the negative image of teens presented in the local newspaper
AUDIENCE   Your community, especially adults
LENGTH   1–2 pages

2. Open Assignment

Select an organization in your community that serves an important role or offers fine service but rarely receives public attention. Write a letter to the editor of the local newspaper in which you praise this organization and its service. Persuade the public to pay more attention to the organization and to support it. You might choose the local public library, a civic recreation center, a museum, or a service organization at your school.

3. Cooperative Learning

In a small group, brainstorm about issues appropriate for letters to the editor. Each group member should write a letter to the editor about one of the issues. Then the group should pretend they are the editors of the local paper. Read the letters, and evaluate them. Consider how well each writer succeeded in presenting a strong argument in a calm, reasonable manner. Writers should participate in the discussion of their own letters, helping to assess effectiveness. Decide which letters to publish and which to revise. Make specific suggestions for improving those that need work.

COMPUTER OPTION

Your school may have computers with graphic design capability. If it does, you and your editorial team can use the computer to design the page layout and graphics for the editorial page discussed in the Cooperative Learning activity.

Writing a Letter to the Editor **287**

Meet One of My Favorite Books

My own grandma, AnadaAki, was born in a tipi during the eighteen eighties. She has come a long way to her present place in life, which includes being the family elder as well as being a devoted fan of the TV serial "As the World Turns." If you heard her British-accented voice calling out for someone to turn on the TV, you would not imagine that she was raised in the household of one of the last great medicine men among the Bloods.

Beverly Hungry Wolf,
The Ways of My Grandmothers

Beverly Hungry Wolf's grandma has something to give you—stories of a past you probably know nothing about. The grandma, AnadaAki, speaks in the pages of the book *The Ways of My Grandmothers.* But how will readers find out about her and hear her wonderful stories? Sometimes people tell others about a book they liked, and the word spreads. Often, though, the best way to learn about new books is through a book review. A reviewer can call your attention to books worth reading.

Uncovering Good Books

Every day, libraries and bookstores offer new books. Finding out which ones are worth reading can be difficult. Reviews can help readers in two ways. They summarize a book's contents, answering every reader's first question: What's it about? They also evaluate the book, telling whether, in the reviewer's opinion, the book is worthwhile. Read the following book review.

Literature Model

*I*t is a compilation of history, social life and customs. . . . There are stories . . . about the lives of her mother and grandmother, and others of her Elders, as well as accounts of some of her own experiences in learning how to live in the traditional [Blackfoot] manner. . . . Apart from its content, which is extremely valuable, one special quality of this work is its depiction of Native [American] people living a happy, normal and fulfilling existence—here are *anybody's* grandmothers, yours, mine, human beings. . . .

Beverly Hungry Wolf is a very good writer. Her book is interesting, moving, and, here and there, pretty funny.

Doris Seale, review of *The Ways of My Grandmothers*
First appeared in *Interracial Books for Children Bulletin*

Here the reviewer summarizes the book's contents, explaining what it is about.

Here she evaluates the book. What does she consider its strengths?

Different people look for different qualities in books. Some enjoy drama and suspense, and others read mainly for information. Some respond to the quality of the writing itself. Many look for new books by their favorite authors. When you review a book you've liked, you often have so many ideas that you have to make choices. Knowing your audience and their interests can help you decide what to include and what to leave out.

• JOURNAL ACTIVITY •
Try It Out

Think of a book that you feel strongly about. List reasons why you like it or don't like it. Then list some people you would try to persuade to read this book, or not to read it, and explain why.

Personalizing a Book

Editing Tip

When editing a book review, be sure to underscore the book title. Use italics if your word-processing program allows you to.

Some reviewers respond to books in a highly personal way—for example, Melinda Eldridge in her review of *The China Year.* The book tells of experiences similar to the reviewer's, so Melinda also tells readers something about herself. Notice how Melinda's use of the first-person point of view makes her review seem all the more personal.

Student Model

What particular part of the main character's experience interested Melinda, and why?

T he best parts of the book . . . are the friendships that evolved during Henrietta's year in China. I know first-hand how much fun it is to have friends from another culture, but I also know how much more painful it is to leave them because you don't know if you'll ever see them again.

The China Year is an excellent book for people of all types and from all walks of life. It stands as great testimony to the wonderful adventures one can have by living outside one's own culture.

Melinda Eldridge, Arlington, Texas
First published in *Stone Soup*

As a book reviewer, you have a wide range of options. You can compare the book to others by the same author or to others of the same type. You can comment on whether the book holds your interest. You can suggest certain types of readers who would enjoy the book. You can relate the book to events in your own experience, as Melinda did. Most readers are interested in a reviewer's personal responses. You can review a book in various ways. The choice is yours.

Activities

Here are some activities to help you apply what you have learned.

1. Guided Assignment

Think of a book you've read in the past that meant something special to you. Think especially of books in which you were able to identify with a character whose experiences were something like yours. Write a review recommending the book to other readers of your own age. If you wish, be specific about the kind of readers you think might enjoy and respond to the book as you did.

PURPOSE	To review a favorite book
AUDIENCE	Your classmates
LENGTH	1–2 pages

2. Open Assignment

Your school has a sister school in Nigeria whose students want to read books showing everyday life in the United States. Choose a book that represents *your* view of living in America. Write a review of one to two pages in which you summarize and recommend the book. Also, explain to your Nigerian readers your personal response to the book and to its view of life in America.

Carol Soatikee, *Students,* 1969

3. Art

Study the painting on this page. Consider whether the figures seem to be together or apart. How do colors and shapes create a certain mood? If you were in this painting, how would you pose? Imagine that your student council wants to buy a painting for the school and they have not seen this one yet. Write a review of the painting for the student council. As you would in a book review, describe the content of the painting and give your opinion of its value. Include reasons for your opinion.

Rachel Carson
from

Silent Spring

Written thirty years ago by scientist Rachel Carson, Silent Spring *begins with this fable that shows how humanity's carelessness and irresponsibility can harm the world today and in the future.*

There was once a town in the heart of America where all life seemed to live in harmony with its surroundings. The town lay in the midst of a checkerboard of prosperous farms, with fields of grain and hillsides of orchards where, in spring, white clouds of bloom drifted above the green fields. In autumn, oak and maple and birch set up a blaze of color that flamed and flickered across a backdrop of pines. Then foxes barked in the hills and deer silently crossed the fields, half hidden in the mists of the fall mornings.

Along the roads, laurel, viburnum and alder, great ferns and wildflowers delighted the traveler's eye through much of the year. Even in winter the roadsides were places of beauty, where countless birds came to feed on the berries and on the seed heads of the dried weeds rising above the snow. The countryside was, in fact, famous for the abundance and variety of its bird life, and when the flood of migrants was pouring through in spring and fall people traveled from great distances to observe them. Others came to fish the streams, which flowed clear and cold out of the hills and contained shady pools where trout lay. So it had been from the days many years ago when the first settlers raised their houses, sank their wells, and built their barns.

Then a strange blight crept over the area and everything began to change. Some evil spell had settled on the community: mysterious maladies swept the flocks of chickens; the cattle and sheep sickened and died. Everywhere was a shadow of death. The farmers spoke of much illness among their families. In the town the doctors had become more and more puzzled by new kinds of sickness appearing among their patients. There had been several sudden and unexplained deaths, not only among adults but even among children, who would be stricken suddenly while at play and die within a few hours.

There was a strange stillness. The birds, for example—where had they gone? Many people spoke of them, puzzled and disturbed. The feeding stations in the backyards were deserted. The few birds seen anywhere were moribund; they trembled violently and could not fly. It was a spring without voices. On the mornings that had once throbbed with the dawn chorus of

Leonard Koscianski, *Whirlwind*, 1992

robins, catbirds, doves, jays, wrens, and scores of other bird voices there was now no sound; only silence lay over the fields and woods and marsh.

On the farms the hens brooded, but no chicks hatched. The farmers complained that they were unable to raise any pigs—the litters were small and the young survived only a few days. The apple trees were coming into bloom but no bees droned among the blossoms, so there was no pollination and there would be no fruit.

The roadsides, once so attractive, were now lined with browned and withered vegetation as though swept by fire. These, too, were silent, deserted by all living things. Even the streams were now lifeless. Anglers no longer visited them, for all the fish had died.

In the gutters under the eaves and between the shingles of the roofs, a white granular powder still showed a few patches; some weeks before it had fallen like snow upon the roofs and the lawns, the fields and streams.

No witchcraft, no enemy action had silenced the rebirth of new life in this stricken world. The people had done it themselves.

This town does not actually exist, but it might easily have a thousand counterparts in America or elsewhere in the world. I know of no community that has experienced all the misfortunes I describe. Yet every one of these disasters has actually happened somewhere, and many real communities have already suffered a substantial number of them. A grim specter has crept upon us almost unnoticed, and this imagined tragedy may easily become a stark reality we all shall know.

For Discussion

1. How did you feel about the town Carson describes?

2. In what ways do you agree or disagree with Carson's view of humanity's impact on the environment?

Readers Respond

This story held my attention throughout. I think Rachel Carson wrote it as she did to let her readers know that everything beautiful doesn't have to stay that way and that we should take nothing for granted in this lifetime. I would recommend this story because I would want my friends to enjoy it as much as I have.

Tashaunda Jackson

The fable from *Silent Spring* is a story about a beautiful town with peaceful surroundings. It seemed as if an evil plague crept over the town, for bad things started happening. The writer's point is that even though the story is fiction, many things like that are happening in America, and people are the cause of them.

I liked the descriptions the best. They were so vivid you could almost see what was happening. I would recommend this story to friends, because it gives them something to ponder.

Alina Braica

Do You Agree?

1. Do you agree that Carson's message is still important today? In your journal, list your ideas about what has been done in recent years to solve environmental problems. Then list some things that still remain to be done.

2. Carson could have started her book by citing dramatic examples of the misuse of chemicals. Instead, she opened with a fable, which is fiction. Do you agree that the fable makes a stronger opener for this nonfiction book? Explain your answer.

Writing Process in Action

Our Future

What does the future look like to you? Look into the future of whole cities and nations, whole oceans and planets. What do you see around you now that seems likely to affect this future?

You have already seen the future that Rachel Carson envisioned more than thirty years ago in *Silent Spring*. The following assignment invites you to write persuasively about how an important current issue might affect the future.

• Assignment •

Context   Your class has decided to publish *Our Future,* a magazine that deals exclusively with how issues of today may affect the future.

Purpose   To write an account of how today's decisions and events will affect the future

Audience   Your classmates and your teacher

Length   3-4 pages

For advice on how to approach this assignment, read the next few pages. Don't feel that you have to remember it all. You can come back to these pages during the writing process, getting help when you need it.

1. Prewriting

It might seem odd, but the best way to find a topic about the future is to look around you today. You need to find an important topic—and one that holds meaning for you—that you can project into the future. What if pollution continues at the current rate for the next hundred years? What if no more wars occur? Ask yourself *what if* questions until you hit on a topic. The chart on the right suggests some more ways to find a topic that interests you.

You may also want to review pages 48–51 for suggestions on freewriting and brainstorming. Remember, your goal is to find a topic that's important today and that could substantially alter the future. It should be an issue you care about, one you'd want to persuade readers to take a stand on.

Finally, before going on, think carefully about your audience. Remember that readers of *Our Future* will expect both logical, closely reasoned depictions of the future and engaging persuasive writing.

Option A

Explore your journal.

Option B

Brainstorm with a friend.

Option C

Freewrite for ideas.

Watching the cars and trucks pour in all day carrying their bottles, papers, and cans for recycling—You can't convince me that this doesn't help people and the environment. We just need to keep it up!

2. Drafting

Before you start to transform your prewriting notes into a draft, look back at the literature selection. How does the first line begin? Read on briefly, watching for word choice and listening to how the words sound when you read them aloud. Using the form of the fable allows Carson to transform her message from a simple description of pollution's dangers to a dire warning about people's tendency to look only at the present.

Like Rachel Carson, you need to think about a powerful form for your writing. Letters, mock advertisements, parables, satires, and short stories offer you possibilities. Pages 272–275 can help you develop your own form for writing. Don't get stuck with writing that's stale and unimaginative!

Your final task before writing is to research your topic to learn exactly how it might influence the future. Again, the strength of your view of the future will depend largely on how much you know about today. Rachel Carson, for example, writes quite explicitly about how present realities influenced her fable for tomorrow:

> *I know of no community that has experienced all the misfortunes I describe. Yet every one of these disasters has actually happened somewhere, and many real communities have already suffered a substantial number of them.*

Pages 264–271 can help you develop and support a convincing argument.

Question A

What is my purpose?

Question B

Do I consider my audience?

Question C

Have I chosen the best, most precise words?

Nuclear man probably recycled some materials. Scholars have not determined, however, if Nuclear man had any ~~system~~ organized system for recycling. It may be ~~that recycling was a~~ is likely haphazard occurrence in the life of Nuclear man. The fact that Nuclear man seemed obsessed with the word garbage suggests that Nuclear man had only the slightest notion of resource management and allocation. —a complex term with many meanings but thought to refer to unrecycled material—

3. Revising

After you've made sure you've followed the assignment, you may want to talk with a peer reviewer. Pages 276–279 can help you do this.

Probably the most important part of your revising is checking for weaknesses in your case. Use this checklist as a guide. Finally, check how your writing flows. Let pages 68–71 and the revision shown on the previous page guide your review.

Checklist

1. *Have I chosen a powerful form?*
2. *Have I stated my argument clearly?*
3. *Have I supported my arguments with sufficient details?*
4. *Have I checked spelling and capitalization?*

4. Editing

Careful editing is essential to persuasive writing. Why? Given the chance to dismiss your argument—because of a misspelling or a grammatical error—some readers will. Use pages 80–83 as a guide to checking your sentences and proofreading for mechanics.

You'll make the editing process easier and more thorough if you check for only one kind of error at a time.

5. Presenting

Are you ready to submit your work to *Our Future*? How do you know? That's a question writers often face. You can ask for help from a peer editor, friend, family member, or teacher, but you have the final say.

Reflecting

Is your vision of the future like your vision of the present? Is your future optimistic or dark, violent or peaceful, comforting or frightening? Try to hear your own writing speak back to you and teach you something about yourself.

Portfolio & Reflection

Summary

Key concepts in persuasive writing include the following:

- Persuasive writing effects change by affecting thoughts and actions.
- Evidence to support a position includes facts, opinions, statistics, examples, and reasons.
- To write persuasively, you need to know what your audience is like.
- Developing a strategy means getting attention, stating a position, and building a case or argument.
- Revising persuasive writing involves examining the amount and quality of the evidence.
- The basic goals of an ad are to attract attention, arouse interest, create desire, and cause action.
- An effective letter to the editor supports an opinion in a calm, businesslike way.

Your Writer's Portfolio

Look over the writing you did for this unit. Choose your two favorite pieces for your portfolio. Look for writing that does the following:

- calls attention to a problem or an issue in an unusual or a surprising way
- supports an opinion about a change you consider especially important
- uses words and ideas appropriate to a specific audience
- uses strong evidence gathered from at least two sources
- summarizes and recommends a book, relating it to the reviewer's experience

Reflection and Commentary

Think about what you learned in this unit. Answer the following questions as you look over the two pieces of writing you chose. Write a page of "Comments on Persuasive Writing" for your portfolio.

1. Which prewriting techniques helped you the most in persuasive writing?
2. Why is knowing one's audience especially important in ad writing and in other persuasive writing?
3. Did you ever change your opinion as a result of writing on a certain topic?
4. Does any of your persuasive writing deserve a larger audience?

Feedback

If you had a chance to respond to the following student comment, what would you say or ask?

The best thing about writing is being able to express your opinions.

Kathy Beil, Libby Middle School,
Spokane, Washington

Part 2

Grammar, Usage, and Mechanics

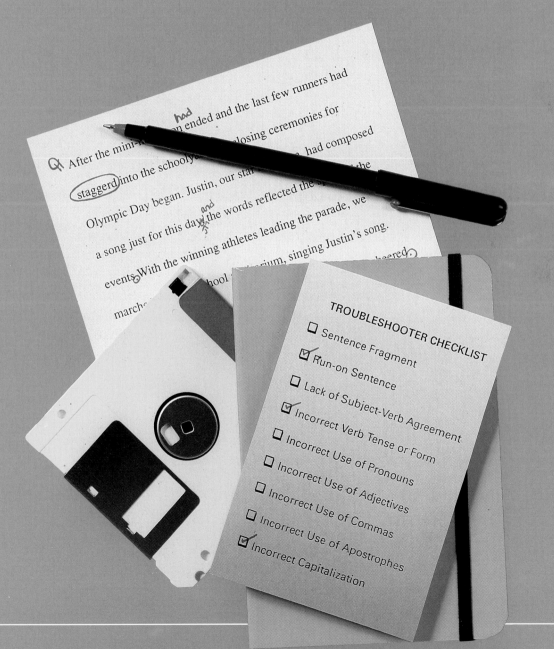

Part 2 Grammar, Usage, and Mechanics

Troubleshooter

This Troubleshooter is designed to help you correct the common errors that your teacher is likely to mark. Use the Table of Contents below to locate quickly a lesson on a specific error. Your teacher may mark errors with the handwritten codes in the left-hand column.

7.1 Sentence Fragment

Fragment that lacks a subject

frag Sol went to the airport. (Wanted to leave today.)

frag Dora jogged to school. (Was late for class.)

frag My car broke down today. (Couldn't start it.)

SOLUTION

Sol went to the airport. He wanted to leave today.

Dora jogged to school. She was late for class.

My car broke down today. I couldn't start it.

Add a subject to the fragment to make a complete sentence.

PROBLEM 2

Fragment that lacks a predicate

frag Jo caught a plane yesterday. (The plane at noon.)

frag Colin baked a cake today. (The cake in the oven.)

frag Tatiana likes that court. (The tennis court in the park.)

Jo caught a plane yesterday. The plane left at noon.

Colin baked a cake today. The cake is in the oven.

Tatiana likes that court. The tennis court in the park is the one she likes.

Add a predicate to make the sentence complete.

PROBLEM 3

Fragment that lacks both a subject and a predicate

frag   Sylvia played the violin. In the symphony orchestra.

frag   My cousin rode his bike. To the store today.

frag   Alex bought new skis. From the sports store.

SOLUTION

Sylvia played the violin in the symphony orchestra.

My cousin rode his bike to the store today.

Alex bought new skis from the sports store.

Combine the fragment with another sentence.

Need More Help?

If you need more help avoiding sentence fragments, turn to pages 328–329.

7.2　Run-on Sentence

PROBLEM 1

Two main clauses separated only by a comma

run-on　Barb went water skiing, she skied behind the boat.

run-on　I stopped reading, my eyes were tired.

SOLUTION A

Barb went water skiing. She skied behind the boat.

Replace the comma with a period or other end mark, and begin the new sentence with a capital letter.

SOLUTION B

I stopped reading; my eyes were tired.

Place a semicolon between the main clauses.

PROBLEM 2

Two main clauses with no punctuation between them

run-on　My dog has fleas he scratches behind his ears.

run-on　Husam bought that book he read it last week.

SOLUTION A

My dog has fleas. He scratches behind his ears.

Separate the main clauses with a period or other end mark, and begin the second sentence with a capital letter.

SOLUTION B

Husam bought that book, and he read it last week.

Add a comma and a coordinating conjunction between the main clauses.

PROBLEM 3

Two main clauses with no comma before the coordinating conjunction

run-on	Samantha went home ⟨and she went to bed early.⟩
run-on	I can go to Roberta's party ⟨but I can't stay long.⟩

SOLUTION

Samantha went home, and she went to bed early.

I can go to Roberta's party, but I can't stay long.

Add a comma before the coordinating conjunction.

If you need more help in avoiding run-on sentences, turn to pages 336–337.

7.3   Lack of Subject-Verb Agreement

PROBLEM 1

A subject that is separated from the verb by an intervening prepositional phrase

agr   One of the radios (are) broken.

agr   The boys in the class (is) singing.

SOLUTION

One of the radios is broken.

The boys in the class are singing.

Ignore a prepositional phrase that comes between a subject and a verb. Make sure that the verb agrees with the subject of the sentence. The subject is never the object of the preposition.

PROBLEM 2

A sentence that begins with here *or* there

agr   There (go) the local train.

agr   Here (is) the students who will write the report.

agr   There (is) oil paintings in the art gallery.

PROBLEM 3

An indefinite pronoun as the subject

agr	Neither of the girls ⟨have⟩ their umbrella.
agr	Many of the books ⟨is⟩ old.
agr	All of my pleading ⟨were⟩ in vain.

Some indefinite pronouns are singular, some are plural, and some can be either singular or plural, depending upon the noun they refer to.

SOLUTION

Neither of the girls has her umbrella.

Many of the books are old.

All of my pleading was in vain.

Determine whether the indefinite pronoun is singular or plural, and make the verb agree.

PROBLEM 4

A compound subject that is joined by and

agr   Posters and balloons (was) strewn around the gym.

agr   The star and team leader (are) Rico.

SOLUTION A

Posters and balloons were strewn around the gym.

If the parts of the compound subject do not belong to one unit or if they refer to different people or things, use a plural verb.

SOLUTION B

The star and team leader is Rico.

If the parts of the compound subject belong to one unit or if both parts refer to the same person or thing, use a singular verb.

PROBLEM 5

A compound subject that is joined by or *or* nor

agr   Either the actor or the actress (appear) onstage.

agr   Neither the tomato nor the bananas (looks) ripe.

agr   Either Mom or Dad (are) driving us to the movie.

agr   Neither my brother nor my uncles (likes) trains.

Either the actor or the actress appears onstage.

Neither the tomato nor the bananas look ripe.

Either Mom or Dad is driving us to the movie.

Neither my brother nor my uncles like trains.

Make the verb agree with the subject that is closer to it.

If you need more help with subject-verb agreement, turn to pages 484–493.

7.4 Incorrect Verb Tense or Form

PROBLEM 1

An incorrect or missing verb ending

tense Have you (reach) all your goals?

tense Last month we (visit) Yosemite National Park.

tense The train (depart) an hour ago.

SOLUTION

Have you reached all your goals?

Last month we visited Yosemite National Park.

The train departed an hour ago.

Add *-ed* to a regular verb to form the past tense and the past participle.

PROBLEM 2

An improperly formed irregular verb

tense The wind (blowed) the rain from the roof.

tense The loud thunder (shaked) the house.

tense Sophia (bringed) the horse back to the barn.

The past and past participle forms of irregular verbs vary. Memorize these forms, or look them up.

SOLUTION

The wind blew the rain from the roof.

The loud thunder shook the house.

Sophia brought the horse back to the barn.

Use the correct past or past participle form of an irregular verb.

PROBLEM 3

Confusion between the past form and the past participle

tense Mimi has rode the horse home from school.

SOLUTION

Mimi has ridden the horse home from school.

Use the past participle form of an irregular verb, not the past form, when you use the auxiliary verb *have*.

Need More Help?

If you need more help with correct verb forms, turn to pages 362–385.

7.5 Incorrect Use of Pronouns

A pronoun that refers to more than one antecedent

pro	Sonia jogs with Yma, but (she) is more athletic.
pro	After the dogs barked at the cats, (they) ran away.
pro	When Sal called out to Joe, (he) didn't smile.

SOLUTION

Sonia jogs with Yma, but Yma is more athletic.

After the dogs barked at the cats, the cats ran away.

When Sal called out to Joe, Joe didn't smile.

Rewrite the sentence, substituting a noun for the pronoun.

Personal pronouns as subjects

pro	Vanessa and (me) like to camp in the mountains.
pro	Georgianne and (them) drove to the beach.
pro	(Her) and Mark flew to London.

Vanessa and I like to camp in the mountains.

Georgianne and they drove to the beach.

She and Mark flew to London.

Use a subject pronoun as the subject part of a sentence.

PROBLEM 3

Personal pronouns as objects

pro   Joel is coming with Manny and (she.)

pro   Please drive Rose and (I) to the store.

pro   The dog brought the stick to Chandra and (I.)

Joel is coming with Manny and her.

Please drive Rose and me to the store.

The dog brought the stick to Chandra and me.

Use an object pronoun as the object of a verb or preposition.

Need More Help?

If you need more help with the correct use of pronouns, turn to pages 392–405.

7.6 Incorrect Use of Adjectives

PROBLEM 1

Incorrect use of good, better, best

> *adj*   Is mountain air (more good) than ocean air?
>
> *adj*   Marla is the (most good) babysitter I know.

SOLUTION

Is mountain air better than ocean air?

Marla is the best babysitter I know.

The comparative and superlative forms of *good* are *better* and *best*. Do not use *more* or *most* before irregular forms of comparative and superlative adjectives.

PROBLEM 2

Incorrect use of bad, worse, worst

> *adj*   Mandy's cold is the (baddest) cold I've ever seen.

SOLUTION

Mandy's cold is the worst cold I've ever seen.

Do not use *more* or *most* before irregular forms of comparative and superlative adjectives.

PROBLEM 3

Incorrect use of comparative adjectives

adj   Twine is (more stronger) than thread.

SOLUTION

Twine is stronger than thread.

Do not use both *-er* and *more* at the same time.

PROBLEM 4

Incorrect use of superlative adjectives

adj   This is the (most hardest) test I've ever taken.

SOLUTION

This is the hardest test I've ever taken.

Do not use both *-est* and *most* at the same time.

If you need more help with the incorrect use of adjectives, turn to pages 416–417.

PROBLEM 1

Missing commas in a series of three or more items

com   We had fish⌒vegetables⌒and bread for dinner.

com   Help me make the beds⌒sweep the floor⌒and
wash the windows.

SOLUTION

We had fish, vegetables, and bread for dinner.

Help me make the beds, sweep the floor, and wash the windows.

When there are three or more items in a series, use a comma after the item that precedes the conjunction.

PROBLEM 2

Missing commas with direct quotations

com   "The concert⌒" said Dora⌒"was loud and boring."

com   "Tomorrow⌒" said Burton⌒"I will read that book."

Missing commas with nonessential appositives

com   Mr. Unser‸our English teacher‸was born in England.

com   Ms. Charo‸my mother's boss‸is taking us to dinner.

PROBLEM 4

Missing commas with nonessential adjective clauses

> *com*   Devin who arose early smelled the eggs and bacon.

SOLUTION

Devin, who arose early, smelled the eggs and bacon.

Determine whether the clause is truly not essential to the meaning of the sentence. If it is not essential, set off the clause with commas.

PROBLEM 5

Missing commas with introductory adverb clauses

> *com*   When the whistle blows the workday is over.

SOLUTION

When the whistle blows, the workday is over.

Place a comma after an introductory adverbial clause.

If you need more help with commas, turn to pages 540–545.

PROBLEM 1

Singular possessive nouns

apos   (Beths) dress is from France.

apos   (My boss) report is on (Angelas) desk.

apos   (My gerbils) fur is brown and white.

SOLUTION

Beth's dress is from France.

My boss's report is on Angela's desk.

My gerbil's fur is brown and white.

Use an apostrophe and an -*s* to form the possessive of a singular noun, even one that ends in -*s*.

PROBLEM 2

Plural possessive nouns ending in -s

apos   The (boys) shirts are too big for them.

apos   My (horses) manes are long and thick.

apos   My (parents) friends joined them for dinner.

The boys' shirts are too big for them.

My horses' manes are long and thick.

My parents' friends joined them for dinner

Use an apostrophe alone to form the possessive of a plural noun that ends in -*s*.

PROBLEM 3

Plural possessive nouns not ending in -s

apos   The (childrens) books are in the library.

apos   The (womens) meetings are in this building.

The children's books are in the library.

The women's meetings are in this building.

Use an apostrophe and an -*s* to form the possessive of a plural noun that does not end in -*s*.

PROBLEM 4

Possessive personal pronouns

apos   This new tape is (her's,) but the CD is (their's.)

This new tape is hers, but the CD is theirs.

Do not use an apostrophe with any of the possessive personal pronouns.

Confusion between its *and* it's

apos   The bird built (it's) nest in the oak tree.

apos   I want to know if (its) going to be sunny today.

The bird built its nest in the oak tree.

I want to know if it's going to be sunny today.

Do not use an apostrophe to form the possessive of *it*. Use an apostrophe to form the contraction of *it is*.

If you need more help with apostrophes and possessives, turn to pages 550–551.

7.9 | Incorrect Capitalization

PROBLEM 1

Words referring to ethnic groups, nationalities, and languages

cap   Many (canadian) citizens speak (french.)

SOLUTION

Many Canadian citizens speak French.

Capitalize proper nouns and adjectives that refer to ethnic groups, nationalities, and languages.

PROBLEM 2

The first word of a direct quotation

cap   Devon said, ("the) new highway will run through town."

SOLUTION

Devon said, "The new highway will run through town."

Capitalize the first word in a direct quotation that is a complete sentence. A direct quotation gives the speaker's exact words.

Need More Help?

If you need more help in capitalizing, turn to pages 524–531.

Pierre-Auguste Renoir, *Woman Reading*, 1892

8.1 Kinds of Sentences

A **sentence** is a group of words that expresses a complete thought.

Different kinds of sentences have different purposes. A sentence can make a statement, ask a question, give a command, or express strong feeling. All sentences begin with a capital letter and end with a punctuation mark. The punctuation mark at the end of the sentence is determined by the purpose of that sentence.

A **declarative sentence** makes a statement. It ends with a period.

> Edgar Allan Poe wrote suspenseful short stories.

An **interrogative sentence** asks a question. It ends with a question mark.

Our class is reading "The Raven" by Edgar Allan Poe.

> Did Poe also write poetry?

Was it fun?

An **exclamatory sentence** expresses strong feeling. It ends with an exclamation point.

> What a great writer Poe was!

An **imperative sentence** gives a command or makes a request. It ends with a period.

> Read "The Pit and the Pendulum."

It sure scared me!

Édouard Manet, Illustration to
E. A. Poe's "The Raven," c. 1875

Read some of his other poems.

Exercise 1

Identifying Kinds of Sentences Write each sentence.
Write whether the sentence is *declarative, interrogative,
exclamatory,* or *imperative.*

1. Edgar Allan Poe was born in Boston in 1809.
2. Did you know that Poe lost his parents at a very
   early age?
3. The boy lived with his foster parents.
4. What impressive writing Poe produced!
5. Find out more about Poe.

Exercise 2

Capitalizing and Punctuating Sentences Write
each sentence. Add capital letters and punctuation marks
where they belong.

1. is it true that Edgar Allan Poe wrote the first
   detective story
2. his character C. Auguste Dupin, a private detective,
   appears in "The Purloined Letter," a story
3. tell me if you have read "The Raven," one of Poe's
   most famous poems
4. what a harrowing ending this poem has
5. Poe's writings are very popular in Europe
6. Did the young man go to college in Virginia
7. poe is highly regarded for his literary criticism
8. he lived in Philadelphia during a part of his career

Writing Link

Briefly summarize a detective or mystery story that
you have read. Try to use at least three of the four kinds
of sentences.

8.2 Sentences and Sentence Fragments

Every sentence has two parts: a subject and a predicate.

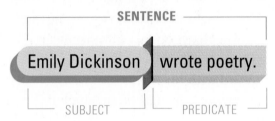

SENTENCE

Emily Dickinson wrote poetry.

SUBJECT — PREDICATE

The **subject part** of a sentence names whom or what the sentence is about.

The **predicate part** of the sentence tells what the subject does or has. It can also describe what the subject is or is like.

A sentence must have both a subject and a predicate to express a complete thought. A group of words that does not have both parts is an incomplete sentence, or sentence fragment.

A **sentence fragment** is a group of words that lacks either a subject, a predicate, or both. A fragment does not express a complete thought.

You often use fragments when talking with friends or writing personal letters. Some writers use sentence fragments to produce special effects. You should use complete sentences, however, in anything you write for school or business.

Correcting Sentence Fragments		
Fragment	**Problem**	**Sentence**
Her sister.	The fragment lacks a predicate. *What did her sister do?*	Her sister discovered the poems in the attic.
Wrote about her emotions.	The fragment lacks a subject. *Who wrote about her emotions?*	This gifted poet wrote about her emotions.
Of meaning.	The fragment lacks both a subject and a predicate.	Her poems contain many layers of meaning.

Identifying Sentences and Sentence Fragments
Write each item. If it is a sentence, underline the subject part once and the predicate part twice. If it is a fragment, write *fragment*, and explain why it is a fragment.

1. Emily Dickinson lived in Amherst, Massachusetts, her entire life.
2. At her parents' home.
3. Few of her poems were published during her lifetime.
4. Considered one of the greatest American poets.
5. You should study her poems carefully.
6. Dickinson's sister collected her poems.
7. This famous poet.
8. Insisted on complete privacy.
9. Her poems reflect her intensely emotional nature.
10. Many readers are attracted to her highly original style.
11. Dickinson's poetry comments on all matters of life.
12. Wrote about love and beauty.
13. Dickinson analyzes her emotions poetically.
14. So much fine work, despite her lonely way of life.
15. With echoes of clear, precise observation.
16. Her way of writing gives every word weight.
17. Almost every one of her poems includes startling insights.
18. To every possible human concern.

Writing Link

Recall a poem you have enjoyed reading. Describe in a paragraph what you like most about the poem. Make sure your sentences all have subjects and predicates.

8.3　Subjects and Predicates

A sentence consists of a subject and a predicate, which together express a complete thought. Both a subject and a predicate may consist of more than one word.

Complete Subject	Complete Predicate
Dickens's **novels**	**are** still popular today.
My English **teacher**	**wrote** an article on Dickens.

The **complete subject** includes all of the words in the subject of a sentence.

The **complete predicate** includes all of the words in the predicate of a sentence.

Not all of the words in the subject or the predicate are of equal importance.

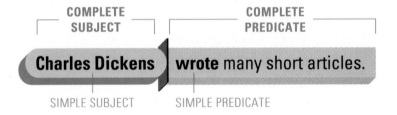

The **simple subject** is the main word or group of words in the complete subject.

The simple subject is usually a noun or a pronoun. A **noun** is a word that names a person, a place, a thing, or an idea. A **pronoun** is a word that takes the place of one or more nouns.

The **simple predicate** is the main word or group of words in the complete predicate.

The simple predicate is always a verb. A **verb** is a word that expresses an action or a state of being.

Sometimes the simple subject is also the complete subject. Similarly, the simple predicate may also be the complete predicate.

Identifying Subjects and Predicates   Write each sentence. Draw a vertical line between each complete subject and complete predicate. Then underline each simple subject once and each simple predicate twice.

GRAMMAR HINT

The complete subject can be replaced by a single word—*I*, *you*, *he*, *she*, *it*, *we*, or *they*.

1. Charles Dickens wrote many great novels during his lifetime.
2. The English novelist remains a very popular writer.
3. He created memorable characters in novels about social injustice.
4. This very popular writer lived in poverty as a child.
5. Dickens lived with his family in London.
6. He labored in a shoe polish factory at an early age.
7. The English courts sent Dickens's father to debtors' prison.
8. His family needed money after the imprisonment of his father.
9. Dickens found work for a short while as a court stenographer.
10. He took notes at court for two years.
11. Dickens also reported news for a local newspaper.
12. He published short articles on life in London.
13. At first Dickens published his writing under a different name.
14. The best articles appeared in his first book, *Sketches by Boz*.
15. My favorite Dickens novel is *Hard Times*.

Writing Link

Imagine that you make your living by writing novels. Describe a typical day in your life. Make sure that each of your sentences has a subject and a predicate.

8.4   Identifying Subjects and Predicates

In most sentences the subject comes before the predicate.

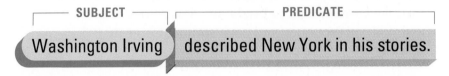

SUBJECT — PREDICATE

Washington Irving | described New York in his stories.

Other kinds of sentences, such as questions, begin with part or all of the predicate. The subject comes next, followed by the rest of the predicate.

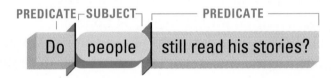

PREDICATE ┌SUBJECT┐ ─── PREDICATE ───

Do | people | still read his stories?

To locate the subject of a question, rearrange the words to form a statement.

Predicate	Subject	Predicate
Did	Irving	write many funny stories?
	Irving	did write many funny stories.

The predicate also precedes the subject in sentences with inverted word order and in declarative sentences that begin with *Here is, Here are, There is,* or *There are.*

┌PREDICATE┐ ─── SUBJECT ───

There is | Irving's original manuscript.

In requests and commands the subject is usually not stated. The predicate is the entire sentence. The word *you* is understood to be the subject.

UNDERSTOOD SUBJECT ─── PREDICATE ───

(You) | Look for the author's name on the cover.

Identifying the Subject   Rewrite each of the following sentences so that the subject comes first. If the sentence is a command, write *(You)* before it.

1. There is a Washington Irving story with roots in German folklore.
2. Did Washington Irving live from 1783 to 1859?
3. Does Irving use a particular writing style in this tale?
4. Read Irving's satire on New York.
5. Examine Irving's humorous sketches of New York society first.
6. Did he write during his stay in England?
7. Did Irving devote himself completely to literature?
8. Has the class discussed his short story "The Legend of Sleepy Hollow"?
9. There are four books based on his travels in Spain.
10. Study his style of writing.
11. Did Irving's *Sketch Book* bring new importance to the short story?
12. Here is the *Sketch Book of Geoffrey Crayon.*
13. Do critics regard his short stories as his best achievement?
14. Discuss how Irving's writings influenced other writers.
15. On the shelf is a collection of his short stories.
16. Under the dictionary lies Irving's biography.
17. Did you read all of Irving's stories?

Writing Link

Describe a trip you've taken that was particularly memorable. What do you remember the most about the trip? Find the subjects in your sentences.

8.5 Compound Subjects and Compound Predicates

A sentence may have more than one simple subject or simple predicate.

A **compound subject** has two or more simple subjects that have the same predicate. The subjects are joined by *and*, *or*, or *but*.

COMPOUND SUBJECT

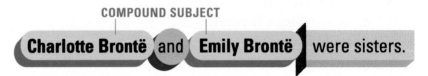

Charlotte Brontë and **Emily Brontë** were sisters.

When the two simple subjects are joined by *and* or by *both . . . and,* the compound subject is plural. Use the plural form of the verb to agree with this plural compound subject.

In sentences with simple subjects joined by *or,* however, the compound subject may be singular or plural. The verb must agree with the nearer simple subject.

> **Charlotte** or **Emily** was a poet as well as a novelist.
> **Charlotte** or her **sisters** are famous British novelists.

In the first sentence, *Emily* is the nearer subject, and so the singular form of the verb is used. In the second sentence *sisters* is the nearer subject, and so the plural form is used.

A **compound predicate** has two or more simple predicates, or verbs, that have the same subject. The verbs are connected by *and*, *or*, or *but*.

COMPOUND PREDICATE

Many students **read** the novel *Jane Eyre* and **enjoy** it.

The compound predicate in this sentence consists of *read* and *enjoy*. Both verbs agree with the plural subject.

GRAMMAR HINT

To see if a sentence has a compound subject joined by *and*, replace the subject with *they* or *we*.

Exercise 6

Identifying Compound Subjects and Predicates
Write each sentence. Write whether the sentence has a *compound subject* or a *compound predicate*.

1. Charlotte or Emily Brontë is one of the great nineteenth-century novelists.
2. Anne and Emily are not as well known as their sister Charlotte.
3. Many readers have read and enjoyed their books.
4. Some scholars buy and sell rare editions of their books.
5. The Brontë sisters and their brother are famous.

Exercise 7

Making Subjects and Verbs Agree Write each sentence. Use the correct form of the verb in parentheses.

1. Emily Brontë's poems or her one novel (deserve, deserves) attention.
2. *Wuthering Heights* or her poetic works (draw, draws) praise from critics.
3. Her writing (show, shows) an understanding of people and (reveal, reveals) her love of England.
4. Critics and other readers (discuss, discusses) and (praise, praises) her one novel.
5. Critics or other readers (pay, pays) more attention to Charlotte Brontë's work.

Writing Link

Write a paragraph about a particular book. Describe what you like most about it. Use some compound subjects and predicates in your writing.

8.6 Simple and Compound Sentences

A **simple sentence** has one subject and one predicate.

SIMPLE SENTENCE

Eudora Welty lived in Jackson, Mississippi.

A simple sentence may have a compound subject, a compound predicate, or both, as in the following example.

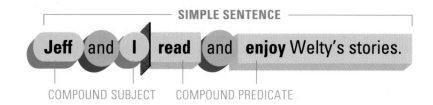

SIMPLE SENTENCE

Jeff and I read and enjoy Welty's stories.

COMPOUND SUBJECT   COMPOUND PREDICATE

A **compound sentence** is a sentence that contains two or more simple sentences joined by a comma and a coordinating conjunction or by a semicolon.

A compound sentence has two complete subjects and two complete predicates.

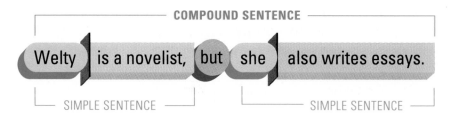

COMPOUND SENTENCE

Welty is a novelist, but she also writes essays.

SIMPLE SENTENCE   SIMPLE SENTENCE

A run-on sentence is two or more sentences incorrectly written as one sentence. To correct a run-on, write separate sentences, or combine the sentences as shown below.

| Correcting Run-On Sentences ||
Run-on	Correct
Welty wrote novels she wrote essays. Welty wrote novels, she wrote essays.	Welty wrote novels. **S**he wrote essays. Welty wrote novels, **and** she wrote essays. Welty wrote novels**;** she wrote essays.

Identifying Simple and Compound Sentences
Write whether each sentence is *simple*, *compound*, or *run-on*. If it is a run-on sentence, rewrite it correctly.

1. Percy Bysshe Shelley lived and wrote in the nineteenth century.
2. He was a Romantic poet his wife, Mary Shelley, was a novelist.
3. Three of his famous poems are "Ozymandias," "Ode to a Skylark," and "Adonais"; and *Frankenstein* was Mary Shelley's most famous novel.
4. Percy traveled in Europe and visited friends.
5. Percy Shelley made friends with other poets; John Keats was one of those friends.
6. William Godwin was another friend, Shelley liked his daughter.
7. Mary Godwin and Percy Shelley met and fell in love.
8. Mary's father was a famous philosopher, her mother worked for women's rights.
9. Percy respected Mary's father and visited him often.
10. Percy and Mary married and went to Europe.
11. Mary and Percy were friendly with the poet Byron.
12. Byron wrote long, beautiful poems; some of them are almost epic in scope.
13. Byron was one of the greatest Romantic poets students still study his work.

Writing Link

Write an explanation of how your state's tourist attractions could inspire a writer. Point out your state's best features. Use both simple and compound sentences.

Grammar Workshop

Subjects, Predicates, and Sentences

Russell Baker wrote about his early life in the autobiographical memoir *Growing Up.* In the following excerpt he describes his reaction to having his work read publicly for the first time. The passage has been annotated to show some examples of the kinds of subjects, predicates, and sentences covered in this unit.

Literature Model

from GROWING UP

by Russell Baker

"Now boys," he said, "I want to read you an essay. This is titled 'The Art of Eating Spaghetti.'"

And he started to read. My words! He was reading *my words* out loud to the entire class. What's more, the entire class was listening. Listening attentively. Then somebody laughed, then the entire class was laughing, and not in contempt and ridicule, but with openhearted enjoyment. Even Mr. Fleagle stopped two or three times to repress a small prim smile. . . .

For the first time, light shone on a possibility. It wasn't a very heartening possibility, to be sure. Writing couldn't lead to a job after high school, and it was hardly honest work, but Mr. Fleagle had opened a door for me. After that I ranked Mr. Fleagle among the finest teachers in the school.

My mother was almost as delighted as I when I showed her Mr. Fleagle's A-Plus and described my triumph. Hadn't she always said I had a talent for writing?

- Complete predicate
- Simple subject
- Simple predicate
- Compound sentence
- Complete subject
- Interrogative sentence

Writing Sentences from Fragments.   Correct each fragment by writing a complete sentence.

SAMPLE   His mother said it. Could write.
ANSWER   His mother said it. He could write.

1. Baker wrote an essay. About eating spaghetti.
2. He was reading my words out loud to the entire class. Listened attentively.
3. Soon the entire class was laughing. With genuine and honest good humor.
4. Mr. Fleagle had opened a door for me. Was one of the finest teachers in the school.
5. I showed my mother the A-Plus. This new accomplishment.
6. Today Baker's newspaper column is read by millions of people. Hundreds of newspapers.

Identifying Subjects and Predicates   Rearrange the words in each question to form a statement. Then underline each complete subject once and each complete predicate twice.

SAMPLE   Was the story about spaghetti?
ANSWER   The story was about spaghetti.

1. Had Baker's mother encouraged him to become a writer?
2. Did Baker's teacher like his essay?
3. Did the class enjoy the essay?
4. Was the class laughing at Baker?
5. Was Mr. Fleagle one of the finest teachers in Baker's school?
6. Was Baker's mother pleased with her son?

Writing Compound Sentences   Combine each pair of simple sentences to form a compound sentence. Use the coordinating conjunction *and, but,* or *or.*

SAMPLE   Baker is a newspaper columnist. He has also written a number of books.

ANSWER   Baker is a newspaper columnist, and he has also written a number of books.

1. Russell Baker grew up in Baltimore. His first job was with a Baltimore newspaper.
2. Baker thought Mr. Fleagle wouldn't like what he wrote. Mr. Fleagle liked it very much.
3. Mr. Fleagle read Baker's story to the class. The class enjoyed it.
4. Baker could have asked his teacher not to read the story. He could have left the room.
5. Baker knew that writing wouldn't get him a job after high school. He loved to write anyway.

Proofreading   The following passage is about American artist Joseph Raffael, whose work appears on the opposite page. Rewrite the passage, correcting the errors in spelling, capitalization, punctuation, grammar, and usage. There are ten errors in all.

Joseph Raffael

[1] Joseph Raffael is a California artist known for his brightly colored paintings of landscapes, fish, flowers and tropical birds. [2] In the painting on the opposite page however, Raffael has taken a different approach. [3] The painting is a portrait of the artist and his son, whom appear almost as if they was posing for a photograph.

[4] The strong contrast among light and dark in the ➡

painting add to the effect, giving it the acidental quality of a snapshot. [5] Raffael is experimanting with the different qualities of light and of color. [6] The colors—from the warm yellow to the deep purple are as much the subject of the painting as the artist and his sun.

Joseph Raffael, *Joseph and Reuben,* **1984**

Unit 8 Review

Subjects, Predicates, and Sentences

Kinds of Sentences

[pages 326–327]

Write each sentence. Use punctuation marks where needed. Then write whether the sentence is *declarative*, *interrogative*, *imperative*, or *exclamatory*.

1. Where was Lorraine Hansberry born
2. The critics recognized the high quality of her work
3. What a moving play it is
4. Read Hansberry's play first
5. How accomplished a writer she was

Sentences and Fragments; Subjects and Predicates; Identifying the Subject

[pages 328–333]

Write each group of words that forms a complete sentence. Underline the complete subject once and the complete predicate twice. Write *(You)* before a command. If the group of words is not a complete sentence, write *fragment*.

6. Pearl S. Buck grew up in China.
7. Returned to the United States.
8. She developed an understanding of the Chinese people.
9. Her real name, Pearl Sydenstricker.
10. The Nobel Prize in 1938.

Compound Subjects and Predicates; Simple and Compound Sentences

[pages 334–337]

Write each sentence. If the sentence has a compound subject, draw one line under each simple subject. If the sentence has a compound predicate, draw two lines under each simple predicate. If it is a compound sentence, circle each simple sentence.

11. Carl Sandburg wrote poetry and created stories for children.
12. This poet and biographer is still popular today.
13. "Chicago" is Sandburg's most famous poem; "Fog" is also popular.
14. History inspired Walt Whitman, and Whitman greatly inspired Carl Sandburg.
15. Sandburg's nonfiction books and poetry volumes earned him several literary awards.

Writing for Review

Pearl Buck wrote about China. Write a paragraph describing a country you would like to study. Use all four kinds of sentences and some compound sentences.

Nouns

William H. Johnson, *Three Great Freedom Fighters*, c. 1945

9.1   Kinds of Nouns

Look at the incomplete sentence below. Decide which of the words in the box that follows can complete the sentence.

The historian wrote about many famous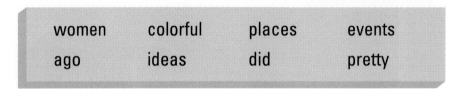

women	colorful	places	events
ago	ideas	did	pretty

The words *women, ideas, places,* and *events* can complete the sentence. These words are called nouns.

A **noun** is a word that names a person, place, thing, or idea.

There are two basic kinds of nouns: proper nouns and common nouns.

A **proper noun** names a *specific* person, place, thing, or idea.

A **common noun** names *any* person, place, thing, or idea.

The first word and all other important words in proper nouns are capitalized.

Common nouns can be either concrete or abstract.

Concrete nouns name things that you can see or touch.

Abstract nouns name ideas, qualities, or feelings that cannot be seen or touched.

Kinds of Nouns		
Common		**Proper**
Abstract	Concrete	
truth	document	Supreme Court
courage	crown	Queen Victoria
time	snow	December
history	museum	Museum of Anthropology
heritage	buffalo	Native American

Exercise 1

Identifying Nouns Write each noun that appears in the following sentences. Indicate whether each is a *common noun* or a *proper noun*. Remember to capitalize each proper noun.

1. A baby named isabella began life as a slave in the united states.
2. Slavery was allowed in the united states before the civil war.
3. Isabella worked very hard as a child.
4. The master chose a husband for Isabella.
5. Isabella had thirteen children.
6. Isabella later became a free person.
7. Then isabella took the name sojourner truth.
8. This brave crusader worked for the freedom of women and african americans.
9. Sojourner truth traveled around the country.
10. Sojourner talked about the evils of slavery.
11. The brave woman spoke to large numbers of people in many states.
12. The speaker faced danger on many occasions.
13. Sojourner Truth became famous as a result of her many speeches.
14. Sojourner met with president abraham lincoln at the white house.
15. After her visit with the president, Sojourner stayed in washington, d.c.

Writing Link

Think of a famous person you would like to meet. In a paragraph explain why you would like to meet him or her. Use both common and proper nouns.

9.2 Compound Nouns

The noun *storybook* is made up of two words: *story* and *book*. Such a noun is called a compound noun.

Compound nouns are nouns that are made up of two or more words.

Compound nouns can be one word, like *storybook,* or more than one word, like *ice cream.* Others are written as two or more words joined by hyphens, like *mother-in-law.*

Compound Nouns	
One word	housekeeper, showcase, bookmark, football, storybook
Hyphenated	mother-in-law, runner-up, great-grandmother, kilowatt-hour
More than one word	dining room, ice cream, maid of honor, music box

To form the plural of compound nouns written as one word, add *-s* or *-es*. To form the plural of compound nouns that are hyphenated or written as more than one word, make the most important part of the word plural.

Forming Plural Compound Nouns		
	Singular	**Plural**
One word	Add **-s** or **-es**.	football**s**, leftover**s**, bookmark**s**, strongbox**es**
Hyphenated	Make the most important part of the word plural.	great-grandmother**s**, runner**s**-up, mother**s**-in-law
More than one word	Make the most important part of the word plural.	maid**s** of honor, music box**es**

Whether the compound noun is singular or plural, the verb must agree with it.

> The sister-in-law **writes** books.   The sisters-in-law **write** books.

Exercise 2

Making Compound Nouns Plural   Write the plural form of each compound noun below.

1. lifeguard
2. vice-principal
3. golf club
4. master-at-arms
5. sweet potato
6. father-in-law
7. sheepskin
8. attorney general

Exercise 3

Using Plural Compound Nouns   Write each sentence. Use the plural form of the compound noun in parentheses to complete each sentence.

1. The White House is the official residence for each of our (commander in chief).
2. All (vice-president) have had another residence.
3. Many (sergeant-at-arms) guard the White House.
4. John Adams was the first of the (chief executive) to live there.
5. (Sightseer) flock to the White House.
6. (Editor in chief) of leading newspapers must show passes to enter the White House grounds.
7. Almost all the (first family) have changed the White House in some way.
8. President Franklin D. Roosevelt had small (swimming pool) added to the residence.
9. Under President John F. Kennedy (guidebook) to the building's history were published.

GRAMMAR HINT

Some compound nouns are written as one word (lifeguard), some are written as two or more words (attorney general), and some are written with hyphens (great-grandmother). In your writing be sure to check a dictionary to see which form is correct.

Writing Link

Describe what you would do first if you were elected president of the United States. Use some compound nouns.

9.3 Possessive Nouns

A noun can be singular, naming only one person, place, thing, or idea; or it can be plural, naming two or more. A noun can also show ownership or possession of things or qualities. This kind of noun is called a possessive noun.

A **possessive noun** names who or what owns or has something.

Possessive nouns can be common nouns or proper nouns. They can also be singular or plural. Notice the possessive nouns in the following sentences:

> **Rita** has a book on history.
> **Rita's** book is new.
>
> Read the **books**.
> Note the **books'** major themes.

Posessive nouns are formed in one of two ways. To form the possessive of most nouns, you add an apostrophe and -*s* (*'s*). This is true for all singular nouns and for plural nouns not ending in -*s*. To form the possessive of plural nouns already ending in -*s*, you add only an apostrophe. These rules are summarized in the chart below.

Forming Possessive Nouns		
Nouns	**To Form Possessive**	**Examples**
Most singular nouns	Add an apostrophe and **-s** (**'s**).	a girl—a girl**'s** name a country—a country**'s** products
Singular nouns ending in **-s**	Add an apostrophe and **-s** (**'s**).	Lewis—Lewis**'s** explorations Chris—Chris**'s** homework
Plural nouns ending in **-s**	Add an apostrophe (**'**).	animals—animals**'** habits the Joneses—the Joneses**'** car
Plural nouns not ending in **-s**	Add an apostrophe and **-s** (**'s**).	women—women**'s** history children—children**'s** history

Exercise 4

Forming Possessive Nouns   Write the possessive form of each underlined word or group of words.

1. <u>Queen Elizabeth</u> reign
2. <u>documents</u> pages
3. <u>Arizona</u> landscape
4. <u>citizens</u> rights
5. <u>Dickens</u> work
6. <u>people</u> choice
7. <u>King Charles</u> laws
8. <u>women</u> rights

GRAMMAR HINT

To see if a noun is possessive, try replacing the noun with a possessive personal pronoun: *his, her, its,* or *their.* If you can, the noun is likely to be possessive.

Exercise 5

Using the Possessive   Write each sentence, using the correct possessive form of the noun in parentheses.

1. Meriwether Lewis was one of (Virginia) famous people.
2. He shared many (children) love of exploring.
3. Lewis served as President (Jefferson) personal secretary.
4. Jefferson guided (Lewis) preparations for an expedition.
5. Lewis and William Clark explored the (nation) uncharted territory.
6. Lewis depended on (Clark) skill at map making.
7. The (expedition) route ran through the Louisiana Territory and the Oregon region.
8. The team spent more than two (years) time in the Northwest.
9. The (men) bravery won great praise.

Writing Link

Imagine that you've been exploring the wilderness for the last two years. What would you miss the most? The least? Use some possessive nouns.

Distinguishing Plurals, Possessives, and Contractions

Most plural nouns, most possessive nouns, and certain contractions end with the letter -*s*. As a result they sound alike and can be easily confused. Their spellings and meanings are different, however.

Noun Forms and Contraction		
	Example	**Meaning**
Plural Noun	The **students** wrote a play.	more than one student
Plural Possessive Noun	The **students'** play is good.	the play of the students
Singular Possessive Noun	I saw the **student's** play.	the play of one student
Contraction	The **student's** the author.	The student is the author.

A **contraction** is a word made by combining two words into one and leaving out one or more letters. An apostrophe shows where the letters have been omitted.

In the chart below, notice that the plural nouns do not have an apostrophe. The plural possessive nouns end with an apostrophe. The singular possessive nouns end with an apostrophe and an -*s*. You can tell these words apart by the way they are used in a sentence.

Noun Forms and Contractions			
Plural Nouns	**Contractions**	**Singular Possessive Nouns**	**Plural Possessive Nouns**
speakers	speaker's	speaker's	speakers'
women	woman's	woman's	womens'
echoes	echo's	echo's	echoes'
countries	country's	country's	countries'

Using Plurals, Possessives, and Contractions

Write each sentence, using the word in parentheses that correctly completes the sentence.

1. Herman (Melville's, Melvilles) a great American writer.
2. Herman (Melville's, Melvilles) life was full of adventure.
3. Melville traveled on sailing (ships, ship's) as a young man.
4. The (sailor's, sailors') lives were full of challenges.
5. Did Melville keep a record of his (experience's, experiences)?
6. Melville began his (adventures', adventures) as a cabin boy in 1837.
7. The young (man's, mans') destination was Liverpool.
8. (Liverpool's, Liverpools') an important city in Great Britain.
9. Special ships hunted (whales', whales) at this time.
10. These whaling (ships', ships) crews searched the world for whales.
11. (Whales, Whales') blubber provided many products.
12. Melville joined a whaling (ships, ship's) crew in 1841.
13. He visited the beautiful (islands, islands') of the Pacific Ocean.
14. Melville wrote (books', books) about his experience.
15. The public enjoyed this (writers', writer's) work.

Writing Link

In Melville's day whale hunting was big business and a great adventure. Discuss why you think people's attitudes toward whale hunting have changed since then.

9.5　Collective Nouns

A **collective noun** names a group that is made up of individuals.

Collective Nouns			
committee	audience	swarm	club
family	team	crowd	orchestra
flock	class	jury	herd

Nouns and verbs always must show agreement in sentences. Collective nouns, however, present special agreement problems. Every collective noun can have either a singular meaning or a plural meaning. If you speak about the group as a unit, then the noun has a singular meaning. If you want to refer to the individual members of the group, then the noun has a plural meaning.

The **crowd move** to their favorite spots.

The **crowd cheers**.

> The **crowd cheers** the passing parade. [refers to group as a unit, singular]
> The **crowd move** to their favorite spots along the parade route. [individual members, plural]

When you are thinking of the group as a unit, use a collective noun and the form of the verb that agrees with a singular noun. When you want to refer to the individual members of the group, use the collective noun and the form of the verb that agrees with a plural noun.

To help you determine whether a collective noun in a sentence is singular or plural, substitute the word *it* for the collective noun and any words used to describe it. If the sentence still makes sense, the collective noun is singular. If you can substitute *they*, the collective noun is plural.

> **The team** works on its project. [it, singular]
> **The team** work on their separate projects. [they, plural]

Using Collective Nouns   Write each of the following sentences, and underline the collective noun. Complete each sentence by using the correct form of the verb in parentheses.

1. The class (describes, describe) their vacations.
2. The whole class (meets, meet) at 2:00 P.M.
3. The family (takes, take) a trip to Valley Forge.
4. The film club (compares, compare) their personal opinions of the movie.
5. Girl Scout Troop 39 (presents, present) a tribute to athletes.
6. The committee (argues, argue) among themselves over the mayor's suggestion.
7. The audience (cheers, cheer) their favorite contestants.
8. The orchestra (performs, perform) my favorite symphony.
9. The football team (practices, practice) together every afternoon.
10. The herd (returns, return) to the same meadow each year.
11. The crowd (claps, clap) their hands to the music.
12. The public (supports, support) its local basketball team.
13. The whole wolf pack (roams, roam) the countryside.
14. The audience (finds, find) their way to the best seats.
15. The jury (reaches, reach) its verdict.

Writing Link

Describe one of the student organizations that you have at your school. Mention how often it meets, what it does, and who belongs to it. Use at least one collective noun.

9.6 Appositives

An **appositive** is a noun that is placed next to another noun to identify it or add information about it.

> James Madison's wife, **Dolley**, was a famous first lady.

The noun *Dolley* adds information about the noun *wife* by giving the wife's name. *Dolley* in this sentence is an appositive.

An **appositive phrase** is a group of words that includes an appositive and other words that describe the appositive.

> Madison, **our fourth president**, held many other offices.

The words *our fourth* describe the appositive *president*. The phrase *our fourth president* is an appositive phrase. It adds information about the noun *Madison*.

An appositive or appositive phrase can appear anywhere in a sentence as long as it appears next to the noun that it identifies.

> **Our fourth president**, Madison held many other offices.
> Many historians have studied the life of Madison, **our fourth president**.

An appositive phrase is set off from the rest of the sentence with one or more commas. If, however, the appositive is needed to identify the noun, you do not use commas. If the appositive simply provides extra information, you do use commas.

> Madison's friend **Thomas Jefferson** was president before him.
> Madison's father, **James Madison,** was a plantation owner.

Since Madison had more than one friend, the name Thomas Jefferson is needed to identify this particular friend. No commas are needed. Since Madison had only one father, however, the father's name is not needed to identify him. Then commas are used.

Identifying Appositives   Write each sentence. Under-line each appositive or appositive phrase, and circle the noun that it identifies. Add commas where needed.

1. James Madison grew up on a plantation Montpelier.
2. He attended Princeton a college in New Jersey.
3. Madison a dedicated student completed college in two years.
4. He first held office in his home colony Virginia.
5. In 1776 Thomas Jefferson another young politician served in the first state assembly with Madison.
6. Madison a devoted patriot served in the Continental Congress.
7. He also represented his home state Virginia at the Constitutional Convention of 1787.
8. Madison a believer in strong government played an active role at the convention.
9. He wrote *The Federalist* with his colleagues Hamilton and Jay.
10. A series of letters to newspapers *The Federalist* still offers the best explanation of the Constitution.
11. Madison and his friend Jefferson formed a new political party.
12. This party the Democratic-Republican party was the forerunner of the present Democratic party.
13. Madison was appointed secretary of state by his closest friend Thomas Jefferson.

GRAMMAR HINT

Here's another way to think about punctuating appositives: Is the appositive *essential* or *not essential* to the meaning of the sentence? If it is essential, do not use commas. If it is not essential, use commas.

Writing Link

Imagine that you witnessed the Constitutional Convention. Describe your reaction to your state's acceptance of the Constitution, using appositives in your sentences.

Grammar Workshop

Nouns

Barbara Jordan by James Haskins is a biography of the first African-American woman from Texas to serve in the United States Congress. The following passage contains an excerpt from Jordan's keynote speech at the 1976 Democratic National Convention. The passage has been annotated to show some of the kinds of nouns covered in this unit.

Literature Model

from BARBARA JORDAN

by James Haskins

"One hundred and forty-four years ago, members of the Democratic Party first met in convention to select a presidential candidate. Since that time Democrats have continued to convene once every four years and draft a party platform and nominate a presidential candidate. . . .

"But there is something different about tonight. There is something special about tonight. What is different? What is special? I, Barbara Jordan, am a keynote speaker."

She was interrupted by wild applause and cheering, and she would be interrupted again and again as she spoke of the problems of the country and her hopes for America. . . . The overwhelming response was one of pride, not just from women because she was a woman, not just from blacks because she was black, not just from Democrats or from Texans, but from all segments of the population, because she was an American.

Common noun
Appositive
Singular noun
Concrete noun
Plural noun
Proper noun
Abstract noun

Using Possessives and Contractions   The following sentences are based on the passage from *Barbara Jordan*. Write each sentence, inserting apostrophes to correctly punctuate the possessive nouns and contractions.

SAMPLE   The audience cheered Jordans speech.
ANSWER   The audience cheered Jordan's speech.

1. The applause and cheers expressed the Democrats pride in the congresswoman from Texas.
2. Jordan spoke about her hopes for Americas future.
3. She also talked about womens rights.
4. The impressive speech united all segments of the countrys population.
5. Jordans still a notable force in American politics.

Using Collective Nouns   The following sentences are about political conventions. Each sentence contains a collective noun. Write each sentence, using the form of the verb in parentheses that agrees with the noun.

SAMPLE   The audience (roars, roar) its approval during the keynote speech.
ANSWER   The audience roars its approval during the keynote speech.

1. A committee (chooses, choose) the convention city.
2. The group (meets, meet) to draft its party's policies.
3. Then the committee (states, state) their opinions.
4. During the convention, the party (nominates, nominate) its candidates for president and vice-president.
5. After both candidates have been nominated, the team (delivers, deliver) their speeches.

Using Appositives   The following sentences are about Barbara Jordan's life. Write each sentence, correctly inserting the appositive or appositive phrase shown in parentheses. Remember to add a comma or commas where needed. In some cases more than one answer may be possible.

SAMPLE   Barbara Jordan received her law degree from Boston University. (a lawyer)

ANSWER   Barbara Jordan, a lawyer, received her law degree from Boston University. **OR**
A lawyer, Barbara Jordan received her law degree from Boston University.

1. Jordan served in the House of Representatives from 1973 to 1979. (a Texas Democrat)
2. Barbara Jordan has worked tirelessly to promote the good of the country. (a role model for all Americans)
3. She worked to pass legislation banning discrimination and dealing with another important issue. (the environment)
4. Jordan was also asked to address the Democratic National Convention in 1992. (a powerful speaker)
5. The audience's response to Jordan's speech was a tribute to a notable American. (a standing ovation)

Proofreading   The following passage is about the artist Henri Matisse, whose work appears on the following page. Rewrite the passage, correcting the errors in spelling, capitalization, punctuation, grammar, and usage. There are ten errors in all.

Henri Matisse
[1]The French artist Henri matisse (1869–1954) was the leader of the Fauves a group of painters who began the ➡

first important art movement of the twentieth century. [2]These painters' used bright colors and simple designs to produce patterns and a sense of movement in his work.

[3]Matise made no atempt to represent reality in his colorful paintings or in the compositions he made out of paper cutouts. [4]For example, *La Négresse* one of Matisse's cutouts represents a dancer surrounded by dark birds. [5]The vivid colors and bold shapes suggest an energy much like Barbara Jordans'. [6]The dancer, prowd and tall among the birds and flowers, possesses strength and dignity.

Henri Matisse, *La Négresse*, 1952

Nouns

Kinds of Nouns

[pages 344–347]

Write the nouns in each sentence. Write *common noun* after each common noun and *proper noun* after each proper noun. Write whether any common nouns are *compound nouns*. Then write the plural form of each compound noun.

1. Alfred Hitchcock was a great director.
2. His suspense films thrilled two generations of audiences.
3. *The Birds* was a huge success at the box office.
4. The soundtrack of *Vertigo* features music by Bernard Herrmann.
5. No screenplay was too big a challenge for Hitchcock.

Plurals, Possessives, and Contractions

[pages 348–351]

Write each of the following sentences. Use the correct word in parentheses to complete the sentence. Then write whether the noun is *plural, singular possessive, plural possessive,* or a *contraction*.

6. Walt (Whitman's, Whitmans') poems are as popular as ever.
7. Today most (readers', readers) consider him a genius.
8. In his own lifetime (readers', readers) reactions were more mixed.
9. I borrowed (Charles', Charles's) copy of *Leaves of Grass.*
10. This (anthologys', anthology's) a treasure chest of great poetry.

Collective Nouns; Appositives

[pages 352–355]

Circle each collective noun, and write whether its meaning is *singular* or *plural*. Then underline each appositive or appositive phrase. Add commas where needed.

11. Aristotle the ancient Greek philosopher was born in 384 B.C.
12. His greatest work the *Metaphysics* is an enduring classic.
13. Aristotle tutored Alexander the Great a powerful general.
14. Our class loves to talk about philosophy.
15. My family are not all avid readers.

Writing for Review

Imagine that you are a famous film director. Write a brief summary of the plot of your next film. Describe it in a way that will convince your classmates that they must see the film when it comes out.

Betsy Graves Reyneau, *Paul Robeson,* 1943–1944

10.1 Action Verbs

ACTION VERB

You may have heard of the movie director's call for "lights, camera, *action!*" The actions in movies and plays can be named by verbs. If a word expresses action and tells what a subject does, it is an action verb.

An **action verb** is a word that names an action. It may contain more than one word.

Notice the action verbs in the following sentences.

> The director **shouts** at the members of the cast.
> The lights **flash** above the stage.
> The audience **arrives** in time for the performance.
> Several singers **memorize** the lyrics of a song.

She **acted** as if . . .

Action verbs can express physical actions, like shouting and arriving. They can also express mental activities, such as memorizing and forgetting.

Action Verbs	
Physical	shout, flash, arrive, own, talk, hit, applaud, praise
Mental	remember, memorize, forget, appreciate

Have, has, and *had* are action verbs, too, when they name what the subject owns or holds.

> The actors in this play already **have** their uniforms.
> The director **has** a script in her back pocket.
> The theater **has** a trapdoor.
> Rosa **had** a theater program from 1959.

. . . she **remembered** her lines.

Identifying Action Verbs   Write each sentence.
Underline each action verb, and write whether it expresses
a *physical* or a *mental* action.

1. Eugene O'Neill's father, an actor, toured the country.
2. O'Neill learned about the theater from his father.
3. O'Neill's father sent him to Princeton University.
4. Soon O'Neill developed an interest in the sea.
5. He returned home after two years of travel.
6. Later, a drama teacher at Harvard University
   inspired O'Neill to write.
7. O'Neill knew the value of his own work.
8. He journeyed to Cape Cod for the summer.
9. A group of friends admired this new playwright.
10. They used a stage in their town for theatrical
    productions.
11. O'Neill wrote many plays while in Connecticut.
12. He joined a group of performers and writers.
13. The young O'Neill worked long hours.
14. On some days O'Neill walked along the wharves.
15. Sometimes he met friends along the way.
16. The playwright considered ideas for new plays.
17. In 1936 he won the Nobel Prize for literature.
18. Many theater groups perform his plays each year.
19. Audiences like the dramatic situations.
20. Most of the plays express dark moods.
21. Actors enjoy the challenging roles.

Writing Link

Imagine that you are the leading actor or actress in
a play. Describe opening night. Use action verbs to
describe physical and mental actions.

10.2 Transitive and Intransitive Verbs

In some sentences the predicate consists of only a verb.

> The actor **remembered**.

Usually sentences provide more information. The predicate often names who or what received the action of the verb.

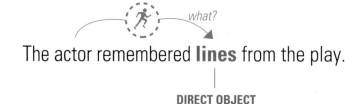

The actor remembered **lines** from the play.

DIRECT OBJECT

In the sentence above, *lines* tells what was remembered. It is the direct object.

A **direct object** receives the action of a verb. It answers the question *whom?* or *what?* after an action verb.

Some sentences have a compound direct object. That is, a sentence may have more than one direct object.

> We saw **Maurice** and **Inez** in the audience.

When an action verb transfers action to a direct object, it is transitive. When an action verb has no direct object, it is intransitive.

A **transitive verb** has a direct object.

An **intransitive verb** does not have a direct object.

Many action verbs can be transitive or intransitive. Such verbs can be labeled transitive or intransitive only by examining their use in a particular sentence.

> The audience **applauds** the actors. [transitive]
> The audience **applauds** loudly. [intransitive]

Exercise 2

Distinguishing Transitive and Intransitive Verbs

Write each sentence. Underline each action verb once. If the verb has a direct object, write *transitive*. If it does not, write *intransitive*. Underline each direct object twice.

1. Many famous actors rehearse in this fine old theater.
2. A stagehand moves the scenery.
3. The heavy red velvet curtain falls quietly.
4. The entire group enjoys the tour of the theater.
5. The director inspected the scenery, costumes, and lights.
6. Many people bought tickets to the new play.
7. The almost silent audience watched.
8. Nearly all the people liked the music and the drama.
9. At the end of the play, everyone clapped wildly.
10. Some enthusiastic spectators even cheered.
11. The majority of the critics enjoyed the performance.
12. They wrote favorable reviews.
13. The musical show succeeded.
14. In fact, the director won an award for it from a theater guild.
15. At the awards ceremony the director spoke.
16. The cast and their guests listened carefully.
17. He thanked the producers.
18. A newspaper reporter asked some questions.
19. The director inspected the scenery.
20. He praised the actors.

GRAMMAR HINT

Only sentences with transitive verbs can be turned into a *whom?* or *what?* question whose answer is the object of the verb.

Writing Link

Think of the last play or concert you attended. Describe the performance, using transitive and intransitive verbs.

10.3 Verbs with Indirect Objects

Words that answer the question *whom?* or *what?* after an action verb are called direct objects.

> Amalia wears a **costume**.

Sometimes both a direct object and an indirect object follow an action verb.

An **indirect object** answers the question *to whom?* or *for whom?* an action is done.

Friends sent the **actors** flowers.

to whom?

INDIRECT OBJECT

The direct object in the sentence above is *flowers*. The indirect object is *actors*. *Actors* answers the question *to whom?* after the action verb *sent*.

Some sentences have a compound indirect object.

> The audience gave the **cast** and the **orchestra** an ovation.

An indirect object appears only in a sentence that has a direct object. Two easy clues can help you recognize an indirect object. First, an indirect object always comes before a direct object. Second, you can add the preposition *to* or *for* before the indirect object and change its position. The sentence will still make sense.

> Friends sent the **actors flowers**.
> Friends sent flowers **to the actors**.

You know that in the first sentence *actors* is the indirect object because it comes before the direct object and because it can be placed behind the preposition *to,* as in the second sentence.

Distinguishing Direct and Indirect Objects   Write each of the following sentences. Underline each direct object once. If the sentence contains an indirect object, underline it twice.

1. None of the musicians know the composition.
2. The orchestra leader brings the musicians the music.
3. For several days the orchestra leader teaches the orchestra a song.
4. The sopranos learn their part first.
5. The audience loves the musical comedy.
6. That famous director frequently gives performers acting lessons.
7. She also gives children lessons in the afternoon.
8. She wrote plays for many years.
9. Now she shows her students her special acting techniques.
10. The theater offers young people interesting opportunities.
11. Students ask actors and directors questions about different roles.
12. A director and the producers bring shows success.
13. She offers her students advice about their careers.
14. The aspiring actors memorize scripts.
15. The young writer sold a producer and a director his idea.
16. The theater club offers subscribers a discount.

Writing Link

What character in a play, short story, or novel would you like to perform on stage? Describe how you would interpret the role. Use direct and indirect objects .

10.4 Linking Verbs and Predicate Words

A **linking verb** connects the subject of a sentence with a noun or adjective in the predicate.

Bess Powell **was** the director.

LINKING VERB

LINKING
VERB

The verb *was* is a form of the verb *be.* It links the word *director* to the subject. It tells what the subject is.

A **predicate noun** is a noun that follows a linking verb. It tells what the subject is.

A **predicate adjective** is an adjective that follows a linking verb. It describes the subject by telling what it is like.

Sometimes a sentence contains a compound predicate noun or a compound predicate adjective.

The set designer was a **carpenter** and an **electrician.**
　　[compound predicate noun]
He is **stern** but **kind.** [compound predicate adjective]

Some of the more common linking verbs are listed below.

Common Linking Verbs			
be	appear	turn	smell
become	look	taste	sound
seem	grow	feel	

Many of these verbs can be used as action verbs, also.

The director grew angry. [linking verb]
The director grew a beard. [action verb]

Identifying Action and Linking Verbs and Predicate Nouns and Adjectives   Write each sentence. Underline each verb, and write whether it is an *action verb* or a *linking verb*. If it is a linking verb, write whether it is followed by a *predicate noun* or a *predicate adjective*.

GRAMMAR HINT

To see whether a verb is a linking verb, replace it with the correct form of *be: Janine* grew *tired. Janine* was *tired.*

1. William Shakespeare was a great playwright and poet.
2. Famous actors appear in his plays all over the world.
3. Characters in Shakespeare's plays seem universal.
4. Some of the characters were actually historical figures.
5. Some costumes in Shakespeare's plays look odd.
6. The styles of earlier times appear strange today.
7. Many of Shakespeare's plots sound farfetched.
8. Some of the characters are more popular than others.
9. In *Romeo and Juliet* a character drinks poison.
10. In *Othello* the main character grows jealous.
11. Some members of Shakespeare's original casts were children.
12. The children played women's roles.
13. Films of Shakespeare's plays are plentiful and popular.
14. Great actors and actresses perform complex roles.
15. Laurence Olivier and John Barrymore were great Hamlets.
16. More recently Mel Gibson played Hamlet.

Writing Link

Write an imaginary interview with a playwright. Use action and linking verbs.

10.5 Present and Past Tenses

The verb in a sentence tells what action took place. It also tells you when the action took place. The form of a verb that shows the time of the action is called the **tense** of the verb.

The **present tense** of a verb names an action that happens regularly. It can also express a general truth.

> The actor **wins** awards.

In the present tense the base form of a verb is used with all subjects except singular nouns and the words *he, she,* and *it.* When the subject is a singular noun or *he, she,* or *it, -s* is usually added to the verb. Remember that a verb in a sentence must agree in number with its subject.

Present Tense Forms of the Verb *Walk*	
Singular	**Plural**
I **walk.**	We **walk.**
You **walk.**	You **walk.**
He, she, *or* it **walks.**	They **walk.**

The **past tense** of a verb names an action that already happened.

The past tense of many verbs is formed by adding *-ed* to the verb.

> The actors **practiced** their lines.

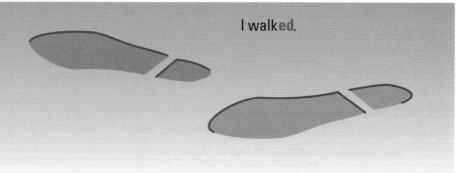

I walk**ed**.

I walk.

Exercise 5

Distinguishing Present and Past   Write each sentence. Use the correct tense of the verb in parentheses. Then write whether it is in the *present* or *past.*

1. Many people (attend) the theater yesterday.
2. My sister and I (discuss) the plot afterward.
3. Now the show (start) on time every day.
4. Later we (purchase) tickets for tomorrow's opera.
5. Yesterday the reviewer in the *Herald* (compare) the lead performer with Caruso.
6. Enrico Caruso (live) at the beginning of the twentieth century.
7. He (appear) in many operas throughout the world.
8. Caruso (arrive) in America in 1903.
9. Sometimes he (pass) out free tickets to poor people.
10. Caruso (earn) more money than any other singer at the time.
11. He always (maintain) a warm affection for his many fans.
12. Caruso often (play) tricks on his fellow performers.
13. He (possess) a dynamic personality.
14. Today singers still (talk) about his wonderful voice.
15. Now some people (listen) to his crude recordings.
16. Some modern singers (copy) the great singer's style and technique.
17. That great Italian tenor (inspire) singers for many years.

Writing Link

Discuss your favorite singer. In a paragraph explain what it is you like about the singer. Use the present and past tenses.

10.6　Main Verbs and Helping Verbs

Verbs have four principal parts that are used to form all tenses. Notice how the principal parts of a verb are formed.

Principal Parts of the Verb *Act*			
Base Form	Present Participle	Past Form	Past Participle
act	acting	acted	acted

You can use the base form itself and the past form alone to form the present and past tenses. The present and past participles can be combined with helping verbs to form other tenses.

A **helping verb** helps the main verb to tell about an action or make a statement.

A **verb phrase** consists of one or more helping verbs followed by a main verb.

> They **are acting** in another play right now.

In the sentence above, the word *are* is the helping verb, and the present participle *acting* is the main verb. Together they form a verb phrase.

The most common helping verbs are *be, have,* and *do.* Forms of the helping verb *be* include *am, is,* and *are* in the present and *was* and *were* in the past. They combine with the present participle of the main verb.

Forms of the helping verb *have* include *have* and *has* in the present and *had* in the past. They combine with the past participle form of a verb.

Have and the Past Participle			
Present		Past	
Singular	Plural	Singular	Plural
I **have** acted.	We **have** acted.	I **had** acted.	We **had** acted.
You **have** acted.	You **have** acted.	You **had** acted.	You **had** acted.
She **has** acted.	They **have** acted.	She **had** acted.	They **had** acted.

Using Helping Verbs and Present and Past Participles
Write each sentence. Use the correct helping verb shown in parentheses. Underline the verb phrase in the sentence, and draw a second line under the participle. Then write whether it is a *present participle* or a *past participle*.

1. Stagehands (are, have) preparing the scenery.
2. They (were, had) started their work before dawn.
3. The director (is, had) joined them later in the day.
4. The star of the show (is, has) arriving now.
5. The press and the public (are, have) expecting an excellent performance.
6. Theater (are, has) remained a popular form of entertainment.
7. People (are, have) buying tickets to many different shows.
8. Some people in theater (are, have) having spectacular success.
9. Television (is, has) exposed many people to drama.
10. Now groups (have, are) performing dramas on television.
11. People (have, are) developed a taste for theater.
12. Audiences (have, are) watching great performances.
13. They (have, are) enjoyed comedies and tragedies.
14. Famous acting companies (are, have) performed on television live.
15. They (are, have) awakened interest in drama.

GRAMMAR HINT
The main verb is always the last verb in a verb phrase. The first verb shows present, past, or future time.

Writing Link

Imagine that you are a drama critic. You have just seen a performance of one of your favorite plays. Write a review of the performance. Use verb phrases.

10.7   Progressive Forms

You know that the present tense of a verb names an action that occurs repeatedly. To describe an action that is taking place at the present time, you use the present progressive form of the verb.

The **present progressive form** of a verb names an action or condition that is continuing in the present.

Althea **is finishing** her song.

The present progressive form of a verb consists of the present participle of the main verb and the helping verb *am, are,* or *is.*

Present Progressive Form	
Singular	**Plural**
I **am leaving**.	We **are leaving**.
You **are leaving**.	You **are leaving**.
He, she, *or* it **is leaving**.	They **are leaving**.

The past progressive names an action that was continuing at some point in the past.

The **past progressive form** of a verb names an action or condition that continued for some time in the past.

The plot **was becoming** scary.

The past progressive form of a verb consists of the present participle and the helping verb *was* or *were.*

Past Progressive Form	
Singular	**Plural**
I **was following**.	We **were following**.
You **were following**.	You **were following**.
He, she, *or* it **was following**.	They **were following**.

Exercise 7

Using Present and Past Progressive Forms Write each sentence. Use the present progressive or past progressive form of the verb given in parentheses.

1. My class (go) to two opera productions a week.
2. The schedule (tire) for some members.
3. They (fall) behind in their schoolwork.
4. Our teacher (plan) a big party for us later.
5. We (see) too many shows last month.
6. We (expect) a period of relaxation.
7. Last year we (study) the comic operas of Gilbert and Sullivan.
8. At that time we (stage) our own productions.

Exercise 8

Using the Progressive Forms Write each sentence. If the verb is in the present tense, change it to the present progressive form. If the verb is in the past tense, change it to the past progressive form.

1. The new theater season begins soon.
2. A committee reads the scripts.
3. The committee looked for something different.
4. One new play caused much excitement.
5. Some of my friends planned their own show.
6. They seek advice from an actress.
7. She stars in a hit show.

Writing Link

Imagine that you could spend a day with your favorite actor or actress. In a letter to a friend describe your day. Use some progressive forms.

10.8   Perfect Tenses

The **present perfect tense** of a verb names an action that happened at an indefinite time in the past. It also tells about an action that happened in the past and is still happening now.

> The actor **has rehearsed** for many hours.
> Nick and Maria **have seen** *Guys and Dolls* five times.

The present perfect tense consists of the helping verb *have* or *has* and the past participle of the main verb.

Present Perfect Tense	
Singular	**Plural**
I **have performed**.	We **have performed**.
You **have performed**.	You **have performed**.
He, she, *or* it **has performed**.	They **have performed**.

The **past perfect tense** of a verb names an action that happened before another action or event in the past.

The past perfect tense is often used in sentences that contain a past tense verb in another part of the sentence.

> We **had** just **arrived** when the play **began**.
> The play **had been rewritten** several times before it **opened**.

The past perfect tense of a verb consists of the helping verb *had* and the past participle of the main verb.

Past Perfect Tense	
Singular	**Plural**
I **had started**.	We **had started**.
You **had started**.	You **had started**.
He, she, *or* it **had started**.	They **had started**.

Exercise 9

Using Present Perfect Tense   Write each sentence. Use the present perfect tense of the verb in parentheses.

1. That actress (perform) in several award-winning plays.
2. Her drama coach (help) her a great deal.
3. The cast (learn) discipline and craft.
4. Our drama club (wait) for the opening of the opera season.
5. The members (plan) weekly theater parties.
6. Some new students (join) the club this year.
7. The club (elect) Tanya president.

Exercise 10

Using the Past Perfect Tense   Write each sentence. Use the past perfect tense of the verb in parentheses.

1. Before the show began, the cast (rehearse) for weeks.
2. Artists (create) the scenery before the opening.
3. Before the first rehearsal our teacher (talk) to us.
4. Before opening night the cast (suffer) from stage fright.
5. We (present) only one show before last year.
6. Until last week every member of the cast (attend) every rehearsal.
7. The director (demonstrate) many valuable techniques.

Writing Link

What kinds of clubs does your school have? Write a description of the kind of club you would like to join. Use the present and past perfect tenses.

10.9 Expressing Future Time

The future tense of a verb is formed by adding the helping verb *will* before the main verb. The helping verb *shall* is sometimes used when the subject is *I* or *we*.

There are other ways to show that an action will happen in the future. *Tomorrow, next year,* and *later* are all words that express a future time. These words are called **time words,** and they are used with the present tense to express future time. Read the sentences below.

> Our show **opens next week**.
> **Tomorrow** we **design** scenery and rehearse.

The present progressive form can also be used with time words to express future actions.

> **Next Friday** our show **is opening**.
> **Soon** we **are ending** rehearsals.

Another way to talk about the future is with the future perfect tense.

The **future perfect tense** of a verb names an action that will be completed before another future event begins.

The future perfect tense is formed by adding *will have* or *shall have* before the past participle of the verb.

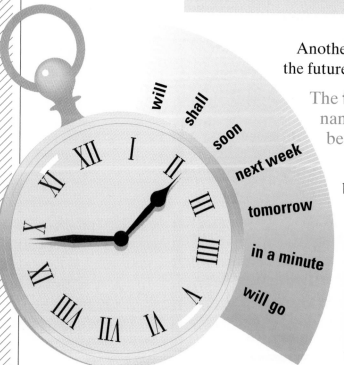

will
shall
soon
next week
tomorrow
in a minute
will go

> Thursday I **shall have performed** six times.
>
> By next week the production **will have closed**.

Expressing Future Time   Write each sentence. Then write whether each underlined verb is in the *present, future, future perfect,* or *present progressive.*

1. Until the show we <u>shall practice</u> every day.
2. Tomorrow I <u>am going</u> to learn my part by heart.
3. I <u>give</u> my first performance next Saturday.
4. Next year I <u>will enter</u> an acting school.
5. Next Monday the class <u>meets</u> for a dress rehearsal.
6. By next week we <u>shall have presented</u> five plays.
7. By the time the show closes, Michael <u>will have sung</u> "Some Enchanted Evening" fifteen times.
8. The cast party <u>is</u> Saturday night.

Identifying Verb Tenses   Write each sentence. Underline the verb or verb phrase, and write whether it is in the *present, future,* or *present progressive.*

1. All the dancers will practice this afternoon.
2. Later today we are changing the second scene.
3. After our show next week we take a break.
4. I will go to the cast party after the show.
5. Later today we are giving a benefit performance.
6. The day after tomorrow my new costume arrives.
7. This evening we are designing the program.
8. We shall be ready on time.

Writing Link

What kinds of future events does your school have planned? Write a paragraph describing one of these events. Be aware of your use of future tenses.

10.10 Active and Passive Voice

A sentence is in the **active voice** when the subject performs the action of the verb.

> George Bernard Shaw **wrote** that play.

A sentence is in the **passive voice** when the subject receives the action of the verb.

> That play **was written** by George Bernard Shaw.

In the first sentence above, the author, George Bernard Shaw, seems more important because *George Bernard Shaw* is the subject of the sentence. In the second sentence *play* seems more important than the name of the author because it is the subject of the sentence.

Notice that the verbs in passive-voice sentences consist of a form of *be* and the past participle. Often a phrase beginning with *by* follows the verb in a passive-voice sentence.

> Plays are performed **by actors**.

The curtain **was drawn** to reveal an empty stage.

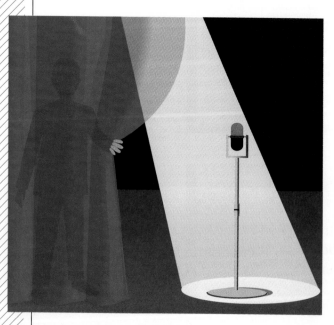

The active voice is usually a stronger, more direct way of expressing your ideas. Use the passive voice only if you want to emphasize the receiver of the action or de-emphasize the performer of the action or if you do not know who the performer is.

> *The Tempest* **was performed**. [You may want to emphasize the play.]
> The curtain **was drawn**. [You may not want to say who did it.]
> The theater **was burned**. [You may not know who did it.]

Exercise 13

Distinguishing Active and Passive Voice Write each sentence. Underline the word that names the receiver of the action. Then write whether the sentence is in the *active* or *passive voice*.

1. *Pygmalion* was written by George Bernard Shaw.
2. Shaw's play is based on an ancient Greek myth.
3. Many people saw the play at the theater.
4. A show at the playhouse was criticized by many in the audience.
5. Critics gave it poor reviews in the newspapers.
6. The script was written by a brilliant playwright.
7. She created strange and different characters.
8. The director did his very best with the material.
9. The director was praised by several critics.
10. The scenery was designed by the author's relatives.
11. Costumes were created by the cast members.
12. The show was produced by members of a local drama club.
13. Most people predicted a short run for the show.
14. The public was surprised by the show's long run.
15. The cast used the criticism as a way of improvement.
16. Many people liked the show.
17. They told their friends about it.
18. Critics reconsidered their reviews.
19. The show was awarded a prize.
20. Now it is performed everywhere.

Writing Link

Imagine that a new play is being presented at your school. Write a review of this play. Try to write your review in the active voice.

10.11   Irregular Verbs

The irregular verbs below are grouped according to the way their past form and past participle are formed.

Pattern	Base Form	Past Form	Past Participle
One vowel changes to form the past and the past participle.	begin	began	begun
	drink	drank	drunk
	ring	rang	rung
	shrink	shrank *or* shrunk	shrunk
	sing	sang	sung
	spring	sprang *or* sprung	sprung
	swim	swam	swum
The past form and past participle are the same.	bring	brought	brought
	buy	bought	bought
	catch	caught	caught
	creep	crept	crept
	feel	felt	felt
	get	got	got *or* gotten
	keep	kept	kept
	lay	laid	laid
	lead	led	led
	leave	left	left
	lend	lent	lent
	lose	lost	lost
	make	made	made
	pay	paid	paid
	say	said	said
	seek	sought	sought
	sell	sold	sold
	sit	sat	sat
	sleep	slept	slept
	swing	swung	swung
	teach	taught	taught
	think	thought	thought
	win	won	won

Using the Past and Past Participle of Irregular Verbs
Write each sentence, using the past tense or the past participle of the verb in parentheses.

1. Earlier the first performance had (begin).
2. I had (lose) my way to the new theater.
3. The star had (sing) two songs before my arrival.
4. I already had (pay), but I could not find the ticket.
5. I have (sit) in the theater for a long time.
6. Unfortunately the manager (leave) for a few minutes.
7. He has (keep) me waiting for ten minutes.
8. Luckily I (bring) a book with me.
9. I finally have (catch) my breath by sitting quietly.
10. One of my friends (bring) me a copy of the program.
11. Finally I (get) in.
12. I (think) the show superb.
13. A famous teacher had (teach) the performers well.
14. At the show's end the members of the audience (spring) to their feet.
15. The leading actor had (win) our hearts.
16. I (feel) happy and sad at the same time.
17. After the performance we had (seek) autographs.
18. The shy star (shrink) from the crowd.
19. At last she (creep) away.
20. She (say) she was tired and wanted to rest.
21. She hadn't (sleep) well the previous night.

Writing Link

Write a paragraph describing a scene from your favorite movie. Use several irregular verbs in the past tense and in one of the perfect tenses.

10.12 More Irregular Verbs

Irregular Verbs			
Pattern	**Base Form**	**Past Form**	**Past Participle**
The base form and the past participle forms are the same.	become come run	became came ran	become come run
The past form ends in -ew, and the past participle ends in -wn.	blow draw fly grow know throw	blew drew flew grew knew threw	blown drawn flown grown known thrown
The past participle ends in -en.	bite break choose drive eat fall give ride rise see speak steal take write	bit broke chose drove ate fell gave rode rose saw spoke stole took wrote	bitten broken chosen driven eaten fallen given ridden risen seen spoken stolen taken written
The past form and the past participle do not follow any pattern.	am, are, is do go tear wear	was, were did went tore wore	been done gone torn worn
The base form, past form, and past participle are the same.	cut let	cut let	cut let

Using the Past and Past Participle of Irregular Verbs
Write each sentence. Use the past tense or the past participle of the verb in parentheses.

1. A prominent actress has (write) about her experiences with stage fright.
2. One night onstage she (become) immobile.
3. Before her appearance on stage, she had (know) her lines by heart.
4. She (take) several slow, deep breaths.
5. She regained her confidence and (throw) herself into the part.
6. Her drama coach had (give) her good advice about stage fright.
7. The actress eventually (come) through with a fine performance.
8. She (draw) on her knowledge of the character's personality.
9. The actress (grow) into the part.
10. She (see) through her character's eyes.
11. She even (wear) similar clothes.
12. By the end of the play, the actress (speak) her lines flawlessly.
13. A majority of theater critics have (choose) her for an award.
14. They say she has (steal) the show.
15. She has (grow) more confident.

Writing Link

Imagine that you are a filmmaker. Describe your latest movie. Use several irregular verbs in the past tense and in one of the perfect tenses.

$\mathcal{G}rammar$Workshop

Verbs

The play *Our Town* by Thornton Wilder focuses on the fictional New England town of Grover's Corners, New Hampshire. The play consists of three acts, each with a single theme. These themes are a typical day in the town, love and marriage, and death. Each act is introduced by the Stage Manager, who also breaks into the action now and then to explain something about the town or its inhabitants. In the excerpt presented here, the Stage Manager sets the stage for the second act. The passage has been annotated to show examples of the kinds of verbs covered in this unit.

Literature Model

from OUR TOWN
by Thornton Wilder

Present perfect tense

Action verb followed by a direct object

Past tense of a regular verb

Past tense of an irregular verb

Passive voice

STAGE MANAGER: Three years have gone by. Yes, the sun's come up over a thousand times. Summers and winters have cracked the mountains a little bit more and the rains have brought down some of the dirt. Some babies that weren't even born before have begun talking regular sentences already; and a number of people who thought they were right young and spry have noticed that they can't bound up a flight of stairs like they used to, without their heart fluttering a little. All that can happen in a thousand days. Nature's been pushing and contriving in other ways, too: a number of young people fell in love and got married. Yes, the mountain got bit away a few fractions of an inch; millions of gallons of water went by the mill; and here and there a new home was set up under one roof.

Identifying Action Verbs and Linking Verbs   Write each sentence. Circle each verb, and write whether it is an *action verb* or a *linking verb*. Then write whether each underlined word is a *predicate noun, predicate adjective, direct object,* or *indirect object*.

SAMPLE   Simon Stimson directs the church <u>choir</u>.
ANSWER   Simon Stimson (directs) the church <u>choir</u>.
         action verb; direct object

1. Joe Crowell delivers the <u>newspaper</u> every morning.
2. Charles Webb is the <u>editor</u> of the local paper.
3. Banker Cartwright is very <u>wealthy</u>.
4. Rebecca Gibbs loves <u>money</u> most of all.
5. Mrs. Webb cooks her <u>family</u> breakfast every morning.

Using Verb Tenses   Rewrite each sentence, using the correct tense of the verb in parentheses.

SAMPLE   By the end of the play, several of the main characters (die).
ANSWER   By the end of the play, several of the main characters will have died.

1. The play (be) first performed in 1938.
2. It (perform) many times since then.
3. In the play George Gibbs (marry) Emily Webb.
4. Doc Gibbs (deliver) a baby by the time his wife and children arose.
5. Wilder (be) remembered by future generations as the writer of *Our Town.*
6. This play (earn) Wilder a Pulitzer Prize.
7. Previously Wilder (win) a Pulitzer Prize for the novel *The Bridge of San Luis Rey.*

Using Verb Tenses   Rewrite each sentence, changing the sentence from the passive voice to the active voice.

SAMPLE   The factory is owned by Banker Cartwright.
ANSWER   Banker Cartwright owns the factory.

1. *Our Town* was written by Thornton Wilder.
2. Each act is introduced by the Stage Manager.
3. The baby was delivered by Doc Gibbs.
4. The newspaper is published by Charles Webb.
5. The choir is directed by Simon Stimson.
6. The dead are remembered by the living.

Proofreading   The following passage is about American artist Roger Brown, whose work appears on the opposite page. Rewrite the passage, correcting the errors in spelling, capitalization, punctuation, grammar, and usage. There are ten errors in all.

Roger Brown

[1] We get another look at American life in the painting on the opposite page [2] The painting is by chicago artist Roger Brown and is characteristic of his work.

[3] The focus is no longer the provinces North of New York. [4] The southern town consists of a row of houses that is backed by sand dunes and palm trees. [5] Beyond the dunes and trees is the ocean and the setting sun. [6] The sun desends and leaves a series of colored concentric circles.

[7] The caracters in this case are reduced to pairs of silhouettes. [8] Each pare consist of a man and a woman. [9] They are either sitting separately in they're homes or walk alone along the sidewalk.

Roger Brown, *Coast of California,* **1987**

Unit 10 Review

Verbs

Transitive and Intransitive Verbs; Direct and Indirect Objects; Linking Verbs

[pages 362–369]

Underline each verb once. If it is an action verb, tell whether it is *transitive* or *intransitive*. If it is transitive, underline the direct object twice. Circle any indirect objects. If the verb is a linking verb with a predicate word, circle the predicate word, and tell whether it is a *predicate noun* or a *predicate adjective*.

1. Tonight the auditorium is a concert hall.
2. Sounds fill the room.
3. Ushers give the guests programs.
4. The room grows dark.
5. The musicians sit quietly.

Tenses and Forms; Main and Helping Verbs

[pages 370–379]

Underline each verb or verb phrase, and circle any helping verbs. Indicate the tense or form: *present, past,* or *future tense; present progressive* or *past progressive form; present perfect, past perfect,* or *future perfect tense.*

6. John is going to rehearsal.
7. Tuesday the show begins at three.
8. We were practicing all week.
9. Ellen has sung her part six times.
10. I shall memorize my part by tomorrow.
11. By Monday we shall have got it right.
12. The costumes look odd.
13. The designers did them over.
14. The director had insisted on it.
15. Marie is singing her song in a little while.

Active and Passive Voice

[pages 380–381]

Underline each verb once and the word that receives the action twice. Write whether the voice is *active* or *passive*.

16. Dance was revolutionized by Isadora Duncan.
17. Duncan studied the motions in nature.
18. Traditional ballet was rejected by Isadora Duncan.
19. Many critics praised her work.
20. Later generations of dancers were inspired by her techniques.

Writing for Review

Write a paragraph about your favorite kind of dance. Use the active voice as much as possible.

Pierre-Auguste Renoir, *Young Girls at the Piano*, 1892

11.1 Personal Pronouns

A **pronoun** is a word that takes the place of one or more nouns and the words that describe those nouns.

Pronouns that are used to refer to people or things are called **personal pronouns.**

Personal pronouns are singular or plural. Some personal pronouns are used as the subjects of sentences. Others are used as the objects of verbs or prepositions.

A **subject pronoun** is used as the subject of a sentence.

> Rita likes books. **She** particularly likes novels.

In the example above, the pronoun *She* replaces the noun *Rita* as the subject of the sentence.

An **object pronoun** is used as the object of a verb or a preposition.

> The novel amuses Rita. The novel amuses **her.** [direct object of the verb *amuses*]
>
> For Raul's birthday Rita gave **him** a novel. [indirect object of the verb *gave*]
>
> Rita presented a biography of Mark Twain to **us.** [object of the preposition *to*]

Personal Pronouns		
	Singular	Plural
Used as Subjects	I	we
	you	you
	he, she, it	they
Used as Objects	me	us
	you	you
	him, her, it	them

Exercise 1

Using Personal Pronouns   Write each sentence. Write the pronoun you could use in place of the underlined word or words. Write whether the pronoun you used is a *subject pronoun* or an *object pronoun*.

1. <u>Sarah Orne Jewett</u> was an American writer of the 1800s.
2. The *Atlantic Monthly* first published <u>Jewett</u>.
3. This author wrote <u>the stories</u> at age nineteen.
4. <u>These stories</u> are about history and tradition.
5. <u>The Jewett family</u> lived amid Maine's many villages.
6. <u>Sarah's father</u> was a doctor with an interest in books and people.
7. Sarah studied <u>books and people</u> with her father.
8. <u>Young Sarah</u> observed people's ways of life.
9. She described <u>the people</u> in her stories.
10. She wrote stories about <u>her experiences</u>.
11. <u>Readers</u> learned about life in New England.
12. Bob wrote a research report on <u>Sarah Jewett</u>.
13. <u>"A White Heron"</u> is Sarah Jewett's best-known story.
14. <u>The heron</u> catches a young girl's attention.
15. The young girl approaches <u>the nest</u>.
16. <u>The wild bird</u> avoids the young girl.
17. "A White Heron" appeals to <u>Robert</u>.
18. <u>Our class</u> had difficulty with the story.
19. Luisa pointed out the theme to <u>our class</u>.
20. Rosa said, "Let <u>Rosa</u> help you."

Writing Link

Imagine that you are a famous writer. Write a paragraph describing some of the characters in a story you are writing. Use personal pronouns.

11.2   Pronouns and Antecedents

Read the following sentences. Can you tell to whom the pronoun *She* refers?

> Louisa May Alcott wrote a novel about a young woman.
> **She** has three sisters.

The sentence is not clear because *She* could refer either to the *young woman* or to *Louisa May Alcott.* Sometimes you must repeat a noun or rewrite a sentence to avoid confusion.

> Louisa May Alcott wrote a novel about a young woman.
> **The young woman** has three sisters.

The noun or group of words that a pronoun refers to is called its **antecedent.**

When you use a pronoun, you should be sure that it refers to its antecedent clearly. Be especially careful when you use the pronoun *they.* Notice this pronoun in the following sentence.

> **They** have two books by Alcott at the school library.

To whom does *They* refer? Its meaning is unclear. The sentence might be corrected in the following way.

> Two books by Alcott are available at the school library.

Be sure every pronoun agrees with its antecedent in number (singular or plural) and gender. The gender of a noun or pronoun may be masculine, feminine, or neuter (referring to things). Notice the pronoun-antecedent agreement below.

> The Marches must face a death in their family. **They** face **it** with courage.

Exercise 2

Using Pronouns and Antecedents Correctly   Write the second sentence in each of the following pairs. Use the correct pronoun in each blank. Then write the antecedent of the pronoun and its number and gender.

1. Louisa May Alcott lived in the Boston area. _____ had many famous neighbors.
2. Alcott's first book contained stories for young children. _____ was called *Flower Fables*.
3. Two more books by Alcott appeared quickly. _____ describe her hospital work and her teaching days.
4. An editor asked Alcott to write a book for girls. The editor finally persuaded _____ .
5. In 1868 Alcott published the first part of *Little Women*. _____ was a success.
6. *Little Women* was very popular in the 1800s. _____ changed people's views on women's role in society.
7. In the novel Jo March is the main character. _____ eventually becomes a writer.
8. The March sisters attend school. _____ also earn money for their family.
9. Jo meets Fritz Bhaer. She ultimately falls in love with _____ .
10. Beth is a musician. _____ dies of a terrible illness.
11. At the library I found Alcott's *An Old-Fashioned Girl*. _____ was published in 1870.
12. We have *Little Men* and *Jo's Boys*. I read _____ .

Writing Link

Describe a book or a screenplay you might like to write. Use personal pronouns in your sentences, and check for correct pronoun-antecedent agreement.

11.3   Using Pronouns Correctly

Subject pronouns are used in compound subjects, and object pronouns are used in compound objects.

SUBJECT

Tina and Sam

> Tina and Sam recently read *Heidi.* **She** and **he** recently read *Heidi.* [*She* and *he* form the compound subject.]
> *Heidi* appealed to Sam and Tina. *Heidi* appealed to **him** and **her**. [*Him* and *her* form the compound object.]

Whenever the subject pronoun *I* or the object pronoun *me* is part of the compound subject or object, it should come last.

> Tina and **I** liked the book. [not *I and Tina*]

read about

Sometimes a pronoun and a noun are used together for emphasis. The form of the pronoun depends on the function of the noun in the sentence.

> We students read the book. [*Students* is the subject, so the subject pronoun *We* is used.]
> The book delighted us readers. [*Readers* is the direct object, so the object pronoun *us* is used.]

Peter and Heidi.

OBJECT

Some sentences make incomplete comparisons. The forms of the pronoun can affect the meaning of such sentences. In any incomplete comparison use the pronoun that would be correct if the comparison were complete.

> Heidi liked Peter more than **she** [did].
> Heidi liked Peter more than [she liked] **her.**

In formal writing use a subject pronoun after a linking verb.

> Heidi's closest friend is **he.**

Using Subject and Object Pronouns Correctly

Write each sentence. Use the correct word or words in parentheses. Then write whether each pronoun is a *subject pronoun* or an *object pronoun.*

1. *Heidi* entertained (we, us) readers.
2. Peter and (her, she) love the mountains.
3. Peter becomes a friend to Heidi's grandfather and (she, her).
4. Grandfather is stern, although no one is kinder than (he, him).
5. (We, Us) readers grow fond of Grandfather.
6. My favorite character is (he, him).
7. Grandfather became almost real to (Juan and I, Juan and me).
8. (She, Her) and Peter tend goats.
9. Heidi says good-bye to (Peter and he, Peter and him).
10. (We, Us) readers feel very sympathetic toward Heidi.
11. In fact, I felt almost as sad as (she, her).
12. Between Peter and (she, her) they help Klara toward recovery.
13. Klara and (she, her) become friends in the city.
14. Heidi's dearest friends are Grandfather and (he, him).
15. Klara cannot walk; so Heidi aids the family and (she, her).
16. (Tom and I, Me and Tom) guessed the ending.

GRAMMAR HINT

To see if a pronoun in a compound subject or object is correct, replace the compound with the correct plural pronoun: *They saw* Otis and me. *They saw* us.

Writing Link

Write a paragraph describing what it would be like to form a special friendship. Be aware of your use of pronouns as you write.

11.4 Possessive Pronouns

You often use pronouns to replace nouns that are subjects and nouns that are objects in sentences. You can use pronouns in place of possessive nouns, too.

A **possessive pronoun** is a pronoun that shows who or what has something. A possessive pronoun may take the place of a possessive noun.

Read the following sentences. Notice the possessive nouns and the possessive pronouns that replace them.

Lisa's class put on a play. **Her** class put on a play.
The idea was Lisa's. The idea was **hers.**

Possessive pronouns have two forms. One form is used before a noun. The other form is used alone. The chart below shows the two forms of possessive pronouns.

Possessive Pronouns		
	Singular	**Plural**
Used Before Nouns	my	our
	your	your
	her, his, its	their
Used Alone	mine	ours
	yours	yours
	hers, his, its	theirs

Unlike possessive nouns, such as *Mei's* or *cats'*, possessive pronouns do not contain an apostrophe.

Do not confuse the possessive pronoun *its* with the word *it's*. *It's* is a contraction, or shortened form, of the words *it is*.

Its subject is William Shakespeare. [possessive pronoun]
It's a famous play by Shakespeare. [contraction of *it is*]

Exercise 4

Identifying Possessive Pronouns   Write each sentence. Underline each possessive pronoun. Then write whether the pronoun *comes before a noun* or *stands alone*.

1. Our class is putting on a play by Shakespeare.
2. He wrote centuries ago, but his plays still thrill audiences.
3. *Hamlet* is Lian's favorite, but *Romeo and Juliet* is mine.
4. Have you seen your favorite play yet?
5. Gina was in *Hamlet,* but it's not a favorite of hers.

Exercise 5

Using Possessive Pronouns   Write each sentence. Replace each underlined word or group of words with the correct possessive pronoun.

1. The teacher said to the class, "<u>This class's</u> play this year will be *Romeo and Juliet.*"
2. The teacher said to Emily, "The part of Juliet is <u>Emily's</u>."
3. Angelo declared excitedly, "The role of Romeo is <u>Angelo's</u>!"
4. "<u>Leroy's</u> role is as Tybalt, Juliet's relative," Leroy explained.
5. In the play the Capulets regard the Montagues as <u>the Capulets'</u> enemy.

Writing Link

What is your favorite play? Imagine that you are a critic. Write a review of a new production of this play. Use possessive pronouns in your review.

11.5 | Indefinite Pronouns

An **indefinite pronoun** is a pronoun that does not refer to a particular person, place, or thing.

> **Each** thinks about the plot.

Most indefinite pronouns are either singular or plural.

Some Indefinite Pronouns			
Singular			**Plural**
another	everybody	no one	both
anybody	everyone	nothing	few
anyone	everything	one	many
anything	much	somebody	others
each	neither	someone	several
either	nobody	something	

In addition, the indefinite pronouns *all, any, most, none,* and *some* are singular or plural, depending on the phrase that follows.

When an indefinite pronoun is used as the subject of a sentence, the verb must agree with it in number.

> **Everyone reads** part of the novel. [singular]
> **Several enjoy** it very much. [plural]
> **Most** of the story **takes** place in England. [singular]
> **Most** of the characters **are** memorable. [plural]

Possessive pronouns often have indefinite pronouns as their antecedents. In such cases, the pronouns must agree in number. Note that the intervening prepositional phrase does not affect the agreement.

> **Several** are presenting **their** interpretations of the novel.
> **Each** of the students has **his** or **her** ideas about its meaning.

Using Indefinite Pronouns   Write each sentence. Use the word or words in parentheses that correctly complete the sentence. Then underline the indefinite pronoun, and write whether the pronoun is *singular* or *plural*.

1. Everyone studies (his or her, their) section of *Alice's Adventures in Wonderland*.
2. Most of the characters (is, are) animals.
3. Some of them (attends, attend) a comical tea party.
4. Nothing (makes, make) sense in Wonderland.
5. Everything in Wonderland (confuses, confuse) Alice.
6. No one (answers, answer) her questions.
7. Many of the characters (talks, talk) peculiarly.
8. Some of them even (speaks, speak) in riddles.
9. Few really (believes, believe) in disappearing cats.
10. None of the characters (looks, look) more bizarre than the Mock Turtle.
11. Several offer Alice (his or her, their) advice.
12. Each has (their, his or her) point of view.
13. Nothing predictable (happens, happen) in Wonderland.
14. Most of the story (occurs, occur) down a rabbit hole.
15. Everybody in class enjoys (his or her, their) reading of *Alice's Adventures in Wonderland*.
16. Much (has, have) been written about the story.
17. All of the critics (praises, praise) it.
18. None of them (gives, give) a bad review.

GRAMMAR HINT

To see whether a word is an indefinite pronoun, replace it with *the*. If the new phrase makes sense, the word is probably a modifier, not a pronoun.

Writing Link

What would you do if you stepped through the looking glass into Wonderland? Write a paragraph describing one day in Wonderland. Use indefinite pronouns.

11.6   Reflexive and Intensive Pronouns

A **reflexive pronoun** refers to a noun or another pronoun and indicates that the same person or thing is involved.

The woman bought **herself** a book by Horatio Alger.

REFLEXIVE PRONOUN

REFLEXIVE PRONOUN

Reflexive pronouns are formed by adding *-self* or *-selves* to certain personal and possessive pronouns.

Reflexive Pronouns	
Singular	**Plural**
myself	ourselves
yourself	yourselves
himself, herself, itself	themselves

Sometimes *hisself* is mistakenly used for *himself,* and *theirselves* for *themselves.* Avoid using *hisself* and *theirselves.*

Reflexive pronouns can also add emphasis. When they are used for that purpose, they are called intensive pronouns.

An **intensive pronoun** is a pronoun that adds emphasis to a noun or pronoun already named.

Horatio Alger **himself** wrote more than one hundred books.
He **himself** wrote *Luck and Pluck* and *Sink or Swim.*

Reflexive and intensive pronouns have special uses. They should never be used as the subject of a sentence or as the object of a verb or preposition.

Yolanda and **I** read *Sink or Swim.* [not *Yolanda and myself*]
It pleased Yolanda and **me.** [not *Yolanda and myself*]

Using Reflexive and Intensive Pronouns Write each sentence. Use the correct pronoun in parentheses. Write whether the pronoun is a *reflexive, intensive, subject,* or *object* pronoun.

1. I (me, myself) wrote a review of a book by Horatio Alger.
2. I found (me, myself) inspired by the characters' adventures.
3. Alger's life (it, itself) seemed like one of his success stories.
4. The characters improve (them, themselves) through work and a bit of luck.
5. Yusuf and Tony (themselves, theirselves) were impressed by the number of Alger's books.
6. Horatio Alger (he, himself) lived from 1832 to 1899.
7. Alger's birthplace (it, itself) attracts visitors.
8. We enjoyed (us, ourselves) during a visit to his home.
9. Alger's stories (them, themselves) usually take place in large cities.
10. A friend and (I, myself) have read ten of Alger's books.
11. Alger thought (hisself, himself) ambitious and moved to New York.
12. Alger's style seems warm and light to (me, myself).
13. For Alger ambition (it, itself) can bring about success.

Writing Link

Cities can be very interesting places. Write a paragraph about a large city you might like to visit. Use reflexive and intensive pronouns.

11.7 Interrogative and Demonstrative Pronouns

An **interrogative pronoun** is a pronoun used to introduce an interrogative sentence.

The interrogative pronouns *who* and *whom* both refer to people. *Who* is used when the interrogative pronoun is the subject of the sentence. *Whom* is used when the interrogative pronoun is the object of a verb or a preposition.

> **Who** borrowed the book? [subject]
> **Whom** did the librarian call? [direct object]
> For **whom** did you borrow the book? [object of preposition]

Which and *what* are used to refer to things.

> **What** interests you?   **Which** is it?

Whose shows that someone possesses something.

> I found a copy of *Great Expectations*. **Whose** is it?

When writing, be careful that you do not confuse *whose* with *who's*. *Who's* is the contraction of *who is*.

A **demonstrative pronoun** is a pronoun that points out something.

The demonstrative pronouns are *this, that, these,* and *those.* *This* (singular) and *these* (plural) refer to something nearby. *That* (singular) and *those* (plural) refer to something at a distance.

that

this

> **This** is an interesting book. [singular, nearby]
> **These** are interesting books. [plural, nearby]
> **That** is a long book. [singular, at a distance]
> **Those** are long books. [plural, at a distance]

Using Interrogative and Demonstrative Pronouns
Write each sentence. Use the correct word given in parentheses.

1. (These, This) is Arturo's favorite book.
2. (Who, Whom) taught Pip about books?
3. (That, Those) are Pip's students.
4. From (who, whom) did you get that copy?

Distinguishing Between Pronouns and Contractions
Write each sentence. Use the correct word given in parentheses, and write whether it is an *interrogative pronoun,* a *demonstrative pronoun,* or a *contraction containing an interrogative pronoun.*

1. (Who, Whom) did Miss Havisham see?
2. (This, These) was the girl at Miss Havisham's home.
3. (Who's, Whose) Miss Havisham?
4. To (who, whom) did Estella get married?
5. (This, What) are Pip's great expectations?
6. (Who's Whose) Pip?
7. (Who, Whom) becomes Pip's guardian?
8. (That, These) is a mystery.
9. (Who's, Which) school does Pip attend?
10. (Whose, Who's) the author of this novel?
11. To (who, whom) does Pip turn for help?

Writing Link

Make a list of questions you would ask a character in a story that you know. Use interrogative and demonstrative pronouns.

Grammar Workshop

Pronouns

The following passage is from a biography of Emily Dickinson by Bonita Thayer. In addition to writing nearly eighteen hundred poems, Dickinson wrote many letters to friends. These letters reveal much about her thinking at different periods of her life. In the passage below, Thayer quotes from Dickinson's letters to Colonel Higginson, a writer and abolitionist (someone who opposed slavery). The passage has been annotated to show examples of the kinds of pronouns covered in this unit.

Literature Model

from EMILY DICKINSON

by Bonita E. Thayer

Indefinite pronoun —— **Some** of Emily's letters to Higginson reveal her feelings about the public in general. "Truth is such a rare thing, it is delightful to tell it," she says in one note. Subject pronoun agrees with its antecedent, *Emily* —— Later **she** asks him, "How do most people live without any thoughts? There are many people in the world— you must have noticed **them** in the street—how do Object pronoun agrees with its antecedent, *many people* —— they live? How do they get strength to put on their clothes in the morning?"

She seemed satisfied with her life as she was living it. Her own thoughts filled her mind and were joined with the thoughts of others whose writings she studied.

"There is no frigate like a book to take us lands away," she wrote. She felt that she could travel the world and meet all the people she wanted to through Possessive pronoun —— books. She never had to leave **her** own home, which she considered to be the best and safest place for her.

Grammar Workshop Exercise 1

Making Pronouns and Verbs Agree   Rewrite each sentence, inserting the word in parentheses that agrees with the indefinite pronoun.

SAMPLE   Some of her poetry (is, are) deceptively simple.
ANSWER   Some of her poetry is deceptively simple.

1. Many (consider, considers) Dickinson one of the best American poets.
2. Few of her poems (was, were) published during her lifetime.
3. Did anyone (influence, influences) her writing?
4. Much (has, have) been written about how she never left home.
5. Most of her poems (is, are) very brief.
6. Several of us (enjoy, enjoys) her work.
7. All of her work (is, are) interesting.

Grammar Workshop Exercise 2

Using Pronouns   Rewrite each sentence, using the correct pronoun in parentheses.

SAMPLE   Emily Dickinson and (her, she) never left home.
ANSWER   Emily Dickinson and she never left home.

1. Dickinson and (he, him) wrote each other frequently over the years.
2. In one year Dickinson (she, herself) wrote 366 poems.
3. (Who, Whom) was the most important influence on Dickinson's poetry?
4. (That, Those) is the poem I like the most.
5. To (who, whom) did she write, "Truth is such a rare thing, it is delightful to tell it"?
6. In (whose, who's) house did she live her entire life?
7. In one poem Dickinson wrote, "Success is counted sweetest/By (those, they) that ne'er succeed." ➡

8. (We, Us) readers are often left wondering how she could say so much with so few words.
9. Dickinson never thought of herself as a better poet than (he, him).
10. (Whose, Who's) the best poet writing today?
11. I think the best poets of the past are Dickinson and (they, them).

Grammar Workshop Exercise 3

Proofreading   The following passage is about the artist Paul Sierra, whose work appears on the opposite page. Rewrite the passage, correcting the errors in spelling, capitalization, punctuation, grammar, and usage. There are ten errors in all.

Paul Sierra

[1] Paul Sierra was born in Havana Cuba. [2] His parent's wanted himself to become a doctor, but he wanted to be a painter instead. [3] In 1961 Sierra who was 16 at the time, and his family immigrating to the United States and settled in Chicago.

[4] Sierra began formal training as a painter in 1963 and later went to work as a commercial layout artist. [5] He still works in advertising as a creative director. [6] Because he does not have to rely on sales of paintings for his livelihood he is free to paint what he wishes. [7] His interests include photography and filmaking, in addition to painting.

[8] Sierra often incorporates tropical imagery and exotic coloring in his work. [9] His unusual use of color can be seeing in the painting on the opposite page. [10] The images, however, are drawn from the paintings of Edgar Degas. [11] The woman's head, for instance, are taken from a famous portrait done by Degas. [12] The horse and jockey also reflect Degas's fascination with the sport of racing.

Paul Sierra, *Degas' Studio,* **1990**

Pronouns

Pronouns and Antecedents

[pages 392–395]

Use the correct pronoun in each blank. Underline each pronoun's antecedent.

1. Jim Hawkins lived at the Admiral Benbow Inn. _____ was on the coast.
2. The captain was a pirate. _____ stayed at the inn.
3. He told stories to the guests. _____ were afraid of him.
4. He sang songs. Guests sang _____ also.
5. Jim did not think there could be worse pirates. _____ soon met some.

Using Pronouns Correctly

[pages 396–397]

Choose the correct pronoun. Identify it as a *subject pronoun* or an *object pronoun*.

6. (We, Us) like *Romeo and Juliet*.
7. Romeo and (she, her) met at a banquet.
8. The happiest man there was (he, him).
9. Mei and (I, me) have written a play.
10. *Hamlet* inspires (us, we) actors.

Possessive Pronouns; Indefinite Pronouns

[pages 398–401]

Replace the underlined word or words in each sentence with the correct possessive pronoun or pronouns.

11. In *The Wizard of Oz,* <u>Dorothy's</u> home is in Kansas
12. The characters cannot find <u>the characters'</u> way to Oz fast enough.
13. Everyone is presenting <u>everyone's</u> book report.
14. Many students presented <u>many students'</u> ideas on *The Wizard of Oz*.
15. The best report was <u>Verline's</u>.

Reflexive, Intensive, Interrogative, and Demonstrative Pronouns

[pages 402–405]

Choose the correct pronoun. Indicate whether it is *reflexive, intensive, interrogative,* or *demonstrative*.

16. Dickens's fiction mirrored society (itself, himself).
17. Characters reveal (themselves, itself) through words.
18. Of (who, whom) is Estella fond?
19. (Who, Whom) has read this book?
20. (This, These) is the theme.

Writing for Review

Describe a book you have recently read. Use different kinds of pronouns.

Pablo Picasso, *Harlequin*, 1923

12.1 Adjectives

An adjective describes a person, place, thing, or idea. An adjective provides information about the size, shape, color, texture, feeling, sound, smell, number, or condition of a noun or a pronoun.

The **eager**, **large** crowd of visitors examines the **huge** painting.

In the sentence above, the adjectives *eager* and *large* describe the noun *crowd,* and the adjective *huge* describes the noun *painting.*

An **adjective** is a word that modifies, or describes, a noun or a pronoun.

Most adjectives come before the nouns they modify. An adjective can also follow a linking verb and modify the noun or pronoun that is the subject of the sentence.

The painting is **realistic** and **timeless**.

In the sentence above, the adjectives *realistic* and *timeless* follow the linking verb *is* and modify the subject, *painting.* They are called predicate adjectives.

A **predicate adjective** follows a linking verb and modifies the subject of the sentence.

The present participle and past participle forms of verbs may be used as adjectives and predicate adjectives.

Christina's World is a **haunting** painting. [present participle]

Christina's World is **inspired**. [past participle]

Identifying Adjectives Write each sentence. Underline each adjective, and draw an arrow to the noun or pronoun it modifies.

1. Georgia O'Keeffe is a major American artist.
2. Her permanent residence was in the Southwest.
3. O'Keeffe's works hang in numerous museums.
4. The dry desert provided her with interesting material.
5. Objects in her paintings appear transformed.
6. Georgia O'Keeffe spent several years in Wisconsin.
7. She studied art at a large school in Chicago in the early 1900s.
8. She lived for a short time in bustling New York City.
9. As a young woman she seemed restless and ambitious.
10. O'Keeffe had not yet found the right subjects.
11. In 1912 she became aware of the interesting scenery in Texas.
12. She made an eye-opening journey to Amarillo, Texas.
13. O'Keeffe was awestruck by the vast landscapes.
14. The bright flowers and whitened bones of the desert inspired her.
15. The endless Texas landscape seemed filled with strange objects and ghostly figures.
16. Her unique style combined abstract design with realistic scenery.

Writing Link

Describe a favorite painting or photo. Add interest to your writing by using adjectives.

12.2   Articles and Proper Adjectives

The words *a*, *an*, and *the* make up a special group of adjectives called **articles**. *A* and *an* are called **indefinite articles** because they refer to one of a general group of people, places, things, or ideas. *A* is used before words beginning with a consonant sound, and *an* before words beginning with a vowel sound.

a unit	**a** painting	**an** etching	**an** hour

The is called a **definite article** because it identifies specific people, places, things, or ideas.

The valuable statue is **the** only one of its kind.

Proper adjectives are formed from proper nouns. A proper adjective always begins with a capital letter.

The **Italian** statue is on exhibit in **American** museums.
The **Houston** exhibit will begin in February.
The **February** exhibit follows a show of **French** paintings.

Although most proper adjectives are formed from proper nouns by adding one of the endings listed below, some are formed differently. Check the spellings in a dictionary.

Common Endings for Proper Adjectives				
-an	Mexico Mexic**an**	Morocco Morocc**an**	Alaska Alask**an**	Guatemala Guatemal**an**
-ese	China Chin**ese**	Bali Balin**ese**	Sudan Sudan**ese**	Japan Japan**ese**
-ian	Canada Canad**ian**	Italy Ital**ian**	Nigeria Niger**ian**	Asia As**ian**
-ish	Spain Span**ish**	Ireland Ir**ish**	Turkey Turk**ish**	England Engl**ish**

Using *A* and *An* Write each word or group of words. Add the correct indefinite article before it.

1. satellite	**11.** unknown rock
2. electrical storm	**12.** typical day
3. transmitter	**13.** masterpiece
4. vehicle	**14.** awkward age
5. howling wind	**15.** instrument
6. expedition	**16.** high-wire act
7. unicorn	**17.** explanation
8. unique event	**18.** hourly report
9. anonymous writer	**19.** honest effort
10. unexplored part	**20.** activity

Forming Proper Adjectives Rewrite each group of words, using a proper adjective to describe the noun. Change the article if necessary.

1. a drum from Africa	**9.** a bobsled from Alaska
2. a bracelet from Mexico	**10.** a car from Japan
3. a student from China	**11.** a winter in Minnesota
4. a snowstorm in January	**12.** a writer from Ireland
5. a flag from Australia	**13.** a clock from Taiwan
6. a tea from England	**14.** a celebration in July
7. an artist from Poland	**15.** a ring from Bolivia
8. a wedding in April	**16.** a song from Brazil

Writing Link

Describe a foreign country you have studied. Mention location, geographic features, and neighboring countries and cultures. Use both articles and proper adjectives.

12.3 Comparative and Superlative Adjectives

The **comparative form** of an adjective compares two things or people.

The **superlative form** of an adjective compares more than two things or people.

For most adjectives of one syllable and some of two syllables, *-er* and *-est* are added to form the comparative and superlative.

Comparative and Superlative Forms	
Comparative	She is **younger** than the other painter.
Superlative	She is the **youngest** painter in the entire group.

For most adjectives with two or more syllables, the comparative or superlative is formed by adding *more* or *most* before the adjective.

Comparative and Superlative Forms of Longer Adjectives	
Comparative	The one next to it is **more colorful.**
Superlative	The painting in the next room is the **most colorful.**

Never use *more* or *most* with adjectives that already end with *-er* or *-est*. This is called a double comparison.

Some adjectives have irregular comparative forms.

Irregular Comparative and Superlative Forms		
Adjective	**Comparative**	**Superlative**
good, well	better	best
bad	worse	worst
many, much	more	most
little	less	least

Using the Comparative and Superlative Write each sentence. Use the correct comparative or superlative form of the adjective in parentheses.

1. Michelangelo was one of the (great) artists of all time.
2. He was also the (famous) artist of his own time.
3. Are his statues (good) than his paintings?
4. Which is the (fine) statue, *David* or the *Pietà?*
5. Michelangelo's figures were (large) than life.
6. Few paintings are (beautiful) than the one on the ceiling of the Sistine Chapel in Rome.
7. His buildings may be (famous) than his renowned statues and paintings.
8. Pablo Picasso may be the (great) painter of our century.
9. His early paintings are (realistic) than his later work.
10. His cubist works are probably the (famous) of all.
11. Cubism may have been the (original) of Picasso's many styles, yet he explored other approaches to painting.
12. Critics argue over the question of his (good) style of all.
13. They also disagree on his (bad) style.
14. Few artists completed (many) paintings than he did.
15. Of all artists he showed the (quick) response to change.

Writing Link

Imagine that you are an art critic. Briefly compare three imaginary works of art. Include both comparative and superlative adjectives in your writing.

That gallery has modern art.

This gallery contains Impressionist works.

12.4 Demonstratives

The words *this, that, these,* and *those* are called demonstratives. They "demonstrate," or point out, people, places, or things. *This* and *these* point out people or things near to you, and *that* and *those* point out people or things at a distance from you. *This* and *that* describe singular nouns, and *these* and *those* describe plural nouns.

This, that, these, and *those* are called demonstrative adjectives when they describe nouns.

Demonstrative adjectives point out something and describe nouns by answering the questions *which one?* or *which ones?*

The words *this, that, these,* and *those* can also be used as demonstrative pronouns. They take the place of nouns and call attention to, or demonstrate, something that is not named.

Notice the demonstratives in the following sentences.

Demonstrative Words	
Demonstrative Adjectives	**Demonstrative Pronouns**
This painting is my favorite.	**This** is my favorite painting.
I like **these** kinds of paintings.	**These** are the paintings I like.
That portrait is well known.	**That** was the first stage.
He draws **those** sorts of pictures.	**Those** are from his Cubist phase.

The words *here* and *there* should not be used with demonstrative adjectives. The words *this, these, that,* and *those* already point out the locations *here* and *there.*

This painting is by Matisse. [not *This here painting*]

The object pronoun *them* should not be used in place of the demonstrative adjective *those.*

I saw **those** pictures. [not *them pictures*]

Using Demonstratives   Write each sentence, using the correct word or words in parentheses.

1. The artist saw (that, those) things in a new way.
2. (This, This here) painting shows her imaginative style.
3. This (kinds of, kind of) painting has become famous.
4. (This, That) painting over there shows an acrobat.
5. Usually (those, them) colors together would clash.
6. (This, These) are her brushes and palette.
7. (That there, That) painting by Paul Cézanne is influential.
8. (This, This here) is an early work.
9. Cézanne breaks up the dimensions of (this, these) objects.
10. Then he rearranges (these, these here) fragments.
11. This (kind of, kinds of) painting shows his technique.
12. (These, These here) are explorations of space.
13. The angles in (this, this here) picture seem to overlap.
14. These (kinds of, kind of) angles do form solids.
15. The *Pietà* is not (that, that there) kind of sculpture.
16. (This, These) is a fine example of abstract art.
17. Many are familiar with (that, that there) artist.
18. One artist produced all (these, these here) works.
19. (Those, Them) paintings are older than his.
20. (These, These here) pieces are by an unknown artist.

Writing Link

Imagine being a guard at an art museum. Describe the theft of three priceless paintings. Use some demonstrative adjectives and pronouns in your writing.

12.5　Adverbs

An **adverb** is a word that modifies, or describes, a verb, an adjective, or another adverb.

What Adverbs Modify	
Verbs	People handle old violins **carefully.**
Adjectives	**Very** old violins are valuable.
Adverbs	Some violins are played **extremely** rarely.

Adverbs that tell *to what extent* a quality exists are sometimes called **intensifiers.** *Very, quite,* and *almost* are intensifiers.

An adverb may tell *when, where,* or *how* about a verb. The adverbs in the sentences below all modify the verb *play.*

Ways Adverbs Modify Verbs	
How?	Many pianists play **well** with a large orchestra.
When?	Pianists **sometimes** play duets.
Where?	Some pianists play **everywhere** in the country.

When modifying an adjective or another adverb, an adverb usually comes before the word. When modifying a verb, an adverb can occupy different positions in a sentence.

Many adverbs are formed by adding *-ly* to adjectives. However, not all words that end in *-ly* are adverbs. The words *friendly, lively, kindly,* and *lonely* are usually adjectives. Similarly, not all adverbs end in *-ly.*

Adverbs Not Ending in *-ly*			
afterward	often	there	hard
sometimes	soon	everywhere	long
later	here	fast	straight

Identifying Adverbs   Write each sentence. Underline each adverb, and write the word it describes.

1. The early Greeks studied music thoroughly.
2. To the Greeks music and mathematics were very similar.
3. Pythagoras strongly believed in the enormous power of music.
4. His ideas about music were certainly important.
5. People sang choral music often at ancient ceremonies.
6. The notes of each singer were exactly alike.
7. These choruses almost surely sang without accompaniment.
8. Composers later wrote separate parts for different voices.
9. Musicians of the Middle Ages developed part singing rather quickly.
10. Some unusually beautiful music resulted.
11. The parts were highly complex.
12. Modern choruses are very professional groups of singers.
13. These choruses perform everywhere.
14. Many choral singers are totally dedicated to their work.
15. People often overlook this kind of music.
16. Some people await major choral concerts eagerly.

Writing Link

Describe a musical performance you have attended. Use adverbs, including intensifiers, to describe the performance as well as the reaction of the audience.

12.6 Comparative and Superlative Adverbs

The **comparative form** of an adverb compares two actions.

The **superlative form** of an adverb compares more than two actions.

Long adverbs require the use of *more* or *most.*

Comparing Adverbs of More than One Syllable	
Comparative	The audience listened **more attentively** last night than tonight.
Superlative	Last Sunday's audience responded **most enthusiastically** of all.

Shorter adverbs need *-er* or *-est* as an ending.

Comparing One-Syllable Adverbs	
Comparative	Did the pianist play **louder** than the cellist?
Superlative	Did the drummer play the **loudest** of all?

Here are some irregular adverbs.

Irregular Comparative and Superlative Forms		
Adverb	Comparative	Superlative
well	better	best
badly	worse	worst
little (amount)	less	least

The words *less* and *least* are used before both short and long adverbs to form the negative comparative and the negative superlative.

I play **less well.** I play **least accurately.**

Forming the Comparative and Superlative Write the comparative and superlative forms of each of the following adverbs:

1. tenderly
2. fast
3. little
4. easily
5. violently
6. rapidly
7. close
8. gently
9. straight

Using Comparative and Superlative Forms Write each sentence. Use the correct comparative or superlative form of the adverb in parentheses.

1. The performance began (late) tonight than last night.
2. My sister sat (far) from the stage than we did.
3. Several backup singers rehearsed (long) than the piano player.
4. The lead singer sang (badly) last year than this year.
5. The guitarists sang (little) during this concert than during their last one.
6. The drummer played (forcefully) during her solo than before.
7. We heard the first song (clear) of all the songs.
8. The band played (energetically) of all at the end.
9. I clapped (loud) during the second half than during the first.
10. The evening ended (soon) than expected.

Writing Link

In a paragraph compare three of your favorite musical performers. Use as many comparative and superlative adverbs as possible.

12.7 Using Adverbs and Adjectives

Louis Armstrong was a **real** innovator in jazz.

Adverbs and adjectives are often confused, especially when they appear after verbs. A predicate adjective follows a linking verb.

> The musicians are **professional**.

In the sentence above, the predicate adjective *professional* describes *musicians*.

In the sentence below, the adverb *hard* describes the action verb *trains*.

> A musician trains **hard** for a place in a symphony orchestra.

People also sometimes confuse the words *bad, badly, good,* and *well*. *Bad* and *good* are both adjectives. They are used after linking verbs. *Badly* and *well* are adverbs. They describe action verbs. When used after a linking verb to describe a person's health or appearance, *well* is an adjective.

His music was **really** popular.

Distinguishing Adjective from Adverb	
Adjective	**Adverb**
The sound is **bad**. The band sounds **good**. The soloist seems **well**.	The actor sang **badly**. The band played **well**.

People also confuse *real, really; sure, surely;* and *most, almost*. *Real, sure,* and *most* are adjectives. *Really, surely,* and *almost* are adverbs.

Distinguishing Adjective from Adverb	
Adjective	**Adverb**
Music is a **real** art. A pianist needs **sure** hands. **Most** pianos have eighty-eight keys.	Music is **really** popular. Piano music is **surely** popular. Piano strings **almost** never break.

Identifying Adjectives and Adverbs   Write each sentence. Underline the verb twice, and write whether it is an *action verb* or a *linking verb*. Then identify the predicate adjective or adverb that follows each verb.

1. Louis Armstrong was famous as a jazz trumpeter.
2. Armstrong began his music career early in the 1900s.
3. He played the trumpet well during his teens in New Orleans.
4. Armstrong listened carefully to other musicians' styles.
5. He seemed enthusiastic about a new singing style called "scat."
6. Scat was rhythmic in its use of syllables instead of words.
7. He seemed ready for a new career as an actor in motion pictures.
8. Big bands played everywhere.
9. They were extremely popular in the 1930s.
10. Louis Armstrong traveled widely and made a number of hit records.
11. Both the soloists and the conductors of the big bands became widely known.
12. The Dorsey brothers were extremely successful as popular musicians.
13. They worked steadily throughout the 1940s.
14. Dinah Shore sang often with big bands.

Writing Link

Have you ever played a musical instrument or wanted to play one? Write a paragraph describing the instrument. Use both adjectives and adverbs.

12.8 Avoiding Double Negatives

The adverb *not* is a negative word. **Negative words** express the idea of "no." *Not* often appears in a shortened form as part of a contraction. Study the words and their contracted forms below.

Contractions with *Not*		
is not = isn't	cannot = can't	have not = haven't
was not = wasn't	could not = couldn't	had not = hadn't
were not = weren't	do not = don't	would not = wouldn't
will not = won't	did not = didn't	should not = shouldn't

Notice that the apostrophe replaces the *o* in *not* in all but two words. In *can't* both the letter *n* and the letter *o* are dropped. *Will not* becomes *won't*.

Other negative words are listed below. Each negative word has several opposites. These are **affirmative words**, or words that show the idea of "yes."

Negative and Affirmative Words	
Negative	**Affirmative**
never	ever, always
nobody	anybody, somebody
none	one, all, some, any
no one	everyone, someone
nothing	something, anything
nowhere	somewhere, anywhere

Be careful to avoid using two negative words in the same sentence. This is called a **double negative.** You can correct a double negative by removing one of the negative words or by replacing one with an affirmative word. The sentence *The clarinet isn't no new instrument* can be corrected in the following manner.

The clarinet isn't a new instrument.
The clarinet is no new instrument.

Using Negative Words   Write each sentence, using the correct word or words given in parentheses.

1. Didn't (anyone, no one) play pipe organs before Roman times?
2. We (would, wouldn't) hardly recognize the Roman pipe organ today.
3. Aren't there (no, any) old Roman pipe organs still in existence?
4. The pipe organ (was, wasn't) scarcely used outside of churches.
5. Scarcely (no, any) ancient civilizations were without musical instruments.
6. The Egyptians (weren't, were) no exception.
7. Hardly (any, none) of their paintings leave out cymbals and drums.
8. The harp and flute weren't seen (nowhere, anywhere) until centuries later.
9. The zither (was, wasn't) heard nowhere before it was developed in China.
10. Hardly (no, any) ancient lyres are on public display.
11. If you haven't (ever, never) seen a lyre, try an art museum.
12. Some museums have collections of instruments that are rarely played (anymore, no more).
13. These collections have some instruments that can't be seen (nowhere, anywhere) else.

Writing Link

Imagine that you are the lead singer of a musical group. Describe the best performance that you ever gave. Make sure that you avoid using double negatives.

Grammar Workshop

Adjectives and Adverbs

During the 1600s Juan de Pareja became the slave of the great Spanish painter Diego Velázquez. *I, Juan de Pareja*, by Elizabeth Borton de Treviño, tells how the slave became the artist's friend and assistant. In this passage de Pareja explains his duties. The passage has been annotated to show some of the types of adjectives and adverbs covered in this unit.

Literature Model

from I, JUAN DE PAREJA

by Elizabeth Borton de Treviño

One by one, he taught me my duties. First, I had to learn to grind the colors. There were many mortars for **this** work, and pestles in varying sizes. I soon learned that the lumps of earth and metallic compounds had to be softly and **continuously** worked until there remained a powder as fine as the ground rice ladies used on their cheeks and foreheads. It took hours, and sometimes when I was sure the stuff was as fine as satin, Master would pinch and move it between his **sensitive** fingers and shake his head, and then I had to grind some more. Later **the** ground powder had to be incorporated into the oils, and well-mixed, and much later still, I arranged Master's palette for him, the little mounds of color each in its **fixed** place, and he had his preferences about how much of any one should be set out. And, of course, brushes were to be washed daily, in plenty of good **Castile** soap and water. Master's brushes all had to be clean and fresh every morning when he began to work.

Demonstrative adjective

Adverb

Adjective

Article

Past participle used as an adjective

Proper adjective

Grammar Workshop Exercise 1

Using Comparative and Superlative Adjectives
The following sentences are based on the passage from
I, Juan de Pareja. Rewrite each sentence, using the correct comparative or superlative form of the adjective as indicated in parentheses.

SAMPLE   De Pareja was (young) than Velázquez.

ANSWER   De Pareja was younger than Velázquez.

1. Juan de Pareja ground the colors until there remained only the (fine) powder.
2. The artist's fingers were (sensitive) than Juan's.
3. He used the mounds of color on his palette to create some of the (beautiful) paintings of all.
4. Every day Juan de Pareja made sure the artist's brushes were (clean) and (fresh) than Velázquez had left them.
5. Velázquez used the (good) materials he could.

Grammar Workshop Exercise 2

Using Comparative and Superlative Adverbs   The
following sentences are about Diego Velázquez. Rewrite each sentence, using the correct form of the adverb in parentheses.

1. Velázquez represented his subjects (realistically) than had many earlier artists.
2. Of all the techniques the artist's use of rich colors, light, and shadow (clearly) characterized his style.
3. Velázquez produced many works, but he painted portraits (frequently) of all.
4. He traveled (far) than many other artists of his day to study the art of ancient Rome.
5. Although many artists have imitated his style, Velázquez (heavily) influenced modern painters.

Distinguishing Between Adjectives and Adverbs
Rewrite each sentence, using the correct adjective or adverb in parentheses.

1. Velázquez and de Pareja became (good, well) friends.
2. Velázquez recognized his assistant's (real, really) love for art.
3. De Pareja had a (sure, surely) talent for painting.
4. Juan de Pareja served Velázquez (loyal, loyally) until the artist died.
5. The former slave became a (true, truly) artist himself.

Proofreading   The following passage is about Spanish artist Diego Velázquez, whose work appears on the next page. Rewrite the passage, correcting the errors in spelling, capitalization, punctuation, grammar, and usage. There are ten errors in all.

Diego Velázquez

[1]Diego Rodriguez de Silva y Velázquez (1599–1660) was born in Seville Spain. [2]As a young man he studied the style of italian artist Caravaggio, whose realistically figures were painted in contrasting light and dark tones. [3]In 1623 Velázquez becomes the official painter for Spain's King Philip IV. [4]However, the artist's portraits of the royal family seems more like pictures from a personal album then paintings advertising the power of Spain.
[5]In his portraits Veláquez also captures the personalities of her subjects. [6]In his portrat of Juan de Pareja, for example, Velázquez convey the intellagence and dignity of the man who became his lifelong friend.

Diego Velázquez, *Juan de Pareja,* **1650**

Unit 12 Review

Adjectives and Adverbs

Adjectives

[pages 412–419]

Write each sentence. Use the correct word or words given in parentheses. Underline the noun that each of those adjectives modifies.

1. Mary Cassatt was a famous (american, American) painter who spent much of her life living in France.
2. She painted domestic scenes with people in (familiar, familiarly) poses.
3. She shared with the famous French artist Edgar Degas (an, the) interest in Japanese prints.
4. For many artists color is the (most important, important) element of all.
5. (This, This here) artist depicts many different kinds of subjects.

Adverbs

[pages 420–425]

Write each sentence. Underline each adverb once and the word it describes twice.

6. Yehudi Menuhin is a very famous American violinist.
7. Among violinists he has one of the better developed techniques.
8. Menuhin has played well throughout a distinguished career.
9. In addition to his career as a violinist, Menuhin has received extremely good reviews for his conducting.
10. His quite successful career has spanned more than six decades.

Avoiding Double Negatives

[pages 426–427]

Write each sentence. Use the word or words that correctly complete the sentence.

11. Hardly (no one, anyone) is a better jazz singer than Ella Fitzgerald.
12. There (isn't, is) no singer with better voice control and tone.
13. She didn't have (no, any) hit songs until "A Tisket, a Tasket."
14. It seemed she couldn't (never, ever) be beaten in singing contests.
15. She (wasn't, was) barely twenty years old when she became a star.

Writing for Review

Imagine that you are a famous artist or musician. Write a paragraph in which you describe your childhood and how you decided on a career as an artist. Focus on the way in which your experience differed from that of the children with whom you grew up. Include adjectives and adverbs in your writing.

Prepositions, Conjunctions, and Interjections

André Derain, *Charing Cross Bridge*, 1906

13.1 Prepositions and Prepositional Phrases

A **preposition** is a word that relates a noun or a pronoun to some other word in a sentence.

> The boy **by** the window is French.

The word *by* in the sentence above is a preposition. *By* shows the relationship of the word *boy* to the noun *window*.

Commonly Used Prepositions				
about	before	during	off	to
above	behind	for	on	toward
across	below	from	onto	under
after	beneath	in	out	until
against	beside	inside	outside	up
along	between	into	over	upon
among	beyond	like	since	with
around	by	near	through	within
at	down	of	throughout	without

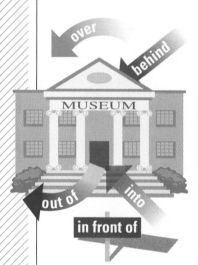

A preposition can consist of more than one word.

> Yasmin will visit Trinidad **instead of** Jamaica.

Compound Prepositions			
according to	aside from	in front of	instead of
across from	because of	in place of	on account of
along with	far from	in spite of	on top of

A **prepositional phrase** is a group of words that begins with a preposition and ends with a noun or pronoun, which is called the **object of the preposition**.

> The painting **near you** is **by a Brazilian artist**.

GRAMMAR HINT

A preposition is always the first word in a prepositional phrase. The preposition is always followed by a noun or a pronoun object.

Exercise 1

Identifying Prepositional Phrases and Objects of Prepositions   Underline each prepositional phrase. Draw a second line under the preposition, and circle the object of the preposition.

1. The Louvre is a famous museum in Paris.
2. Do you know the history of this stately building?
3. The Louvre was once a residence for royalty.
4. Then the royal family moved to Versailles.
5. The galleries throughout the Louvre contain paintings and sculpture.
6. A renovation of the Louvre is under way.
7. Paris, the French capital, is in northern France.
8. Vineyards stretch across the French countryside.
9. Picturesque old churches are scattered about the landscape.
10. Many harbors lie along the Atlantic and Mediterranean coasts.
11. The largest French port, Marseilles, is on the Mediterranean Sea.
12. Ferries travel across the English Channel.
13. The English held Calais for more than two centuries.
14. Many people enjoy winter sports in the French Alps.
15. Several resort cities cluster along the southern coast.
16. Most of the French kings were crowned at the cathedral in Reims.
17. Travelers to Europe will find many museums in London and Paris.

Writing Link

Describe some foreign-made products that you use regularly. For each, give the country of origin.

13.2 Pronouns as Objects of Prepositions

When a pronoun is the object of a preposition, remember to use an object pronoun and not a subject pronoun.

> Dan handed the tickets to Natalie. Dan handed the tickets to **her**.

In the example above, the object pronoun *her* replaces *Natalie* as the object of the preposition *to*.

Sometimes a preposition will have a compound object consisting of a noun and pronoun. Remember to use an object pronoun in a compound object.

> I borrowed the suitcase from Ivan and Vera. I borrowed the suitcase from Ivan and **her**.
>
> Natalie traveled with Ivan and **me**.

Object pronouns are used in the sentences above. In the second sentence *Ivan and her* is the compound object of the preposition *from*. In the third sentence *Ivan and me* is the compound object of the preposition *with*.

If you are unsure about whether to use a subject pronoun or an object pronoun, try saying the sentence aloud with only the pronoun following the preposition.

> I borrowed the suitcase from **her**.
> Natalie traveled with **me**.

The subject pronoun *who* is never the object of a preposition; only the object pronoun *whom* can be an object.

> The man **of whom** I spoke is from Colombia.
> To **whom** did you lend the guidebook?

Using Pronouns as Objects of Prepositions   Write each sentence, using the correct form of the pronoun in parentheses. Be sure each pronoun you choose makes sense in the sentence.

1. Carmen's aunt in Spain sent a post card to David and (her, she).
2. This is the aunt about (who, whom) Carmen and David have told us so much.
3. According to Carmen and (he, him), Spain is a great place to spend a vacation.
4. Carmen showed photographs of the Costa del Sol to Hector and (him, he).
5. There was also one of David and (her, she) in front of the Alhambra in Granada.
6. It was hard to distinguish between Carmen's cousin and (he, him); they look alike.
7. Aside from David, Carmen, and (he, him), no one in our class has been to Spain.
8. Everyone was impressed with the description of the Alcázar given by Carmen and (her, she).
9. Most of (they, them) had never even seen a castle like the Alcázar.
10. The Spanish lived alongside (them, they) for centuries.
11. The strong North African influences were described by David and (she, her).

Writing Link

In a paragraph describe the most interesting place you have visited. Use pronouns as objects of prepositions in your writing.

13.3 Prepositional Phrases as Adjectives and Adverbs

An **adjective phrase** is a prepositional phrase that modifies, or describes, a noun or pronoun.

> A temple **of great size** stands here.
>
> I noticed some men **with heavy suitcases**.

In the first sentence above, the prepositional phrase *of great size* modifies the subject of the sentence, *temple*. In the second sentence the prepositional phrase *with heavy suitcases* describes a noun in the predicate, *men*.

Notice that, unlike most adjectives, an adjective phrase usually comes after the word it modifies.

An **adverb phrase** is a prepositional phrase that modifies, or describes, a verb, an adjective, or another adverb.

Adverb Phrases Modifying a Verb, an Adjective, and an Adverb	
Describes a verb	The tourists travel **in a group**.
Describes an adjective	The temple is stunning **from this view**.
Describes an adverb	It has held up well **for its age**.

An adverb phrase tells *when*, *where*, or *how* an action occurs.

How Adverb Phrases Function	
When?	They left the hotel **in the morning**.
Where?	The excited visitors went **to Japan**.
How?	The large group traveled **by airplane**.

Exercise 3

Identifying Adjective and Adverb Phrases   Write each sentence. Underline each prepositional phrase, and write whether it is an *adjective phrase* or an *adverb phrase*.

1. Most people in Japan follow the traditional customs of their country.
2. The Japanese traditionally bow on certain occasions.
3. They show great respect for their elders.
4. Throughout their history the Japanese have also loved beauty.
5. Their gardens are models of grace and delicacy.
6. Japanese gardens are exceptional in their harmony.
7. Artificial and natural elements blend together as one in their gardens.
8. Soft woven mats cover the floors of many Japanese homes.
9. People customarily wear comfortable slippers inside their homes.
10. The guests of a family receive much kindness and consideration.
11. People sometimes cook on small charcoal stoves.
12. They often prepare bowls of noodles.
13. Diners frequently sit around very low tables.
14. Many Japanese people eat with chopsticks.
15. Hosts serve small cups of fragrant tea.
16. A guide translates the language with care.

GRAMMAR HINT

Adverb phrases can usually be moved to the beginning of the sentence.

Writing Link

Describe the room in your house you like being in the most. Use as many adjective and adverb phrases as you can to explain what makes it so special.

13.4 Conjunctions

A **coordinating conjunction** is a single word used to connect parts of a sentence, such as words or phrases. *And*, *but*, *or*, *for*, and *nor* are coordinating conjunctions.

Using Coordinating Conjunctions	
Compound Subject	Allison **and** Rosita have lived in Mexico City.
Compound Predicate	Tourists shop **or** relax on the beaches.
Compound Object of a Preposition	Amiri went to Brazil **and** Peru.
Compound Sentence	Tom shopped every day, **but** we toured.

To make the relationship between words or groups of words especially strong, use a correlative conjunction.

Correlative conjunctions are pairs of words used to connect words or phrases in a sentence. Correlative conjunctions include *both . . . and*, *either . . . or*, *neither . . . nor*, and *not only . . . but also*.

> Examples of great architecture exist in **both** New York **and** Paris.

When a compound subject is joined by the conjunction *and*, it is a plural subject. The verb must agree with the plural subject.

When a compound subject is joined by *or* or *nor*, the verb must agree with the nearest part of the subject.

> Winema **and** Tanya **are** in Madrid this week.
> Neither the twins **nor** Ann **is** studying Spanish.

GRAMMAR HINT

Coordinating conjunctions always join elements of the same kind—subject with subject, sentence with sentence, or verb with verb.

Exercise 4

Identifying Conjunctions   Underline each conjunction. Write whether it forms a *compound subject*, a *compound predicate*, a *compound object of a preposition*, or a *compound sentence*.

1. Our teacher traveled to France and toured Paris.
2. The tour took a long time, but it was fascinating.
3. A cathedral or a museum in France may be very old.
4. Visitors spend hours in the bookstores and galleries.

Exercise 5

Making Compound Subjects and Verbs Agree
Write each sentence, using the correct verb form. Underline each coordinating or correlative conjunction.

1. An auto or a train (is, are) the best transportation for tourists.
2. Neither our teacher nor her companions (speaks, speak) French.
3. Both a subway and a bus system (serves, serve) Paris.
4. Either a taxi or a subway train (is, are) quick.
5. Two buses and a train (goes, go) to the Eiffel Tower.
6. Sometimes musicians and jugglers (performs, perform) in the subway stations in Paris.
7. Neither the Royal Palace nor the Louvre (is, are) open.
8. Both the Left and the Right banks of the Seine (is, are) parts of Paris.

Writing Link

In a paragraph describe the advantages of living where you do. Note the conjunctions you use.

13.5   Conjunctive Adverbs

You can use a special kind of adverb instead of a coordinating or correlative conjunction to join the simple sentences in a compound sentence.

Many Asians use chopsticks, **but** some use forks.
Many Asians use chopsticks; **however**, some use forks.

Conjunctive adverbs, such as *however* in the sentence above, are usually stronger and more precise than coordinating conjunctions.

A **conjunctive adverb** may be used to join the simple sentences in a compound sentence.

Using Conjunctive Adverbs	
To replace *and*	also, besides, furthermore, moreover
To replace *but*	however, nevertheless, still
To state a result	consequently, therefore, so, thus
To state equality	equally, likewise, similarly

When two simple sentences are joined with a conjunctive adverb, a semicolon always appears before the second sentence. The conjunctive adverb can appear at the beginning, at the end, or in the middle of the second sentence. When it comes at the beginning or end, it is set off with a comma. When it appears in the middle, one comma precedes it, and one follows it.

Chinese people often stir-fry their food; **therefore,** they must cut it into very small pieces.
Stir-frying should be done quickly; the wok must be very hot, **therefore.**
Vegetables cook more quickly than meat; they must, **therefore,** be cooked last.

GRAMMAR HINT

Unlike conjunctions—but like adverbs—conjunctive adverbs can be moved around within the simple sentence.

Exercise 6

Identifying Conjunctive Adverbs   Write each sentence. Underline each conjunctive adverb, and add any needed punctuation.

1. People in different lands often have different eating styles moreover they may use different utensils.
2. Many people in India use bread as a scoop however some use a fork.
3. Chinese cooks cut meat into bite-size pieces similarly they chop or slice most vegetables.
4. Food is bite-size thus a knife isn't needed.
5. Europeans may push their food onto the fork consequently they hold both the knife and the fork while eating.

Exercise 7

Using Conjunctive Adverbs   Write each sentence, filling the blank with a conjunctive adverb that makes sense.

1. Cuisines differ from country to country; _____, they often feature similar dishes.
2. France is rich in dairy products; _____, French cooks use cream and cheese.
3. Indian food is sometimes vegetarian; _____, it is often spicy.
4. Rice is a staple of Chinese cooking; _____, it is a staple of Japanese cooking.

Writing Link

Describe the cuisines that have gone into the melting pot of American cooking. Make sure to use conjunctive adverbs.

13.6 Interjections

Sometimes people express very strong feelings in a short exclamation that may not be a complete sentence. These exclamations are called interjections.

An **interjection** is a word or group of words that expresses strong feeling. It has no grammatical connection to any other words in the sentence.

Interjections are used to express strong feelings, such as surprise or disbelief. They are also used to attract attention.

Any part of speech can be used as an interjection. Some of the more common interjections are listed below.

Common Interjections			
aha	good grief	oh	well
alas	ha	oh, no	what
awesome	hey	oops	whoops
come on	hooray	ouch	wow
gee	look	phew	yes

An interjection that expresses a very strong feeling may stand alone either before or after a sentence. Such interjections are followed by an exclamation mark.

> We are taking a boat ride around Venice. **Hooray!**

When an interjection expresses a milder feeling, it appears as part of the sentence. It is separated from the rest of the sentence by a comma.

> **Wow**, that view of the skyline is spectacular.

You use interjections frequently when you speak. You should use them sparingly when you write, however. Overusing them will spoil their effectiveness.

Identifying Interjections   Write the sentences below, adding punctuation where needed. Underline the interjection in each sentence.

1. Wow Doesn't Venice, Italy, have a lot of canals!
2. Imagine There are hardly any cars in Venice.
3. The city is built upon nearly 120 islands. Phew.
4. Alas we won't have time to visit every island.
5. There's a candy-striped pole up ahead. Oh, no
6. My goodness that was close.
7. Oops Look out for that gondola on your left.
8. Psst what is that bridge?
9. It is the famous Rialto Bridge. Yippee
10. No kidding Shall we visit it after lunch?
11. Good grief I can't believe I lost my camera.
12. Did you visit the Galleria dell'Accademia? Awesome
13. Come on There's a great outdoor restaurant very near the museum.
14. Hey Did you notice how the narrow, winding streets usually lead to a large, airy plaza?
15. Gee did you realize that the Grand Canal is so long?
16. Is rain in the forecast? Ugh
17. Hey the water is rough in this canal.
18. Eek Don't tip us over.
19. Oh, no Don't stand up in the gondola.
20. Whee Let's spend the whole day on this gondola.
21. Oh boy We are going to be spending the afternoon at the Lido.

Writing Link

Write a paragraph about the last time you went to an amusement park. Use some interjections.

13.7   Finding All the Parts of Speech

Each word in a sentence performs a particular job. Each word can be put into a category called a **part of speech**. The part of speech of a word depends on the job the word performs in the sentence. You have learned all eight parts of speech. The sentence below contains an example of each.

> Gee, Venice is astonishingly beautiful, and it has stunning architecture in every quarter.

Parts of Speech		
Word	**Part of Speech**	**Function**
Gee	Interjection	Expresses strong feeling
Venice	Proper noun	Names a specific thing
is	Linking verb	Links *Venice* with the adjective *beautiful*
astonishingly	Adverb	Describes the adjective *beautiful*
beautiful	Adjective	Describes the subject *Venice*
and	Conjunction	Joins two simple sentences
it	Pronoun	Takes the place of a noun
has	Action verb	Names an action
stunning	Adjective	Describes the object, *architecture*
architecture	Common noun	Names a thing
in	Preposition	Relates *architecture* and *quarter*
every	Adjective	Describes the noun *quarter*
quarter	Common noun	Names a thing

Identifying Parts of Speech   Write each underlined word and its part of speech.

1. Moira often <u>travels</u> to <u>foreign</u> countries.
2. <u>In</u> June <u>she</u> will go to Chile.
3. She <u>is</u> <u>especially</u> fond of Greece.
4. <u>Spain</u> is also close to her <u>heart</u>.
5. Next year she <u>plans</u> to visit Japan <u>and</u> Taiwan.
6. New Zealand is <u>also</u> on her list. <u>Wow</u>!

Using Parts of Speech   Complete each sentence below by supplying a word whose part of speech is indicated in parentheses. Be sure your finished sentences make sense.

1. Tony (conjunction) Sadie have been to more (common noun) than any other people I know.
2. (Pronoun) visited (proper noun) last year.
3. (Preposition) January they will (action verb) to Israel and Egypt.
4. Tony thought Portugal (linking verb) (adjective).
5. Tony has been to (correlative conjunction) Turkey (correlative conjunction) Hungary.
6. He has (negative adverb) been to Asia; Sadie, (conjunctive adverb), has been to China twice and Japan three times.

Writing Link

Describe a vacation that you would like to take. Use all the parts of speech in your description of this dream vacation.

Grammar Workshop

Prepositions, Conjunctions, and Interjections

On a Caribbean island a young girl discovers the boat of Christopher Columbus. The passage is annotated to show some of the concepts covered in this unit.

Literature Model

from MORNING GIRL

by Michael Dorris

Preposition

Prepositional phrase (adverb phrase)

Coordinating conjunction

Prepositional phrase (adjective phrase)

Preposition of more than one word

Interjection

Noun as object of preposition

I forgot I was still beneath the surface until I needed air. But when I broke into the sunlight , the water sparkling all around me, the noise turned out to be nothing! Only a canoe! The breathing was the dip of many paddles! It was only *people* coming to visit, and since I could see they hadn't painted themselves to appear fierce, they must be friendly or lost.

   I swam closer to get a better look and had to stop myself from laughing. The strangers had wrapped every part of their bodies with colorful leaves and cotton. Some had decorated their faces with fur and wore shiny rocks on their heads. Compared to us, they were very round. Their canoe was short and square, and, in spite of all their dipping and pulling, it moved so slowly. What a backward, distant island they must have come from. But really , to laugh at guests, no matter how odd, would be impolite, especially since I was the first to meet them. If I was foolish, they would think they had arrived at a foolish place .

Identifying Adjective and Adverb Phrases Write
each sentence. Underline each prepositional phrase, and
write whether it is an *adjective phrase* or an *adverb phrase*.

SAMPLE She splashed through the surf.

ANSWER She splashed <u>through the surf</u>. (adverb phrase)

1. Morning Girl dove into the water without looking.
2. In the distance she heard an unfamiliar sound.
3. The strangers were wrapped in leaves and cotton.
4. Some wore shiny rocks on their heads.
5. Morning Girl swam boldly toward the exotic visitors
   from a distant place.

Identifying Conjunctions Write each sentence.
Underline each conjunction, and write whether it forms a
*compound subject, compound predicate, compound
object of a preposition,* or *compound sentence.*

SAMPLE Their canoe was square, and it was shorter
        than any other canoes she had ever seen.

ANSWER Their canoe was square, <u>and</u> it was shorter
        than any other canoes she had ever seen.
        (compound sentence)

1. She wanted to laugh, but she knew that would be
   impolite.
2. Morning Girl approached the strangers and called
   out a greeting.
3. The strangers either had come to visit or were lost.
4. In spite of all their dipping and pulling, the canoe
   moved very slowly.
5. Morning Girl and her brother Star Boy often played
   together.

Using Conjunctive Adverbs   Substitute the conjunctive adverb in parentheses for each of the underlined conjunctions. Then write each compound sentence. Be sure to punctuate the resulting sentences correctly.

SAMPLE   Morning Girl swam near the ship, <u>but</u> the crew members didn't see her. (although)

ANSWER   Although Morning Girl swam near the ship, the crew didn't see her.

1. She had never seen people dressed as they were, <u>and</u> she didn't know what to make of them. (furthermore)
2. Star Boy collected shells, <u>but</u> he lost them all in a storm. (however)
3. Morning Girl was hot <u>and</u> she swam. (so)
4. The strangers were oddly dressed, <u>and</u> she thought they must have come from a backward island. (therefore)
5. Morning Girl knew it was impolite to laugh at strangers, <u>and</u> Morning Girl didn't want them to think she was foolish. (besides)

Proofreading   The following passage is about the American artist Nereyda García-Ferraz, whose work appears on the opposite page. Rewrite the passage, correcting the errors in spelling, capitalization, punctuation, grammar, and usage. There are ten errors in all.

Nereyda García-Ferraz

[1] Nereyda García-Ferraz was born in Havana, Cuba in 1954. [2] She immigrated to the United States when she was 17.

[3] García-Ferraz draws on her experiences living in a foreign land for many of her work. [4] She paints in a traditional style, using images that has specific ➡

meanings and who often tell a story when they are viewed as a whole.

[5]A painting on this page be titled *Sin Oir—Sin Ver,* which in english means "Without Hearing—Without Seeing." [6] The word in the middle of the painting, on the bottom, *nadabas,* refers to swimming. [7] The use of words, as well as the bright colors, are charateristic of her work. García-Ferraz blends emotion and intellect to produce finished works of art.

Nereyda García-Ferraz, *Without Hearing—Without Seeing,* 1991

Prepositions, Conjunctions, and Interjections

Prepositions and Prepositional Phrases

[pages 434–439]

Underline each prepositional phrase, and write whether it is an *adverb phrase* or an *adjective phrase*. Circle the preposition, and draw a second line under the object of the preposition.

1. Paris is a center of fashion.
2. Many well-known clothes designers work in Paris.
3. Parisian models often work late into the night.
4. Paris is beautiful in the spring.
5. Parisian fashion trends are of interest to my friends and me.

Conjunctions and Conjunctive Adverbs

[pages 440–443]

Underline each connecting word, and write whether it is a *coordinating conjunction*, a *correlative conjunction*, or a *conjunctive adverb*.

6. She has visited Mexico twice but has never been to Mexico City.
7. Both Mexico's beaches and its Aztec ruins are famous.

8. Spanish and many Native American languages are spoken in Mexico.
9. Many languages are spoken in Mexico, and communication can be difficult.
10. Traveling in Mexico is inexpensive; you should go there soon, therefore.

Interjections; Parts of Speech

[pages 444–447]

Identify the part of speech of each underlined word.

11. Next week <u>we</u> are leaving <u>for</u> the Swiss Alps.
12. My, the airline tickets are <u>certainly</u> <u>expensive</u>.
13. Goodness! The cable car <u>ride</u> up the mountain <u>is</u> frightening.
14. <u>Hey</u>, did you catch a glimpse of the <u>Matterhorn</u>?
15. Switzerland <u>has</u> the world's longest road tunnel <u>and</u> its longest stairway.

Writing for Review

Imagine that you are a tourist in Italy. Write a paragraph describing what you would like to see first. Then note the different parts of speech you have used.

UNIT 14

Clauses and Complex Sentences

Thomas Eakins, *Baseball Players Practicing*, 1875

453

14.1 Sentences and Clauses

A **sentence** is a group of words that expresses a complete thought.

A **simple sentence** has one complete subject and one complete predicate.

The **complete subject** names whom or what the sentence is about. The **complete predicate** tells what the subject does or has. Sometimes it tells what the subject is or is like.

Complete Subject	Complete Predicate
The Cincinnati Reds	played their first baseball game in 1869.
This Ohio team	was the first professional baseball team.
The American League	played its first games in 1901.

A **compound sentence** is a sentence that contains two or more simple sentences. Each simple sentence is called a main clause.

A **main clause** has a subject and a predicate and can stand alone as a sentence.

In the compound sentences below, each main clause is in black; the connecting elements are highlighted in red.

Abner Doubleday supposedly invented baseball, but some reject this claim.

Alexander Joy Cartwright established rules; he was a good organizer.

Cartwright improved the game; moreover, many now regard him as the inventor of modern baseball.

Cartwright set up a game in 1846, and eighteen men played.

A comma precedes the conjunction in a compound sentence. A semicolon joins the two main clauses if they are not joined by a conjunction. A semicolon also precedes a conjunctive adverb, such as *moreover*.

Exercise 1

Identifying Simple and Compound Sentences

Identify each sentence as *simple* or *compound*.

1. Alexander Cartwright wrote rules for the Knickerbocker Baseball Club.
2. The first modern baseball game took place in 1846.
3. One team brought the ball, and the other team provided the field.
4. Pitchers threw underhand, but their pitches were slow.
5. The game ended; two men were on third base.
6. The winners were the New York Nines.

Exercise 2

Punctuating Simple and Compound Sentences

Write each sentence, and underline each main clause. Add a comma or a semicolon as needed.

1. Historians have theories about the origin of baseball however, the truth remains a mystery.
2. Did baseball begin as rounders or did it come from cricket?
3. The British played rounders in the early nineteenth century.
4. Cartwright established the rules but Henry Chadwick improved them.
5. Baseball has many serious and devoted fans.

Writing Link

Imagine that you're in spring training for the baseball season. Using simple and compound sentences, describe your practice activities.

14.2　Complex Sentences

A **main clause** has a subject and a predicate and can stand alone as a sentence.

Sometimes sentences have more than one clause, and only one of the clauses is a main clause. The other clause is a subordinate clause.

A **subordinate clause** is a group of words that has a subject and a predicate but does not express a complete thought and cannot stand alone as a sentence. It is always combined with a main clause.

A sentence with a main clause and a subordinate clause is a complex sentence. In each complex sentence below, the main clause is in light type, and the subordinate clause is in dark type.

> Basketball has increased in popularity **since it began in Springfield, Massachusetts.**
> Many basketball fans visit Springfield, **which was the birthplace of basketball.**
> Many people know **that basketball is played by men and women.**

A **complex sentence** is a sentence that has a main clause and one or more subordinate clauses.

Subordinate clauses can function in three ways: as adjectives, as adverbs, or as nouns. In the examples above, the first sentence has an adverb clause that modifies the verb *has increased,* the second has an adjective clause that modifies the noun *Springfield,* and the third has a noun clause that is the direct object of the verb *know.* Such clauses can be used in the same ways that adjectives, adverbs, and nouns are used.

The team waits on the sidelines, **while the substitute warms the bench.**

MAIN CLAUSE　　SUBORDINATE CLAUSE

Exercise 3

Identifying Complex Sentences Write each sentence, and underline the main clause. Then identify each sentence as *complex* or *not complex*.

1. Professional basketball is played during the winter, which was once a dull season for sports.
2. James Naismith developed the game because he saw the need for an indoor sport.
3. A soccer ball was the ball that was first used.
4. The rules of the game were drafted in 1891.
5. Do the rules of the game change when men and women play basketball together?
6. Although the rules for men's and women's basketball are similar, the ball is different.
7. The referee tosses the ball into the air.
8. After the referee tosses the ball, one player from each team jumps within the center circle.
9. Each player tries for the ball.
10. When a team scores, the opposing team takes the ball out of bounds from behind the base line.
11. That team then moves the ball toward the basket that is at the other end of the court.
12. A special excitement belongs to basketball, which is a fast-moving game.
13. Basketball has won many young fans who are dedicated basketball enthusiasts.
14. Many players who are popular have fan clubs.

Writing Link

Imagine that you are watching the first basketball game. In a letter to a friend, describe the game. Use some complex sentences in your letter.

14.3 Adjective Clauses

Sometimes a subordinate clause acts as an adjective.

The aqualung, **which divers strap on,** holds oxygen.

The divers breathe through a tube **that attaches to the tank.**

Each subordinate clause in dark type in these sentences is an adjective clause. An adjective clause adds information about a noun or pronoun in the main clause.

An **adjective clause** is a subordinate clause that modifies, or describes, a noun or pronoun in the main clause of a complex sentence.

An adjective clause is usually introduced by a relative pronoun. Relative pronouns signal that a clause is a subordinate clause and cannot stand alone.

Relative Pronouns			
that	who	whose	what
which	whom	whoever	

An adjective clause can also begin with *where* or *when*.

Divers search for reefs **where much sea life exists.**

A relative pronoun that begins an adjective clause can be the subject of the clause.

Some divers prefer equipment **that is light in weight.**
Willa is a new diver **who is taking lessons.**

In the first sentence above, *that* is the subject of the adjective clause. In the second sentence *who* is the subject of the adjective clause.

Identifying Adjective Clauses   Write each sentence. Underline each adjective clause once and each relative pronoun twice. Circle the noun that each adjective clause modifies.

1. Scuba equipment, which is used for deep diving, gets its name from the term *self-contained underwater breathing apparatus.*
2. Jacques Cousteau, who is famous for underwater exploration, designed the aqualung.
3. Divers sometimes wear weights that strap on.
4. Divers often wear wet suits and rubber fins, which are standard diving equipment.
5. Diving methods, which are now advanced, allow close observation of sea life.
6. Alexander the Great, who lived in the fourth century B.C., used a barrel for diving.
7. Diving bells were the earliest containers that were reliable.
8. The diving bells, which were used in the 1500s, were quite large.
9. Auguste Piccard designed the bathyscaph, which is a diving vehicle.
10. Jacques Piccard, who is Auguste's son, wanted to explore the Gulf Stream.
11. The Gulf Stream, which is a warm undersea water current, flows through the Atlantic Ocean.

Writing Link

Imagine that you are scuba diving in the ocean. Using some adjective clauses, write a paragraph describing your underwater adventure.

14.4 Essential and Nonessential Clauses

Read the sentence below. Is the adjective clause in dark type needed to make the meaning of the sentence clear?

> The woman **who is near the pool** is a good swimmer.

The swimmer **who is in lane six** won last time.

The adjective clause here is essential, or necessary, to the meaning of the sentence. It describes the particular woman who is a good swimmer.

An **essential clause** is an adjective clause that is necessary to make the meaning of the sentence clear. Do not use commas to set off an essential clause from the rest of the sentence.

Notice the adjective clauses in the sentences below.

Our team, **which is undefeated,** is favored to win the championship.

> Swimmers enjoy the pool, **which is extremely clean.**
> The pool, **which is open all week,** is never crowded.

In the sentences above, the adjective clauses are set off by commas. The clauses are nonessential, or not necessary, to the meaning of the sentences. The clauses give only additional information about the nouns that they modify.

A **nonessential clause** is an adjective clause that is not necessary to make the meaning of the sentence clear. Use commas to set off a nonessential clause from the rest of the sentence.

One way to tell whether some clauses are essential or nonessential is to look at the first word. A clause that begins with *which* is usually nonessential. One that begins with *that* is essential.

> Did you see the meet **that** our team won yesterday?
> The meet, **which** began late, ended well after dark.

Exercise 5

Identifying Essential and Nonessential Clauses
Write each sentence, and underline each adjective clause.
Identify the adjective clause as *essential* or *nonessential*.

1. The athletes whom I most admire are swimmers.
2. Our women's team, whose record stands, enters.
3. The contestants who are in blue will swim first.
4. The signal that starts each race is a gunshot.
5. Our school, which has an excellent swimming coach, has a statewide reputation.

Exercise 6

Punctuating Essential and Nonessential Clauses
Write each sentence, and underline each adjective clause.
Identify each clause as *essential* or *nonessential,* and add commas as needed.

1. In the 1800s the Australian crawl which replaced the breast stroke in popularity came into use.
2. In the 1920s Johnny Weissmuller whose other career was acting in movies perfected the front crawl.
3. Weissmuller was the athlete who set sixty-five United States and world records.
4. In 1968 Jim Counsilman studied techniques that swimmers were using.
5. Counsilman whose observations were later published became a world-famous coach.

Writing Link

Imagine taking a swimming lesson. Write a paragraph about what you think the lesson would be like. Use essential and nonessential clauses.

GRAMMAR HINT

Nonessential clauses are like nonessential appositives. They give extra information about the nouns they follow, and they are set off with commas.

Essential and Nonessential Clauses **461**

14.5   Adverb Clauses

Sometimes a subordinate clause is an adverb clause. It may add information about the verb in the main clause. An adverb clause tells *how, when, where, why,* or *under what conditions* the action occurs.

After she bought safe equipment, Lee explored the undersea world.

Scuba divers wear tanks **because they cannot breathe underwater.**

In the first sentence above, the adverb clause *After she bought safe equipment* modifies the verb *explored.* The adverb clause tells *when* Lee explored the undersea world. In the second sentence the adverb clause *because they cannot breathe underwater* modifies the verb *wear.* The adverb clause tells *why* scuba divers wear tanks.

An **adverb clause** is a subordinate clause that often modifies, or describes, the verb in the main clause of a complex sentence.

An adverb clause is introduced by a subordinating conjunction. Subordinating conjunctions signal that a clause is a subordinate clause and cannot stand alone.

Subordinating Conjunctions			
after	before	though	whenever
although	if	unless	where
as	since	until	whereas
because	than	when	wherever

You usually do not use a comma before an adverb clause that comes at the end of a sentence. When an adverb clause introduces a sentence, however, you do use a comma after the adverb clause.

Identifying Adverb Clauses   Write each sentence. Underline each adverb clause once and each subordinating conjunction twice. Circle the verb that each adverb clause modifies.

1. Divers wear wet suits and rubber fins when they swim.
2. They wear wet suits because the water may be cold.
3. After you dive for the first time, you will have more confidence.
4. Divers wear weighted belts when they want to stay underwater for a long time.
5. When divers return to the surface, they should rise slowly and carefully.
6. Interest in the deep seas began when Alexander the Great first went diving.
7. He sat inside a glass barrel as sailors lowered it into the sea.
8. Jacques Piccard designed an underwater craft before he began exploration of the Gulf Stream.
9. Divers can suffer the bends when they rise to the surface too quickly.
10. Because this condition can occur, divers must learn how to control the ascent.
11. Although divers naturally want to reach the surface quickly, they learn to surface slowly.
12. Divers should work with partners when they are diving in unfamiliar waters.

Writing Link

Imagine that you are Alexander the Great. Write a journal entry about your first dive. Use some adverb clauses in your writing.

14.6 Noun Clauses

Subordinate clauses often function as adjectives or adverbs in sentences. Subordinate clauses can also act as nouns. Notice how the noun in dark type in the sentence below can be replaced by a clause.

> **Players** must skate extremely well.
> **Whoever plays ice hockey** must skate extremely well.

The clause in dark type, like the noun it replaces, is the subject of the sentence. Since this kind of clause acts as a noun, it is called a noun clause.

A **noun clause** is a subordinate clause used as a noun.

You can use a noun clause in the same ways that you can use a noun—as a subject, a direct object, an object of a preposition, or a predicate noun. Notice in each sentence below that you could replace the noun clause with the word *it*, and the sentence would still make sense.

How Noun Clauses Are Used	
Subject	**What makes ice hockey exciting** is the speed.
Direct Object	Players know **that the game can be dangerous.**
Object of a Preposition	Victory goes to **whoever makes more goals.**
Predicate Noun	This rink is **where the teams will play.**

Some of the words that can introduce noun clauses are given in the chart below.

Words That Introduce Noun Clauses		
how, however	where	whose
that	which, whichever	why
what, whatever	who, whom	
when	whoever, whomever	

Exercise 8

Identifying Noun Clauses   Write each sentence, and underline each noun clause.

1. That ice hockey began in Canada is not surprising.
2. The fact is that Canadians are still among the best hockey players.
3. There have been some changes in how ice hockey is played.
4. Whoever plays hockey today must wear protective equipment.
5. Do you know which sport is most dangerous?
6. Some people question whether hockey has to be so dangerous.

Exercise 9

Identifying Noun Clauses   Write each noun clause, and label it *subject, direct object, object of a preposition,* or *predicate noun.*

1. Most people know that ice hockey is a game of action.
2. Players must respond quickly to whatever happens.
3. Fast starts, stops, and turns are what the game demands.
4. What the players pursue is the puck.
5. The goalies know that their role is critical.
6. How players respond can be crucial to the game.

GRAMMAR HINT
You can usually replace a noun clause with a pronoun: *He knows* that he should go. *He knows* it.

Writing Link

Imagine that you're watching a hockey game. Write a paragraph describing what you might see and hear. Include some noun clauses.

Grammar Workshop

Clauses and Complex Sentences

In this passage from "The Education of a Baseball Player,"
New York Yankee outfielder Mickey Mantle tells of his weaknesses in playing the field. The passage has been annotated to
show some of the clauses and the sentences covered in this unit.

Literature Model

from THE EDUCATION OF A BASEBALL PLAYER

by Mickey Mantle

Main clause — My fielding, I knew, was often sorry. I had learned
to charge a ground ball well and if I could get an angle
on a ball, I could field it cleanly and get off a fast throw.
My arm was unusually strong, and my throws would
really hum across the diamond. But when a ball came

Complex sentence — straight at me, I was often undone. Somehow it was
almost impossible for me to judge the speed or the
bounce of a ground ball like that. I might back off fool-
ishly, letting the ball play me, and then lose it altogether.

Adverb clause — Or I would turn my head as it reached me, and the ball
would skip by or bounce right into my face. I carried

Simple sentence — around uncounted fat lips in that day from stopping
ground balls with my mouth. And the more often I got
hit, the more I would shy at such a ball. Even the balls I
fielded cleanly did not always mean an out, for I had a
habit of rejoicing so in the strength of my arm that I
would not take the time to get a sure eye on the target.

Compound sentence — I would just let fly with my full strength, and often the
ball would sail untouched into the stands.

Grammar Workshop Exercise 1

Identifying Compound Sentences Write each sentence. Indicate whether the sentence is *simple* or *compound.* If it is compound, underline each main clause. Add commas where needed.

1. As a young boy Mantle frequently played ball from morning to night.
2. His father gave him a professional-model baseball glove for Christmas one year and he cared for it devotedly.
3. Mantle considered himself the worst player on his team.
4. His fielding was erratic and other boys hit better than he did.
5. As a player Mantle was known for not only his powerful hitting but his fast running as well.

Grammar Workshop Exercise 2

Identifying Essential and Nonessential Clauses Write each sentence. Underline each adjective clause. Write whether the clause is *essential* or *nonessential.* Add commas where needed.

1. Mickey was named after the catcher Mickey Cochrane who made it into the Hall of Fame.
2. Mantle's father who worked in the lead mines had played amateur and semipro ball.
3. The baseball glove that his father gave him for Christmas one year cost twenty-two dollars.
4. Mantle who was named the Most Valuable Player three times also played in sixteen All-Star games.
5. Mantle hit 536 home runs during the years that he played with the Yankees.

Grammar Workshop Exercise 3

Identifying Adverb Clauses   Write each sentence. Underline the adverb clause, and circle the word that the clause modifies. Add commas where needed.

SAMPLE   When Mantle joined the Yankees Casey Stengel was the manager.

ANSWER   <u>When Mantle joined the Yankees</u>, Casey Stengel (was) the manager.

1. Mantle considered himself lucky because his father pushed and encouraged him.
2. Mantle was only nineteen years old when the Yankees signed him.
3. Before he joined the Yankees he spent a couple of years in the minor leagues.
4. While he played for the Yankees they were the dominant team in baseball.
5. Mantle was elected to the Hall of Fame as soon as he became eligible.

Grammar Workshop Exercise 4

Proofreading   The following passage is about the American artist Morris Kantor, whose work appears on the opposite page. Rewrite the passage, correcting the errors in spelling, capitalization, punctuation, grammar, and usage. There are ten errors in all.

Morris Kantor

[1]Morris Kantor was an American painter who living during the early part of this century. [2]He came to that country in 1911, and later studied art in New York and Paris.

[3]The painting on the oposite page was done during the Great Depression of the 1930s . [4]*Baseball at night* show a group of Americans from a small town enjoying a game of semiprofessional baseball. [5]Mickey Mantle's ➡

father, Mutt Mantle was playing baseball at about the same time and probably under similar conditions.

[6]Mickey Mantle became a National hero in part because he came from the world of small towns and sandlot baseball that Kantor depict in *Baseball at Night*.

Morris Kantor, *Baseball at Night,* **1934**

Unit 14 Review

Clauses and Complex Sentences

Sentences and Clauses; Complex Sentences

[pages 454–457]

Write each sentence. Write whether it is *simple, compound,* or *complex.* If it is a compound or complex sentence, underline each main clause.

1. The game boccie has been popular since ancient peoples created it.
2. The English developed their version of the game in the 1100s.
3. Germans later created a similar game; they called it *keglers.*
4. Because it can be played anywhere, boccie is a flexible game.
5. The game's playing area has boarded sides and ends.

Adjective, Adverb, and Noun Clauses

[pages 458–459; 462–465]

Write each sentence. Underline each subordinate clause, and write whether it is an *adjective clause,* an *adverb clause,* or a *noun clause.*

6. Fishing is a sport that is popular.
7. People use rods that have bait on the end of the line.
8. They dangle the line in the water while they wait for hungry fish.

9. When people fish in salt water, they use heavy rods, which can bear the weight of large fish.
10. Are there places where the fish are plentiful?

Essential and Nonessential Clauses

[pages 460–461]

Write each sentence. Draw a line under the adjective clause, and write whether it is *essential* or *nonessential.* Add commas as needed.

11. Games that challenge the mind are both fun and educational.
12. Board games which are among the most popular kinds of games are of extremely ancient origin.
13. Since chess is a game of strategy, the winner is usually the one who can plan far ahead.
14. Checkers which many people play has relatively easy rules.
15. Checkers is played on a board that has red and black squares.

Writing for Review

Make up a game. Use each kind of subordinate clause: adjective, adverb, and noun. Include a brief description of your game's rules.

Robert Delaunay, *The Team from Cardiff*, 1913

15.1 Participles and Participial Phrases

A present participle is formed by adding *-ing* to the verb. A past participle is usually formed by adding *-ed* to the verb. Sometimes a participle acts as the main verb in a verb phrase or as an adjective to describe, or modify, nouns or pronouns.

> The player has **kicked** the ball. [main verb in a verb phrase]
> The **kicked** ball soared. [adjective modifying *ball*]

Sometimes a participle that is used as an adjective is part of a phrase. This kind of phrase is called a participial phrase.

> **Cheering for the home team,** the fans were on their feet.
> The ball **kicked by Donnell** soared over the goal post.

A **participial phrase** is a group of words that includes a participle and other words that complete its meaning.

A participial phrase that is placed at the beginning of a sentence is always set off with a comma.

> **Running for the ball,** a player slipped in the mud.

Other participial phrases may or may not need commas. If the phrase is necessary to identify the modified word, it should not be set off with commas. If the phrase simply gives additional information about the modified word, it should be set off with commas.

> The player **kicking the ball** is Donnell.
> Donnell, **kicking the ball,** scored the extra point.

A participial phrase can appear before or after the word it describes. Place the phrase as close as possible to the modified word; otherwise, the meaning of the sentence may be unclear.

The **kicked** ball soared . . .

. . . over the goal.

Exercise 1

Identifying Participles   Write each sentence. Under-line each participle, and write whether it is *part of a verb phrase* or is used as an *adjective.*

1. Soccer can be a challenging game.
2. Many young people are participating in the sport.
3. The size of the playing field for soccer may vary.
4. Have rules for the sport changed over the years?
5. A player on our team has scored the winning goal.

Exercise 2

Identifying Participial Phrases   Underline each participial phrase. Then draw two lines under the word that the phrase describes. Add commas as needed.

1. Attracting huge crowds soccer is a popular sport.
2. The game consists of two teams competing for goals.
3. Playing within certain areas only the goalkeepers can touch the ball with their hands.
4. For other players the only contact permitted by the rules is with their feet, heads, or bodies.
5. The two teams playing the game kick off.
6. The teams rarely stopping during play kick the ball back and forth.
7. Varying their formations players move about the field.
8. By the 1800s English schools playing a similar game had drawn up the first set of rules.

Writing Link

Imagine that you are a famous tennis player. Describe one of your winning games. Use some participial phrases.

15.2 Gerunds and Gerund Phrases

The previous lesson explains that the present participle may be used as an adjective. A verb form ending in -ing may also serve as a noun, in which case it is called a *gerund*.

> The **playing** field is one hundred yards long. [adjective]
> **Playing** is our favorite activity. [gerund]

A **gerund** is a verb form that ends in -*ing* and is used as a noun.

Sometimes a gerund serves as the simple subject of a sentence. At other times a gerund serves as a direct object or as the object of a preposition.

> **Blocking** requires strength. [subject]
> The athletes enjoy **exercising**. [direct object]
> They maintain endurance by **running**. [object of a preposition]

A **gerund phrase** is a group of words that includes a gerund and other words that complete its meaning.

> **Kicking the ball** takes skill.
> A team tries **scoring a touchdown.**
> A touchdown results from **moving the ball across the goal.**

You can identify the three verb forms with -*ing* endings by distinguishing their function in a sentence. A verb form ending in -*ing* may serve as a verb in a verb phrase, as an adjective, or as a noun, in which case it is called a gerund.

> The Giants are **winning** the game. [main verb in verb phrase]
> The **winning** team scores the most points. [adjective]
> **Winning** is always exciting. [gerund]

Exercise 3

Identifying Verbals   Write each sentence. Then write whether the underlined word is the *main verb in a verb phrase*, a *participle used as an adjective*, or a *gerund*.

1. The coach or the captain chooses <u>playing</u> strategies.
2. <u>Passing</u> makes a game exciting.
3. The team members are <u>hoping</u> for a victory.
4. <u>Scoring</u> in football can occur in four different ways.
5. <u>Crossing</u> the opponent's goal line earns a team six points.

Exercise 4

Identifying Gerunds   Underline each gerund or gerund phrase. Write whether it is used as a *subject*, a *direct object*, or an *object of a preposition*.

1. Teams try earning the most points with a touchdown.
2. Kicking works in two different ways in this sport.
3. A team earns three points by kicking a field goal.
4. Teams also try converting for one point after a touchdown.
5. Defending the team's own goal is crucial.
6. A team's defense features blocking and tackling.
7. Passing makes football exciting.
8. Testing your skills is an important part of football.
9. Skilled players increase spectators' enjoyment by adding dramatic action to the game.
10. Winning is also important.

Writing Link

Imagine that you are a sportscaster. Describe an Olympic event. Use some gerunds and gerund phrases.

15.3 Infinitives and Infinitive Phrases

Another verb form that may function as a noun is an infinitive.

> **To referee** requires training.
> Trainees learn **to referee.**

An **infinitive** is formed from the word *to* together with the base form of a verb. It is often used as a noun in a sentence.

The word *to* is not a preposition when it is used immediately before a verb.

> Those young players want **to win.**
> The coach is pointing **to the pitcher.**

In the first sentence the words in dark type form an infinitive. The two words work together as a noun. *To win* names what the players want. In the second sentence the words in dark type form a prepositional phrase. The phrase is used as an adverb that tells *where* the coach is pointing.

Because the word *to* and the base form of the verb can work together as a noun, the two words may appear as the subject of a sentence or as a direct object of an action verb. The direct object receives the action of the verb.

> **To referee** demands patience. [subject]
> Athletes often try **to argue.** [direct object]

An **infinitive phrase** is a group of words that includes an infinitive and other words that complete its meaning.

> A player may try **to influence the call.**

INFINITIVE

The player has **to run.**

She runs
to home base.

PREPOSITIONAL
PHRASE

Identifying Infinitives   Write each sentence. Then write whether each underlined group of words is an *infinitive* or a *prepositional phrase*.

1. <u>To win</u> is the dream of every World Series player.
2. The top team in each division goes <u>to the play-offs</u>.
3. The two winners are invited <u>to the World Series</u>.
4. <u>To excel</u> is each team's goal at these games.

Identifying Infinitive Phrases   Underline each infinitive or infinitive phrase. Indicate whether it is used as a *subject* or as a *direct object*.

1. To play on a team in the American League or the National League is an accomplishment.
2. Most players prefer to play home games.
3. To leave means losing the support of all the home town fans.
4. To play baseball requires knowledge of the structure of the game.
5. The players want to improve their strategies.
6. We've decided to root for the American League team in the World Series.
7. To attend a World Series game is one of my goals.
8. I want to go to Dodger Stadium.
9. Have you learned to pitch a fast ball?

Writing Link

Imagine that you are a sportscaster. Describe an Olympic event that you are interested in. Use infinitives and prepositional phrases with *to* in your description.

Grammar Workshop

Verbals

In 1960 Wilma Rudolph became the first American woman to win three gold medals in track and field at the Olympic games. Shortly before she competed in her first Olympics, however, Rudolph was defeated at a regional high school track meet in Tuskegee, Alabama. In the following passage from "Wilma," an autobiographical essay, Rudolph describes how the defeat at Tuskegee motivated her to win in the future. The passage has been annotated to show some of the types of verbals covered in this unit.

Literature Model

from WILMA

by Wilma Rudolph

I ran and ran and ran every day, and I acquired this sense of determination, this sense of spirit that I would never, never give up, no matter what else happened. That day at Tuskegee had a tremendous effect on me inside. That's all I ever thought about. Some days I just wanted to go out and die. I just moped around and felt sorry for myself. Other days I'd go out to the track with fire in my eyes and imagine myself back at Tuskegee, **beating them all**. Losing as badly as I did had an impact on my personality. **Winning all the time in track** had given me confidence; I felt like a winner. But I didn't feel like a winner any more after Tuskegee. My confidence was shattered, and I was thinking the only way I could put it all together was **to get back the next year and wipe them all out**.

Participial phrase — beating them all

Gerund phrase — Winning all the time in track

Infinitive phrase — to get back the next year and wipe them all out

Grammar Workshop Exercise 1

Using Participles   Rewrite each sentence, inserting the participle or participial phrase in parentheses.

SAMPLE   Rudolph gained confidence. (running hard)
ANSWER   Running hard, Rudolph gained confidence.

1. The track meet at Tuskegee shocked the runner. (previously unbeaten)
2. Rudolph felt like quitting. (shattered by her defeat)
3. She dreamed of winning the meet. (imagining herself back at Tuskegee)
4. The athlete never gave up. (fiercely determined)
5. Rudolph realized that a champion can pick herself up and try again, even after a defeat. (crushing)

Grammar Workshop Exercise 2

Using Gerunds   Write a sentence that answers each question, using the word or words in parentheses.

SAMPLE   What is Wilma Rudolph best known for? (winning three gold medals at the Olympics)
ANSWER   Wilma Rudolph is best known for winning three gold medals at the Olympics.

1. By what means did Rudolph first achieve fame? (competing in the 1956 Olympic games)
2. What is another of Rudolph's achievements? (setting world records in the 100-meter and 200-meter races)
3. What might have prevented Rudolph from pursuing a career in track? (having polio as a young girl)
4. By what means did Rudolph strengthen her muscles after her illness? (running)
5. What is Rudolph's current challenge? (working with young people in sports and educational programs)

Grammar Workshop Exercise 3

Using Infinitives   Write a sentence that answers each question, using the word or words in parentheses.

1. What is the purpose of the hurdle race? (to run and jump over obstacles placed on the track)
2. What must relay racers learn? (to pass the baton smoothly and quickly)
3. What does a high jumper attempt to do? (to leap over an upraised bar)
4. What do throwing events require athletes to do? (to propel an object as far as they can)
5. Why did athletes gather at the first Olympic Games? (to run a foot race)

Grammar Workshop Exercise 4

Proofreading   The following passage is about Jacob Lawrence, whose work appears on the next page. Rewrite the passage, correcting the errors in spelling, capitalization, punctuation, grammar, and usage. There are ten errors in all.

Jacob Lawrence

[1] Jacob Lawrence was born in new jersey in 1917 but growed up in Harlem. [2] Lawrence began studying art in after-school programs and acheived success at an early age. [3] While still in his twentys, Lawrence became the first African-American artist to have a one-man show at the Museum of Modern Art in New York City.

[4] Lawrences' work are characterised by vivid primary colors and highly stylized figures. [5] The artist uses gestures and facial expressions to convey his figures' emotions. [6] In *Study for the Munich Olympic Games Poster,* for example, the relay racers visibly strains to cross the finish line. [7] Like Wilma Rudolph, each runner is determined too win.

Jacob Lawrence, *Study for the Munich Olympic Games Poster,* **1971**

Unit 15 Review

Verbals

Participles and Participial Phrases

[pages 472–473]

Write each sentence. Then underline each participle or participial phrase, and write whether it is used as an *adjective* or as *part of a verb phrase*.

1. The Royal Canadian Air Force has developed an exercise program.
2. The controlled exercises develop strength and endurance.
3. As weeks pass, the routine includes more challenging exercises.
4. People following the routine have profited greatly from it.
5. Exercising at home, Gene has lost ten pounds.

Gerunds and Gerund Phrases

[pages 474–475]

Write each sentence. Then underline each gerund or gerund phrase, and write whether it is used as the *subject, direct object,* or *object of a preposition* in the sentence.

6. Swimming is a recreational activity and a competitive sport.
7. Japan first introduced swimming in formal competitions.

8. Some swimmers develop an interest in racing.
9. Competing in water sports became an international event in 1896.
10. Diving is now an international event also.

Infinitives and Infinitive Phrases

[pages 476–477]

Write each sentence. Then underline each infinitive or infinitive phrase, and write whether it is used as the *subject* or the *direct object* in the sentence.

11. People began to race horses in Egypt around 1500 B.C.
12. To watch the Kentucky Derby, a famous horse race, is a thrill.
13. Many serious horse racers seek to compete in this race.
14. *National Velvet* is about a girl who hopes to enter a world-famous horse race.
15. My niece likes to ride horses at summer camp.

Writing for Review

Write a paragraph describing your favorite form of exercise. Try to use participial phrases, gerund phrases, and infinitive phrases.

Subject–Verb Agreement

Melissa Miller, *Northern Lights,* 1982

16.1   Making Subjects and Verbs Agree

The basic idea of subject-verb agreement is a simple one—a singular noun subject calls for a singular form of the verb, and a plural noun calls for a plural form of the verb. The subject and its verb are said to *agree in number.* Read the sentences below. You can see that the subjects and verbs agree.

Notice that in the present tense the singular form of the verb usually ends in -*s* or -*es.*

The **frogs leap.**
PLURAL SUBJECT   PLURAL VERB

A **frog leaps.**
SINGULAR   SINGULAR
SUBJECT   VERB

Subject and Verb Agreement	
Singular Subject	**Plural Subject**
An **ecologist studies** nature.	**Ecologists study** nature.
The **boy learns** about ecology.	The **boys learn** about ecology.
Judy plants seedlings.	**Judy** and **Kim plant** seedlings.

The verb must also agree with a subject pronoun. Look at the chart below. Notice how the verb changes. In the present tense the -*s* ending is used with the subject pronouns *it, he,* and *she.*

Subject Pronoun and Verb Agreement	
Singular	**Plural**
I **hike**.	We **hike**.
You **hike**.	You **hike**.
He, she, *or* it **hikes**.	They **hike**.

The irregular verbs *be, do,* and *have* can be main verbs or helping verbs. They must agree with the subject, regardless of whether they are main verbs or helping verbs.

I **am** a ranger. They **are** tagging a bear. He **is** digging.
She **does** well. She **does** climb cliffs. They **do** garden.
He **has** gear. He **has** saved birds. They **have** traveled.

Identifying Subject and Verb Agreement   Write each sentence. Complete it by choosing the correct form of the verb in parentheses.

1. The day (was, were) perfect for a visit to the bog.
2. The students always (enjoy, enjoys) field trips.
3. Bogs (contain, contains) acidic soil and many mosses.
4. Swamps (is, are) similar to bogs.
5. The acidity (tell, tells) you about the type of bog.
6. A bog (is, are) usually smaller than a swamp.
7. Ecosystems (is, are) communities of living and nonliving factors.
8. An ecosystem (include, includes) the surrounding air.
9. An ecosystem (has, have) distinct cycles.
10. Water (is, are) an important part of all ecosystems.
11. An ecologist (do, does) a great deal of fieldwork.
12. Bogs often (provide, provides) interesting ecosystems.
13. This bog (have, has) supported a rare ecosystem.
14. A unique fungus (grow, grows) in this bog.
15. Many creatures (live, lives) in bogs.
16. Ecosystems (consist, consists) of many different combinations of plants and animals.
17. Our survival (do, does) depend upon the painstaking work of the ecologists.
18. Their important research often (have, has) a great impact on our view of our planet.

GRAMMAR HINT

The verb *be* is the only verb in English that has different forms in the past tense: *was* [singular], *were* [plural].

Writing Link

Write a paragraph about an imaginary animal that could live in a bog. Make sure that each of your verbs agrees with its subject.

16.2 Problems with Locating the Subject

Making a subject and its verb agree is easy when the verb directly follows the subject. Sometimes, however, a prepositional phrase comes between the subject and the verb.

The **desert**, except in the polar regions, **becomes** very hot.

In the sentence above, *except in the polar regions* is a prepositional phrase. The singular verb *becomes* agrees with the subject of the sentence, *desert,* not with the plural noun *regions,* which is the object of the preposition.

Inverted sentences are those in which the subject follows the verb. Inverted sentences often begin with a prepositional phrase. Do not mistake the object of the preposition for the subject.

In the desert **roam herds** of camels.

In inverted sentences beginning with *Here* or *There,* look for the subject after the verb. *Here* or *There* is never the subject.

There **is** a high **mountain** near the desert.
Here at the top **are** many damp **rocks**.

By rearranging each sentence so that the subject comes first, you see the subject and verb in their usual order.

A high **mountain** there **is** near the desert.
Many damp **rocks are** here at the top.

In some interrogative sentences an auxiliary verb may come before the subject. Look for the subject between the auxiliary verb and the main verb.

Do any **deserts contain** large animals?

Exercise 2

Identifying the Correct Verb Form Write each sentence. Complete it by choosing the correct form of the verb in parentheses.

1. The plains near the North Pole (is, are) very cold.
2. The temperature in these zones (is, are) usually below zero.
3. In this area (live, lives) many animals.
4. During the brief summers (grow, grows) a rare moss.
5. In the moss (nest, nests) many birds.
6. There (is, are) little rainfall during the summer.
7. Does snow (provide, provides) the needed moisture?

Exercise 3

Making Subjects and Verbs Agree Write each sentence. Underline the subject once and its verb twice. If they agree, write *correct*. If they do not agree, correct the verb.

1. The savanna, with its waving grasses, lie next to the desert.
2. It is on the margin of the trade-wind belts.
3. In the savanna lives many large animals.
4. The savanna, except in its rainy summers, are dry.
5. In Africa are the largest savannas.
6. Do savannas exist everywhere in the world?
7. There is many giraffes in the grassland.

Writing Link

Write a paragraph describing your preparations for a camping trip to the savanna. Keep subject-verb agreement in mind as you write.

16.3 Collective Nouns and Other Special Subjects

It is sometimes difficult to tell whether certain special subjects are singular or plural. For example, collective nouns follow special agreement rules. A collective noun names a group. The noun has a singular meaning when you speak about a group that acts as a unit. The noun has a plural meaning when you are showing that each member of the group acts as an individual. The meaning of the noun determines whether you use the singular or plural form of the verb.

The **team agrees** to save papers. [one group, singular]
The **team agree** to store them in their homes. [individuals, plural]

Certain nouns, such as *mathematics* and *news*, end in *-s* but take a singular verb. Other nouns that end in *-s* and name one thing, such as *trousers* and *pliers*, take a plural verb.

Mumps is a disease that is spread through the air. [singular]
Scissors are not practical for shredding. [plural]

When the subject refers to an amount as a single unit, it is singular. When it refers to a number of units, it is plural.

Ten years seems a long time. [single unit]
Ten years have passed since you left. [individual units]
Five cents is the deposit on one bottle. [single unit]
Five cents are in my hand. [individual units]

A title of a book or work of art is considered singular even if the subject within the title is plural.

***Recycling Successes* is** now a best-selling book. [one book]

The team . . .

. . . **collect** cans and bottles at the shore.

The team . . .

. . . **collects** cans and bottles for recycling.

Identifying the Correct Verb Form Write each sentence. Complete it by choosing the correct form of the verb in parentheses.

1. The committee (decide, decides) to recycle paper.
2. The committee (decide, decides) among themselves.
3. The audience (leave, leaves) when they are bored.
4. The audience (want, wants) more drastic measures.
5. News (is, are) being made at this town meeting.
6. Even eyeglasses (is, are) recyclable.
7. *Seven Ways to Recycle Newspapers* (is, are) the book we need.
8. The class (discuss, discusses) their different opinions about pollutants.
9. The group (discuss, discusses) the problem of landfills.
10. The herd of goats (graze, grazes) at the landfill.
11. The herd (is, are) all healthy.
12. One million gallons (is, are) a large amount of pollutants.
13. *Energy Alternatives* (is, are) an important book.
14. Five hundred dollars (was, were) handed to the mayor for the town's recycling program.
15. *Fragile Lands* (do, does) seem a significant film.
16. The class (is, are) working on a group project.
17. The group (see, sees) a movie about landfills.
18. Two years (seem, seems) a long time for recovery.

GRAMMAR HINT

You can determine whether to use a singular or plural verb by substituting *it* or *they* for the collective noun.

Writing Link

Write about a recycling drive held by your school or community. What kinds of things would you recycle? Be sure your subjects and verbs agree.

16.4   Indefinite Pronouns as Subjects

An **indefinite pronoun** is a pronoun that does not refer to a specific person, place, or thing.

Some indefinite pronouns are singular. Others are plural. When they are used as subjects, the verbs must agree in number with these indefinite pronouns. Study the indefinite pronouns in the chart below.

Indefinite Pronouns			
Singular			**Plural**
another	everybody	no one	both
anybody	everyone	nothing	few
anyone	everything	one	many
anything	much	somebody	others
each	neither	someone	several
either	nobody	something	

Some indefinite pronouns may be singular or plural, depending on the phrase that follows. They include *all, any, most, none,* and *some.*

Notice how indefinite pronouns are used below.

Nobody lives without oxygen. [singular]
Many study the process of respiration. [plural]
Some of her lawn **is** brown. [singular]
Some of the ferns **are** large. [plural]

Often a prepositional phrase follows an indefinite pronoun that can be singular or plural. To determine whether the pronoun is singular or plural, look at the object of the preposition. For example, in the third sentence above, *some* refers to *lawn*. Because *lawn* is singular, *some* is singular. In the fourth sentence *some* refers to *ferns*. Because *ferns* is plural, *some* is plural.

Identifying the Correct Verb Form Write each sentence. Complete it by choosing the correct form of the verb in parentheses.

1. Much of the process of respiration (is, are) complex.
2. Few completely (understand, understands) it.
3. Many (study, studies) the two types of oxygen exchange.
4. Much (happen, happens) during the two processes.
5. Someone (explain, explains) the respiratory system.
6. Another of our problems (is, are) water pollution.
7. One (need, needs) understanding of the solutions.
8. Some of them (improve, improves) the water supply immediately.
9. Many (provide, provides) sensible approaches.
10. Either of the processes (clean, cleans) the water equally well.
11. Both of them (call, calls) for further study.
12. Neither (is, are) apparently preferable.
13. Most of the higher animals (have, has) lungs.
14. All of the oxygen exchange (occur, occurs) there.
15. Most of *Processes* (is, are) clearly written.
16. Nobody (deny, denies) the value of the project.
17. Many of the volunteers (work, works) diligently.
18. Any of the projects (need, needs) extra volunteers.
19. Most of the people (support, supports) conservation.
20. Several of the volunteers (suggest, suggests) ideas.

Writing Link

Write about an antipollution measure that you would like to see implemented. Use some indefinite pronouns in your writing.

16.5   Agreement with Compound Subjects

A compound subject contains two or more simple subjects that have the same verb. Compound subjects require either a singular or a plural verb, depending on how the parts of the subject are joined. When two or more simple subjects are joined by the coordinating conjunction *and* or by the correlative conjunction *both . . . and,* the verb is plural.

> New York, Denver, **and** London have smog.
> **Both** automobiles **and** factories **create** smog.
> Air inversion **and** the absence of wind **aid** the conditions.

In all of these sentences, the reference is to more than one place, thing, or idea.

Occasionally *and* is used to join two words that are part of one unit or refer to a single person or thing. In these cases, the subject is considered to be singular. In the sentence below, notice that *captain* and *leader* refer to the same person. Therefore, the singular form of the verb is used.

> The captain **and** leader of the air-testing team **is** Joan.

When two or more subjects are joined by the coordinating conjunctions *or* or *nor,* or the correlative conjunction *either . . . or* or *neither . . . nor,* the verb agrees with the subject that is closest to it.

> The city **or** the state **responds** to pollution complaints.
> **Either** smoke **or** gases **cause** the smog.

In the first sentence *responds* agrees with *state,* which is the subject closer to the verb. The verb is singular because the subject is singular. In the second sentence *cause* agrees with *gases,* which is the closer subject. *Gases* requires a plural verb.

Identifying the Correct Verb Form   Write each sentence. Complete it by using the correct form of the verb in parentheses.

1. A savanna and a desert (is, are) next to each other.
2. A rain forest or a desert (make, makes) a good study site.
3. Jungles, forests, and bogs (has, have) different characteristics.
4. Neither Caldwell nor the girls (want, wants) to study swamps.
5. Plants and animals in a community (is, are) interdependent.
6. Food, water, and air (is, are) essential to life.
7. Both food and oxygen (come, comes) from plants.
8. Neither science nor industry (want, wants) natural resources wasted.
9. Both days and seasons (change, changes) natural systems.
10. Either zoology or botany (provide, provides) a good background.
11. Either mathematics or other sciences (give, gives) support.
12. The teacher and leader of the group (have, has) been an expert on ecological issues for years.
13. Too much rain or drought (do, does) affect the area.
14. States, cities, and towns (have, has) responsibilities.

GRAMMAR HINT

If a compound subject contains *and,* check for agreement by replacing the subject with a plural pronoun:
Cal and Jan *go.*
They *go.*

Writing Link

People affect nature. Describe what you think your neighborhood looked like before people changed it. Use some compound subjects.

Usage **Workshop**

Subject-Verb Agreement

To learn about bats, journalist Diane Ackerman accompanied a world authority on the subject to a cave in Texas. In the following excerpt from her essay "Bats," the writer observes an emergence of Mexican free-tailed bats. The passage has been annotated to show some examples of subject-verb agreement covered in this unit.

Literature Model

from BATS

by Diane Ackerman

Agreement between a singular subject and verb in an inverted sentence

Agreement between a plural pronoun subject and a plural verb

Agreement between a plural subject and a verb that have a prepositional phrase between them

In the early evening, I take my seat in a natural amphitheater of limestone boulders, in the Texas hill country; at the bottom of the slope is a wide, dark cave mouth. Nothing stirs yet in its depths. But I have been promised one of the wonders of our age. Deep inside the cavern, twenty million Mexican free-tailed bats are hanging up by their toes. They are the largest known concentration of warm-blooded animals in the world. Soon, at dusk, all twenty million of them will fly out to feed, in a living volcano that scientists call an "emergence. . . ."

A hawk appears, swoops, grabs a stray bat out of the sky, and disappears with it. In a moment, the hawk returns, but hearing his wings coming, the bats in the column all shift sidewise to confuse him, and he misses. As wave upon wave of bats pours out of the cave, their collective wings begin to sound like drizzle on autumn leaves.

Making Verbs Agree with Their Subjects   The
following sentences are based on the passage from
"Bats." Rewrite each sentence, choosing the correct
form of the verb in parentheses.

SAMPLE   The bats, sleeping deep inside the cave,
          (hangs, hang) upside down by their toes.
ANSWER   The bats, sleeping deep inside the cave,
          hang upside down by their toes.

1. There (is, are) about twenty million Mexican free-
    tailed bats in the cave.
2. Eager to observe the bats, the team (takes, take)
    their seats among the limestone boulders.
3. From out of nowhere (appears, appear) a hawk.
4. A wave of bats (emerges, emerge) from the cave.
5. (Does, Do) the bats (tries, try) to attack the hawk?
6. "Bats" (is, are) an entertaining and informative essay.

**Making Verbs Agree with Indefinite Pronoun
Subjects**   The following sentences are about bats.
Rewrite each sentence, choosing the correct form of the
verb in parentheses.

SAMPLE   Everyone (has, have) an opinion about bats.
ANSWER   Everyone has an opinion about bats.

1. Many (fears, fear) the animals.
2. Few (knows, know) very much about them.
3. Much (remains, remain) to be learned about bats.
4. Some (uses, use) high-frequency sounds to navigate
    in the dark.
5. Most of these sounds (extends, extend) beyond the
    range of human hearing.

Making Verbs Agree with Compound Subjects

Rewrite each sentence, choosing the correct form of the verb in parentheses.

1. Neither the flying fox nor the vampire bat (hibernates, hibernate) in winter.
2. Both snakes and hawks (preys, prey) on bats.
3. Vision and sense of smell (helps, help) some bats find food at night.
4. Fruit or insects (provides, provide) food for bats.

Proofreading The following passage is about American artist Leonard Koscianski, whose work appears on the next page. Rewrite the passage, correcting the errors in spelling, capitalization, punctuation, grammar, and usage. There are ten errors in all.

Leonard Koscianski

[1]Many of Leonard Koscianski's paintings reflects his concern with issues affecting the earths future, such as enviromental pollution. [2]koscianski believes that human society imposes an artificial order on the world. [3]The result may be a disruption of the balence of nature.

[4]In *Forest Spirit,* for example, the artist represents the natural order in the forest, where a hawk swoops down to attack a hiden prey. [5]Like the mexican free-tailed bat in "Bats," the prey may be siezed and killed. [6]Although this killing may seem cruel to some people, Koscianski suggests that such activity is neccesary to maintain the natural balance. [7]Besides, nature allows the hunted to fight back. [8]Like most of the bats in Ackerman's essay, the hawks prey may be able to protect itself and escape.

Leonard Koscianski, *Forest Spirit,* **1991**

Subject-Verb Agreement

Making Subjects and Verbs Agree

[pages 484–487]

Write each sentence. Underline the subject once and its verb twice. If they agree, write *correct*. If they do not agree, correct the verb.

1. The Cousteau Society aids other environmental groups.
2. They sponsors scientific studies.
3. The researchers reports on issues of concern.
4. Pollution threatens everyone.
5. It poison the undersea world.
6. Conservation of our resources are vital.
7. There is many examples of irresponsibility.
8. Theories about our world include the Gaea hypothesis.
9. Believers in this theory sees the earth as a living being.
10. Here are a new view of our interactions.

Collective Nouns; Indefinite Pronouns; Compound Subjects

[pages 488–493]

Write each sentence. Complete the sentence by choosing the correct form of the verb in parentheses.

11. The class (investigate, investigates) possible methods of protecting a variety of endangered species.
12. The Wildlife Federation (maintain, maintains) an exhaustive list of the species in danger.
13. The committee (grow, grows) more vocal about their concerns.
14. Everyone (recognize, recognizes) not only the ugliness of litter but also its potential threat to public health.
15. Many of us (take, takes) the litter laws seriously.
16. However, some of our neighbors (do, does) not.
17. Builders and city planners (design, designs) environments.
18. Both pure air and pure water (is, are) requirements.
19. Neither safety nor health (is, are) unimportant.
20. A park or playgrounds (improve, improves) the surroundings.

Writing for Review

Write a paragraph about what you and your friends can do to clean up your neighborhood. Make sure that the subject and the verb in each sentence agree.

UNIT 17
Glossary of Special Usage Problems

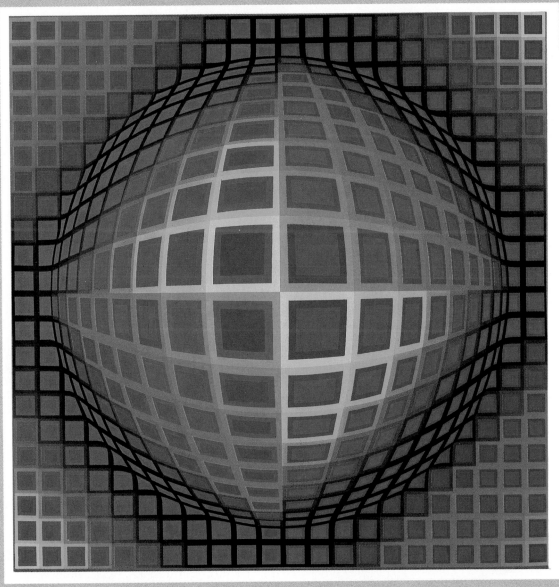

Victor Vasarely, *Vega–Nor*, 1969

499

17.1　Using Troublesome Words I

Like all languages English contains a number of confusing expressions. The following glossary will help you understand some of the more troublesome ones.

Word	Meaning	Example
accept except	"to receive" "other than"	We do not readily **accept** new ideas. Few **except** scientists understand them.
all ready already	"completely prepared" "before" or "by this time"	They are **all ready** for new ideas. Ideas have **already** changed.
all together altogether	"in a group" "completely"	The planets **all together** weigh less than the sun. Most stars are **altogether** too distant to study.
a lot	"very much" *A lot* is two words. Its meaning is vague; avoid using it.	**A lot** of stars can't be seen. [vague] Thousands of stars can't be seen. [more precise]
beside besides	"next to" "in addition to"	In May the moon appeared **beside** Mars. **Besides** Saturn, Jupiter and Uranus have rings.
between among	Use *between* for two people or things. Use *among* when talking about groups of three or more.	Mercury is **between** Venus and the sun. Meteor trails are seen **among** the stars.
bring take	"to carry from a distant place to a closer one" "to carry from a nearby place to a more distant one"	Astronomers **bring** exhibits to schools. Students will **take** the model planets home.
can may	indicates ability expresses permission or possibility	We **can** see Pluto with a telescope. **May** we see the charts?
choose chose	"to select" "selected"	**Choose** a planet to study. Last year we **chose** Mars.

Exercise 1

Choosing the Correct Word   Write each sentence. Choose the correct word or words in parentheses.

1. Our galaxy is one (among, between) many.
2. There may be more galaxies (beside, besides) the ones we know.
3. Many people (accept, except) the idea that space is endless.
4. (Can, May) we use that telescope?
5. (Bring, Take) a compass to the lab when you go.
6. Galaxies are (all together, altogether) too numerous.

Exercise 2

Using the Correct Word   Write each sentence. Use the correct word or words from the lesson. A definition of the word appears in parentheses.

1. We _____ see Pluto through this telescope. (have the ability)
2. Before today we'd observed every planet _____ Pluto. (other than)
3. Scientists have _____ learned a great deal about comets. (by this time)
4. They will _____ our class a meteorite. (carry to a closer place)
5. We will _____ the meteorite home. (carry to a farther place)

Writing Link

Our galaxy is called the Milky Way. Read about another galaxy in the universe, and write a paragraph describing it. Use some of the words from the lesson.

17.2   Using Troublesome Words II

Word	Meaning	Example
fewer	Use with nouns that can be counted.	There are **fewer** sunspots this year.
less	Use with nouns that cannot be counted.	Mars has **less** gravitational force than Earth.
formally formerly	the adverb form of *formal* "in times past"	The sun is **formally** a star. Pluto was **formerly** thought to be a moon of another planet.
in into	"inside" indicates movement from outside to a point within	Our sun is **in** the Milky Way. Meteorites fall **into** the atmosphere.
its it's	the possessive form of *it* the contraction of *it is*	A comet wobbles in **its** orbit. **It's** difficult to see Neptune.
lay lie	"to put" or "to place" "to recline" or "to be positioned"	**Lay** the charts on the table. Layers of dust **lie** on the moon.
learn teach	"to receive knowledge" "to give knowledge"	Astronauts **learn** astronomy as part of their training. Many astronomers **teach** at colleges.
leave let	"to go away" "to allow"	We will **leave** after the eclipse. The school **let** us use the compass.
loose lose	"not firmly attached" "to misplace" or "to fail to win"	Scientists gather **loose** particles in space and bring them back to study. Comets **lose** particles.
many much	Use with nouns that can be counted. Use with nouns that cannot be counted.	We know the weight of **many** stars. **Much** of the weight is gas.
precede proceed	"to go or come before" "to continue"	Compasses **preceded** telescopes. *Voyager 2* will **proceed** to Neptune.

Exercise 3

Choosing the Correct Word   Write each sentence. Choose the correct word in parentheses.

1. There are (many, much) kinds of telescopes.
2. Astronomers were (formally, formerly) limited by crude optics.
3. Reflecting telescopes allow the viewer to see deep (in, into) space.
4. A telescope's power is determined by the size of (its, it's) lens.
5. Our astronomy club is (formally, formerly) organized.

Exercise 4

Using the Correct Word   Write each sentence. Use the correct word from the lesson. A definition of the word appears in parentheses.

1. Volcanoes _____ erupted on the moon. (in times past)
2. I can _____ on the ground for hours, looking at the sky. (recline)
3. _____ that telescope stand where it is! (allow)
4. A _____ lens will make a telescope inoperable. (not firmly attached)
5. Astronomers _____ from space probes. (receive knowledge)

Writing Link

How many star formations can you identify when you look at the sky at night? Describe the formations you are familiar with. Use some of the words from the lesson.

17.3 Using Troublesome Words III

Word	Meaning	Example
quiet	"calm" or "motionless"	It is very **quiet** in outer space.
quite	"completely" or "entirely"	It is **quite** dark in outer space.
raise	"to cause to move upward"	**Raise** heavy binoculars with a tripod.
rise	"to move upward"	The stars **rise** into view.
set	"to place" or "to put"	She **set** the camera down carefully.
sit	"to place oneself in a seated position"	Let's **sit** and watch the sky.
than	introduces the second part of a comparison	The sun is denser **than** the earth.
then	"at that time"	Choose a planet, and **then** locate it.
their	the possessive form of *they*	Ask **their** advice about lenses.
they're	the contraction of *they are*	**They're** using special night lenses.
theirs	"that or those belonging to them"	**Theirs** is a reflecting telescope.
there's	the contraction of *there is*	**There's** also a refractor telescope in our observatory.
to	"in the direction of"	Let's go **to** the observatory.
too	"also" or "excessively"	Why don't you come, **too**?
two	the number after one	We have only **two** telescopes in our observatory.
where at	Do not use *at* after *where*.	**Where** is the Milky Way? [not *Where is the Milky Way at?*]
who's	the contraction of *who is*	**Who's** a famous astronomer?
whose	the possessive form of *who*	**Whose** discoveries are the most significant?
your	the possessive form of *you*	I liked **your** essay about Mars.
you're	the contraction of *you are*	**You're** looking at the North Star.

Choosing the Correct Word Write each sentence. Choose the correct word in parentheses.

1. Jupiter's moons look static, but (they're, their) always in orbit.
2. Pluto is smaller (than, then) the other planets.
3. (Who's, Whose) bringing the camera to the site?
4. (Set, Sit) the tripod over there.
5. Each of the planets is (quite, quiet) different in color.
6. (Your, You're) sure to see Venus tonight.
7. (Who's, Whose) count of Saturn's rings is correct?
8. Most observers (sit, set) in deck chairs.

Using the Correct Word Write each sentence. Use the correct word from the lesson. A definition of the word appears in parentheses.

1. Our friends will bring _____ compass and camera. (possessive form of *they*)
2. The telescope is _____. (that belonging to them)
3. The observation site is on a _____ hill. (calm)
4. The night sky can be _____ stunning. (completely)
5. The stars will _____ soon. (move upward)
6. We will _____ our eyes and our spirits. (cause to move upward)
7. _____ our watch will begin. (at that time)
8. I hope it's not _____ cold. (excessively)

Writing Link

In a paragraph describe the planet you find most interesting. Use some of the words from the lesson.

Usage Workshop

Glossary of Special Usage Problems

In her essay "Star Fever" Judith Herbst discusses people's age-old fascination with stars. In the following passage, Herbst considers the worlds that may lie beyond our vision. She also explains the usefulness of the stars. The passage has been annotated to show some usage items covered in this unit.

Literature Model

from STAR FEVER

by Judith Herbst

Lie, meaning "to recline"

I love the stars. Sometimes I lie awake at night and think about them. I imagine that they all have planets with strange forms of life. I see red, rugged landscapes bathed in the glare of two suns, one swollen and scarlet, the other a cold steel blue. I see steamy tropical planets covered with silver vines that snake in and out of silver trees. I see planets with methane oceans and iron mountains. It's not so crazy. They could be out there, you know. . . .

The contraction of *it is*

The stars not only mark the seasons, they also tell you where north, south, east, and west are. Stars " rise " in the east and "set" in the west, so all you have to do is look for the appearance of a new constellation. If you see one that wasn't there an hour before, you're facing east. Once you know east it's a snap to find the other three directions. Just look behind you for west, to the right side for south, and to the left for north.

Rise, meaning "to move upward"

The contraction of *you are*

As you can imagine, without the compass the early sailors absolutely relied on the stars to find their way around. There are no landmarks on the high seas.

Making Usage Choices   The following sentences elaborate on ideas suggested by the passage from "Star Fever." Rewrite each sentence, choosing the correct word in parentheses.

SAMPLE   (Beside, Besides) marking the seasons, stars can also be used to tell directions.

ANSWER   Besides marking the seasons, stars can also be used to tell directions.

1. The stars (can, may) be used as a means to navigate only when the sky is clear.
2. On an overcast night (fewer, less) stars are visible in the sky.
3. Chinese navigators were (all ready, already) using magnetic compasses to guide their ships by the 1100s.
4. Some of the objects we see (between, among) the stars are planets.
5. Do you (accept, except) the idea that there may be life on other planets?

Making Usage Choices   Rewrite each sentence, choosing the correct word in parentheses.

1. (Many, Much) stars formed more than 10 billion years ago.
2. The color of a star's light depends on (its, it's) surface temperature.
3. As a star dies, it slowly begins to (loose, lose) material and shrink.
4. About one hundred ball-like clusters of stars (lay, lie) around the center of the Milky Way galaxy.
5. People can (learn, teach) about stars at a planetarium.

Making Usage Choices   The following sentences are about the sun. Rewrite each sentence, choosing the correct word in parentheses.

1. The sun is nearer to the earth (than, then) any other star is.
2. Scientists have learned (quiet, quite) a bit about other stars by studying the sun.
3. (Theirs, There's) a solar telescope in Tucson, Arizona, that helps astronomers study the sun's light.
4. (Who's, Whose) studies in the early 1500s revealed the true relationship between the earth and the sun and challenged earlier scientists' findings?
5. Polish astronomer Nicolaus Copernicus challenged (their, they're) beliefs about the sun.
6. Today scientists continue to (raise, rise) questions about the sun and its impact on people.

Proofreading   The following passage is about Fernand Léger, whose work appears on the next page. Rewrite the passage, correcting the errors in spelling, capitalization, punctuation, grammar, and usage. There are ten errors in all.

Fernand Léger

[1] French painter Fernand Léger (1881–1955) used an abstract style of art. [2] This style combine several fragmented aspects of a object in a single painting. [3] léger frequently used cubes and other forms to create mechanical figures that repersented the new machines developed in the early 1900s. [4] In these paintings the artist explored the role of human beings in the industriel world.

[5] In *The Creation of the World* Léger present his vision of a world produced by machines? [6] Laying ➡

beneath a moon and a handful of stars, Légers world recalls the planets that Judith Herbst imagined in "Star Fever." [7] Perhaps the strange images in the painting may actualy exist under some distant star.

Fernand Léger, *The Creation of the World,* **c. 1925**

Glossary of Special Usage Problems

Using Troublesome Words I

[pages 500–501]

Complete each sentence by choosing the correct word or words in parentheses.

1. *Voyager 2* is (between, among) the many spacecraft still functioning.
2. Some astronomers do not (accept, except) Pluto as a true planet.
3. Find Jupiter (between, among) Mars and Saturn.
4. We are (all ready, already) to go stargazing.
5. (Can, May) Venus be seen tonight?

Using Troublesome Words II

[pages 502–503]

Write each sentence. Use the correct form of the glossary word that is defined in the parentheses.

6. Our teacher will ____ us make a model of Saturn. (allow)
7. The surface of Mars ____ under a blanket of rust. (is positioned)
8. The rings of Saturn are ____ bands of dust. (not firmly attached)
9. We ____ about stars by using a spectroscope. (receive knowledge)
10. They ____ binoculars on the table. (placed)

Using Troublesome Words III

[pages 504–505]

Write each sentence. Complete the sentence by choosing the correct word from the parentheses.

11. Pluto's orbit is more erratic (than, then) any other planet's.
12. Astronomers believe (there's, theirs) only winter on Pluto.
13. Giant gas flares (raise, rise) from the surface of the sun.
14. The colors of Saturn's rings are (quite, quiet) beautiful.
15. Astronomers say (their, they're) learning more from *Voyager 2.*
16. Is (your, yours) one of the most respected astronomers?
17. Is (your, you're) class going to the planetarium?
18. (Set, sit) our display of pictures in the exhibit case.
19. There are (two, too) basic types of tripod mountings.
20. You will be able to see Jupiter if you (raise, rise) the telescope a little.

Writing for Review

Imagine that you have discovered a new planet. Using some of the words from the glossary, describe your discovery.

Diagraming Sentences

Paul Klee, *Twittering Machine*, 1922

18.1 Diagraming Simple Subjects and Simple Predicates

The basic parts of a sentence are the subject and the predicate. To diagram a sentence, first draw a horizontal line. Then draw a vertical line that crosses and extends below the horizontal line.

To the left of the vertical line, write the simple subject. To the right of the vertical line, write the simple predicate. Capitalize any words that are capitalized in the sentence. Do not include punctuation, however.

People are working.	People | are working

The positions of the subject and the predicate in a diagram always remain the same.

Operators sat by the machines.	Operators | sat
By the machines **sat operators.**	operators | sat

GRAMMAR HINT

The simple predicate may contain one or more helping verbs. Be sure to include any helping verbs in a diagram of a simple predicate.

Exercise 1

Diagraming Simple Subjects and Simple Predicates
Diagram each simple subject and simple predicate.

1. People arrived early.
2. They started the machines.
3. Other people were standing around.
4. Four women have arrived late.
5. Most factories are busy.
6. Finally lunchtime arrived.
7. The workers ate lunch.

The simple subject and simple predicate of the four kinds of sentences are diagramed below. Notice that the location of the simple subject and simple predicate in a sentence diagram is always the same, regardless of the word order in the sentence.

DECLARATIVE
People use many machines.

People	use

INTERROGATIVE
Do people use many machines?

people	Do use

IMPERATIVE
Use this machine.

(you)	Use

EXCLAMATORY
What a loud noise **it makes!**

it	makes

Notice that in an interrogative sentence the subject often comes between the two parts of a verb phrase. In an imperative sentence the simple subject is the understood *you.*

Exercise 2

Diagraming Sentences   Diagram the simple subject and the simple predicate of each sentence.

1. Where do people use machines?
2. Machines exist in homes, office buildings, and hospitals.
3. What amazing things machines can do!
4. Listen to the radio.
5. Some machines perform several tasks.
6. Do you use a computer?
7. Try this program.
8. What a fast printer you have!

18.3 Diagraming Direct and Indirect Objects

A direct object is part of the predicate. In a sentence diagram, place the direct object to the right of the verb. Notice that the vertical line between the verb and the direct object does not extend below the horizontal line.

Computers solve **problems**.

| Computers | solve | problems |

Computers process **data**.

| Computers | process | data |

An indirect object is also part of the predicate. It usually tells to whom or for whom the action of a verb is done. An indirect object comes before a direct object in a sentence. Place the indirect object on a line below and to the right of the verb. Then join it to the verb with a slanted line.

Operators feed **computers** data.

| Operators | feed | data |
                     \ computers

GRAMMAR HINT

Diagram a direct object after the verb on the horizontal line. Diagram an indirect object, however, on a horizontal line below the verb.

Exercise 3

Diagraming Sentences   Diagram the simple subject, the simple predicate, and the direct object of each sentence. Diagram any indirect objects as well.

1. People solve problems every day.
2. A computer will provide answers.
3. An idea enters your mind.
4. You collect the information.
5. The method gives you the answer.
6. You offer someone the results.
7. The operator gives the computer a problem.

In a diagram place adjectives and adverbs on slanted lines beneath the words they modify.

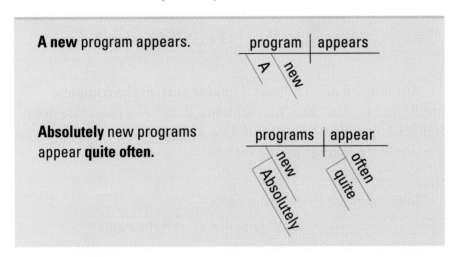

A prepositional phrase can function as either an adjective or an adverb. Study the diagram of a prepositional phrase below.

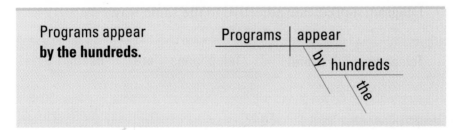

Exercise 4

Diagraming Sentences   Diagram each sentence.

1. Many people use computers regularly.
2. An extremely efficient computer works very quickly.
3. You very probably use electricity at home.
4. Computers have changed our way of life.
5. You might have a computer at home.

GRAMMAR HINT

Diagram a preposition on a slanted line that has a tail. This line connects the object of the preposition to the word the phrase modifies.

Diagraming Predicate Nouns and Predicate Adjectives

You have learned that in a sentence diagram the direct object is placed after the action verb.

People use telephones.

| People | use | telephones |

A predicate noun follows a linking verb in the complete predicate of a sentence. In a sentence diagram a predicate noun is placed after the linking verb. Use a slanted line to separate the predicate noun from the verb.

Telephones are useful **instruments.**

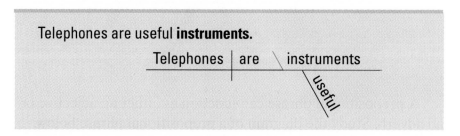

Diagram a predicate adjective in the same way.

Telephones are **useful**.

| Telephones | are \ useful |

GRAMMAR HINT

Place on the horizontal line only the single subject, the simple predicate, direct objects, predicate nouns, and predicate adjectives.

Exercise 5

Diagraming Sentences   Diagram each sentence.

1. The telephone is a recent invention.
2. Alexander Graham Bell was the inventor.
3. Telephones have become common.
4. Some calls are international.
5. Early telephones looked odd.
6. The first big change was the dial.
7. A much later improvement was the undersea cable.

18.6 Diagraming Compound Sentence Parts

Coordinating conjunctions such as *and, but,* and *or* are used to join words, phrases, or sentences. When you diagram compound parts of a sentence, you place the second part of the compound below the first. You write the coordinating conjunction on a dotted line connecting the two parts.

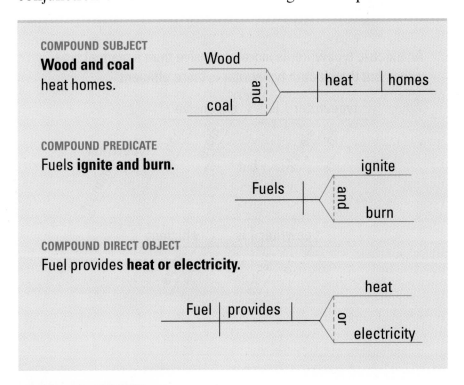

COMPOUND SUBJECT
Wood and coal heat homes.

COMPOUND PREDICATE
Fuels **ignite and burn.**

COMPOUND DIRECT OBJECT
Fuel provides **heat or electricity.**

Exercise 6

Diagraming Sentences   Diagram each sentence.

1. Oil and electricity are expensive.
2. Prices for fuels rise and fall.
3. Some families have used windmills or solar energy.
4. Stoves and furnaces provide heat.
5. Heated air or heated water circulates through the house.

18.7   Diagraming Compound Sentences

When you diagram compound sentences, diagram each clause separately. If the main clauses are connected by a semicolon, use a vertical dotted line to connect the verbs of each clause. If the main clauses are connected by a conjunction such as *and, but,* or *or,* place the conjunction on a solid horizontal line, and connect it to the verbs of each clause by vertical dotted lines.

An electric typewriter is more expensive than a manual typewriter, **but** the electric typewriter is more efficient.

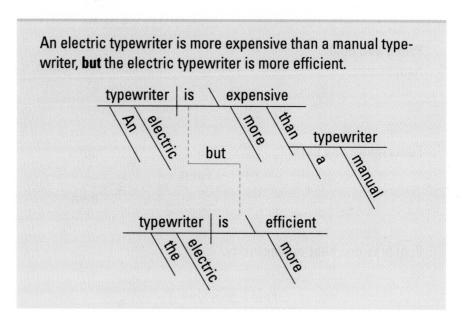

Exercise 7

Diagraming Sentences   Diagram each sentence.

1. C. L. Sholes experimented with typewriters in 1867, and he patented a typewriter in 1868.
2. E. Remington marketed the machine in 1874, and soon other firms manufactured typewriters.
3. Businesses use the larger typewriters, but students prefer portable typewriters.
4. Word processors have extensive capabilities, and they have display screens.

Diagraming Complex Sentences with Adjective and Adverb Clauses

When you diagram a complex sentence with an adjective clause, draw a dotted line between the relative pronoun introducing the clause and the word it modifies in the main clause. Diagram the relative pronoun according to its function in its own clause.

ADJECTIVE CLAUSE
People **who cooked** used enormous stoves.

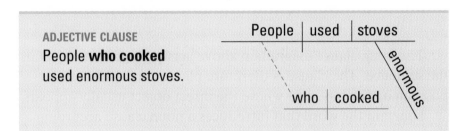

When you diagram a complex sentence with an adverb clause, draw the connecting line between the verb in the adverb clause and the word it modifies in the main clause. Then write the subordinating conjunction on the connecting line.

ADVERB CLAUSE
When people cooked, they used enormous stoves.

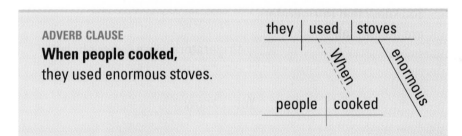

Exercise 8

Diagraming Sentences   Diagram each sentence.

1. People once used only stoves that burned wood.
2. Such stoves required attention while they were in use.
3. People who cooked on those stoves worked hard.
4. Families manually inserted the wood that these stoves required.
5. As the wood burned, ashes and dirt accumulated.

GRAMMAR HINT

When diagraming an adverb clause, always remember to write the subordinating conjunction on the dotted line.

18.9   Diagraming Noun Clauses

Noun clauses can be used in place of nouns as subjects, direct objects, objects of prepositions, or predicate nouns.

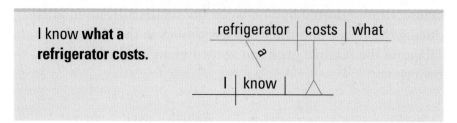

I know **what a refrigerator costs.**

The noun clause diagramed above acts as the direct object in the sentence. The clause is therefore placed on a "stilt" in the position on the base line where the direct object usually appears.

Diagram the word that introduces a noun clause according to its function within the clause. In the noun clause above, the word *what* is the direct object. Sometimes the word that introduces the noun clause is not truly part of either the noun clause or the main clause. Place such a word on its own line.

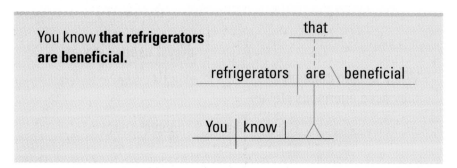

You know **that refrigerators are beneficial.**

Exercise 9

Diagraming Sentences   Diagram each sentence.

1. Whoever uses a refrigerator should be appreciative.
2. That iceboxes were helpful is undeniable.
3. People eagerly awaited what the iceman delivered.
4. When refrigeration began may surprise you.
5. People in the last century knew how it worked.
6. That the machinery was impractical was true.

18.10 Diagraming Verbals I

When diagraming a participle or a participial phrase, the line on which the participle is placed descends diagonally from the word the participle modifies and then extends to the right horizontally. The participle is written on a curve.

The machine, **humming loudly**, cooled the air rapidly.

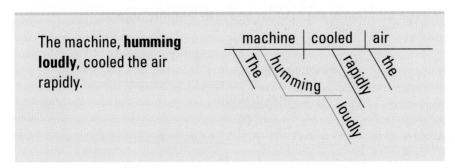

When diagraming a gerund or a gerund phrase, place the gerund on a "step." Set the step on a "stilt," positioning the stilt according to the role of the gerund. (A gerund can be a subject, an object of a verb or a preposition, or an appositive.)

Cleaning the air is another job of the machine.

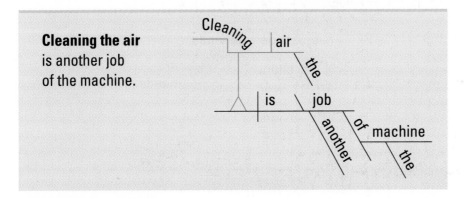

Exercise 10

Diagraming Sentences   Diagram each sentence.

1. Cooling the air was the subject of much research.
2. The machine cooled the heated air.
3. Controlling the temperature is not an easy task.
4. The circulating air cools everyone.

18.11　Diagraming Verbals II

When an infinitive or an infinitive phrase is used as a noun, diagram it as you would a prepositional phrase, and then place it on a "stilt" in the appropriate position.

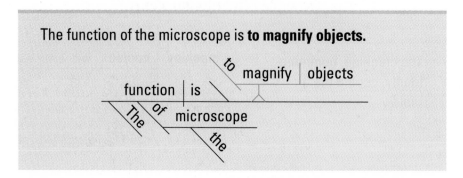

The function of the microscope is **to magnify objects.**

When an infinitive or an infinitive phrase is used as either an adjective or an adverb, diagram it as you would a prepositional phrase.

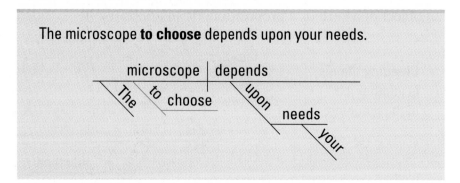

The microscope **to choose** depends upon your needs.

GRAMMAR HINT

Diagram the *to* that begins an infinitive or an infinitive phrase in the same position in which you would diagram a preposition.

Exercise 11

Diagraming Sentences　Diagram each sentence.

1. The Romans may have used glass crystal to magnify objects.
2. To discover the compound microscope was Janssen's mission.
3. Be sure to use microscopes carefully.
4. Sloan's job is to prepare the microscope for use.

Capitalization

Nancy Schutt, *Jacob Lawrence,* 1986

523

19.1 Capitalizing Sentences, Quotations, and Salutations

A capital letter appears at the beginning of a sentence. A capital letter also marks the beginning of a direct quotation and the salutation and closing of a letter.

RULE 1: Capitalize the first word of every sentence.

Many people helped our country gain independence.
Among them were George Washington, Thomas Jefferson, and Benjamin Franklin.

RULE 2: Capitalize the first word of a direct quotation that is a complete sentence. A direct quotation gives a speaker's exact words.

Travis said, "**A**nother one of those people was Paul Revere."

RULE 3: When a quoted sentence is interrupted by explanatory words, such as *she said*, do not begin the second part of the sentence with a capital letter.

"I read a famous poem," said Kim, "**a**bout Paul Revere."

When the second part of a quotation is a new sentence, put a period after the interrupting expression, and begin the second part of the quotation with a capital letter.

"I know that poem," said Sarah. "**M**y class read it last week."

RULE 4: Do not capitalize an indirect quotation. An indirect quotation does not repeat a person's exact words and does not appear in quotation marks. It is often preceded by the word *that*.

The teacher said **the** poem was written by Lange How.
Travis said **that** another man rode with Paul Revere.

RULE 5: Capitalize the first word in the salutation and closing of a letter. Capitalize the title and name of the person addressed.

Dear **M**rs. **A**dams   **Y**ours truly,

Capitalizing Sentences, Quotations, and Salutations

Write each sentence. Use capital letters where needed. If an item contains no error, write *correct*.

1. we wanted to learn more about Paul Revere.
2. "let's go to the library," said Lisa, "and see what we can find."
3. one book about Paul Revere says, "he designed the first issue of Continental money."
4. Hasan said that he was a silversmith and an engraver.
5. "he designed the colonies' first official seal," said Hasan. "then he engraved it."
6. "did you know that he took part in the Boston Tea Party?" asked Lisa.
7. "he is best known," said Hasan, "for warning the people that the British were coming."
8. we read that on his famous ride Paul Revere was accompanied by William Dawes.
9. "isn't it funny," said Hasan, "that Dawes is not known for this deed?"
10. "yes, it is," Lisa agreed. "the famous poem about the ride mentions only Paul Revere."
11. we decided to submit our report to a magazine.
12. Hasan began the letter, "dear sir or madam."
13. "we have written a report on Paul Revere," we wrote. "we would like to submit it to you."
14. they said that they would publish it.

Writing Link

If you could talk to any historical figure, who would it be? What would you say to each other? Write an imagined conversation.

19.2 Capitalizing Names and Titles of People

A common noun is the general name of a person, place, or thing. A common noun is not capitalized. A proper noun names a particular person, place, or thing and is capitalized.

RULE 1: Capitalize the names of people and the initials that stand for their names.

Lucretia Mott   E. C. Stanton

RULE 2: Capitalize a title or an abbreviation of a title when it comes before a person's name or when it is used in direct address.

In 1918 President Wilson planned the League of Nations.
"Has peace been declared, General?"

Do not capitalize a title that follows or is a substitute for a person's name.

Woodrow Wilson was president during World War I.

RULE 3: Capitalize the names and abbreviations of academic degrees that follow a person's name. Capitalize *Jr.* and *Sr.*

Martin Greer, Ph.D.   Eve Tanaka, M.D.   Carl Healy Sr.

RULE 4: Capitalize words that show family relationships when used as titles or as substitutes for a person's name.

We have pictures of Aunt Meg marching for women's rights.
In 1902 Grandmother was a suffragist.

Do not capitalize words that show family relationships when they follow a possessive noun or pronoun.

Maria's cousin wrote about women's suffrage.
My aunt has told me about the women's movement.

RULE 5: Always capitalize the pronoun *I.*

History is the subject I like best.

Exercise 2

Capitalizing Proper Names and Titles   Write each item, using capital letters where needed.

1. miss lucy stone
2. benjamin davis jr.
3. sonia fox, d.d.s.
4. emmeline g. pankhurst
5. maury kilbridge, ph.d.
6. peter ashike, m.a.
7. dr. michael thomas
8. general robert e. lee
9. sir walter raleigh
10. j. p. slaughter

Exercise 3

Using Capital Letters   Write each sentence, using capital letters where needed for names, titles, and abbreviations.

1. Without susan b. anthony women might not have the vote today.
2. With elizabeth cady stanton and m. j. gage, anthony wrote *History of Woman Suffrage.*
3. My great-grandmother once met miss anthony.
4. Later she met president wilson.
5. "Should women vote, mr. wilson?" she asked.
6. A shy man, woodrow wilson did not care to comment.
7. My great-grandmother and my great-grandfather knew the importance of the right to vote.
8. A colonel in the army, aunt helen owes a debt of gratitude to the women's movement.
9. My uncle and i often tease, "Do you think women belong in the military, colonel?"

We have a picture of our **great aunt Meg.**

Here is **Great Aunt Meg** marching for women's rights.

Writing Link

Write a paragraph describing a relative or a close friend, and highlight something unique about that person.

The names of specific places are proper nouns and are capitalized. Do not capitalize articles and prepositions that are part of geographical names, however.

RULE 1:   Capitalize the names of cities, counties, states, countries, and continents.

    Chicago   Dade County   Hawaii

RULE 2:   Capitalize the names of bodies of water and geographical features.

    Dead Sea   Gulf of Mexico   Rocky Mountains

RULE 3:   Capitalize the names of sections of the country.

    New England   Midwest   the Northwest

RULE 4:   Capitalize compass points when they refer to a specific section of the country.

    the West Coast   the West   the Northwest

Do not capitalize compass points when they indicate direction.

    Milwaukee is north of Chicago.

Do not capitalize adjectives derived from words indicating direction.

    southerly wind   northern Texas

RULE 5:   Capitalize the names of streets and highways.

    River Road   West Side Highway

RULE 6:   Capitalize the names of buildings, bridges, and monuments.

    Golden Gate Bridge
    Lincoln Memorial

You are now entering North Dakota.

Great West Highway

This way north

Capitalizing Place Names   Write each word or group
of words, using capital letters where needed.

1. northern illinois
2. world trade center
3. spain
4. arabian desert
5. northern california
6. front street
7. national boulevard
8. carlsbad caverns
9. nebraska
10. atlantic ocean
11. yellowstone river
12. yankee stadium
13. pennsylvania avenue
14. mediterranean sea

Using Capital Letters   Write each sentence, using
capital letters where needed for geographical names.

1. The louisiana purchase covered 827,987 square miles.
2. The united states bought the land from france.
3. It extended from canada to mexico.
4. The land was bordered by the mississippi river on the
   east and by the rocky mountains on the west.
5. The purchase of the land doubled the size of the
   united states of america.
6. It also ended French control of the mississippi valley.
7. The Americans had wanted only a small piece of
   land that allowed access to the west.
8. Now Americans could move farther west.
9. Someday the country might extend to the west coast.

Writing Link

Write a brief paragraph about the place where you
live. Name the region of the country in which it is located
and any nearby landmarks.

19.4 Capitalizing Other Proper Nouns and Adjectives

Many nouns besides the names of people and places are proper nouns. Adjectives that are formed from proper nouns are called proper adjectives. For example, the proper adjective *Cuban* is formed from the proper noun *Cuba*.

RULE 1: Capitalize the names of clubs, organizations, businesses, institutions, and political parties.

American Bar Association   Farragut Middle School

RULE 2: Capitalize brand names but not the nouns following them.

Smoothies lotion   Neato sneakers

RULE 3: Capitalize the names of important historical events, periods of time, and documents.

Vietnam War   Renaissance   Gettysburg Address

RULE 4: Capitalize the names of days of the week, months of the year, and holidays. Do not capitalize names of the seasons.

Friday   July   Thanksgiving Day   winter

RULE 5: Capitalize the first word, the last word, and all important words in the title of a book, play, short story, poem, essay, article, film, television series, song, magazine, newspaper, and chapter of a book.

Profiles in Courage   "The Necklace"   *Newsweek*

RULE 6: Capitalize the names of ethnic groups, nationalities, and languages.

Vietnamese   Chilean   German

RULE 7: Capitalize proper adjectives that are formed from the names of ethnic groups and nationalities.

Chinese cooking   Japanese flag

GRAMMAR HINT

Capitalize the name of a period of time if it is formed from a person's name—for example, *Victorian novels* (from *Queen Victoria*).

Exercise 6

Capitalizing Proper Nouns and Adjectives Write the following items. Use capital letters where needed.

1. sunnyvale school
2. *reader's digest*
3. english
4. magna charta
5. "yankee doodle"
6. egyptian history
7. american red cross
8. girl scouts
9. wheatola cereal
10. *boston globe*
11. boston tea party
12. memorial day

Exercise 7

Using Capital Letters Write each sentence, using capital letters where needed for proper nouns and adjectives. Write *correct* if the sentence has no errors.

1. The emancipation proclamation ended slavery in the South.
2. President Abraham Lincoln wrote this document in the summer of 1862.
3. Lincoln issued it during the civil war.
4. Lincoln is also famous for the Gettysburg address, a short speech he delivered in november 1863.
5. The Thirteenth Amendment, ratified in december 1865, ended slavery in the United States.
6. The Fourteenth Amendment to the constitution was also ratified soon after the war.
7. The war was well documented in *harper's weekly*.

Writing Link

Write a paragraph about your favorite holiday. Describe the origin of the holiday and what you do to celebrate it.

Mechanics Workshop

Capitalization

Morning Star, Black Sun by Brent Ashabranner details the efforts of the Northern Cheyenne to preserve their cherished homeland. In the following passage from the book, Joe Little Coyote, a young Northern Cheyenne man, relates the story of how his people had obtained their reservation. The passage has been annotated to show some of the rules of capitalization covered in this unit.

Literature Model

from MORNING STAR, BLACK SUN

by Brent Ashabranner

Title coming before a person's name

Name of a person

Name of a body of water

First word of a direct quotation that is a complete sentence

Place name

"When General Miles—the Indians called him Bear Coat—decided to help my ancestors get a reservation," Joe Little Coyote said, "he picked a group of Cheyenne under Chief Two Moons and a troop of soldiers and told them to ride through the country until they found good land for a reservation. The Cheyenne rode straight to the Tongue River, and they said that was the land they wanted. The soldiers wanted them to look further, to be sure they had found the best place. They were afraid General Miles might think they hadn't done their job right. But the Cheyenne said, 'No. This will be our land.'"

Then Joe Little Coyote said, "Our spiritual history is here, in this land, and in Bear Butte where Sweet Medicine received the Sacred Arrows. This is more than a reservation. This is our homeland." And he added, "You don't sell your homeland."

Mechanics Workshop Exercise 1

Capitalizing Sentences   Rewrite each sentence, correcting any errors in capitalization.

SAMPLE Joe Little Coyote said, "our spiritual history is in this land."

ANSWER Joe Little Coyote said, "Our spiritual history is in this land."

1. "My ancestors got the reservation," he explained, "With the help of General Miles."
2. Chief Two Moons said That the land along the Tongue River was the land they wanted.
3. the soldiers asked the Cheyenne, "do you want to look further?"
4. the Cheyenne said that the land near the Tongue River would be their home.
5. Joe Little Coyote said, " you don't sell your homeland."

Mechanics Workshop Exercise 2

Capitalizing Proper Nouns   The following sentences are about Joe Little Coyote. Rewrite each sentence, correcting any errors in capitalization.

SAMPLE Joe Little coyote went to harvard.

ANSWER Joe Little Coyote went to Harvard.

1. Joe returned to the land by the tongue river.
2. He worked to preserve Their Reservation.
3. Joe told the young people that their ancestors had come from bear butte.
4. The young man explained, "My Grandfather and my Father settled in this valley."
5. Generations of northern cheyenne have lived on the land that general Miles gave them.

Capitalizing Proper Nouns and Proper Adjectives
Rewrite each sentence, correcting any errors in capitalization.

1. The cheyenne once lived together.
2. In the early 1830s they split into two groups—the northern and the southern cheyenne.
3. In 1876 the northern cheyenne fought the settlers in the midwest who tried to take away their land.
4. The cheyenne and the sioux defeated lieutenant colonel custer in the Battle of the little Bighorn.
5. The american government gave the northern cheyenne a reservation in montana in 1884.

Proofreading The following passage is about artist Robert Henri, whose work appears on the next page. Rewrite the passage, correcting the errors in spelling, capitalization, punctuation, grammar, and usage. There are ten errors in all.

Robert Henri

[1]Robert Henri (1865–1929) was an american portrait and cityscape painter who's subjects sparkle with life. [2]The artist painted ordinary and exotic people rather then the rich and famous. [3]His paintings of urbin life helped portray a newer, more modern era.
[4]Henri's aim in painting were to capture feeling and sensation. [5]In *Portrait of Po Tse (Water Eagle)* this spirit is conveyed through the subjects' expressive, dignified face. [6]Dressed in traditionel clothes, the subject shows pride in his Native american heritage. [7]like Joe Little Coyote in *Morning Star, Black Sun,* the subject in the portrait cherishes his Homeland.

Robert Henri, *Portrait of Po Tse (Water Eagle),* **c. 1916–1925**

Capitalization

Capitalizing Sentences and Quotations

[pages 524–525]

Write each sentence. Use capital letters where needed.

1. the French gave us the Statue of Liberty on July 4, 1884.
2. in 1924 the statue became a national monument.
3. "this majestic copper statue," said Otis, "stands on Liberty Island."
4. immigrants saw the statue as they approached New York Harbor.
5. Colleen said, "my grandparents saw the statue from their ship."

Capitalizing Names and Titles of People

[pages 526–527]

Write each sentence. Use capital letters where needed.

6. As a girl shirley chisholm studied hard.
7. Mr. and mrs. chisholm took pride in their daughter's achievements.
8. In 1959 shirley chisholm, m.a., became an educational consultant.
9. Later she became known as congress-woman chisholm.
10. She was aunt jean's congresswoman.

Capitalizing Names of Places and Other Proper Nouns and Adjectives

[pages 528–531]

Write each sentence. Use capital letters where needed.

11. Thomas edison, an american inventor, was born in milan, ohio.
12. Edison worked for a company called the grand trunk railway.
13. Later he printed a newspaper known as the *weekly herald.*
14. He tested the phonograph he invented by reciting "mary had a little lamb."
15. Later he organized the edison general electric company.
16. During world war I he worked for the united states government.
17. Few americans are more famous.
18. Communication between the east coast and the west coast greatly improved because of his inventions.
19. The french government awarded him the Legion of Honor.
20. In 1960 new york university elected him to its hall of fame.

Writing for Review

Imagine you have just made a great invention. Describe it in a journal entry. Use some proper nouns and adjectives.

Punctuation

Vincent van Gogh, *Summer Evening, Wheatfield with Setting Sun*, 1888

20.1 Using the Period and Other End Marks

Different end marks are used with the different types of sentences. The period is used for declarative and imperative sentences. The question mark is used for interrogative sentences, and the exclamation point is used for exclamatory sentences.

RULE 1: Use a period at the end of a declarative sentence. A declarative sentence makes a statement.

Tractors perform many jobs on a farm.
Tractors pull plows.
I worked on a farm last summer.

RULE 2: Use a period at the end of an imperative sentence. An imperative sentence gives a command or makes a request.

Turn the key. [command]
Please start the motor. [request]

RULE 3: Use a question mark at the end of an interrogative sentence. An interrogative sentence asks a question.

When was the first tractor built?
Were you aware of that?
Do modern tractors have both speed and power?

RULE 4: Use an exclamation point at the end of an exclamatory sentence. An exclamatory sentence expresses strong feeling.

What a powerful tractor that is!
How fast it moves!
What an amazing machine that is!

RULE 5: Use an exclamation point at the end of an interjection. An interjection is a word or group of words that expresses strong emotion.

Wow!	My goodness!	Hi!	Hey!
Hooray!	Oh, boy!	Oops!	Phew!

Exercise 1

Using End Marks   Add the correct end mark to each sentence, and then write whether each sentence is *declarative, imperative, interrogative,* or *exclamatory.*

1. Please tell me about the history of tractors
2. Read about tractors in your book
3. The first tractor was used in the 1870s
4. This tractor was driven by steam
5. Was this machine very large
6. Could it haul and pull heavy loads
7. Can you believe that this tractor could pull as many as forty plows
8. Please tell me about the early days of farming
9. Open your history book
10. Read about the fascinating techniques used by ancient farmers
11. The early Egyptians developed the first large-scale irrigation system
12. What a tremendous advancement this was
13. Each year the Nile River overflowed its banks
14. Farmers discovered they could grow crops by using this water
15. Did farmers prosper when the Nile overflowed
16. In 3000 B.C. Egyptian farmers invented the ox-drawn plow
17. This plow helped Egyptian farmers produce a great deal of food

To recognize an imperative sentence, remember that the complete predicate is the entire sentence. The word *you* is the understood subject of all imperative sentences.

Writing Link

Think about one invention that helped make farming easier, and describe its effect in a paragraph. Use the three end marks in your sentences.

20.2　Using Commas I

Commas make sentences easier to understand because they signal a pause or separation between parts of a sentence.

and　clog city streets.

RULE 1:　Use commas to separate three or more items in a series.

Cars, buses, and trucks clog city streets.

RULE 2:　Use a comma to show a pause after an introductory word.

Yes, most cities have few parking garages.

RULE 3:　Use a comma after two or more introductory prepositional phrases.

In the fall of 1991, Frank M. Jordan was elected mayor.

RULE 4:　Use a comma after an introductory participle and an introductory participial phrase.

Plagued by deficits, many cities need state aid.

RULE 5:　Use commas to set off words that interrupt the flow of thought in a sentence.

A large city, as you can see, employs many police officers.

RULE 6:　Use a comma after conjunctive adverbs such as *however, moreover, furthermore, nevertheless,* and *therefore.*

The city is growing; therefore, the city payroll must grow.

RULE 7:　Use commas to set off an appositive if it is not essential to the meaning of a sentence.

Alpine Inc., this city's oldest company, joined a large cartel.

RULE 8:　Use commas to set off names used in direct address.

Tony, are you going downtown?

Exercise 2

Using Commas   Add a comma or commas where needed to the following sentences. Write *correct* if the sentence needs no changes.

1. Yes cities offer many different places to live.
2. Some people live in apartment buildings private homes and town houses.
3. In the middle of the city you can see skyscrapers.
4. Some buildings are neat clean and attractive.
5. Other buildings are dirty and neglected.
6. The city has a large population.
7. Traveling away from the center of the city you can find less crowded living conditions.
8. Many people in cities do not have large back yards.
9. Yolanda did you know that San Diego is one of the nation's fastest growing cities?
10. A big city in my opinion is the best place to live.
11. Norm do you prefer the city or the country?
12. Does Jo your new friend enjoy living in the city?
13. Pausing a moment to consider my answer I responded that she likes the city.
14. Moreover she has never lived in the country.
15. Eva dislikes the city; nevertheless she refuses to move.
16. Country houses you might imagine have more land.
17. I hope Maya you can find a big house in the country.
18. The suburbs I suppose would be a good alternative Maya.

Writing Link

Where would you rather live—the city or the country? Write about the advantages of one or the other. Use commas in your sentences.

20.3   Using Commas II

Use commas correctly in sentences with clauses. A clause is a group of words that has a subject and a predicate and is used as part of a sentence.

RULE 9:   Use a comma before *and, or,* or *but* when it joins main clauses.

Farming is a business, and farmers need to make a profit.
Farmers must sell their crops, or they cannot afford to replant.
Farming can be rewarding, but it is hard work.

RULE 10:   Use a comma after an introductory adverb clause. Adverb clauses begin with subordinating conjunctions such as *after, although, as, because, before, considering (that), if, in order that, since, so that, though, unless, until, when, whenever, where, wherever, whether,* or *while.*

When the weather is too dry, farmers have problems.
If there is no rain, crops can be ruined.

Do not use a comma with an adverb clause that comes at the end of a sentence.

Farmers have problems when the weather is too dry.
Crops can be ruined if there is no rain.

RULE 11:   Use a comma or a pair of commas to set off an adjective clause that is nonessential. An adjective clause is nonessential when it is not necessary to the meaning of the sentence. This means that the clause merely gives additional information. Adjective clauses often begin with the relative pronouns *who, whom, whose, which,* or *that.*

Dairy cows, which are common on farms, are raised for their milk.

Do not use a comma or pair of commas to set off an essential clause from the rest of the sentence. An adjective clause is essential when it is necessary to the meaning of the sentence.

The animal that is raised for milk is the dairy cow.

Using Commas with Clauses   Write each sentence. Add a comma or commas where needed. Write *correct* if the sentence needs no changes.

1. Agriculture offers many careers but only some of these careers involve farm work.
2. Farmers may grow crops or they may raise animals.
3. Before they plant crops farmers prepare the soil.
4. Whenever weeds appear farmers must act quickly.
5. Insects that harm crops can be controlled.

Using Commas with Subordinate Clauses   Write each sentence. Underline each subordinate clause and add any needed commas.

1. Pest control which is very expensive remains important to farmers.
2. Boll weevils which feed on cotton plants are a pest.
3. Farmers guard against the boll weevil since it harms cotton crops.
4. Some predators that we call helpful aid farmers.
5. As long as people have been farming the ladybug has been a helpful predator.
6. Wasps which people usually fear also help farmers by eating caterpillars.
7. Farmers need the help of predators because these insects aid in pest control.

Writing Link

   If you could work in agriculture, what would you like to do? Use subordinate clauses in writing your answer.

20.4 Using Commas III

Several rules for using commas—among those the rules for punctuating dates and addresses—are a matter of standard usage.

RULE 12: Use commas before and after the year when it is used with both the month and the day. Do not use a comma if only the month and the year are given.

> The antipollution project began on May 25, 1992, and lasted a year.
> The first meeting was held in July 1992.

RULE 13: Use commas before and after the name of a state or a country when it is used with the name of a city. Do not use a comma after the state if it is used with a ZIP code.

> Speakers came from Palo Alto, California, to speak at the meeting.
> The address on the envelope was as follows: 123 Ridge Road, Orange, CT 06477.

RULE 14: Use a comma or pair of commas to set off an abbreviated title or degree following a person's name.

> One expert on pollution and health is Jay Carr, M.D.
> Peter Fujita, Ph.D., wrote a book on pollution.

RULE 15: Use a comma before *too* when *too* means "also."

> Water pollution creates problems, too.

RULE 16: Use a comma or commas to set off a direct quotation.

> Dr. Flores said, "Pollution causes serious problems in our cities."
> "We will try," said Joan, "to fight pollution."

RULE 17: Use a comma after the salutation of a friendly letter and after the closing of both a friendly and a business letter.

> Dear Sharon,   Your friend,   Yours truly,

RULE 18: Use a comma to prevent misreading.

> Instead of three, four panelists discussed pollution.

Using Commas Add commas to the sentences below, or write *correct* if the sentence needs no changes.

1. A letter from Austin Texas arrived today.
2. Larry said "We are going to have a meeting soon."
3. "Is Dr. Jean Loubet" asked Evan "a physician?"
4. Jean Loubet Ph.D. is an expert on pollution.
5. His new book will be published in June 1994.

Using Commas Add any needed commas to each of the following numbered items.

[1] 109 National Boulevard
[2] Los Angeles California 90034
[3] September 30 1993

[4] Dear Aunt Patricia

[5] Last week my teacher said "We can all do more to stop pollution." [6] I think that students can help too. [7] I said to Yoko "Let's make posters for the Stop Pollution Fair." [8] The fair will be like the one that was held on January 5 1992 in Denver Colorado. [9] Alex Gafar M.A. will speak on recycling.

[10] Much love
Antonia

Writing Link

Write a letter to the editor of your school newspaper urging students to show more concern for the environment. Use commas correctly.

20.5   Using Semicolons and Colons

RULE 1:   Use a semicolon to join the parts of a compound sentence when a coordinating conjunction such as *and, or, nor,* or *but* is not used.

> Many people in Africa farm small pieces of land; these farmers raise food for their families.

RULE 2:   Use a semicolon to join parts of a compound sentence when the main clauses are long and are subdivided by commas, even if these clauses are already joined by a coordinating conjunction.

> Herding is an important job for the Dinka, Masai, and Turkana; but plowing, planting, and harvesting are also crucial tasks.

RULE 3:   Use a semicolon to separate main clauses joined by a conjunctive adverb such as *consequently, furthermore, however, moreover, nevertheless,* or *therefore.* Be sure to use a comma after a conjunctive adverb.

> Many African farmers grow crops on family-owned farms; however, in some areas farmers work on land owned by the government.

RULE 4:   Use a colon to introduce a list of items that ends a sentence. Use a phrase such as *these, the following,* or *as follows* before the list.

> African farmers grow the following: corn, millet, and sorghum.

> Do not use a colon immediately after a verb or a preposition.

> Some farmers work with hoes, knives, and digging sticks.

RULE 5:   Use a colon to separate the hour and the minute when you write the time of day.

> Many farmers start working at 5:15 in the morning.

RULE 6:   Use a colon after the salutation of a business letter.

> Dear Sir or Madam: Dear Ms. Ngai:

GRAMMAR HINT

Use a semicolon (not a comma) to join together two main clauses that have closely related meanings.

Exercise 7

Using Semicolons and Colons   Write each sentence. Add a semicolon or a colon where needed.

1. I received a letter from my cousin she wrote about her work in Africa.
2. Jill told me that Africa could be divided into these regions deserts, tropical jungles, and farmlands.
3. She wrote, "It's 745 in the evening."
4. Jill mentioned the following products of Tanzania cotton, coffee, and sugar.
5. Jill finds life in Africa fascinating nevertheless, she misses the United States.

Exercise 8

Using Semicolons and Colons   Add a semicolon or a colon where needed in the following numbered items.

[1]Dear Mr. Bishop

[2]I am buying a farm for my venture I will need farming equipment. [3]I will have to buy plows, tractors, and spreaders. [4]In the near future I will also need the following items seed, fertilizer, and more machinery. [5]I am now pricing equipment therefore, if you are interested in doing business with me, please supply me with a list of your prices.

Sincerely yours,
Eleni

Writing Link

Write a letter to a friend proposing a business venture. Use a colon and a semicolon in your sentences.

20.6 Using Quotation Marks and Italics

Quotation marks enclose a person's exact words as well as the titles of some works. Italic type—a special slanted type that is used in printing—identifies titles of other works.

RULE 1: Use quotation marks before and after a direct quotation.

"A nomad is a person who wanders," May said.

RULE 2: Use quotation marks with a divided quotation.

"Most nomads," said Ali, "travel by animal or on foot."

RULE 3: Use a comma or commas to separate a phrase such as *he said* from the quotation itself. Place the comma outside opening quotation marks but inside closing quotation marks.

"Most nomads," Betsy explained, "raise animals."

RULE 4: Place a period inside closing quotation marks.

José said, "Some nomads move their animals through deserts."

RULE 5: Place a question mark or an exclamation point inside the quotation marks when it is part of the quotation.

Bo asked, "Do nomads travel to find water for their herds?"

RULE 6: Place a question mark or an exclamation point outside the quotation marks when it is part of the entire sentence.

Did Ms. McCall say, "Write an essay on nomads"?

RULE 7: Use quotation marks for the title of a short story, essay, poem, song, magazine or newspaper article, or book chapter.

"Dusk" [short story]   "Mending Wall" [poem]   "Skylark" [song]

RULE 8: Use italics (underlining) to identify the title of a book, play, film, television series, magazine, or newspaper.

The Sea Wolf [book]   *Julius Caesar* [play]   *Newsweek* [magazine]

Exercise 9

Punctuating Titles   Correctly add quotation marks or underlining for italics to each of the items below.

1. Nanook of the North (film)
2.. New York Times (newspaper)
3. The Eternal Nomad (poem)
4. The Old Man and the Sea (book)
5. Dream-Children (essay)
6. Star Trek (television series)
7. The Skin of Our Teeth (play)

Exercise 10

Using Quotation Marks and Italics   Add quotation marks, italics, and other punctuation marks where needed in the following sentences.

1. Frieda asked Have you read the article in our textbook
2. Bonnie shouted What an interesting article on nomads that was
3. Nomadic herders live mainly in Africa and Asia said Sylvia but they also are found in other areas
4. The Lapps live in Lapland said Ms. Ito.
5. Did Ms. Ito say Lapland is in Scandinavia
6. Barry asked Have you read the article on Lapps in National Geographic
7. No I answered but I read about them in a book

"Most nomads,"

said Ali,

"travel by animal or on foot."

Writing Link

Write a dialogue between two people debating the advantages and drawbacks of nomadic life as you imagine it.

20.7 Using the Apostrophe

An apostrophe shows possession; the missing letters in a contraction; and the plurals of letters, numbers, or words.

RULE 1: Use an apostrophe and an *s* (*'s*) to form the possessive of a singular noun.

girl + **'s** = girl**'s**   Francis + **'s** = Francis**'s**

RULE 2: Use an apostrophe and an *s* (*'s*) to form the possessive of a plural noun that does not end in *s*.

women + **'s** = women**'s**   mice + **'s** = mice**'s**

RULE 3: Use an apostrophe alone to form the possessive of a plural noun that ends in *s*.

girls + **'** = girl**s'**   Johnsons + **'** = Johnson**s'**

RULE 4: Use an apostrophe and an *s* (*'s*) to form the possessive of an indefinite pronoun.

anyone + **'s** = anyone**'s**   somebody + **'s** = somebody**'s**

Do not use an apostrophe in a possessive pronoun.

That map is **theirs**.
The books on the table are **hers**.

RULE 5: Use an apostrophe to replace letters that have been omitted in a contraction. A **contraction** is a word that is made by combining two words into one by leaving out one or more letters.

it + is = it**'s**   you + are = you**'re**
there + is = there**'s**   did + not + didn**'t**

RULE 6: Use an apostrophe to form the plurals of letters, figures, and words when they are used as themselves.

three *t***'s**   five *6***'s**   *and***'s**, *if***'s**, and *but***'s**

RULE 7: Use an apostrophe to show missing numbers in a date.

the class of **'87**

Exercise 11

Using the Possessive Form   Write the possessive form of each of the words below.

1. cities
2. nation
3. everybody
4. children
5. Mr. Schultz
6. dogs
7. man
8. Sharice
9. woman
10. geese
11. classes
12. teacher
13. Alex
14. someone
15. oxen
16. Jim

Exercise 12

Using Apostrophes   Write each sentence. Use apostrophes where they are needed. Write *correct* if the sentence needs no changes.

1. This citys outlook is uncertain.
2. Ours is an uncertain future.
3. Today cities arent built beneath the earth.
4. Its strange to think of underground cities.
5. Perhaps well see cities floating on the water.
6. Many city planners ideas are unusual.
7. Their reports usually are filled with too many *ifs*.
8. Tomorrows cities are a mystery to us.
9. No city can plan its future exactly.
10. All of our visions are full of *maybes*.

Writing Link

Imagine that you have been transported by a time machine into a futuristic city. Write your impressions in a journal. Use apostrophes in your sentences.

20.8 Using Hyphens, Dashes, and Parentheses

RULE 1: Use a hyphen to show the division of a word at the end of a line. Always divide the word between its syllables.

> Forests and their products are of the greatest impor-
> tance to people.

RULE 2: Use a hyphen in compound numbers.

> eighty-seven coats   thirty-nine trees

RULE 3: Use a hyphen in a fraction that is used as a modifier. Do not use a hyphen in a fraction used as a noun.

> Forest rangers receive **one-half** pay upon retirement. [modifier]
> **One half** of all tree diseases are caused by fungi. [noun]

RULE 4: Use a hyphen or hyphens in certain compound nouns.

> great-grandfather   brother-in-law   attorney-at-law

RULE 5: Hyphenate a compound modifier only when it precedes the word it modifies.

> It's a **well-maintained** park.   It is **well maintained**.

RULE 6: Use a hyphen after the prefixes *all-*, *ex-*, and *self-*. Use a hyphen to separate any prefix from a word that begins with a capital letter.

> all-powerful   self-educated   pre-Columbian

RULE 7: Use a dash or dashes to show a sudden break or change in thought or speech.

> Mrs. Poulos—she lives nearby—helps the park attendants.

RULE 8: Use parentheses to set off material that is not part of the main statement but that is, nevertheless, important to include.

> In tropical rain forests dozens of species of plants may grow in one square mile (2.6 square kilometers) of land.

Using Hyphens   Write each item. Use a hyphen where needed. Write *correct* if the item needs no hyphens.

1. two thirds majority
2. three fourths of the council
3. exchampion
4. self knowledge
5. well loved author
6. all inclusive
7. great aunt
8. sixty five
9. mid American
10. postwar

Using Hyphens, Dashes, and Parentheses   Add any needed hyphens, dashes, or parentheses to the following sentences. Write *correct* if the sentence needs no changes.

1. Before people began to clear the forest for farms and cities, forests covered about one half of the earth.
2. Dr. Orzeck he is an expert on ecology spoke about deforestation.
3. His presentation was well documented.
4. People have used wood products since the beginning of time but more about that later.
5. One tree may have as many as forty two uses.
6. Prehistoric people obtained food by hunting and gathering wild plants in the forest.
7. Later many Native Americans showed European settlers new ways to use the forest.
8. Deer were once well protected animals.

Writing Link

In a paragraph discuss some of the products that can be made from what forests provide. Use hyphens, dashes, and parentheses.

National
Aeronautics and
Space
Administration

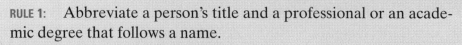

20.9 Using Abbreviations

RULE 1: Abbreviate a person's title and a professional or an academic degree that follows a name.

Mr. Roy Wells **Jr.**   Rosa Mendoza, **M.D.**   Lou Alex, **Ph.D.**

RULE 2: Abbreviate the names of certain organizations and government agencies, using capital letters and no periods.

World Health Organization   **WHO**

RULE 3: Use the abbreviations *A.M.* and *P.M.* and *B.C.* and *A.D.*

7:15 **A.M.**   9:30 **P.M.**   40 **B.C.**   **A.D.** 476

RULE 4: Abbreviate calendar items only in charts and lists.

Sun.   Tues.   Wed.   Mar.   Aug.   Sept.

RULE 5: In scientific writing abbreviate units of measure.

inch(es) **in.**   pound(s) **lb.**   kilometer(s) **km**   liter(s) **l**

RULE 6: In informal writing abbreviate street names.

Street **St.**   Avenue **Ave.**   Road **Rd.**   Drive **Dr.**

RULE 7: In informal writing and on envelopes, use Postal Service abbreviations for the names of states.

Postal Service Abbreviations

		District of		Louisiana	LA	New Hampshire	NH	South Carolina	SC
		Columbia	DC	Maine	ME	New Jersey	NJ	South Dakota	SD
		Florida	FL	Maryland	MD	New Mexico	NM	Tennessee	TN
Alabama	AL	Georgia	GA	Massachusetts	MA	New York	NY	Texas	TX
Alaska	AK	Hawaii	HI	Michigan	MI	North Carolina	NC	Utah	UT
Arizona	AZ	Idaho	ID	Minnesota	MN	North Dakota	ND	Vermont	VT
Arkansas	AR	Illinois	IL	Mississippi	MS	Ohio	OH	Virginia	VA
California	CA	Indiana	IN	Missouri	MO	Oklahoma	OK	Washington	WA
Colorado	CO	Iowa	IA	Montana	MT	Oregon	OR	West Virginia	WV
Connecticut	CT	Kansas	KS	Nebraska	NE	Pennsylvania	PA	Wisconsin	WI
Delaware	DE	Kentucky	KY	Nevada	NV	Rhode Island	RI	Wyoming	WY

Exercise 15

Using Abbreviations Write the correct abbreviation for each underlined item.

1. <u>after Christ</u> 2000
2. David Parker <u>Junior</u>
3. 153 <u>kilometers</u>
4. <u>October</u> 23
5. <u>Thursday</u>
6. 1066 <u>before Christ</u>
7. <u>Young Women's Christian Association</u>
8. <u>Senator</u> Al Moreno
9. ninety-eight <u>pounds</u>
10. Saratoga <u>Road</u>
11. 67 Ryer <u>Avenue</u>
12. Sam Blie <u>Senior</u>
13. Duluth, <u>Minnesota</u>
14. Lewis Wright, <u>Medical Doctor</u>

The abbreviation B.C. (before Christ) always follows the date: *336 B.C.* A.D. (*anno Domini,* Latin for "the year of the Lord") always comes before the date: *A.D. 66.*

Exercise 16

Using Abbreviations Abbreviate each underlined item in the following sentences.

1. The letter was addressed to 48 Bolton <u>Street</u>, Madison, <u>Wisconsin</u>.
2. It contained information from <u>Representative</u> Rita Tapahonso.
3. <u>Mister</u> Ed Jones is teaching ecology.
4. Last year classes met from 9:30 <u>in the morning</u> until 3:30 <u>in the afternoon</u>.
5. Scheduled speakers included <u>Doctor</u> Robin Oren.
6. Also present will be a representative of the <u>Geological Society of America</u>.
7. Classes begin in <u>September</u>.
8. My adviser will see me on <u>Friday</u>.

Writing Link

Write a formal letter inviting a friend to a lecture on rock climbing. Use several acceptable abbreviations.

20.10 Writing Numbers

In charts and tables, numbers are always written as figures. However, in an ordinary sentence, numbers are sometimes spelled out and sometimes written as numerals.

RULE 1: Spell out numbers that you can write in one or two words.

My dad had not visited his hometown for **twenty-five** years.

RULE 2: Use numerals for numbers of more than two words.

Approximately **250** people used to live in his hometown.

RULE 3: Spell out any number that begins a sentence, or reword the sentence so that it does not begin with a number.

Nine thousand two hundred people now live in Dad's hometown.

RULE 4: Write very large numbers as a numeral followed by the word *million* or *billion*.

The population of the United States is about **248 million**.

RULE 5: If related numbers appear in the same sentence, use all numerals.

Of the **435** graduates, **30** have received a scholarship to college.

RULE 6: Spell out ordinal numbers (first, second, and so forth).

Jan is the **sixth** person to use the new library.

RULE 7: Use words to express the time of day unless you are writing the exact time with the abbreviation A.M. or P.M.

Classes begin at **nine o'clock**.
They end at **2:45** P.M.

RULE 8: Use numerals to express dates, house and street numbers, apartment and room numbers, telephone numbers, page numbers, amounts of money of more than two words, and percentages. Write out the word *percent*.

May **24, 1887**   **62** Oak Drive   Room **307**   **98** percent

Writing Numbers   Use the correct form for writing numbers in the sentences below. Write *correct* if a sentence needs no changes.

1. My father graduated from Red Bank Regional High School with the class of nineteen hundred sixty-one.
2. His class recently had a reunion after thirty years.
3. The party began at seven-thirty P.M.
4. The reunion was held in room forty-two, the old cafeteria.
5. 220 people came to the reunion.
6. More than 50% of the graduates attended.
7. Each alumnus contributed twenty dollars.
8. The party lasted until one o'clock.
9. My father graduated 5th in his class.

Writing Numbers   In the following paragraph use the correct form for writing numbers.

[1] In nineteen hundred ninety-one the population of the United States was approximately 248 million. [2] The estimated population of North America was three hundred ninety million. [3] North America has the 3rd largest population of the world's continents. [4] Asia has the largest, with fifty-nine percent. [5] More than three billion people live in Asia. [6] Africa ranks 2nd in the world's population.

Writing Link

Write a letter accepting an invitation to your sixth-grade class reunion. Observe the rules for using numbers in sentences.

$\mathscr{M}$echanics Workshop

Punctuation

Tourists see a place differently from the way local inhabitants do. In *A Small Place* Jamaica Kincaid writes about her homeland, the small Caribbean island of Antigua. In the following passage from the book, Kincaid looks at the island through the eyes of a tourist. She describes the island's beauty and discusses its history. She also expresses her hopes for the future of Antigua. The passage has been annotated to show some of the rules of punctuation covered in this unit.

Literature Model

from A SMALL PLACE

by Jamaica Kincaid

Comma before *and* used to join main clauses

Semicolon to join parts of a compound sentence without a conjunction

Dash to show an interrupted thought

Comma after two introductory prepositional phrases

Oh, but by now you are tired of all this looking , and you want to reach your destination—your hotel, your room. You long to refresh yourself ; you long to eat some nice lobster, some nice local food. You take a bath, you brush your teeth. You get dressed again; as you get dressed, you look out the window. That water — have you ever seen anything like it? Far out, to the horizon, the color of the water is navy-blue; nearer, the water is the color of the North American sky. From there to the shore , the water is pale, silvery, clear, so clear that you can see its pinkish-white sand bottom. Oh, what beauty! Oh, what beauty! You have never seen anything like this. You are so excited. You breathe shallow. You breathe deep.

Mechanics Workshop Exercise 1

Using Punctuation Correctly   Rewrite each sentence, inserting end marks, commas, semicolons, colons, quotation marks, and italics.

SAMPLE   Antigua a Caribbean island is popular with tourists

ANSWER   Antigua, a Caribbean island, is popular with tourists.

1. In A Small Place Jamaica Kincaid imagines a typical tourist's reaction to Antigua's beautiful beaches
2. What an island paradise said the tourist
3. Antigua's attractions include the following clear water sandy beaches and warm climate
4. Is the water really pale silvery and clear
5. Tourists enjoy Antigua's warm climate however long periods of drought sometimes strike the island

Mechanics Workshop Exercise 2

Using Punctuation Correctly   Rewrite each sentence, inserting apostrophes, hyphens, dashes, and parentheses as needed.

SAMPLE   St. John's is Antigua and Barbudas capital.

ANSWER   St. John's is Antigua and Barbuda's capital.

1. The country of Antigua and Barbuda has a total land area of 171 square miles 442 square kilometers.
2. Redonda an uninhabited island is also part of the island country.
3. Most of the countrys population lives on the island of Antigua.
4. The majority of the people descendants of black Africans speak English.
5. The country is a self governing nation.

Using Abbreviations and Numbers   Rewrite each sentence, correcting the errors in abbreviations and numbers.

1. Mister Vere Cornwall is the prime minister of Antigua and Barbuda.
2. About two percent of the people live on Barbuda, the smaller island.
3. The islands receive about 45 in. of rain annually.
4. 2 deaths and 80 million dollars in property damage resulted when Hurricane Hugo struck in 1989.
5. The island's hospitals need qualified Drs.

Proofreading   The following passage describes *Interior at Nice,* the painting by Henri Matisse that appears on the next page. Rewrite the passage, correcting the errors in spelling, capitalization, punctuation, grammar, and usage. There are ten errors in all.

Interior at Nice

[1] The young woman featured in Interior at Nice sits in front of a window on a hotel balcony in France. [2] With her back to the sea she gazes at the observer. [3] The sun reflects off the sea and bathe the room in silvery light. [4] Intense pinks blues and grays help convey the atmosphere of warmth.

[5] Like Jamaica Kincaid, Henri Matisse has captured a momant during an afternoon by the sea. [6] The picture on the hotel wall a picture within the picture duplicates the figure of the woman on the balcony. [7] The observers' attention is drawn to the woman. [8] Perhaps, like the tourist in *A Small Place,* the woman in the painting has retired to her room to refresh themselves.

Henri Matisse, *Interior at Nice,* **1921**

Unit 20 Review

Punctuation

End Marks and Other Punctuation

[pages 538–553]

Write each sentence. Add end marks, commas, semicolons, colons, quotation marks, italics, apostrophes, hyphens, dashes, and parentheses where needed.

1. The United States said John leads the world in corn production
2. How important rice is to China
3. Which cities have the most museums art galleries and theaters
4. John Muir tramped through much of the United States he spent six years in the Yosemite Valley.
5. Muir wrote the following book The Mountains of California.
6. Yes lets do it right now.
7. Read Robert Frosts poem A Time to Talk
8. His well educated father in law spent thirty nine dollars on books.
9. John Steinbeck 1902–1968 wrote the novel The Grapes of Wrath.
10. Steinbeck he was also a writer of short stories is my favorite novelist.

Using Abbreviations

[pages 554–555]

Write each sentence. Use the correct abbreviation for the underlined word or words in each sentence.

11. Cassie took the dog to Elena Mendoza, <u>Doctor of Veterinary Medicine</u>.
12. <u>Mister</u> John Hope <u>Junior</u> will speak.
13. Jerry is working for the <u>United States Department of Agriculture</u>.
14. The store is only twenty <u>feet</u> away.
15. Take me to 707 Melrose <u>Road</u>, Baton Rouge, <u>Louisiana</u>.

Writing Numbers

[pages 556–557]

Write each sentence. Use the correct form for writing numbers in each sentence.

16. 334 areas make up the National Park System.
17. More than 300,000,000 people visit our national parks each year.
18. Camping is permitted in 3% of our national parks.
19. We went camping with 25 people.
20. There were 100 other families there, but ours was the tenth in line.

Writing for Review

Write a paragraph about a camping trip you would like to take. Try to use as many elements of punctuation as you can.

Grammar Through Sentence Combining

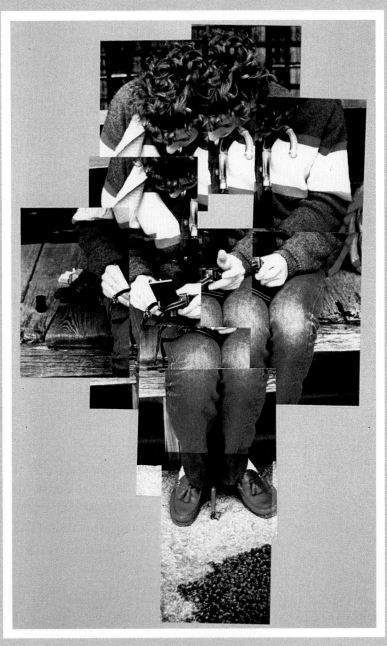

David Hockney, *Gregory Loading His Camera, Kyoto, February 1983*

21.1 Prepositional Phrases

Prepositional phrases are effective tools for sentence combining. They describe nouns and verbs, just as adjectives and adverbs do. Furthermore, because they show relationships between words, prepositional phrases can usually express more complicated ideas than adjectives or adverbs.

> EXAMPLE
> **a.** The landscape has undergone a change.
> **b.** This change is **for the worse**.
> **c.** This is **according to Rachel Carson**.
>
> **According to Rachel Carson**, the landscape has undergone a change **for the worse**.

The new information from sentences *b* and *c* is added to sentence *a* in the form of prepositional phrases. In the new sentence the prepositional phrase *According to Rachel Carson* modifies the verb *has undergone,* while the prepositional phrase *for the worse* modifies the noun *change.* Prepositional phrases follow the nouns they modify. Prepositional phrases that modify verbs can precede or follow the verbs they modify. (For a list of common prepositions, see page 434.)

A **prepositional phrase** is a group of words that begins with a preposition and ends with a noun or pronoun. Prepositional phrases modify nouns, verbs, and pronouns.

Exercise 1

Combining Sentences with Prepositional Phrases
The following sentences are based on an excerpt from *Silent Spring* by Rachel Carson, which you can find on pages 292–294. Combine each group of sentences, so that the new information is turned into a prepositional phrase. In the first few items the new information is in dark type.

1. a. Carson describes a mythical town.
   b. The town was one **of great natural beauty**. ➡

2. **a.** Prosperous farms surrounded the town.
   b. The farms were dotted **with rich productive fields.**
3. **a.** Birds filled the trees and bushes.
   b. The birds were **of many different kinds**.
4. **a.** A blight covered the land.
   b. The blight was one of unknown origin.
5. **a.** Silence now reigned in the springtime.
   b. It reigned as the birds disappeared.
6. **a.** The countryside changed dramatically.
   b. It turned into a scene of mysterious mourning.

Exercise 2

Combining Sentences   Rewrite the following paragraph. Use prepositional phrases to combine sentences. Make any other changes in wording that you feel are necessary.

No one place has suffered all the tragedies described by Carson. However, each blight has occurred somewhere. The blights are upon the environment. Each one might have occurred in this country, or it might have been in other parts of the world. Many communities have undergone several of these misfortunes. This fact is without exaggeration. Carson writes of a "grim specter." This specter is upon our landscape. Carson writes in her book *Silent Spring*. The tragedy might become a reality. The tragedy is that of the mythical town. The reality is for all of us. This is according to Rachel Carson.

Invitation to Write

Imagine a *what if . . .?* situation. For example, what would it be like if there were no television? Write two paragraphs describing your *what if* situation and its effects.

21.2   Appositives

Appositives allow you to combine sentences in a compact and informative way. Appositives and appositive phrases identify or reveal something new about a noun or pronoun.

> EXAMPLE   **a.** Maya Lin designed the Vietnam Veterans Memorial.
> **b.** Maya Lin was **an architecture student**. [, + ,]
>
> Maya Lin, **an architecture student,** designed the Vietnam Veterans Memorial.

The appositive phrase *an architecture student* tells us more about *Maya Lin.* The appositive is set off with commas because it gives additional information. If an appositive supplies essential information, it is not set off with commas. (For more information on appositives, see pages 354–355.)

An **appositive** is a noun placed next to another noun to identify it or give additional information about it. An **appositive phrase** includes an appositive and other words that describe it.

Exercise 3

Combining Sentences with Appositives   The following sentences are based on "Always to Remember" by Brent Ashabranner, which you can find on pages 240–246. Combine each group of sentences so that the new information is turned into an appositive or appositive phrase. In the first few items the new information is in dark type; the information in brackets indicates that you should add a comma or commas to the new sentence.

1. **a.** Congress had authorized the Vietnam Veterans Memorial.
   b. The memorial was to be **a monument to the war's dead and missing soldiers**. [,] ➡

2. a. Over one thousand contestants submitted plans.

  b. This number of contestants was **a record number for a design competition**. **[,+,]**

3. a. The winner was Maya Lin.

  b. She was **the daughter of the dean of fine arts at Ohio University**. **[,]**

  c. The dean was **Henry Huan Lin.[,+,]**

4. a. Maya Lin studied architecture at Yale University.

  b. She was valedictorian in high school. **[,+,]**

5. a. In France she was impressed by a memorial.

  b. The memorial was the work of the architect.

  c. The architect was Sir Edwin Lutyens.

Exercise 4

Combining Sentences   Rewrite the paragraph below. Use appositives and appositive phrases to combine sentences. Make any changes in wording you feel necessary.

   Before making her design, Maya Lin visited the monument's proposed site. The site was Constitution Gardens in Washington, D.C. During her visit the park was being enjoyed by many people. These people were both Washington, D.C., residents and tourists. Lin did not want to destroy a living, beautiful park with a grim monument. That monument would be a structure out of harmony with its surroundings. Instead, her design fits in with the park's landscape. Her final design was a long wall of polished black stone.

Invitation to Write

   Research a famous monument or statue that interests you. Then write a paragraph explaining how that monument came to be built.

21.3 Adjective Clauses

Adjective clauses are useful in combining sentences. When two sentences share information, one of them can be made into an adjective clause that modifies a word or phrase in the other.

EXAMPLE **a.** Lyddie began her working day long before breakfast.
b. Lyddie **labored in a cloth factory. [, who . . . ,]**

Lyddie, **who labored in a cloth factory,** began her working day long before breakfast.

The new information from sentence *b*, *labored in a cloth factory,* becomes an adjective clause modifying *Lyddie* in sentence *a*. The pronoun *who* now connects the clauses. Notice the commas in the new sentence. Adjective clauses that add nonessential information require commas. Adjective clauses that add essential information do not require commas. (For more information on adjective clauses, see pages 458–459.)

An **adjective clause** is a subordinate clause that modifies a noun or pronoun in the main clause. The relative pronouns *who, whom, whose, which, that,* and *what* are used to tie the adjective clause to the main clause.

Exercise 5

Combining Sentences with Adjective Clauses The following sentences are based on an excerpt from *Lyddie* by Katherine Paterson, which you can find on pages 176–182. Combine each group of sentences so that the new information is turned into an adjective clause. In the first items the new information is in dark type. The information in brackets indicates the relative pronoun to use and whether a comma or commas are needed.

1. a. The girls began their working day long before breakfast. ➡

b. The girls **labored in the cloth factory**. [who]

2. a. Lyddie found a job in a cloth factory.

b. Lyddie **had come from the country**. [, who . . . ,]

3. a. The overseer pulled the cord to the leather belt.

b. The belt **set the factory machinery into motion**. [that]

4. a. The girls had to rush back at seven-thirty.

b. The girls were released at seven for breakfast.

5. a. By the end of the day, Lyddie was too tired to think about the regulations.

b. These were the rules that all the girls had to learn.

Exercise 6

Combining Sentences   Rewrite the paragraph below, using adjective clauses to combine sentences. Make any other changes in wording or punctuation you think necessary.

Betsy read out loud from the novel *Oliver Twist*. *Oliver Twist* was written by Charles Dickens. The novel tells the story of a hungry boy. The boy is punished for asking for more food at a poorhouse. Lyddie heard the description of Oliver's punishment. The man reminded her of the factory overseer. The man scolded Oliver. The overseer had frightened her that very day. Lyddie now wanted to hear the whole story of Oliver. Lyddie had before been too tired to speak. Betsy read on until the curfew bell. Betsy's voice grew hoarse with fatigue.

Invitation to Write

Think of a story or poem that moved or excited you when you first read it. Write a paragraph describing this experience and explaining your response.

21.4   Adverb Clauses

Adverb clauses are a frequently used and highly effective way to combine sentences. Adverb clauses help you establish clear relationships between two or more ideas or actions. For example, you can use adverb clauses to show that one action causes another or follows another.

> EXAMPLE   **a.** Mr. Reese drilled the team thoroughly.
> **b.** They would soon be playing for the championship. [**since**]
>
> Mr. Reese drilled the team thoroughly **since they would soon be playing for the championship**.

In the new sentence the adverb clause *since they would soon be playing for the championship* explains why Mr. Reese drilled them so thoroughly. Note that the subordinating conjunction *since* makes the cause-effect relationship very clear. An adverb clause can occupy several positions within a sentence. If it begins the sentence, it is followed by a comma. (For more information on adverb clauses, see pages 462–463.)

An **adverb clause** is a subordinate clause that often modifies or describes the verb in the main clause. Adverb clauses are introduced by subordinating conjunctions such as *after, although, as, before, if, since, when, whenever, wherever,* and *while*.

Exercise 7

Combining Sentences with Adverb Clauses   The following sentences are based on "The Game" by Walter Dean Myers, which you can find on pages 88–92. Use adverb clauses to combine each group of sentences. In the first few items the information in brackets signals the subordinating conjunction and the punctuation you should use. ➡

1. **a.** The narrator's team was warming up for the championship game. [**As . . . ,**]
   b. They tried not to look at their opponents at the other end of the court.
2. **a.** The other team dominated the game's opening minutes.
   b. They passed and shot the ball extremely well. [**because**]
3. **a.** The narrator's team made a few mistakes. [**When . . . ,**]
   b. Mr. Reese, the coach, called timeout to give the players a rest.
4. **a.** Mr. Reese seemed as calm and reassuring as he usually was.
   b. His team was not playing well. [**although**]
5. **a.** The team returned to the floor [**When . . . ,**]
   b. They began to play much better.
   c. Mr. Reese had given them clear directions. [**because**]
6. **a.** The other team took the ball and immediately tried a slick move.
   b. The narrator's team was ready and handily outmaneuvered them.
7. **a.** The narrator was in the right place at just the right time.
   b. He made his first basket.
8. **a.** Mr. Reese urged the team to stay cool.
   b. They were losing by seven points.
9. **a.** A basketball player is fouled in the process of making a shot.
   b. He gets two foul shots, not one.
10. **a.** The narrator's team won the game.
    b. They were happy and proud.
    c. They had beaten a very rough team.

Exercise 8

Combining Sentences   Rewrite the following paragraphs. Use adverb clauses to combine sentences. ➡

Make any other changes in punctuation or wording that you feel are necessary to improve the flow of the paragraph.

The opposing side was tricked by the "Foul him!" strategy. The narrator's team got the ball. The score was tied. The narrator did not realize it at the time. There were just four minutes left in the game. Sam and Chalky, two good players, came back in. They outscored the other team by four points. The narrator's team won the championship.

The narrator's teammates were given their first-place trophies. They began to jump up and down and slap each other on the back. They had an extra trophy. They gave it to their cheerleaders. The coach shook each player's hand. Then he invited the players' parents and the cheerleaders into the locker room. Mr. Reese made a little speech to the group. He said he was proud of the team. They had worked so hard to win. Mr. Reese finished speaking. The parents and cheerleaders gave the team a round of applause. The narrator started to cry. He often did this. However, this time he was not embarrassed. Leon was crying even more. For the next few days the narrator and his friends were walking on air. They saw someone in the street. They would just "walk up and be happy."

Invitation to Write

Write a paragraph describing a game or other competitive event, such as a debate or spelling bee, that you recently saw or participated in. Try to make your readers feel as if they had actually been present at the event. Use the above passage as an example.

Part 3

Resources and Skills

Part 3 Resources and Skills

Unit 22 Library and Reference Resources

22.1 The Sections of a Library

Learning how a library is organized can help you unlock a wealth of information. Although no two libraries are exactly alike, all libraries group like things together. Adult books are in one section. Children's books are in another. Novels and stories are usually separate from information books. Magazines and newspapers have their own section. So do videos and audiotapes. Turn the page to see how a typical library is organized.

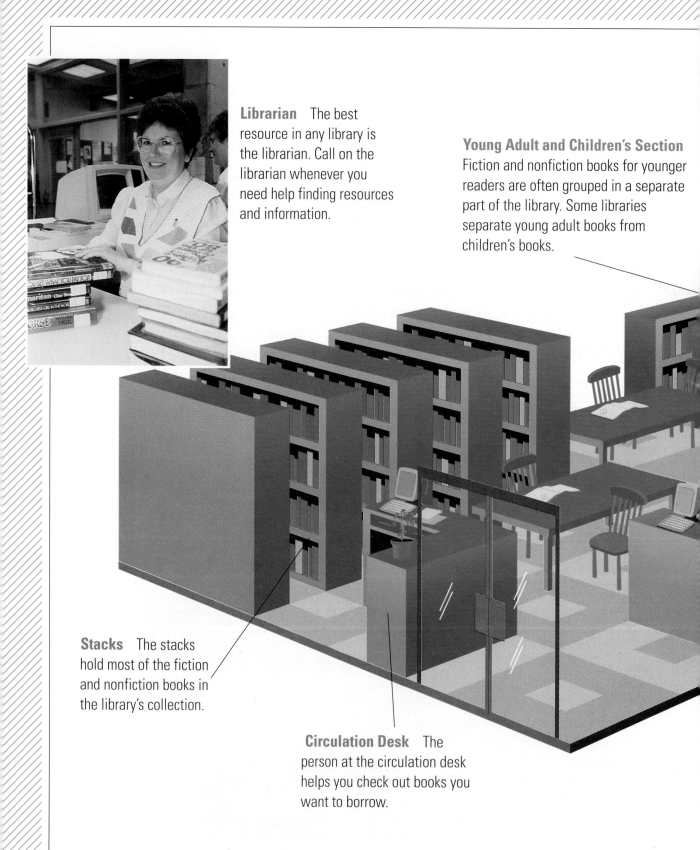

Librarian The best resource in any library is the librarian. Call on the librarian whenever you need help finding resources and information.

Young Adult and Children's Section Fiction and nonfiction books for younger readers are often grouped in a separate part of the library. Some libraries separate young adult books from children's books.

Stacks The stacks hold most of the fiction and nonfiction books in the library's collection.

Circulation Desk The person at the circulation desk helps you check out books you want to borrow.

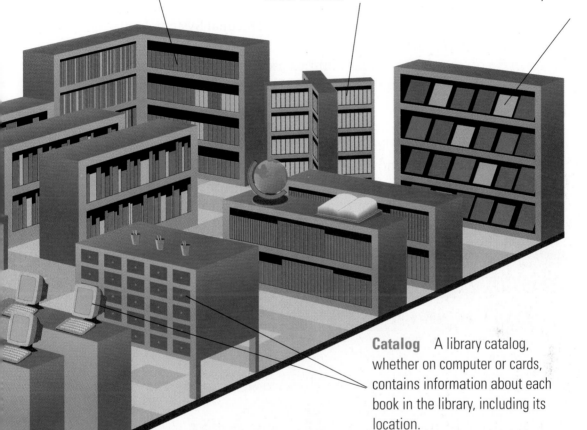

Reference In the reference area you can find encyclopedias, dictionaries, atlases, almanacs, and other reference works.

Audio-Visual Materials Videos, audiotapes, and compact discs are grouped in the audio-visual section.

Newspapers and Periodicals Newspapers and periodicals, including magazines and journals, are usually found in one section of the library.

Catalog A library catalog, whether on computer or cards, contains information about each book in the library, including its location.

Exercise 1

In which section of the library might you find these items?

1. A compact disc of the musical *Cats*
2. The magazine *American Heritage*
3. *To Kill a Mockingbird* (a novel)
4. The *Dictionary of American Biography*
5. The video of *The Call of the Wild.*

The Sections of a Library **577**

22.2　Call Number Systems

If you walk through the stacks in the library, you will see that the books are labeled with numbers and letters. These numbers and letters are part of the system the library uses to organize its collection.

Many libraries use the Dewey Decimal System. Under this system, a library uses numbers to group books into ten categories of knowledge. Other libraries use the Library of Congress System. The Library of Congress System uses letters, then numbers, to group books.

Find out which system your library uses. You don't have to memorize the letters and numbers for these systems. It's best, however, to know how each system works. You also should know where your library has posted the chart that identifies and explains the system they use. Both systems are shown in the chart below.

Library Classification Systems			
Dewey Decimal System		**Library of Congress System**	
Numbers	Major Categories	Letters	Major Categories
000–099	General works	A, Z	General works
100–199 200–299	Philosophy Religion	B	Philosophy, religion
300–399	Social sciences	H, J, K, L	Social sciences, political science, law, education
400–499	Language	P	Language
500–599	Science	Q	Science
600–699	Technology	R, S, T, U, V	Medicine, agriculture, technology, military and naval sciences
700–799	The arts, recreation	M, N	Music, fine arts
800–899	Literature	P	Literature
900–999	History, geography	C-G	History, geography, recreation

Each general category contains subcategories. The first number or letter always indicates the main category and will be followed by other numbers or letters. The diagram below shows how each system works.

How the Two Systems Work		
Dewey Decimal	**Description**	**Library of Congress**
700	A book about art	N
750	A book about painting (a subcategory of art)	ND
759	A book about Spanish painting (a subcategory of painting)	ND800
759.609	*The Story of Spanish Painting*	ND804

Exercise 2

1. Suppose a library used the Dewey Decimal System. What number (in the hundreds) would it use to show the category of each of the following books?

   a. *A History of Colonial America*
   b. *Science for the Nonscientist*
   c. *Language Made Easy*
   d. *World Religions*
   e. *The Novels of Charles Dickens*

2. At your school or neighborhood library, find an interesting book in each section listed below. Write down the book's title, topic, and full Dewey Decimal or Library of Congress call number.

   a. 200–299 or B   c. 400–499 or P   e. 900–999 or C
   b. 300–399 or H   d. 500–599 or Q

22.3   Library Catalogs

So many books, so little time! Maybe you've had this thought as you begin your research at the library. The library catalog makes searching for books easier and saves you time.

Using a Computer Catalog

Many libraries use computers to catalog their books. Computer catalogs allow readers to search for books by author, by title, or by subject. For example, suppose you are looking for books by the writer Milton Meltzer.

1. Type in the author's name: *Meltzer, Milton.*
2. You will see a list of all the books in the library by this author. Each book will have a call number.
3. Type the call number of the book you are interested in to get more information about it.
4. Information about the book will appear, as shown below.

Computer catalogs give step-by-step instructions for each kind of search. Just follow the on-screen directions to use the catalog. If you run into trouble, ask a librarian for help.

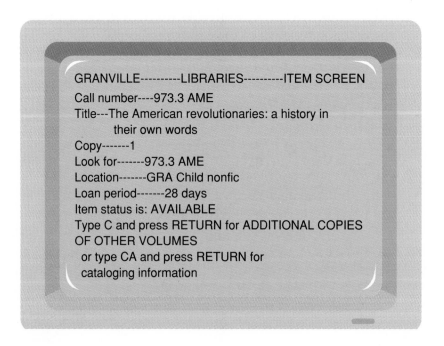

```
GRANVILLE----------LIBRARIES----------ITEM SCREEN
Call number----973.3 AME
Title---The American revolutionaries: a history in
          their own words
Copy-------1
Look for-------973.3 AME
Location-------GRA Child nonfic
Loan period-------28 days
Item status is: AVAILABLE
Type C and press RETURN for ADDITIONAL COPIES
OF OTHER VOLUMES
  or type CA and press RETURN for
  cataloging information
```

Using a Card Catalog

In libraries that use card catalogs, you will find groups of deep, narrow drawers. The drawers contain rows of cards like those below. These catalog cards are in alphabetical order according to title, author, and subject.

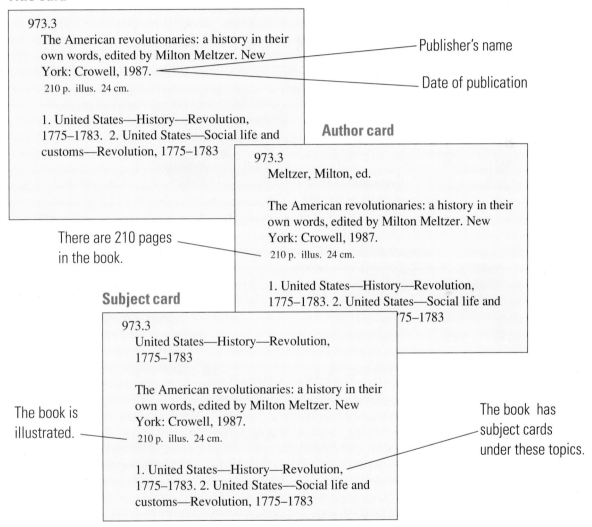

Title card

973.3
The American revolutionaries: a history in their own words, edited by Milton Meltzer. New York: Crowell, 1987.
210 p. illus. 24 cm.

1. United States—History—Revolution, 1775–1783. 2. United States—Social life and customs—Revolution, 1775–1783

— Publisher's name
— Date of publication

Author card

973.3
Meltzer, Milton, ed.

The American revolutionaries: a history in their own words, edited by Milton Meltzer. New York: Crowell, 1987.
210 p. illus. 24 cm.

1. United States—History—Revolution, 1775–1783. 2. United States—Social life and
75–1783

There are 210 pages in the book.

Subject card

973.3
United States—History—Revolution, 1775–1783

The American revolutionaries: a history in their own words, edited by Milton Meltzer. New York: Crowell, 1987.
210 p. illus. 24 cm.

1. United States—History—Revolution, 1775–1783. 2. United States—Social life and customs—Revolution, 1775–1783

The book is illustrated.

The book has subject cards under these topics.

Nonfiction books usually have three catalog cards: an author card, a title card, and one or more subject cards. Most fiction books have an author card and a title card. The call number of the book is near the upper-left corner of each card. The same call number is on the spine of the actual book.

Finding a Book

When you have located a book you want in the catalog, write down the call number shown on the card or computer screen. Note the area in the library where the book is shelved. You will use this information to locate the book.

In the stacks, signs on the shelves tell which call numbers are included in each row. Books with the same call number are alphabetized by the author's last name or by the first author's last name when there is more than one author.

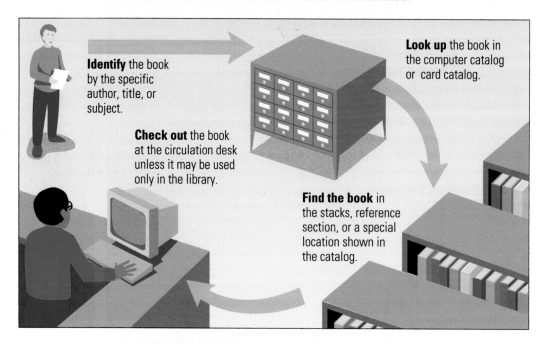

Identify the book by the specific author, title, or subject.

Look up the book in the computer catalog or card catalog.

Check out the book at the circulation desk unless it may be used only in the library.

Find the book in the stacks, reference section, or a special location shown in the catalog.

Exercise 3

Use the card catalog or computer catalog to find a book about any five of the following topics. List the author, title, and call number of each book you find.

1. The brain
2. The development of television
3. Poetry by X. J. Kennedy
4. Marsupials
5. The Spanish language
6. Professional football
7. Mountains
8. The mind

22.4 Types of Reference Works

When you look up the answer to a question or read a book to find information for social studies class, you are doing research. When you check with friends who know more than you do about your bike, you are doing research. For research you need experts. You'll find the opinions and discoveries of many experts in the reference materials in your library.

Reference works are designed to help you locate specific information quickly. You may be doing research for a class project, looking for a single fact, or just feeling curious about a topic. Whatever your purpose is, the reference area offers many interesting resources.

The chart below describes some general types of reference sources found in most libraries. Find out where each of these kinds of references is kept in your public library. Locate those references that are available in your school library or classroom as well.

Using General Reference Works to Answer Questions		
Questions	**Where to Look for an Answer**	**Examples of Sources**
When did Henry Ford introduce the Model T?	**Encyclopedias** include general information on a variety of topics.	• *World Book Encyclopedia* • *Grolier Encyclopedia* • *Encyclopaedia Britannica*
What major cities are on the Ohio River?	**Atlases** are collections of maps. They often include special maps on climate, population, and other topics.	• *Hammond Contemporary World Atlas* • *The Rand McNally Atlas of World Exploration*
Who received the Nobel Peace Prize in 1979?	**Almanacs** provide lists, statistics, and other information on recent and historical topics.	• *Information Please Almanac* • *Guinness Book of World Records*
Where was Mark Twain born?	**Biographical reference works** include biographies of notable persons, both past and present.	• *Dictionary of American Biography* • *Webster's Biographical Dictionary*

Encyclopedias

You will find one-volume encyclopedias and sets made up of many volumes. Encyclopedias may be either general or specialized. General encyclopedias contain articles about all branches of knowledge. Specialized encyclopedias present articles in a specific area of knowledge, such as history, science, or the arts. Two examples of specialized encyclopedias are the *McGraw-Hill Encyclopedia of Science and Technology,* and *The New York Times Encyclopedia of Film.*

Most encyclopedias are organized alphabetically. To find all of the articles with information on your topic, look up the topic in the index. The index is usually the last volume of a multi-volume encyclopedia. It contains an alphabetical listing of topics. After each topic you will find the subjects related to the topic you are investigating. The index tells you the volume and page number of the article where you will find the information. Sometimes the index refers you to a different topic heading for a list of articles.

Many encyclopedia entries end with a list of books that contain additional information. These books may be available at your library. The entry may also list other related articles in the encyclopedia.

Atlases

Atlases are collections of maps. General atlases contain maps of all parts of the world. In a general atlas, you can find map information about population, industry, farming, and other topics for all parts of the world. These atlases may also contain graphs, charts, and pictures. For example, the *National Geographic Atlas of the World* includes satellite images of the earth's major regions.

Some atlases are specialized. They may cover one part of the world, such as a single country. Others have maps on a special topic, such as population, the environment, or animals. Travelers often rely on atlases that show highways, national parks, and places of interest to tourists. Historical atlases contain maps for different periods in history and various parts of the world.

Almanacs and Yearbooks

If you're looking for very current information or statistics, consult almanacs and yearbooks. These references contain the most recent available information on a variety of topics. A new edition is published every year.

Two widely used almanacs are the *Information Please Almanac* and the *World Almanac and Book of Facts.* Both cover a wide range of information, from baseball statistics to the latest scientific discoveries. Much of the information is presented in the form of lists or tables.

A yearbook is a book issued each year by some encyclopedia publishers to update their regular encyclopedia volumes. It contains articles about events and developments of that year. The yearbooks for an encyclopedia generally follow the *Z* volume or the Index volume on the reference shelf.

Biographical Dictionaries

Biographical dictionaries contain information on important people. Some of these dictionaries include living persons as well as persons from history. These references may have many volumes or may be contained in a single book.

In the larger, multivolume dictionaries, such as the *Dictionary of American Biography,* entries are lengthy and give a detailed life history. An example of a shorter reference is *Webster's Biographical Dictionary.* In this work the entries are much briefer, sometimes only a few lines long. An example is shown below. Biographical dictionaries are useful when you need information about particular people.

> **Cra´zy Horse´** (krā´zē hôrs´) Indian name **Tashunca-Uitco.** 1849?–1877. American Indian chief, of the Oglala tribe of the Sioux, in battle of Little Big Horn, in which Custer was killed (1876); surrendered; killed while resisting imprisonment (Sept. 5, 1877).

Exercise 4

1. Name the type of reference work in which you would expect to find answers to the following:

   a. Who was the Olympic champion in the women's long jump in 1988?

   b. Of what country is Jakarta the capital?

   c. What occupations did Samuel Clemens follow before becoming a writer?

   d. In what state is the Painted Desert located?

   e. What was Sputnik, and why was it important?

2. Use a library reference to write the answers to any *two* of the above questions.

Sometimes you may want up-to-date information about a topic. A magazine may be an interesting and useful reference in this case. One of the best sources for finding magazine articles on almost any subject is the *Readers' Guide to Periodical Literature.* The guide indexes articles from over 175 magazines by author and subject.

Using the Readers' Guide

Each hard-bound volume of the *Readers' Guide* contains a year's entries. New paperback indexes are published every two weeks, and larger paperback indexes are published every three months. The following annotated excerpt from the *Readers' Guide* shows you how to read the information in the index.

BLACK HIGH SCHOOL STUDENTS *See* Black students ——— Cross-reference
BLACK HISTORY *See* Blacks—History
BLACK HISTORY MONTH ——— Subject
    Black History Month calendar. H. C. Harrison. il
        American Visions 7:54–64 F/Mr '92
    Black History Month cites discovery, exploration of
        America by heroic blacks. il *Jet* 81:22–3 F 17 '92
    Black History Month fete at White House boosts Bush's
        spirits. il por *Jet* 81:4–5 Mr 9 '92 ——— Date
    Black History Month: stars reveal their favorite heroes
        in black history. C. Waldron. il *Jet* 81:60–2 F 24 '92 ——— Article title
    Now you see them. . . [books published during Black His-
        tory Month] il *Newsweek* 119:60–2 Mr 9 '92
BLACK HOLES (ASTRONOMY)
    How to find a black hole. F. Flam. il *Science* 255:794–5 F 14 '92
    Hubble captures a violent universe [core of two galaxies] ——— Volume
        R. Cowen. il *Science News* 141:52 Ja 25 '92
    New evidence for black holes in Milky Way. R. Cowen. ——— Author
        Science News 141:101 F 15 '92
    New strategy in the hunt for black holes [Hubble Space
        Telescope photographs core of M87 galaxy; study by
        Todd Lauer and Sandra Faber] F. Flam. il *Science* ——— Magazine title
        255:537–8 Ja 31 '92 ——— Pages
    No black hole in SS 433. il *Sky and Telescope* 83:249–50 Mr '92
        Caricatures and cartoons ——— Subheading
    Science Classics. L. Gonick. il *Discover* 13:78–79 Ja '92

Finding an Article in a Periodical

The *Readers' Guide* lists more magazines than any single library owns. Check to see which periodicals are available at your library. Then look up the topic that interests you. Find an entry you would like to investigate. Write the name of the magazine, its date, the article title, and the page numbers. This is the information you will use to locate the article.

If the article is from a recent issue, you will probably find it on open shelves in the periodicals section. Articles from older issues are generally stored as bound volumes or microforms. Microforms are tiny photographs of printed pages arranged on small film cards (called microfiche) or on strips of film (called microfilm). Each type of microform is viewed on a special machine that enlarges the pages so they can be read or printed. A librarian can help you locate microforms and use the viewing equipment.

Exercise 5

Using the excerpts from the *Readers' Guide* on the previous page, answer the following questions:

1. What is the name of the magazine that contains the article "No Black Hole in SS 433"?
2. Under what topic would you find articles about black high school students?
3. Could you use this excerpt of the *Readers' Guide* to find a cartoon about black holes? Explain.
4. On what pages of *American Visions* would you find a calendar of events for Black History Month?
5. Who wrote an article about the Hubble telescope photographing the core of two galaxies? In what magazine was the article published?

22.6   Other Print and Nonprint Media

While books are the heart of most library collections, libraries offer several kinds of media. The word *media* (singular *medium*) means methods of communication, such as newspapers, magazines, movies, and television. The media are often divided into two types—print and nonprint.

Print Media

Magazines and newspapers, like books, are print media. Both news magazines, such as *Time,* and special-interest magazines, such as *Photography,* are good sources for up-to-date information. Since they are printed often (usually weekly or monthly), magazines can provide more recent information than most books. Whatever special interests or research needs you have, there's likely to be a magazine that can help you.

Current newspapers cover recent events of national and local interest, but older issues can also be a good source of information. Some libraries keep copies of local newspapers from as far back as the 1800s. These old issues can be useful if you are doing research on a historical period. Check your library to find out what newspapers are available there. Microforms are used to store back issues of both newspapers and magazines. For more information on using microforms, see page 588.

Some Types of Magazines	
Types of Magazines	**Examples**
News magazines	*Newsweek, U.S. News and World Report, Time*
General-interest magazines	*Reader's Digest, National Geographic, Atlantic*
Special-interest magazines	*Photography, House and Garden, Bicycling, MacUser*
Magazines for younger readers	*National Geographic World, Zillions, Sports Illustrated for Kids*

Nonprint Media

Most libraries now offer videotapes of movies, travelogues, and instructional (how-to-do-it) films. Audiotapes and compact discs (CDs) contain sound recordings. Besides music of all types, they hold plays and readings of poetry and fiction. Compact discs also store printed information such as periodical indexes and encyclopedias. These CDs are fed into a computer, which provides very fast searches for information.

Using Nonprint Media		
Type of Media	**Information Available**	**Equipment Needed**
Microforms	Back issues of newspapers and magazines	Microform viewer or viewer/printer (at the library)
Videotapes	Movies, documentaries, travel and instructional films	VCR and television set
Laser discs	Movies, documentaries, travel and instructional films	Laser disc player and television set
Audiotapes	Music, readings, dramas, language lessons	Audiocassette player
Compact discs	Same as audiotapes Information sources	CD player and stereo system CD player and computer

Exercise 6

In which print or nonprint medium would you expect to find each of the following items? More than one answer may be appropriate in some cases.

1. An article describing a new type of computer
2. Recorded Russian lessons for travelers
3. A documentary about the canal era in Ohio
4. An article about a student from your school who just won a national award
5. *The Grolier Encyclopedia* on computer

22.7   The Dictionary

You English words
I know you:
You are light as dreams,
Tough as oak,
Precious as gold,
As poppies and corn,
Or an old cloak . . .

These lines by Edward Thomas hint at the richness of the English language. You can enrich your knowledge of English by frequent use of the dictionary—an essential tool for a writer.

The Dictionary

A dictionary is an alphabetical listing of words with definitions and often with word origins and other information. Most dictionaries fall into one of the categories below.

Types of Dictionaries		
Type	**Characteristics**	**Examples**
Unabridged Dictionaries	• 250,000 or more entries • Detailed word histories • Detailed definitions • Found mostly in libraries	• *Random House Dictionary of the English Language* • *Webster's Third New International Dictionary*
College Dictionaries	• About 150,000 entries • Detailed enough to answer most questions on spelling or definitions • Widely used in schools, homes, and businesses	• *Random House Webster's College Dictionary* • *American Heritage Dictionary of the English Language* • *Webster's New World Dictionary*
School Dictionaries	• 90,000 or fewer entries • Definitions suitable for students' abilities • Emphasizes common words	• *The Scribner's Dictionary* • *Webster's School Dictionary*

The illustrations show how to use two helpful dictionary features. Guide words help you locate words quickly. The pronunciation key can help you sound out a word.

Guide words show the first and last entry on the page. Use them to zero in on the word you are seeking.

The pronunciation key uses well-known words to interpret the pronunciation symbols.

foot soldier / fore-and-aft

foot soldier, a soldier trained or equipped to fight on foot; infantryman.
foot·sore (foot´sôr´) *adj.* having sore or tired feet, as from much walking.
foot·step (foot´step´) *n.* **1.** a step or tread of the foot: *a baby's first awkward footsteps.* **2.** the sound made by this: *I heard his footsteps in the hall.* **3.** the distance covered in a step.
　to follow in someone's footsteps. to imitate or follow the same course as someone: *Dan followed in his father's footsteps and became a teacher.*

for·bid·ding (fər bid´ing) *adj.* looking unfriendly or dangerous; frightening; grim: *The old house was dark and forbidding.* —**for·bid´ding·ly,** *adv.*
for·bore (fôr bôr´) the past tense of **forbear** .
for·borne (fôr bôrn´) the past participle of **forbear** .
force (fôrs) *n.* **1.** power, strength, or energy: *The batter struck the ball with great force. The force of the explosion broke windows in the nearby buildings.* **2.** the use of such power, strength, or energy; violence: *The sheriff dragged the outlaw off by force.* **3.** the power to convince, or control: *The force of her argument won*

oneself from (doing something): refrain from: *Tom could not forbear smiling at his embarrassed friend.* [Old English *forberan* to hold back.]
for·bear² (fôr´ber) another spelling of **forebear.**
for·bear·ance (fôr berəns) *n.* **1.** the act of forbearing. **2.** self-control or patience: *Jim showed great forbearance during his long illness.*
for·bid (fər bid´) *v.t.,* **for·bade** or **for·bad, for·bid·den** or *(archaic)* **for·bid, for·bid·ding.** to order not to do something; refuse to allow; prohibit: *I forbid you to go out. The school forbids eating in the classrooms.*

fore-and-aft (fôr´en aft´) *adj.* from bow to stern of a ship: *a fore-and-aft sail.*

at; āpe; cär; end; mē; it; īce; hot; ōld; fôrk; wood; fōōl; oil; out; up; turn; sing; thin; this; hw in white; zh in treasure. The symbol ə stands for the sound of a in about, e in taken, i in pencil, o in lemon, and u in circus.

Other useful features are located in the front and back pages of the dictionary. In the front you can find a complete pronunciation key, a list of abbreviations used in entries, and information about punctuation and capitalization. Some dictionaries include a short history of the English language. In the back of the dictionary you may find sections with biographical and geographical entries. Some dictionaries include such information with the regular word listings.

Entry Word

A dictionary entry packs a great deal of information into a small space. By becoming familiar with the basic elements of an entry, you'll find it easier to explore new words.

The entry word is the first element in each entry. It is printed in bold type, which makes it easy to find the beginning of an entry. The entry word shows how to divide a word of more than one syllable. Notice how *flourish* is divided by the dot. Not every dictionary entry is a single word. Some entries are two words, such as *cuckoo clock,* and some, such as *T-shirt,* are hyphenated.

————— Entry word

flour (~~flour~~, flou′ər) *n.* **1.** soft, powdery substance obtained by grinding and sifting grain, esp. wheat, used chiefly as a basic ingredient in baked goods and other foods. **2.** any soft powdery substance. —*v.t.* to cover or sprinkle with flour. [Form of FLOWER in the sense of "finest part" (of the grain).]

————— Definition
————— Pronunciation

flour·ish (flur′ish) *v.i.* **1.** to grow or develop vigorously or prosperously; thrive: *Crops flourish in rich soil. His business is flourishing.* **2.** to reach or be at the peak of development or achievement: *a civilization that flourished thousands of years ago.* —*v.t.* **1.** to wave about with bold or sweeping gestures; brandish: *to flourish a sword; to flourish a baton.* **2.** to display ostentatiously; flaunt. —*n.* **1.** a brandishing: *He bowed to her with a flourish of his hat.* **2.** ostentatious or dramatic display or gesture: *She entered the room with a flourish.* **3.** decorative stroke or embellishment in writing. **4.** elaborate, ornamental passage or series of notes, as a trill or fanfare, added to a musical work. [Old French *floriss-,* a stem of *florir* to flower, bloom, going back to Latin *florere* to flower, bloom] —**Syn.** *v.i.* see **prosper.**

————— Part of speech
————— Word origin
Synonym reference. You can find a list of synonyms for flourish in the entry for prosper.

Pronunciation

The pronunciation of a word follows the entry word. It is written in special symbols that allow you to sound out the word. If you are not sure how to pronounce a syllable, check the pronunciation key, which is usually at the bottom of the page. The simple words in the key show the sounds of the most common symbols. To see a complete pronunciation key, turn to the front pages of the dictionary. Some words have more than one pronunciation; the most common is generally shown first.

Part of Speech

Every dictionary entry indicates a word's part or parts of speech. For example, in the entry for *flourish, v.i.* stands for *intransitive verb* and *v.t.* for *transitive verb.* The letter *n.* stands for *noun.* What would you expect the abbreviations for adjective and adverb to be? A list of the abbreviations is located in the front of the dictionary.

Definition

The definition, or meaning, of the word is the heart of the entry. Many words have more than one meaning. These meanings are usually numbered from most common to least common. Some unabridged and college dictionaries, however, use a different method. They give definitions from the earliest-known meaning to the most recent meaning. Look at the sample entries on page 593 to see how the definitions of *flourish* are numbered.

Word Origins

The word origin is a brief account of how the word entered the English language. Many words, like *flourish,* were used in more than one language before entering English. For example, look at the *flourish* entry. The source of the word is Latin. The word then moved into Old French. English speakers borrowed it from Old French. Many dictionaries use abbreviations for the language from which a word comes, such as *L.* for Latin. A list of these abbreviations is located at the front of the dictionary.

Exercise 7

Use the dictionary entries in this lesson to answer the following questions:

1. How many definitions does this dictionary include for the verb form of the word *flourish?*
2. Which meaning of *flourish* is implied in the following sentence? *The students flourished their handmade signs at the rally.*
3. Does the first syllable of *flourish* rhyme with the first syllable of *flower, flurry,* or *Florence?*
4. Which of the meanings shown for *flour* do you find in the following sentence? *I floured the chicken before putting it into the oven.*
5. What was the meaning of the Latin word that was the original source of *flourish?*

More than 150 years ago a British doctor, Peter Mark Roget [rō zhā´], developed a thesaurus. A thesaurus is a dictionary of synonyms—words with similar meanings. Since that time, the thesaurus has grown and changed.

Using a Thesaurus

Roget organized his thesaurus by categories. Then he listed the categories in an index. When you use this type of thesaurus, you find the category you want in the index. The index will refer you to the lists of synonyms you want.

The excerpt below is from another kind of thesaurus, one in which the words are arranged like those in a dictionary. In a dictionary-style thesaurus the word entries are in alphabetical order.

> *Part of speech is indicated.*

Clever *adjective*
1. Mentally quick and original: *The child is clever but not brilliant.*
   Syns: alert, bright, intelligent, keen, quick-witted, sharp, sharp-witted, smart.
   —*Idiom* smart as a tack (*or* whip).
2. Amusing or pleasing because of wit or originality: *made the audience laugh with a few clever, offbeat comparisons.*
   Syns: scintillating, smart, sparkling, sprightly, witty.
3. DEXTEROUS.
4. SHARP.
clew *noun* SEE **clue.**
cliché *noun*
A trite expression or idea: *a short story marred by clichés.*
   Syns: banality, bromide, commonplace, platitude, stereotype, truism.
cliché *adjective* TRITE.
click *noun* SNAP.
   click *verb*
   1. RELATE.
   2. SNAP.
   3. SUCCEED.

> *Synonyms are grouped by definition.*

> *Usage examples are given.*

> *In this thesaurus capital letters indicate a cross-reference to another entry. More synonyms are found under the cross-reference entry.*

Finding Synonyms

Knowing how the thesaurus is arranged can help you find the exact word you need. You can see from the samples on the previous page that each definition is followed by several synonyms or by a cross-reference to another entry. Synonyms, you recall, are words that have *similar* meanings. The thesaurus can help you distinguish among many synonyms to find the most exact one.

The words in capital letters lead you to further synonyms. If you look up a word shown in capital letters, you will find a definition and many additional synonyms. *Dexterous,* for example, means *clever,* but in a specific way: exhibiting or possessing skill or ease in performance. Your expert handling of a bike might be called dexterous. Conversation on a talk show may be clever, but it is not necessarily dexterous.

Most libraries will have more than one type of thesaurus available. A similar resource, a dictionary of synonyms, is also available to help you locate the most precise word. Two examples are *Webster's New Dictionary of Synonyms* and *Webster's New World Dictionary of Synonyms.*

Many thesauruses list antonyms—words with opposite meanings—as well as synonyms. Your library may have *Webster's Collegiate Thesaurus,* which includes antonyms. For more information on synonyms and antonyms, see pages 609–610.

Exercise 8

Use a thesaurus to find two synonyms for each word below. Then write an original sentence to illustrate the meaning of each synonym. Check the exact meaning of each word in a dictionary before you use it in a sentence.

1. speak (verb)
2. run (verb)
3. thin (adjective)
4. foam (noun)
5. shiny (adjective)

Vocabulary and Spelling

23.1 Words from American English

People all over the world use the word *okay*. It began, however, as an American-English word. How did *okay* become so widespread? Citizens of many nations borrowed this word from American travelers. Speakers of one language will often borrow words from speakers of another language they come into contact with.

Words from Native Americans

English colonists began settling in North America in the early 1600s. They often borrowed Native American words to name foods, plants, and animals new to them. Some examples are the words *pecan*, *hickory*, *squash*, *moose*, *chipmunk*, and *skunk*.

Europeans also borrowed Native American words to name natural features and places. The Mississippi River's name, for example, comes from Algonquian words meaning "great water." More than half the states and many cities and counties have names with Native American origins. Hawaii's name came from its original Polynesian settlers.

Kayak

Raccoon

States with Native American Names		
Alabama	Kansas	Oklahoma
Alaska	Kentucky	Oregon
Arizona	Massachusetts	North Dakota
Arkansas	Michigan	South Dakota
Connecticut	Minnesota	Tennessee
Idaho	Mississippi	Texas
Illinois	Missouri	Utah
Indiana	Nebraska	Wisconsin
Iowa	Ohio	Wyoming

Other Early Loan Words

Europeans from France and Spain were in America even before the English. English speakers had already borrowed many words from the French in Europe. As American English developed, its speakers borrowed more French words in North America. Other new English words came from the Spanish and from Spanish-speaking Mexicans in the Southwest. Some examples of these words of French and Spanish origin are included in the chart below.

Some American-English Loan Words	
Sources	**Words**
French	toboggan, pumpkin, bayou, prairie, dime, chowder
Spanish	mustang, ranch, rodeo, stampede, cafeteria, canyon
Dutch	sleigh, cole slaw, Santa Claus, cookie, boss, waffle
African	gumbo, voodoo, juke, jazz, tote
German	hamburger, noodle, pretzel, kindergarten, semester
Yiddish	kosher, bagel, klutz, kibitzer, schmaltz
Italian	macaroni, spaghetti, pizza, ravioli

Americans are often called Yankees or Yanks. The word came from Dutch colonists in America in the 1600s. The Dutch called New Englanders Yankees. (The name was considered an insult at the time.) The Dutch colony of New Netherland and its port city, New Amsterdam, were taken over by the British. The British renamed the colony and the city New York. The Dutch lost their American colony, but they left a number of their words in American English.

Most of the Africans in colonial America were brought here as slaves. Their contribution to the English language included such words as *gumbo*, *voodoo*, and *juke* (as in *juke box*). The origin of the word *jazz* is uncertain, but it, too, may have come from an African language. These and some other words that became part of American English are shown in the chart above.

Rodeo

Words from Immigrants

Over the centuries millions of immigrants—Italians, Poles, Czechs, Greeks, Chinese, Filipinos, Haitians, Cubans, and many more—came to America. They passed on some of their customs and some of their words to Americans. These words became part of American English. Often the use of the words spread from the United States throughout the English-speaking world. Some examples are included in the chart on the previous page.

Juke box

Words Made in America

Americans have also contributed new words that did not originate in another language. *Okay* is an example of a word that was "made in the U.S.A." Inventions and customs that started in America often led to new words. Some examples are *refrigerator, telephone, jeep, inner city, flow chart, zipper, laser,* and *airline.* Like *okay,* these words are now used throughout the world. Can you think of any other words that were probably made in America?

Exercise 1

Work with a small group. Develop a list of more English words that originated in America. The words can have come from Native American languages or from the languages of immigrants to America. They might be words invented by Americans.

Begin by looking at the place names in your area. Where did the names of mountains, rivers, counties, or cities come from? Look in your library for books or articles on the origins of place names. Think about the names of foods you eat that originated in other countries. If family members or friends are recent immigrants, ask them if they know of any American English words that came from their language. Use your dictionary to check the origins of words on your list.

Techno-Talk

What do the words *nylon, silo,* and *gearshift* have in common? All these words—and countless others—entered the English language as a result of developing technology. New machines, products, and processes required a new vocabulary.

Technical words enter the language by different routes. Some words are coined. A coined word is simply created—none of its parts have any meaning by themselves. For instance, in 1938 scientists developed synthetic fiber, and the word *nylon* was coined as a name for it.

Another route into English is through borrowing. The word *silo* was borrowed into English in 1881 as a name for an airtight container for fodder. The word is Spanish in origin and carries the same meaning in that language.

Another way languages gain new technical words is by compounding. The word parts *gear* and *shift* have existed in English for a long time. It was only because of developing technology that they were combined to name a part of an automobile transmission. Other examples of combining include *transmission* (from Latin word parts) and *telephone* (from Greek word parts). Some words for new inventions originated as names of people; *Ferris wheel* is an example.

CHALLENGE

What new technology uses the word silo? *Think of another technology that named a product a* tweeter. *How do the original meanings of these words fit the new ways in which they are used?*

Tele—
far off
or distant
television
telephone
telescope
telecast
telephoto

Name That Invention

Create several names for the imaginary inventions listed below. Use any of the sources for word formation.

1. a car for air, water, and all surfaces
2. a thermal container that will biodegrade within twelve hours
3. earphones that don't "leak" noise and that allow for loud music without damage to hearing

23.2 Context Clues

Do you check your dictionary every time you read or hear a new word? Probably not—most people don't. The best way to build your vocabulary is to learn new words as you come across them. However, you don't have to have a dictionary in your pocket at all times. You often can learn the meaning of a new word by looking for clues in the context. The words and sentences around the word are its context.

Using Specific Context Clues

Context clues help you unlock the meaning of an unfamiliar word. Sometimes the context actually tells you what the word means. The following chart shows three types of specific context clues. It also gives examples of words that help you identify the type of context clue.

Using Specific Context Clues		
Type of Context Clue	Clue Words	Example
Comparison The thing or idea named by the unfamiliar word is compared with something more familiar.	also same likewise similarly identical	A *rampant* growth of weeds and vines surrounded the old house. The barn was <u>likewise</u> covered with uncontrolled and wild growth.
Contrast The thing or idea named by the unfamiliar word is contrasted with something more familiar.	but on the other hand on the contrary unlike however	Thank goodness Martin didn't *bungle* the arrangements for the party; <u>on the contrary</u>, he handled everything very smoothly and efficiently.
Cause and effect The unfamiliar word is explained as a part of a cause-and-effect relationship.	because since therefore as a result consequently	<u>Because</u> this rubber raft is so *buoyant*, it will float easily, and we won't have to worry about its sinking.

Using the General Context

How do you figure out an unfamiliar word if there are no specific context clues? With a little extra detective work you often can find general clues in the context. Look at the two sentences below. What context clues help you understand the meaning of the word *liaison*?

Note that the word *commu-nication helps you figure out that being a liaison means acting as a line of communica-tion between two groups.*

Joel was chosen student <u>liaison</u> to the faculty. Everyone hoped his appointment would improve communication between the students and the teachers.

Joel is a liaison from one group (the students) to another (the faculty).

Exercise 2

Divide the words below between you and a partner. Use a dictionary if necessary to find the meanings of your words. Then write a sentence using each one. Your sentences should contain context clues to help a reader figure out the meanings of the words. Try to use different types of context clues in the sentences.

Next, exchange papers with your partner and read his or her sentences. Try to use your partner's context clues to understand the words from the list. Discuss whether and how your context clues helped you and your partner understand the meanings of each other's words.

1. depreciate
2. collaborate
3. fathom (noun)
4. abode
5. crucial
6. olfactory
7. refulgence
8. fathom (verb)
9. omnipotent
10. brinkmanship

As Stale as Day-old Bread

If you listen to a cassette tape over and over, most likely you'll get tired of listening to it. Hearing a cliché is something like listening to that cassette tape.

Clichés are expressions your reader has heard many times before. All clichés, though, were once fresh and original. In fact, they were so fresh and original that people used them over and over. Some clichés have been in use for centuries. For example, the phrase *sweeter than honey* originated around 700 B.C. That's when the ancient Greek poet Homer said, "From his tongue flowed speech sweeter than honey."

Another person whose original phrases have turned into clichés was the English poet and playwright William Shakespeare (1564–1616). If you've ever been stubborn about something, you might have said, "I'm not going to budge an inch." That idea comes from Shakespeare's play *The Taming of the Shrew.* Sometimes clichés are slight alterations of the writer's original words. *Cool as a cucumber,* for example, can be traced to the playwrights Francis Beaumont and John Fletcher. Their phrase in the seventeenth-century play *Cupid's Revenge* was "cold as cucumbers."

One way or another, we all get edited.

CHALLENGE

Rewrite the following without the clichés:

Beyond a shadow of a doubt, too many clichés will put you in hot water. Sad but true, a cliché sticks out like a sore thumb. Avoid clichés like the plague.

Do These Clichés Ring a Bell?

Look up the following clichés in *Bartlett's Familiar Quotations* or another reference book, and record the sources.

1. as old as the hills
2. a word to the wise
3. busy as a bee
4. few and far between
5. all in all

"I'm not going to budge an inch."

Context Clues **603**

23.3   Prefixes and Suffixes

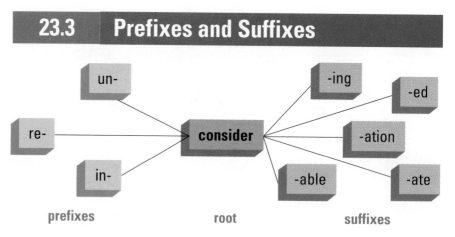

prefixes   root   suffixes

The illustration above shows how words parts can be put together to form many different words. These word parts are called roots, prefixes, and suffixes.

Roots

The root of a word carries the main meaning. Some roots (like the word *consider* above) can stand alone. Others (like *lect*, shown in the chart below) make little or no sense without a prefix or suffix. Knowing the meanings of roots can help you figure out the meanings of unfamiliar words.

Word Roots		
Roots	**Words**	**Meanings**
bio means "life"	biography biosphere	the story of a person's life part of the atmosphere where living things exist
dent means "tooth"	dentist trident	person who treats diseases of the teeth spear with three prongs, or teeth
flex or *flec* means "to bend"	flexible reflect	easily bent to bend back (light)
lect means "speech"	lecture dialect	a speech form of a language spoken in a certain region
tele means "distant"	television telescope	device for receiving pictures from a distance device for viewing distant things

Prefixes

Adding a prefix can change, or even reverse, the meaning of a root word (for example, *belief—disbelief*). In English, a number of prefixes have the same, or nearly the same, meaning. For example, *dis-*, *un-*, and *in-* all can mean "not" or "the opposite of." On the other hand, some prefixes have more than one meaning. The prefix *in-* can also mean "into," as in the word *incise* ("to cut into").

The chart below shows some common prefixes and their meanings. Notice in the example words how the prefixes change the root words' meanings. Learning these prefixes can help you figure out unfamiliar words.

Prefixes			
Categories	**Prefixes**	**Words**	**Meanings**
Prefixes that reverse meaning	*un-* means "not" or "the opposite of"	unnatural unhappy	not natural not happy
	in- means "not" or "the opposite of"	inconsiderate intolerant	not considerate not tolerant
	il- means "not" or "the opposite of"	illegal illogical	not legal not logical
	im- means "not" or "the opposite of"	immoderate imbalance	not moderate lacking balance
	ir- means "not" or "the opposite of"	irregular irreplaceable	not regular not able to be replaced
Prefixes that show relations	*pre-* means "before"	prepay prearrange	to pay in advance to arrange beforehand
	post- means "after"	postdate postpone	to assign a later date to delay until a later time
	sub- means "below" or "beneath"	submarine subway	an underwater boat an underground way or passage
	co- means "with" or "partner"	copilot cooperate	relief or second pilot to work with others

Suffixes

Like prefixes, suffixes change the meanings of roots. Like prefixes, they can have more than one meaning. They can have the same meaning as one or more other suffixes. Unlike prefixes, however, suffixes can also change the part of speech of a root word. For example, adding the suffix *-ness* to *quick* (an adjective) makes it into *quickness* (a noun). Adding *-ly* to *quick* makes *quickly* (an adverb).

Learning suffixes and how they change a root word can help build your vocabulary. The following chart shows a sample of common suffixes. As you look at it, try to think of other words to which each suffix might be added.

Suffixes			
Categories	**Suffixes**	**Words**	**Meanings**
Suffixes that mean "one who does [something]"	*-er, -or*	worker sailor	one who works one who sails
	-ee, -eer	employee profiteer	one who is employed one who profits
	-ist	pianist chemist	one who plays the piano one who works at chemistry
	-ian	physician	one who practices medicine (once called "physic")
Suffixes that mean "full of"	*-ful*	joyful wonderful	full of joy full of wonder
	-ous	furious courageous	full of fury (anger) full of courage
Suffixes that mean "in the manner of" or "having to do with"	*-ly*	happily secretly	in the manner of being happy in the manner of a secret
	-y	windy icy	having to do with wind having to do with ice
	-al	musical formal	having to do with music having to do with form

When suffixes are added to words, the spelling of the word may change. For example, when -ous is added to *fury*, the *y* in *fury* is changed to *i* to make the word *furious*. See pages 617–619 to learn more about the spelling of words that have suffixes added to them.

Exercise 3

Write a word containing each root listed below. Try to use a word that is not used in the word-roots chart. Then write a definition of each word. Check your dictionary if necessary.

1. bio
2. dent
3. flec or flex
4. tele

Exercise 4

Write a word to fit each of the definitions below. Each word should have a prefix or a suffix or both. Underline the suffixes and prefixes in the words. Use the charts in this lesson and a dictionary for help.

1. full of beauty
2. to behave badly
3. to fail to function correctly
4. below the earth
5. one who is a specialist in mathematics
6. a note written at the end of a letter, after the main part of the letter is complete (often abbreviated)
7. not able to be measured
8. in the manner of being not perfect
9. to live or exist together at the same time and in the same place
10. in the manner of being not happy

Weird Old Words

If someone called you a popinjay, would you be pleased? Do you like to show off a little when you know you look good? A popinjay is a vain, strutting person. The word is old-fashioned and not used much today, but the type of personality it describes isn't old-fashioned at all.

Words come and go in any language. If there's no evidence that a word has been used since about 1750, some dictionaries label it obsolete. An example of an obsolete word is an older definition of *popinjay*: a "parrot." No one today uses *popinjay* instead of *parrot*. So this meaning for the word is obsolete.

Many words have disappeared from English. Some vanish completely: *egal* once meant "equal," and a *prest* was money one person was forced to lend another. Neither word is used now. Other obsolete words leave traces. For example, a horse that could be hired out for riding was called a hackney or hack. This meaning of *hack* is now obsolete, but modern English does have a related word. Taxis are often called hacks. It's easy to trace this connection, since people hire taxis today, not riding horses, when they want to get around town.

The next time you pick up your dictionary, keep in mind that it's a work in progress.

CHALLENGE

Words vanish, and one reason may be that they aren't really needed to do the job. List a synonym for each of these obsolete words: joyance, impressure, argument *(meaning an outward sign).*

Gone but Not Forgotten

Think of a modern word related to each of the old words below. The definitions in parentheses should give you a clue or two. A college dictionary will also help.

1. grue (to shiver)
2. gruel (to exhaust)
3. lorn (forsaken, abandoned)
4. yelk (yellow)

You want your writing to be as clear as you can make it. How can you be sure you have written just the right word to express exactly what you mean? Becoming familiar with synonyms and antonyms—and knowing how to locate them—can help you in your writing. At the same time, you can increase your vocabulary.

Synonyms

Partly because of the borrowings from other languages, English speakers can choose from many words to express the same idea. These words that have the same, or nearly the same, meanings are called synonyms.

The important thing to remember is that synonyms rarely mean *exactly* the same thing. When searching for just the right word, the best place to find synonyms is in a thesaurus. (See pages 595–596 for information on how to use a thesaurus.) To use the right word, not *almost* the right word, check your dictionary for the definitions of synonyms, and notice the usage examples given.

For example, suppose you're writing about someone who spoke before a group. You look up synonyms for the word *speech* and find *address* and *oration*. *Speech* is a more general choice than *address* and *oration*. A speech may or may not be formal. An address is a prepared formal speech. An oration is even more formal and is always given at a special occasion. For example, you may have read Abraham Lincoln's Gettysburg Address. Before Lincoln gave that famous address, another speaker gave a two-hour oration.

fast
rapid
quick
fleet
speedy
swift

Knowing synonyms also helps make your writing more interesting. Writing that uses tired, colorless clichés—no matter how precise—is almost always boring. Use your knowledge of synonyms to substitute lively verbs and adjectives for lifeless, dried-out words.

Antonyms

Antonyms are words with opposite or nearly opposite meanings. The easiest way to form antonyms is by adding a prefix meaning "not." *Un-, il-, dis-, in-,* and *non-* are all prefixes that reverse the meaning of a root. They form antonyms, such as *untrue, illegible, disbelief, insufficient,* and *nonfat.* Sometimes an antonym can be made by changing the suffix. For example, *cheerful* and *cheerless* are antonyms.

As with synonyms, the important thing to keep in mind when choosing an antonym is finding exactly the right word. You need to check your dictionary to make sure you are using the right word for your context. When making an antonym by adding a prefix, make sure you check the dictionary. Be sure you are using the right prefix.

fast

slow

Exercise 5

For each of the following words, write two synonyms. Then write a sentence using one of the synonyms in each group. Use your dictionary and thesaurus as needed.

1. difficulty   **3.** confusion   **5.** slow (adjective)
2. nice   **4.** idea

Exercise 6

Replace the underlined word or words in each of the following sentences with an antonym. Use a thesaurus and a dictionary if you wish.

1. Jeremy's <u>good health</u> seems to be changing.
2. Andrea looks especially <u>pale</u> tonight.
3. That was the <u>most difficult</u> test I've ever taken.
4. Jake <u>closed</u> his eyes and saw the man who had been chasing him for so many days.
5. This fruit is so <u>dried out</u> I can't eat it.

Eating Your Words–a Great Diet?

Can you ever gain weight from eating your words? As a matter of fact, people don't generally sit down to a meal of their words. That's because they know that the expression *eat your words* really means "to take back something you've said." It's an idiom.

Let's look at some idioms and pull them apart. If you have decided to *put up with* something, where do you put it? If you *go back on* a promise, where have you gone? The point is, you can't understand an idiom just by putting together the meanings of the parts.

Idioms are a pretty big part of everybody's vocabulary. Some idioms are so ordinary that we hardly give them a thought—such as *to put over (a trick* or *a joke),* or *to come down with (a sickness).* Others add color to language. For example, you might keep a secret *up your sleeve* or *under your hat.*

Idioms arise in various ways. Some are translations from other languages. Many more probably started out having a word-for-word meaning. Later, people changed the meaning to include other situations. For example, at one time *to break the ice* only meant "to cut through river ice in the winter to make a path for ships and boats." In the 1700s the phrase's meaning extended to the process of starting a conversation.

Idio-Matic

How many idioms do you know? Test your idiom vocabulary. Match the following idioms with their meanings.

1. in the pink	a. gloomy
2. draw the line	b. get angry
3. in the dumps	c. healthy
4. a good egg	d. set a limit
5. hit the ceiling	e. nice person

23.5 Homographs and Homophones

If you're like most people, you may have to think for a minute about whether to write *principal* or *principle* when you're talking about the head of your school. Or you might write *there* in your essay when you mean *their*. When someone points out your mistake, you think, "I knew that!" Some words sound alike but are spelled differently. Others are spelled the same but have different meanings.

Homographs

Words that are spelled alike but have different meanings and sometimes different pronunciations are called homographs. The root *homo* means "same," and *graph* means "write" or "writing." *Homograph,* therefore, means "written the same" (in other words, spelled alike).

Fly and *fly* are homographs. You can swat a fly or fly a plane. Although the two words are spelled alike, they have different meanings. The following chart shows some common homographs used in sample sentences. See if you can tell how the homographs in each group differ in meaning.

Homographs
Ed finished the test with one *minute* left before the bell.   To build very small model airplanes, one must enjoy *minute* details.
It's difficult to *row* a canoe upstream.   We sat in the third *row* of seats in the balcony.   We had a terrific *row* yesterday, but today we're getting along fine.
I hope I pick the winning *number*.   This snow is making my feet *number* by the minute.
Abby tried to *console* her little sister when their cat died.   The television *console* has speakers built into it.
Don't let that *wound* on your arm get infected.   Jim *wound* the rope around the tree branch.

Homophones

Homophones are words that *sound* alike but are spelled differently and have different meanings. *Write* and *right* are homophones. The chart below shows some common homophones with their spellings and meanings.

Homophones			
Words	**Meanings**	**Words**	**Meanings**
sight site cite	act of seeing or ability to see a location to quote an authority	scent cent sent	an odor one one-hundredth of a dollar past tense of *send*
read reed	the act of reading the stalk of a tall grass	bore boar	to tire out with dullness a male pig
four fore	the number following three located at the front	main mane	most important long hair on an animal's neck
mail male	letters delivered by post the sex opposite the female	blue blew	the color of a clear sky past tense of *blow*
real reel	actual, not artificial a spool used to wind on	would wood	past tense of *will* hard material that makes up a tree

Exercise 7

Write the homophone from the parentheses that best completes each of the following sentences.

1. Jackie tried to (real, reel) in the fish.
2. The lion is the (main, mane) attraction at the zoo.
3. Chiyo thought that the speech was a (boar, bore).
4. This is the (cite, sight, site) on which the museum will be built.
5. What is that strange (scent, cent, sent) in the air?
6. A wild (bore, boar) can be dangerous if it attacks.
7. Sol (sighted, sited, cited) a thesaurus as his source.
8. Do I detect the (scent, cent, sent) of roses?

When Is a Noun Not a Noun?

The labels on the figure below are nouns that name body parts. English lets you put these same words into action as verbs. Here's how—from head to toe.

You can *head* a committee, *eye* a bargain, or *nose* a car into a parking space. You can *shoulder* a burden, *elbow* your way through a crowd, *hand* over the key, *knuckle* down to work, *thumb* a ride, *back* into a room, *foot* the bill, and *toe* the mark.

For hundreds of years, speakers of English have used these nouns and many others as verbs. Some words shifted in the other direction, from verb to noun. Today you can *walk* on a *walk*, *park* in a *park,* and *pitch* a wild *pitch.* Some shifts involve pronunciation. Notice which syllable you accent:

Will you *perMIT* me to drive?
Yes, when you get a *PERmit.*

Does your garden *proDUCE* carrots?
No, I buy *PROduce* at the market.

Still another shift involves nouns that became adjectives, as in the following: Sara unlocked the *steel* door. Tom wore a *straw* hat. Marty made *onion* soup.

So, when is a noun not a noun? When it's used as a verb or an adjective. The only way to identify such a word is to use it in a sentence.

CHALLENGE

Suppose you got this written message: Ship sails today. *What does it mean? Put the* before *ship; then put the* before *sails. Why can this sentence have two different meanings?*

head

nose

shoulder

hand

elbow

thumb

toe

foot

Double Duty

Use these clues to identify some words that have two functions.

1. *noun:* a very young person
   verb: to pamper
2. *verb:* to walk with regular steps
   noun: music with a steady beat
3. *verb:* throw pictures onto a screen
   noun: special work in science class

23.6 Spelling Rules

You may not know it, but you might have something in common with Noah Webster (of dictionary fame). He wanted to simplify the spelling of American English. He convinced people that the British *gaol* should be spelled *jail* in American English. He also got rid of the *k* in the British *picnick*, *musick*, and *frolick*. Webster especially disliked silent letters. He tried to get people to accept *iland* (*island*), *hed* (*head*), and *bilt* (*built*), among others.

However, most people didn't like Webster's spelling reforms. So today we have a system of spelling filled with rules and exceptions and words spelled nothing like the way they are pronounced. Using a dictionary to check spelling is the best way to avoid mistakes.

Common Spelling Rules

You won't always have a dictionary handy to check your spelling. Memorizing some of the following spelling rules will ensure that you spell most words correctly even when you don't have a dictionary.

Spelling *ie* and *ei*   The letter combinations *ie* and *ei* are found in many English words, and they often cause confusion in spelling. The problem is that two words might have the same vowel sound—long *e*— but one word might be spelled *ie* while the other is spelled *ei*. You can master the spelling of these words by memorizing the rhyme below.

Rule	Examples
Put *i* before *e*	achieve, retrieve, grieve
except after *c*	deceive, receipt, ceiling
or when sounded like *a*, as in *neighbor* and *weigh*.	eighty, veil, freight
Exceptions: species, weird, either, neighbor, seize, leisure, protein, height	

Spelling Unstressed Vowels   The unstressed vowel sound in many English words can cause spelling problems. Dictionary pronunciation guides represent this unstressed vowel sound by a special symbol called a schwa(ə).Listen to the unstressed vowel sound in the word *about*. This vowel sound can be spelled in more than a dozen ways—with any vowel letter and with several combinations of vowel letters—but it always sounds the same. Here are a few examples. Pronounce each word, and listen for the sound represented by the underlined letter or letters:

> *canv<u>a</u>s, ang<u>e</u>l, penc<u>i</u>l, rid<u>i</u>cule, cart<u>o</u>n, medi<u>u</u>m, enorm<u>ous</u>, anc<u>ie</u>nt, pig<u>eo</u>n, courag<u>eou</u>s.*

Notice that you hear the schwa sound only in unstressed syllables.

   As always, the best way to make sure of your spelling is to check a dictionary. When you can't use a dictionary, you might be able to figure out the spelling of the unstressed vowel sound. Think of a related word in which the vowel is stressed. For example, the word *informative* has an unstressed vowel, which happens to be spelled *a*. However, if you don't know that, you might think of the related word *information*, in which the vowel is stressed and sounds like an *a*. The chart below shows some additional examples of how to apply this process.

Spelling Unstressed Vowels		
Unknown Word	**Related Word**	**Word Spelled Correctly**
popul_rize	popul**a**rity	popularize
plur_l	plur**a**lity	plural
aut_mation	aut**o**	automation
influ_nce	influ**e**ntial	influence
not_ble	not**a**tion	notable
form_l	form**a**lity	formal
practic_l	practic**a**lity	practical
pol_r	pol**a**rity	polar
inhabit_nt	habit**a**tion	inhabitant
hospit_l	hospit**a**lity	hospital

Adding Prefixes   Adding prefixes to words usually doesn't present any spelling problems. Keep the spelling of the word, and attach the prefix. If the prefix ends in the same letter as the first letter of the word, keep both letters. Some common examples include the following:

co- + pilot = copilot   dis- + service = disservice
il- + legal = illegal   co- + operate = cooperate

Suffixes and the Final *y*   Adding suffixes to words that end in *y* can often cause spelling problems. The following rules will help you:

- When a word ends in a consonant + *y*, change the *y* to *i*.
  imply + -es = implies   reply + -ed = replied
  pry + -ed = pried   apply + -es = applies

- If the suffix begins with an *i*, keep the *y*.
  supply + -ing = supplying   fly + -ing = flying

- When a word ends in a vowel + *y*, keep the *y*.
  toy + -ing = toying   stay + -ing = staying
  delay + -ed = delayed   prey + -ed = preyed

Doubling the Final Consonant   When adding suffixes to words that end in a consonant, you sometimes double the final consonant. In other cases you simply add the suffix without doubling the consonant.

Double the final consonant when a word ends in a single consonant following one vowel and

- the word is one syllable
  strip + -ed = stripped   sad + -er = sadder
  shop + -ing = shopping   ship + -ed = shipped
  war + -ing = warring   tap + -ed = tapped

- the word has an accent on the last syllable, and the accent remains there after the suffix is added
  occur + -ence = occurrence   repel + -ing = repelling
  forget + -able = forgettable   commit + -ed = committed
  upset + -ing = upsetting   refer + -ed + referred

Do not double the final consonant when

- the accent is not on the last syllable
  flavor + -ing = flavoring
  envelop + -ment = envelopment
  remember + -ing = remembering

- the accent moves when the suffix is added
  refer + -ence = reference
  fatal + -ity = fatality

- two vowels come before the final consonant
  remain + -ed = remained   floor + -ing = flooring
  lead + -ing = leading   train + -ed = trained

- the suffix begins with a consonant
  master + -ful = masterful   dark + -ness = darkness
  tear + -less = tearless   leader + -ship = leadership
  loyal + -ty = loyalty   flat + -ly = flatly
  great + -ness = greatness

- the word ends in two consonants
  bring + -ing = bringing   stick + -ing = sticking
  inspect + -or = inspector   hunt + -ed = hunted
  attach + -ment = attachment
  great + -ness = greatness

  SPECIAL CASE: When a word ends in *ll,* and the suffix *-ly* is added, drop one *l.*
  dull + -ly = dully   full + -ly = fully

Suffixes and the Silent *e*   Noah Webster did his best to get rid of the silent letter *e* in American-English spelling. He succeeded in changing *axe* to *ax.* However, he lost the battle to change *give* to *giv,* and he failed to change the spellings of other words ending in silent *e.* The public was not willing to give up spellings with which they were familiar.

The silent *e* can still cause spelling problems, especially when you add a suffix to a word that ends in a silent *e.* Sometimes the silent *e* is dropped when adding a suffix, and sometimes it is kept. The following chart shows the rules for adding suffixes to words that end in silent *e.*

Adding Suffixes to Words That End in Silent *e*	
Rule	**Examples**
When adding a suffix that begins with a consonant to a word that ends in silent *e*, keep the *e*. **Common exceptions**	state + -ment = statement complete + -ly = completely awe + -ful = awful judge + -ment = judgment
When adding -*ly* to a word that ends in *l* plus a silent *e*, always drop the *e*.	able + -ly = ably sensible + -ly = sensibly remarkable + -ly = remarkably
When adding *y* or a suffix that begins with a vowel to a word that ends in a silent *e*, usually drop the *e*. **Common exceptions**	state + -ing = stating nose + -y = nosy lime + -ade = limeade mile + -age = mileage
When adding a suffix that begins with *a* or *o* to a word that ends in *ce* or *ge*, keep the *e* so the word will retain the soft *c* or *g* sound.	exchange + -able = exchangeable trace + -able = traceable
When adding a suffix that begins with a vowel to a word that ends in *ee* or *oe*, keep the *e*.	disagree + -able = disagreeable shoe + -ing = shoeing flee + -ing = fleeing

Forming Compound Words   The rule for spelling compound words is very simple. In most cases, just put the two words together. Seeing two consonants together, such as *hh*, *kk*, or *kb*, may seem odd. The English language does not have many words with these combinations. However, the rule is to keep the original spelling of both words, no matter how the words begin or end.

foot + lights = footlights   fish + hook = fishhook
busy + body = busybody   book + keeper = bookkeeper
book + bag = bookbag   light + house = lighthouse

Some compound words, such as *hand-me-down* and *forty-niners,* are hyphenated. Others, like *honey bear* (but not *honeybee*), are spelled as two words. Use a dictionary when in doubt.

Forming Plurals   The way plurals are formed in English is generally simple, and the rules are fairly easy to remember. The most common way to form plurals is to add *-s* or *-es*. The following chart shows the basic rules, their exceptions, and example words.

Rules for Plurals		
If the Noun Ends in	**Then Generally**	**Examples**
ch, *s,* *sh,* *x,* or *z*	add *-es*	witch → witches toss → tosses flash → flashes ax → axes buzz → buzzes
a consonant + *y*	change *y* to *i* and add *-es*	story → stories folly → follies
a vowel + *y*	add *-s*	play → plays jockey → jockeys
a vowel + *o*	add *-s*	studio → studios rodeo → rodeos
a consonant + *o*	generally add *-s* **Common exceptions** but sometimes add *-es*	piano → pianos photo → photos hero → heroes veto → vetoes echo → echoes
f or *ff*	add *-s* **Common exceptions** change *f* to *v* and add *-es*	staff → staffs chief → chiefs thief → thieves leaf → leaves
lf	change *f* to *v* and add *-es*	self → selves half → halves
fe	change *f* to *v* and add *-s*	life → lives knife → knives

A few nouns form plurals in a special way. Most of these special cases should not give you any problems in spelling. If you do not already know the irregular forms, such as *goose—geese*, you can memorize them. The following chart lists the special rules for plurals and gives some examples.

Special Rules for Plurals	
Special Case	**Examples**
To form the plural of proper names, add either *-s* or *-es,* following the general rules for plurals.	Smith → Smiths Jones → Joneses Perez → Perezes
To form the plural of one-word compound nouns, follow the general rules for plurals.	homemaker → homemakers blackberry → blackberries latchkey → latchkeys
To form the plural of hyphenated compound nouns or compound nouns of more than one word, generally make the most important word plural.	father-in-law → fathers-in-law lunch box → lunch boxes chief of state → chiefs of state
Some nouns have irregular plural forms and do not follow any rules.	goose → geese mouse → mice tooth → teeth child → children
Some nouns have the same singular and plural forms.	deer → deer sheep → sheep fish → fish

Improving Spelling Skills

Spelling rules will help you spell new words correctly. You can further improve your spelling skills by developing a method for learning these words.

Keep a notebook of unfamiliar words or words that are hard to spell. When you write, take note of any words you have trouble spelling, and add them to your notebook. As you come across new words, add them to your list. When you master the spelling of a word, cross the word off your list. Follow the steps on the next page to learn to spell those difficult words.

Say It	**Visualize It**	**Write It**	**Check It**
Look at the printed word or the word as it is written in your notebook. Say it out loud. Say it a second time, pronouncing each syllable clearly.	Close your eyes, and imagine seeing the word printed or written. Picture how the word is spelled.	Look at the printed word again, and write it two or three times. Then write it again without looking at the printed word.	Check what you have written against the printed word. Did you spell it correctly? If not, go through the process again until you can spell it correctly.

Exercise 8

Find the misspelled word in each sentence and write its correct spelling.

1. Mr. Harrison, the bookkeeper, has applyed for a government grant to buy new computers.
2. The book describes the lifes of famous artists.
3. Hector is fullly aware that we have to proceed with the polar expedition.
4. Stefanie spends her leisure time with the Walshs.
5. Kevin should be in the barnyard shoeing one of the remainning horses.
6. The zookeeper believes he will succeed in transfering the monkeys from the old cages without any problems.
7. The librarian has suggested two referrence books that should contain photos of wolves.
8. The summer weather has been so changeable that everyone is completly convinced we will have an unusually bad winter.
9. The puffs of clouds in the springtime sky reminded me of sheeps in a meadow.
10. The recent recurrence of fighting between the two warring nations is upseting to everyone who hopes for a peaceful settlement.

Vowel Switch

Spelling in English can be a real mystery. Why should the first vowel sounds in *pleasant* and *please* be spelled the same even though they are pronounced differently? Why not spell the sound in *pleasant* with just an *e,* as in *pen* and *red*?

Here's the scoop: Sometime between 1400 and 1600 the pronunciation of certain vowels underwent a change. The vowel in *please* was pronounced like the e in *pen,* only it was longer. This sound gradually shifted to a long ā sound as in *pane.* Meanwhile, the long vowel ā had begun to take on the long ē sound as in *feed,* while the long vowel ē had begun to take on the long ī sound as in *ride.* Similar changes occurred in the other long vowels. These pronunciation changes are called the Great Vowel Shift.

Meanwhile, the short vowels (as in *pleasant*) did not change. Because spelling didn't always keep up with pronunciation changes, the words *please* and *pleasant* were still spelled with the same vowel even though *please* was now pronounced like *plays.* Later some words like *please* changed again. By about 1700 most people pronounced *please* the way you pronounce it today.

So the next time you're puzzled by English spelling, remember that the way a word is spelled sometimes holds a clue to its history.

CHALLENGE

Some spellings have changed to reflect pronunciation changes. One example appears several times on this page. Can you find it?

Shifty Vowels

Which of the following word pairs demonstrate the Great Vowel Shift?

1. crime, criminal
2. mouse, mice
3. breathe, breath
4. serene, serenity
5. die, death

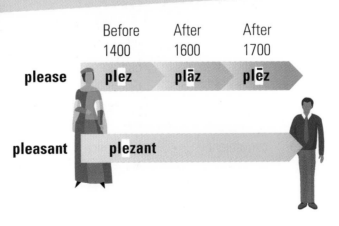

	Before 1400	After 1600	After 1700
please	plez	plāz	plēz
pleasant	plezant		

23.7 Becoming a Better Speller

Spelling the *really* difficult words—such as *pusillanimous* (meaning "cowardly")—is usually not too much of a problem. The reason is that when you use such words (which is not often), you will probably look them up in the dictionary.

What about the less difficult but more common words that you use often? Following is a list of such words. See if any of them are words you have had trouble spelling. What words would you add to the list?

Words Often Misspelled			
absence	curiosity	incidentally	pneumonia
accidentally	develop	incredibly	privilege
accommodate	definite	jewelry	pronunciation
achievement	descend	laboratory	receipt
adviser	discipline	leisure	recognize
alcohol	disease	library	recommend
all right	dissatisfied	license	restaurant
analyze	eligible	maintenance	rhythm
answer	embarrass	mischievous	ridiculous
attendant	environment	misspell	schedule
ballet	essential	molasses	separate
beautiful	February	muscle	sincerely
beginning	fulfill	necessary	souvenir
beneficial	foreign	neighborhood	succeed
business	forty	niece	technology
cafeteria	funeral	noticeable	theory
canceled	genius	nuisance	tomorrow
canoe	government	occasion	traffic
cemetery	grammar	original	truly
changeable	guarantee	pageant	unanimous
choir	height	parallel	usually
colonel	humorous	permanent	vacuum
commercial	hygiene	physical	variety
convenient	imaginary	physician	various
courageous	immediate	picnic	Wednesday

Spelling and Misspelling

Do you have trouble remembering the spellings of common words? How many *c*'s and *m*'s are in *recommend* and *accommodate*? Is it *separate* or *seperate*? Words like these cause many people problems. The following techniques will help you learn to spell troublesome words.

- Use rhymes (such as "*i* before *e* except after *c* . . .") and memory tricks (such as "there's *a rat* in *separate*").
- Pay special attention to words likely to be confused with other words. Below are some examples. You can find more in the list of homophones on page 613.

Words Often Confused	
accept except	Marianne will not *accept* the nomination for class president. All the students *except* Barry were on time.
affect effect	This cold weather can *affect* my sinuses. The space program could have an *effect* on future generations.
formally formerly	The new president was *formally* introduced to the student body. Ananda *formerly* lived in southern California.
its it's	Since *its* walls collapsed, the mine entrance has been closed. *It's* been a long time since I saw Winston so happy.
stationary stationery	The radio transmitting station is mobile, not *stationary*. Her *stationery* is decorated with tiny blue flowers.
thorough through	They completed a *thorough* revision of the student handbook. *Through* the window we could see them coming up the path.
than then	The final draft of my story is much better *than* the first draft. What happened *then*?
their there they're	What was the outcome of *their* first game? The address you are looking for is over *there*. The team members say *they're* happy with the new gym.
weather whether	I hope the *weather* stays nice for the picnic. I'm not sure *whether* it was luck or skill, but I made the team.

Work with one or two other students. Choose three words from the list of Words Often Misspelled on page 624 of this lesson. Develop a memory aid that will help you spell each word. Share your completed memory aids with the class.

Write the word in the parentheses that correctly completes each sentence.

1. The school decided to change the name of (its, it's) football team.
2. One of the test questions asked for an (effect, affect) of the Civil War.
3. Pete (formerly, formally) played on a soccer team at his old school.
4. If you leave your books (their, there, they're), they may get lost.
5. The cat pushed (its, it's) way through the swinging door.
6. Use your best (stationery, stationary) for the thank-you notes.
7. Have you decided what dress (your, you're) going to wear to the party?
8. The detective was very (thorough, through) in his investigation of the crime.
9. We would like to know (whether, weather) it will rain or be sunny on the day of our field trip.
10. The two dogs need to have (their, there, they're) coats brushed after being out all day.
11. I've never been (formerly, formally) introduced to the new counselor.
12. The three girls said that (their, there, they're) going to go swimming.

Unit 24 Study Skills

24.1 Using Book Features

Imagine you're writing a research paper on the Civil War. You've narrowed your topic to the Battle of Gettysburg, focusing on Pickett's Charge, a key event in the three-day battle. You find that the library has many books on the Battle of Gettysburg—but you certainly can't read them all.

How do you decide which books will be the most useful? Looking at certain pages in the front or back of a book will help you narrow your choice.

The pages shown below are valuable tools in discovering which books may hold the material you need. The title page and table of contents appear in the front, before the main text of the book. You'll find the index in the back.

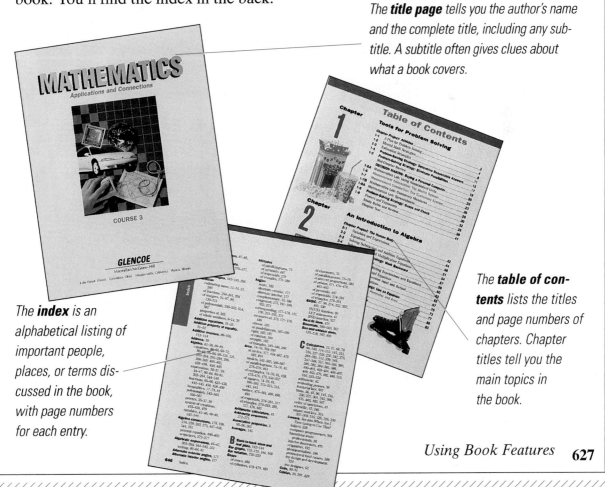

The **title page** tells you the author's name and the complete title, including any subtitle. A subtitle often gives clues about what a book covers.

The **index** is an alphabetical listing of important people, places, or terms discussed in the book, with page numbers for each entry.

The **table of contents** lists the titles and page numbers of chapters. Chapter titles tell you the main topics in the book.

Many books include other informative sections separate from the main text. The copyright page follows the title page. It tells you the year in which the book was published. Also in the front of a book, you may find a foreword, a preface, or an introduction. In the back of some books are glossaries for definitions and pronunciations of unusual words. The chart below shows you how to use some of these parts of a book.

Using a Book Effectively	
Questions	**Where to Look for the Answer**
Who is the author of this book?	The title page contains the author's name and the complete title.
Will this book contain information about my topic?	The table of contents identifies the main topics.
Will this book contain recent information about my topic?	The copyright page tells when a book was published or updated.
Will I find the people, places, and events I'm researching in this book?	The index is an alphabetical listing of people, places, events, and other topics covered in the book.

Exercise 1

Use this textbook to answer all but the first of the following questions:

1. Suppose you were studying how the human heart functions and wanted to find a definition of *atrium.* In what part of a science book would you look?
2. On what page or pages of this book are synonyms discussed?
3. In what year was this book published?
4. What is the title of Unit 10?
5. Does this book discuss homographs and, if so, on what pages?

24.2 Skimming, Scanning, and Careful Reading

What if you needed information about the structure of the human heart? What would you do? Most likely, you would read a book about your topic. There are several different ways to read for information. Using the right reading style for a particular purpose can save valuable time.

Skimming

When you want to know if a book covers the information you need, skimming is a good technique. Skimming can be very helpful in your research or when previewing or reviewing. While skimming, you glance over the text to find the main ideas. To skim a text, you look at the chapter titles, words in italic or bold type, and the topic sentence of each paragraph. Without taking too much time, you can grasp the most important ideas in a given chapter. For instance, the sample notes below might be made by skimming a detailed chapter on the makeup of the human heart.

Heart has two sections—right and left sides.
Right side pumps blood from body through lungs.
Left side pumps blood from lungs through body.
Blood enters right side, or *atrium*, through two veins, called *superior vena cava* and *inferior vena cava*.
Blood carrying oxygen flows from lungs to left atrium through *pulmonary veins*.

Scanning

When you are searching for specific information, you can use the technique of scanning. Scanning is a rapid form of skimming. While scanning, you move your eyes quickly over a page, looking for key words. When you locate the information you want, you read carefully for specific details.

Careful Reading

Careful reading is a third way to read for information. When you use this technique, you read the text slowly. You pay close attention to all details to make sure you clearly understand the information presented. Read carefully when learning material for the first time, such as when studying a new chapter in a science textbook. If you just skim or scan your textbook chapter the first time you read it, you won't learn as much as you need to. You also probably won't understand the technical terms you read. Then, when you have a quiz or a test, you'll find yourself in trouble.

You also practice careful reading when preparing to explain material to someone else. Suppose you were going to present an oral report on the human circulatory system. Any book you find explaining the circulatory system would probably include medical information unfamiliar to you. The only way to fully understand the content is to read slowly and carefully. Read a passage several times until you fully understand it. If you don't understand what you will be speaking or writing about, your audience won't understand it either. Also, keep a dictionary nearby so you can look up any unfamiliar words.

Exercise 2

Decide which reading technique—skimming, scanning, or careful reading—should be used in each of the following situations. Explain each decision.

1. You find a library book on a topic that interests you. You wonder whether the book is worth reading.
2. You've been asked to read the first half of a chapter in your science textbook before tomorrow's class.
3. You need information about the causes of the American Revolution for a report you are writing. You need to decide which of the ten books on the American Revolution you've found would best fit your needs.

24.3   Summarizing

Explaining the main ideas of something in your own words is called summarizing. Every time you tell a friend about a movie you saw or a book you read, you are summarizing. You might summarize yesterday's science lesson to a friend who was sick that day. Summarizing saves time. You also might find that explaining or summarizing something for someone else helps you understand it better.

When to Summarize

Though you often make informal summaries, there are also times when you need to make formal ones. When researching material for a report, for instance, you need to summarize the important ideas. You also might summarize information you hear in a lecture, speech, or film presented in class. After you take notes on what you read or hear, you can summarize the main ideas for reference or review.

You can also use summarizing as a study tool when reading or reviewing material in your text. Writing passages from a textbook in your own words can help you better understand and remember the material. The following chart shows when and why you might summarize material.

When to Summarize	
Situation	**Purpose**
Preparing a written or oral research report	To include important ideas from your reading in your report
Reading textbook material	To better understand and remember ideas from the textbook
Listening to lectures or speeches	To write a report or prepare for a test on ideas from the lecture or speech
Viewing a film or video documentary	To write a report or prepare for a test on ideas from the film

How to Summarize

When you write a summary, put the ideas in your own words. Concentrate on the main ideas, leaving out examples and supporting details. Look below at the example of an original text and one student's summary of it. Notice what details are left out and how the student's language differs from the original.

Abraham Lincoln (1809–1865), considered one of our greatest presidents, preserved the Union at a time of unrest during the Civil War. With the United States facing disintegration, he showed that a democratic form of government can endure.

One of Lincoln's most important qualities was his understanding. Lincoln realized that the Union and democracy had to be preserved. Lincoln was also a remarkable communicator, able to clearly and persuasively express ideas and beliefs in speech and writing. His most famous speech was the brief but powerful Gettysburg Address. His first and second inaugural addresses were also very significant.

Abraham Lincoln, one of our greatest presidents, is best remembered for holding the Union together through the Civil War. He is noted for his understanding and his ability to communicate effectively and persuasively.

Exercise 3

With a partner, choose a film or television documentary, a lesson or chapter from a book, or an encyclopedia article about a subject that interests you. Read or discuss the material, and then work together to write a summary. Identify the main ideas, and put them in your own words. Decide whether to use any direct quotes. Share your completed summary with the class.

24.4　Making Study Plans

Studying may not be your favorite activity but, like it or not, studying is essential to doing well in school. But what about free time? Everyone would like more time off each week. Practicing good study habits will improve your schoolwork and increase your free time.

Setting Goals

A good study plan begins with goal setting. Review your assignments, and then set your goals for each class. Break down your assignments into short-term and long-term goals. Short-term goals can be completed in one study session; long-term goals will take several sessions. Break down your long-term goals into smaller tasks. Be realistic about what you can get done in each study session.

The chart below shows some short-term and long-term goals, and how long-term goals can be broken down.

Setting Goals	
Short-Term Goals	1 learning a short list of spelling or vocabulary words 2 reading several pages in your textbook 3 completing a math exercise for homework
Long-Term Goals	1 completing a research report *short-term tasks* • find library materials • do prewriting • write rough draft • revise draft • prepare final report 2 preparing for a unit test *short-term tasks* • read Chapter 22 • read Chapter 23 • review key terms

Effective Study Time

Once you've determined your goals, set a reasonable deadline for reaching each goal. Write the deadline in a study-plan calendar that includes your regular activities and assignments. When you schedule your study time, keep your deadlines and your other activities in mind. Don't schedule too many deadlines for the same day. Look at the following studying tips. What other tips could you add?

Tips on Studying

1. Study at the same time and in the same place each day. Also, keep your study tools, such as pencils, pens, notepads, and dictionaries, in the same place.

2. Take a short break after reaching each goal.

3. Begin study time with your most difficult assignment.

4. Focus on one assignment at a time.

5. Try a variety of study methods, such as reading, summarizing what you have read, developing your own graphic aids (like clusters), or discussing material with a study partner.

Exercise 4

Keep a "study log" for two weeks. Record the beginning and ending time of each study session, even if it's only fifteen minutes at lunch. Write down what you study each day, and comment on how effective your studying is. You may want to include observations on circumstances that affect your study on a particular day. (For example: It was raining, so I was glad to be inside studying; I had a headache, so I had trouble concentrating.) At the end of the two weeks, take a good look at your study log. Identify the factors that contributed to your most effective use of study time.

24.5 The SQ3R Method

Do you sometimes spend hours reading your textbook only to find that you immediately forget most of what you read? Do you find that, even though you study hard, you often do not do well on tests? The SQ3R method can help make your study time more productive.

SQ3R is an effective method for improving your ability to read and remember written information. SQ3R stands for the steps in the process: survey, question, read, record, and review. Using this method can help you study more efficiently and remember more of what you read. The diagram shows how the SQ3R method works.

Survey	**Question**	**Read**	**Record**	**Review**
Preview the material by skimming. Read heads, highlighted terms, and the first sentence of each paragraph. Look at all pictures and graphs.	Ask questions about the material. Your questions might begin with *who, what, when, where, why,* and *how.*	Read the selection carefully. Identify the main idea of each section. Take notes, and add questions to your list.	Write answers to your questions without looking at the text. Make brief notes about additional main ideas and facts.	Check your answers in the text. Continue to study the text until you can answer all questions correctly.

The SQ3R method works with any subject. Practice the method, and make it a habit. Once you thoroughly learn the SQ3R method and use it regularly, you will

- remember more of what you read,
- better understand the material by developing specific questions about it, and
- be better prepared to participate in class.

Survey

The purpose of surveying, or previewing, the material is to get a general idea of what it is about. The main ideas are sometimes contained in section headings or subheadings. Read each heading and subheading, and skim the entire material. (See page 629 for hints on skimming.) If the material does not include headings, skim each paragraph to find its topic sentence. It will often be the first sentence of the paragraph.

Sometimes important ideas in the text are shown in bold or italic print. Make sure you note these carefully. When previewing, also take note of all pictures, charts, graphs, and maps. Examine them to see how the graphic aids fit in with the text. Read the title and caption for each one.

Question

Before you read, prepare a list of questions you want to be able to answer after reading the material. Having a list of questions before you begin helps you focus on the important ideas. Use questions that begin with *who, what, when, where, why,* and *how.* For example, suppose you're reading a chapter on the Battle of Gettysburg for your history class. You might write questions such as these: Who were the opposing generals in the battle? When did the battle take place? What was the outcome? Develop at least one question for each main idea before you read. Also, look at any review questions at the end of each chapter or lesson.

Read

Once you have prepared your list of questions, you are ready to read through the material carefully. (See page 630 for tips on careful reading.) As you read, look for answers to the questions on your list. Take brief notes about the main ideas. (See pages 638–639 for more information on taking notes.) For example, your notes might include "Battle of Gettysburg fought July 1–3, 1863. Confederate General Robert E. Lee; Union General George G. Meade. Turning point of Civil War." Add more questions to your list as they are raised during your reading. Make sure you thoroughly understand all the ideas. If the ideas are complicated and you are having difficulty, read the material through two or three times. Don't go on to the next chapter or section until you have mastered the material in your current reading.

Record

When you complete your reading, write the answers to your questions without looking at the book or article. If there is a large amount of material, you may wish to stop and answer your questions after you finish reading each section. Answering the questions from your memory will test whether you have thoroughly learned the material. If you have difficulty answering the questions, reread the material. Then try to answer the questions again without looking at the text. Make sure your questions apply to the material. If the material you're studying does not thoroughly answer the questions, revise your questions to fit the text.

Review

Check the answers to your questions against the material you've read. Did you answer them all correctly? If not, review the material to find the answers. Try rewriting some of the questions you missed, or write several new questions that cover the same material. Review the material again, and then answer the new questions. Check your answers against the material. If you miss some of these questions, go through the process again, rewriting questions and reviewing the material until you are able to correctly answer all questions. Save your review questions and answers. You can use them later to study or review for tests.

Exercise 5

Work with a small group of classmates. Each member should choose an event from American history, then find an encyclopedia article or a passage from a book about that event. Study your material, using the SQ3R method. Allow each member to give a brief oral report to the group on the material studied. Group members may evaluate one another's reports and discuss how the SQ3R method helped them.

24.6 Gathering and Organizing Information

Can you remember the important ideas from a discussion you heard two weeks ago? Probably not. Unless you took notes, you've probably forgotten what was said. Note taking is important, because people usually forget most of what they hear. Taking notes and organizing them helps clarify what you hear or read. Well-written notes also come in handy when you're studying for a test or writing a report.

Taking Notes

Taking notes isn't always easy, whether you are working from a lecture, a film or video shown in class, or from research material. You may find you are either trying to write down too much or not enough. Taking notes requires special skill.

The notes you take while listening are important for your later review. They'll help you understand and remember what you hear. The notes you take while reading will allow you to review the important ideas from a source. With good notes, you won't have to go back to a source and reread it.

Tips for Taking Notes

While Listening
1. Take down only main ideas and key details.
2. Listen for transitions and signal words.
3. Use numerals, abbreviations, and symbols for speed, making sure that later you can understand what you have written.

While Writing
1. Take notes only on material that applies directly to your topic.
2. Use a card for each piece of information, and record the source of the information at the top of the card.
3. Summarize as much as possible.
4. Use direct quotations only for colorful language or something that's particularly well phrased.

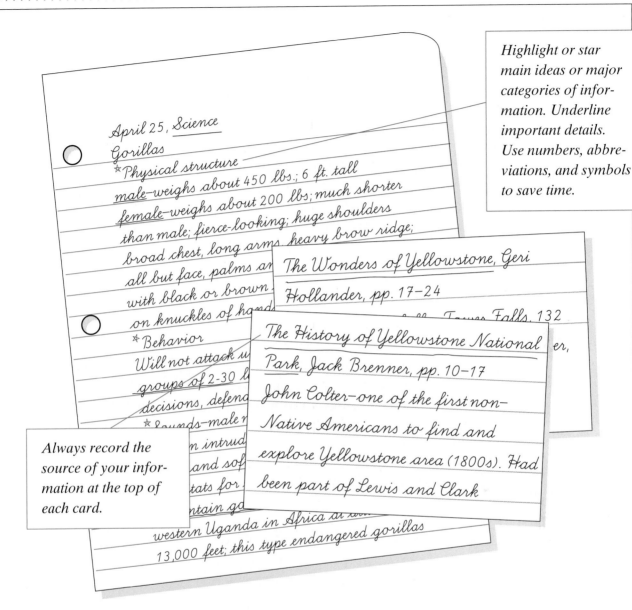

April 25, Science
Gorillas
★Physical structure
male—weighs about 450 lbs.; 6 ft. tall
female—weighs about 200 lbs; much shorter
than male; fierce-looking; huge shoulders
broad chest, long arms, heavy brow ridge;
all but face, palms an
with black or brown.
on knuckles of hand
★Behavior
Will not attack u
groups of 2-30 l
decisions, defend
★Sounds—male

The Wonders of Yellowstone, Geri
Hollander, pp. 17-24
Tower Falls, 132

The History of Yellowstone National
Park, Jack Brenner, pp. 10-17
John Colter—one of the first non-
Native Americans to find and
explore Yellowstone area (1800s). Had
been part of Lewis and Clark

n intrud
and sof
tats for
ntain g
western Uganda in Africa at
13,000 feet; this type endangered gorillas

Outlining

Once you complete your research, put your note cards in order and prepare an outline. The order you use depends on the kind of paper you are writing. If you're writing a paper on historical events, you might use chronological order, or the order in which events happen. A science paper might be ordered by cause and effect.

Group together your note cards that cover similar topics, Each group will become a main topic. Within each group put similar cards into subgroups. These will become your subtopics.

As your outline develops, you may find that you need to do more research. You may also find that you do not need all the notes you have taken. Set aside any note cards that don't apply to your outline. Examine the sample outline below.

Yellowstone National Park

I. The History of Yellowstone

   A. Earliest Explorers

      1. John Colter

         a. member of the earlier Lewis and Clark expedition

         b. first non-Native American to see Yellowstone

         c. visited in early 1800s

      2. Jim Bridger

         a. famous "mountain man" and explorer

         b. visited the region about 1830

   B. Washburn Expedition

      1. confirmed earlier reports of natural wonders

      2. worked to make area a national park

II. Yellowstone's Natural Beauty

Use Roman numerals to number the main topics, or big ideas of your paper.

Indent and use letters and numbers for subtopics and their divisions. Do not use subtopics or divisions unless you have at least two.

Exercise 6

Working with a small group of classmates, look through a magazine such as *National Geographic* or *Discover.* Choose an article that interests all of you. Have each member of the group read the article individually, take notes on it, and write a detailed outline. Then compare notes and outlines, discussing the differences.

Imagine trying to explain to someone, using just words, how a car engine works. A simple description of a process may seem confusing or incomplete. However, a picture or diagram can make it much easier for people to understand how something works.

Tables and Graphs

Many books use graphic aids such as tables and graphs to present figures or other data that are hard to explain with words alone. Table and graphs organize information and make it more understandable.

Tables   Tables allow you to group facts or numbers into categories so that you can compare information easily. The left-hand column of a table lists a set of related items. Across the top of the table are column headings that describe the items in each column. With this arrangement, you can read a table horizontally or vertically, and you don't have to read all the information to find the piece you need. For example, in the table below, you can easily find the population growth of the five largest U.S. cities. Looking across the rows, you can see how a particular city's population increased or decreased over the years. Looking down the columns, you can compare the populations in the different years listed.

\ Population of Largest U.S. Cities						
Rank	City	1950	1960	1970	1980	1986
1	New York City	7,891,984	7,781,984	7,895,563	7,071,639	7,262,700
2	Los Angeles	1,970,358	2,479,015	2,811,801	2,966,850	3,259,340
3	Chicago	3,620,962	3,550,404	3,369,357	3,005,072	3,009,530
4	Houston	596,163	938,219	1,233,535	1,595,138	1,728,910
5	Philadelphia	2,071,605	2,002,512	1,949,996	1,688,210	1,642,900

Source: *U.S. Bureau of the Census*

Bar Graphs   In bar graphs each quantity is shown as a bar. The length of the bar indicates the amount, making it easy to visually compare the amounts. Bar graphs can have horizontal bars or vertical bars, depending on how many categories are being compared. Look at the bar graph below. Use the graph to compare the sales figures for different types of athletic shoes sold in the United States.

Each bar represents a different type of athletic shoe. The height of each bar shows the total sales for one type of shoe.

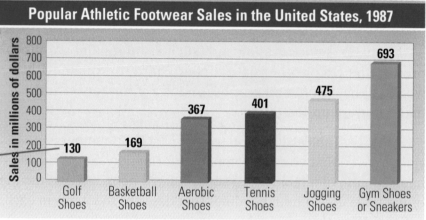

By comparing the lengths of the bars, you see that gym shoes, or sneakers, outsold all other types of athletic shoes in 1987.

Source: *Statistical Abstract of the United States,* 1989

Line Graphs   Line graphs help the reader to see at a glance whether certain numbers are rising, falling, or going up and down. They also show the period of time in which these changes take place. The line graph at the left shows the amount of solid waste thrown away between 1960 and 1985. The amount of garbage, in millions of tons, is listed along the left-hand side, or vertical axis. The years are shown along the bottom, or horizontal axis. By following the line, you can

Amounts are shown along the vertical axis. Horizontal lines make it easy to locate the amount for a given year.

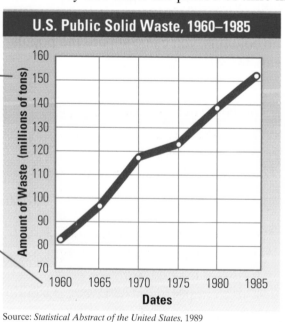

Years are shown along the horizontal axis. Vertical lines on the graph make it easy to see where the year intersects the graph line.

Source: *Statistical Abstract of the United States,* 1989

quickly see that the amount of garbage thrown away in the United States kept rising over the years given.

Circle Graphs   Circle graphs, or pie charts, begin with a circle representing the whole of something. The parts are shown as slices of a pie, with each slice representing part of the whole. Because a circle graph shows parts of a whole, information is often presented as percentages. For instance, instead of representing the population of North America in numbers of people, a circle graph might show it as a percentage of the total world population.

The circle graph on this page uses the same information as the bar graph on the opposite page. The whole circle represents the total of athletic shoes sold in the United States in 1987. The graph is then divided into the different types of athletic shoes. The sizes of the slices allow you to easily compare the portions of total sales for each type of shoe.

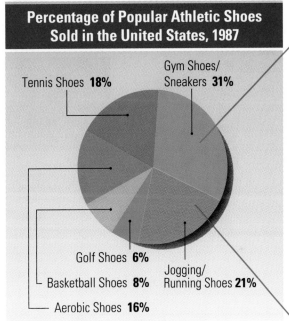

Percentage of Popular Athletic Shoes Sold in the United States, 1987

Tennis Shoes **18%**

Gym Shoes/ Sneakers **31%**

Golf Shoes **6%**

Basketball Shoes **8%**

Aerobic Shoes **16%**

Jogging/ Running Shoes **21%**

Source: *Statistical Abstract of the United States,* 1989

Ordinary gym shoes, or sneakers, are represented by a slice that is 31 percent of all athletic shoes sold in 1987.

The next largest slice, representing jogging or running shoes, accounts for 21 percent of all athletic shoes sold in 1987.

Diagrams

Diagrams may illustrate the steps in a process or show how the parts of an object work together. You might find it difficult to learn about a complex process by reading about it or by listening to someone give an explanation. You might not be able to follow all the stages or understand all the parts without the help of a diagram.

In a diagram each part of the object or process is labeled, sometimes with an explanation of its function. The diagram on the next page, for example, shows how heat energy is turned into electricity. Notice how each important part is labeled. Note also how the arrows show the movement of water and energy.

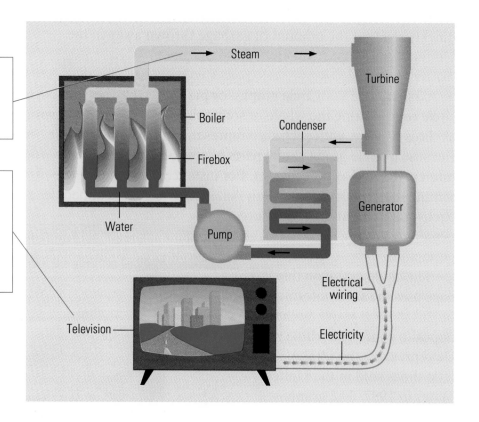

Arrows show movement of water through its complete cycle.

Diagram labels tell the name of each part of the process, but not all the details within that process.

Exercise 7

Work with a classmate on one of the following projects. Display your completed project in class.

1. Find out the high temperature for each day of the preceding week. Draw the appropriate graph showing the week's temperatures. Then write a brief paragraph explaining the graph.
2. Find the total number of games won by five competing athletic teams this season. Develop an appropriate graphic showing the number of games won by each of the five teams. Then write a brief paragraph explaining your graphic.

Do you ever call your best friend on the phone? Of course you do. Friends call each other all the time. Do you look up your friend's number in the phone book every time you call? Not if you have it memorized. Memorizing phone numbers is easy, but what about things you need to know in school? You can memorize information for school as easily as you memorize a friend's phone number.

How to Memorize

Different people have different "learning styles," or methods, of memorizing. One thing may work for one person, but not for someone else. The following are two techniques for memorizing. Try them and see what works better for you.

The most common technique for memorizing is repetition. You keep reading a passage aloud until you've got it memorized. You could also write the material over and over. If you combine your writing with reading aloud, you may memorize even more quickly. If you learn better by hearing, tape record as you read. Play back the tape as many times as necessary until you have memorized the information.

Visualizing is another method of memorizing. Use it to memorize small pieces of information, such as phone numbers, formulas, or the spelling of words. Look at the information. Then close your eyes and "see" the number or word in your mind. Visualize it in an interesting or humorous way. If you can get a unique picture in your mind, you're more likely to be able to visualize it again.

Tricks for Memorizing

Using memory games or tricks is another way to remember information. There are many different tricks or games you can use. Try making a sentence out of words that start with the first letter of each item in a list you want to memorize. Or make up a name using those same letters. You could also try writing a rhyme. Look at the chart below. When you need to memorize something, try some of these memory tricks to remember the material.

Tricks for Remembering	
Purpose	**Memory Aid**
To remember the number of days in each month of the year	Thirty days has September, April, June, and November. All the rest have thirty-one, Except February alone, Which has twenty-eight. In leap year, coming once in four, February then has one day more.
To remember the year Columbus sailed to the Americas	In fourteen hundred and ninety-two, Columbus sailed the ocean blue.
To remember that the order of the planets from the sun is **M**ercury, **V**enus, **E**arth, **M**ars, **J**upiter, **S**aturn, **U**ranus, **N**eptune, and **P**luto	**M**y **v**ery **e**xcellent **m**other **j**ust **s**erved **u**s **n**ine **p**izzas.
To remember that the person who runs a school is a *principal*, not a *principle*	The princi<u>pal</u> is my <u>pal</u>.

Exercise 8

Develop a memory trick to remember the parts of the sun: core, photosphere, chromosphere, corona. Work on your own or with a classmate or two.

Exercise 9

With a partner choose at least two words from the list of Easily Confused Words on page 624 in Lesson 23 .7. Develop ways to memorize each word.

Taking Tests

25.1   Strategies

No one said it would be easy. Studying for and taking a test is hard work. Still, you can learn some strategies that will help you prepare for and take tests. These strategies can help make you less uncomfortable and perhaps more confident in a test-taking situation.

Preparing for a Test

Preparing for a test begins well before the day of the test. Before you study, try to find out what information will be on the test. Then make a test-studying schedule. Include time for reviewing your class notes, homework, quizzes, and textbook. As you study, jot down questions that you think might be on the test. Try to answer these questions after writing them. If some questions are difficult to answer, spend some extra time looking up the answers.

When you think you know the material, work with another student or a group of students. Test these students with your study questions. Explaining the answers to someone else will help you learn the information. In addition, ask the students in your group to test you with questions they wrote. They may have come up with some you hadn't thought of yourself.

Taking a Test

You need to make careful use of the limited time for a test. First, make sure you understand all the test directions. Then estimate how much time each test section will take. Begin with the sections that will take less time, and don't spend too much time on one section. Planning your test time wisely may help you answer all of the questions. The chart on the following page offers suggestions for budgeting your time.

Tips for Budgeting Time During a Test

1. Read the directions carefully. Be sure you understand them before you begin the test.

2. Begin with the section of the test that will take the least amount of time.

3. Answer easier items first. Skip the ones you can't answer.

4. Return to the more difficult items when you have answered everything else.

5. Use any time left over to check your answers. Check the numbers to be sure you didn't write an answer in the wrong place.

Exercise 1

Practice using the test-taking skills you have learned in this lesson. Write the letter of the response that best answers these questions.

1. Which of these strategies is a good way to prepare for a test?
   a. Save all studying until the night before you take the test.
   b. Allow plenty of time to review the material.
   c. Sleep with your book under your pillow.
   d. none of the above
2. Which items should you answer first on a test?
   a. the last ones
   b. the first ones
   c. the easy ones
   d. the difficult ones
3. Which of these is *not* a good test-taking strategy?
   a. Skip the items you know.
   b. Read the directions carefully.
   c. Begin with a section that won't take much time.
   d. Check your answers.

You have just found out that your upcoming exam in science will include true-false, multiple-choice, matching, fill-in, short-answer, and essay questions. Don't panic. Learning a few simple strategies for answering these types of questions can help you deal with them.

True-False Items

True-false items can be tricky. A single item may include both true and untrue information. You must read the whole statement carefully before answering. If *any* part of the statement is not true, the answer to the item should be *false.* Look at the statement below.

> California has more people and more land than any other state in the United States.

California does have more people than any other state. However, Alaska is the largest state in area. The statement is false.

Multiple-Choice Items

Multiple-choice items include either an incomplete sentence or a question, and three or four responses. You need to pick the response that best completes the sentence or answers the question. Read the tips below for answering multiple-choice items. Then answer the question that follows.

- Read each item carefully to know what information you are looking for.
- Read all responses before answering. Sometimes an answer may seem correct, but a response that follows it may be better.
- If permitted, cross out answers you know are incorrect.
- Be careful about choosing responses that contain absolute words, such as *always, never, all,* or *none.* Since most statements have exceptions, absolute statements are often incorrect.

Who was the first woman nominated by a major political party to be vice president of the United States?

a. Sandra Day O'Connor

b. Shirley Chisholm

c. Geraldine Ferraro

d. Barbara Jordan

Matching Items

To complete a matching item, you must match items found in one group to items in another. For example, you might have to match terms with their definitions, cities with their countries, or causes with their effects. A good way to tackle these types of questions is to compare the groups. Do they contain the same number of items? Will every item be used only once? Complete easier items first. If you are allowed to write on your test copy, cross out each item after you use it. When you get to the harder items, you will have fewer choices left.

Read the following example. Match the events or documents in the first column with the dates in the second. Use each date only once.

___ 1. U.S. Civil War begins   a. 1950

___ 2. Korean War begins   b. 1945

___ 3. U.S. Constitution   c. 1861

___ 4. Emancipation Proclamation   d. 1789

                                      e. 1863

Fill-in Items

To complete a fill-in item, you need to fill in a blank or blanks in a sentence. Your answer must make the sentence true and must be grammatically correct. Rereading the sentence with your answer included will help you determine whether you have made the correct choice. Look at the fill-in question below.

> 1. A cold–blooded vertebrate that has gills early in life and then develops lungs later in life is an _____.
>
> 2. The three states in which matter exists are _____, _____, and _____.

The blank is preceded by the word an, *so the answer must be singular and begin with a vowel. The answer is* amphibian.

Note that three responses are called for and that their order is not important. The correct answers are solid, liquid, *and* gas.

Short-Answer Items

In responding to short-answer items, you must provide specific information. Your answer should be clear and easy to understand. The best way to write it is in complete sentences. For example, look at the question and answer below.

> Why are the first ten amendments to the United States Constitution known as the Bill of Rights?

The question asks for an explanation. In your answer you must tell why the amendments are called the Bill of Rights.

> *The first ten amendments are called the Bill of Rights because they preserve and protect specific rights of the people.*

Note that the answer is written in a complete sentence.

Essay Questions

Essay questions usually require an answer that is at least one paragraph long. To answer an essay question, take time to think about your main idea and the details that will support it. Also allow yourself time to write and revise your answer.

Exercise 2

Read the passage below. Use the test-taking strategies you have learned to answer the questions that follow.

Most of the paper we use today comes from trees. After the bark has been removed, the wood is ground up and mixed with water. This mixture is called wood pulp. The wet pulp is pressed into layers by machines, which dry the pulp on a series of screens and large rollers. The dried paper is then wound onto rolls.

Different types of paper are made from a variety of materials that are mixed with the pulp. These include wax, plastic, rags, and wastepaper. Making wastepaper into usable paper products is called recycling. Recycling is an important way to save trees.

1. Is the following statement true or false?
   Paper comes from paper plants.
2. Which of the following is not normally used in the making of paper?
   a. wax **b.** plastic **c.** wood pulp **d.** bark
3. Fill in the correct response: Before paper is made, the ____ of a tree must be removed.
4. Correctly match the items in the first column with those in the second.
   1. wood pulp   **a.** added to wood pulp
   2. screens   **b.** saves trees
   3. wax, plastic, rags   **c.** ground wood plus water
                            d. what the pulp is dried on
5. What is an important reason why you should use recycled paper?

Standardized tests, such as the Iowa Test of Basic Skills and the California Test of Basic Skills, are given to groups of students around the country. Knowing what kinds of questions might be on the tests can help you relax and concentrate on doing well.

Reading Comprehension

Reading-comprehension items measure how well you understand what you read. Each reading-comprehension section includes a written passage and questions about the passage. Some questions will ask you to identify the main idea. Others will ask you to draw conclusions from information in the passage. Practice your skills by reading the passage below and answering the questions.

If you have ever been to a sushi bar, you have had an experience that is new to most Americans. Sushi is a Japanese delicacy created from raw fish, seasoned rice, pickles, seaweed, and horseradish. At a sushi bar customers sit at long counters and watch expert chefs prepare sushi by hand. The chefs shape some pieces one at a time. They slice other pieces from a long roll of rice, fish, and seaweed.

1. What is the best title for this paragraph?
   a. Japanese Traditions
   b. What Is a Sushi Bar?
   c. Raw Fish Is Good for You
   d. Japanese Cooking

The paragraph focuses on describing a sushi bar. The best title is b.

2. What is sushi made of?
   a. horseradish
   b. raw fish and rice
   c. seaweed and pickles
   d. all of the above

If you reread the paragraph's second sentence carefully, you will see that d *is the correct choice.*

Vocabulary

Vocabulary items are usually multiple-choice. Some items ask you to choose the correct meaning of a word used in a sentence. Others may ask you to choose the word that best completes a sentence or a definition. If you are unfamiliar with the word, look for context clues to help you with the meaning. Also, look for prefixes, suffixes, and roots that may be familiar. For example, you may not know what the word *dentifrice* means. If you recognize the root *dent,* you might guess that it is related to *denture* and *dentist.* If you were asked to choose among *boardwalk, can opener, toothpaste,* or *sherbet,* which definition would you choose?

Now try these sample test questions.

The correct answer would be toothpaste.

Context clues can help you guess the meaning of ambivalent. *Jeremy can't decide between two things. The answer is* c.

Note that Mae Ling wants her brother to make sense. Rational *probably means "sensible." Choice* a *is correct.*

The word biplane *contains two parts: the prefix* bi-, *meaning "two," and the root word. Choice* b *makes the most sense.*

Choose the letter of the correct definition of or the synonym for each underlined word.

1. Jeremy could not make up his mind whether to go to the circus or to the baseball game. He was <u>ambivalent.</u>

   a. carefree
   b. feeling angry
   c. having two conflicting wishes
   d. having no energy

2. "Please be <u>rational</u>!" insisted Mae Ling. It annoyed her when her brother made no sense at all.

   a. sensible b. confused c. eager d. polite

3. Samuel planned to perform tricks with his <u>biplane</u> in the county fair competition.

   a. a plane with three sets of wings
   b. a plane with two sets of wings
   c. a glider
   d. a car with two sets of wheels

Analogies

Analogy items test your understanding of the relationships between things or ideas. On a standardized test you may see an analogy written as *animal : whale :: tool : hammer.* The single colon stands for "is to"; the double colon reads "as." The relationship among the words is that the category *animal* includes the whale, and the category *tool* includes the hammer.

This chart shows some word relationships you might find in analogy tests.

Word Relationships in Anology Tests		
Type	**Definition**	**Example**
Synonyms	Two words have the same general meaning.	vivid : bright :: dark : dim
Antonyms	Two words have opposite meanings.	night : day :: tall : short
Use	Words name a user and something used.	writer : pen :: chef : spoon
Cause and Effect	Words name a cause and its effect.	heat : boil :: cold : freeze
Category	Words name a category and an item in it.	fruit : pear :: flower : rose
Description	Words name an item and a characteristic of it.	baby : young :: sky : blue

Try to complete these sample analogies.

1. violin : orchestra :: clown : ___

    a. saxophone b. juggler c. make-up d. circus

2. weeping : sadness :: laughter : ___

    a. comedian b. joy c. yelling d. discomfort

Identify the relationship. A violin is a part of an orchestra. A clown is a part of a ___. The correct answer is circus.

Although a *may seem like the right choice, it is not a feeling, as is* sadness. *The correct answer is* b.

Grammar, Usage, and Mechanics

Standardized tests measure your understanding of correct grammar, usage, and mechanics by asking you to identify errors. You will be given a sentence with portions underlined and lettered. Or you will be given a sentence with numbered sections. In either case you will be asked to identify the section that contains an error. Most tests include one choice that states the sentence has no errors.

Before you complete the sample questions, study this list of common errors included in standardized grammar tests:

- errors in grammar
- incorrect use of pronouns
- subject-verb agreement
- wrong verb tenses
- misspelled words
- incorrect capitalization
- punctuation mistakes

Now choose the section in each item that contains an error.

In section c the preposition on *is incorrect.*

1. Both he and I will be foreign exchange students
   a   b
   on Mexico City in the fall. no error
   c   d   e

Section b includes a double negative, there wasn't… nothing.

2. Ernie always said there wasn't really nothing like
   a   b
   jumping into an icy cold lake in Colorado. no error
   c   d   e

3. Mr. Anglim said enthusiastically, "our school has just
   a   b
   bought a new computer." no error
   c   d

The first word of a quoted sentence is always capitalized. The correct choice is b.

4. Frida Kahlo was a Mexican artist who painted
   a
   beautiful, dreamlike senes of her life. no error
   b   c   d

5. When John Henry was a little baby, he sat on his
   a   b
   father's knee and plays with a hammer. no error
                     c   d

6. We really should ought to thank Grandma for the
   a   b
   presents she sent to us. no error
   c   d

The word scenes *is misspelled in the third section. Therefore,* c *is the correct choice.*

The phrase should ought to *is incorrect. Either* should *or* ought to *could be used, but not both. So* a *is the answer.*

The action in this sentence is taking place in the past. The verb should be played, *not* plays. *Choice* c *is correct.*

Taking a Standardized Test

Standardized tests are different from classroom tests. Instead of writing your answers on the test itself, you will be provided with a separate answer sheet. Since answer sheets are usually graded electronically, you should be careful to avoid stray marks that might be misread.

Some standardized tests do not subtract points for incorrect answers. If this is true for the test you are taking, try to give an answer for every item. You might improve your test score by guessing correctly. But don't just guess wildly. Eliminate options that you know are wrong before making a guess.

If you can't answer a question, don't waste time thinking about it. Go on to the next one. You can come back to the unanswered question later if you have time.

Reading-Comprehension Items   Read the passage below and answer the questions that follow it.

> Medical Research Secretary. Two years' experience in related field required. Must type 50 words per minute. Please send resumé and salary requirements to Tulane University.

1. Where would you most likely find the above paragraph?
   a. the help-wanted page of a newspaper
   b. a teen diary
   c. a science textbook
   d. the front page of a newspaper

2. What experience would be most acceptable?
   a. a typist in a bank
   b. a chemist at a laboratory
   c. a cashier at a supermarket
   d. all of the above

Vocabulary Item   Find the best synonym for the underlined word.

3. We have to make a <u>unified</u> effort, or we will never win the election.
   a. shared   b. difficult   c. untried   d. mighty

Analogy Item   Complete the analogy.

4. flock : geese :: _____ : wolves
   a. herd   b. pack   c. collection   d. sheep

Grammar, Usage, and Mechanics Item   Identify the section that contains an error.

5. <u>The entire side of the mountain</u> <u>exploded into the</u>
            a   b
   <u>air when Mt. St. Helens was erupted.</u> no error
                    c   d

Unit 26 Listening and Speaking

26.1 Effective Listening

Understanding what you hear begins with good listening skills. It's often hard to listen when people are talking and moving around or when other noises attract your attention. But you can learn how to tune out distractions and tune in to what is being said. You can improve your listening skills and increase your ability to understand.

Listening in Class

What happens when you don't understand how to do your homework assignment? It's difficult to do a good job when you don't understand what's expected of you. Learning how to listen better will make tasks that depend on understanding directions much simpler. The following tips will help you improve your listening skills to better understand what you hear.

Tips for Effective Listening

1. First, determine the type of information you are hearing. Are you listening to a story, or is someone giving you directions? Knowing what you are listening for makes understanding easier.

2. Take notes. Identify the main ideas as you hear them, and write them in your own words.

3. Take a note if you hear a statement that tells when you will need the information you are listening to.

4. If you don't understand something, ask a question. Asking questions right away helps avoid confusion later on.

5. Review your notes as soon as possible after the listening experience. Reviewing them soon afterward will allow you to fill in any gaps in your notes.

Listening to Persuasive Speech

What type of argument most easily persuades you? Is it one that includes facts and logical conclusions or one that appeals to your emotions? Speakers who want to persuade you may concentrate on emotional appeals. They may even use faulty thinking to persuade you to accept their opinions.

Faulty Thinking   Faulty thinking may be intentional or unintentional. That is, the speaker may be trying to deceive you or simply may not be thinking clearly. It's up to you, the listener, to analyze the speaker's statements and arguments. Are they well thought out, or are they flawed? Following are some examples of statements you might hear from a political candidate. However, you can find examples of faulty thinking in other kinds of persuasive speeches as well.

Questioning What You Hear	
Statements	**Questions**
Every child in America will have food on the table if I'm elected.	This is a broad statement. Do you think any one candidate can keep such a promise?
Don't vote for my opponent. His brother was investigated by the IRS two years ago.	What was the nature of the investigation? What were its results? Should a candidate be judged by someone else's activities?
I have the support of the great governor of our state in my campaign for senator.	Does the support of the governor prove a person is qualified to be senator? Is the governor a political ally of the candidate?
Voters in three states claim health care is important. I listen to America.	Might voters in some other states have different needs?

Speaker's Bias   Speakers may try to persuade audiences to agree with them by presenting only one side of an issue. Such speeches are biased, or slanted, in favor of one opinion. Always listen with a questioning attitude. Ask yourself if the speaker is dealing with all sides of the issue. Maybe the speaker is giving only the facts that support one opinion.

Be alert for speeches that show bias, such as the first example below. The other example is more objective. As you read, notice the facts each speaker uses.

BIASED SPEAKER: You should vote in favor of the proposed tax increase on gasoline. This tax will give the government enough revenue to rebuild the nation's crumbling highway system. It will provide many thousands of new jobs in the construction industry. It also will help us reduce the national debt. Our country needs this tax increase.

UNBIASED SPEAKER: This tax increase has faults as well as benefits. True, it will help rebuild highways and provide more jobs in highway construction. But it will also place a burden on those who must drive to make a living. The added cost of gas may drive many independent truckers and drivers out of work. People who take buses may find themselves paying higher fares.

The biased speaker gives only arguments in favor of the tax increase. The unbiased speaker admits that the arguments of the biased speaker are valid. However, this speaker points out that the increase will also have some negative effects.

Listening to Radio and Television News

Do you ask questions when you listen to the news? You might be surprised at how much there is to question. It's important to sort out facts from opinions in print, radio, and television news coverage. Doing so will help you evaluate the news coverage for truthfulness and accuracy. It will help you form your own unbiased opinion about what's being said.

Journalists are supposed to be objective. This means that they should not let their own opinions affect what they report and how they report it. This is sometimes a difficult thing to do. For example, a news commentator may call someone an "influential senator." Is the senator really influential, or is the commentator only expressing an opinion? The answer will help you evaluate anything the senator says. It will also help you evaluate what the commentator says about the senator.

Journalists are taught to provide sources for their information. Often it's important to know where the information in a news item came from. For example, suppose you heard the following two items on a newscast. Which would you be more likely to believe?

- Certain unnamed sources reported today that the President would not seek a second term of office.
- The President's chief of staff announced this afternoon that the President plans to seek a second term.

Journalists also try to present information that is complete. In their reports they usually try to answer the questions *what, who, when, where, how,* and *why.* If you carefully read or listen to almost any news story, you will see that it answers questions such as these:

- *What* happened?
- *Who* was involved?
- *When* did it happen?
- *Where* did it happen?
- *How* did it happen?
- *Why* did it happen? (or *Why* is it important?)

The questions may not always follow the above order, but they will all be answered. They'll usually be answered in the first paragraph of a newspaper story or the first minute or so of a radio or television newscast.

When you listen to a news broadcast, you can evaluate the quality of the reporting. Ask yourself some questions, such as the following:

- Was the report complete?
- Is all the information provable, or are some statements only opinions?
- Is any of the report based on faulty thinking?
- If an opinion is expressed, does the reporter tell whose opinion it is?
- Did the reporter identify the sources of the information?

Following are some other examples of how asking questions will help you evaluate a news broadcast.

Evaluating News Statements	
Sample Statements	**Questions to Ask**
The candidate has a liberal voting record on defense spending.	What is a liberal voting record? Who defines *liberal?* Does the candidate's record match the definition?
A reliable source stated that the company has been dumping toxic waste into the river.	Who is the source? How reliable is he or she? Did the source actually see the dumping?
One eyewitness stated that the defendant fired three shots.	Who is this witness? Where was the witness at the time? Does the witness know the defendant?
An expert claims we are in a recession.	Who is the expert? In what field is he or she an expert? Was any proof provided? Do other experts agree?
The tobacco company denies any proven relationship between smoking and illness.	Doesn't the company have an interest in denying the relationship? On what facts does the company base its statement?
Last winter's frost is driving the price of fruit upward.	Is there a proven relationship between the frost and rising fruit costs? Are there other possible reasons for the rising costs?

Exercise 1

Divide into small groups. Each group will form a news broadcast team. Select one person to be the news anchor. Other members of the group can be reporters on special assignments.

Decide which current events in your school or neighborhood to cover. Assign a story to each person. Students should research their stories and write short reports to deliver during a news broadcast of no more than ten minutes. Rehearse your newscast within the group, then present it to the class. Other members of the class should evaluate each broadcast.

26.2   Interviewing Skills

If you wanted answers to three or four questions on the topic of fly fishing, what would be an efficient way to get them? Would you read about the topic in an encyclopedia or interview a neighbor who is a fly fisher? In an encyclopedia you'd have to sift through much information to get to the facts you want. In an interview your questions could be answered directly as you asked them. An interview with an expert can often provide you with exactly the right amount of information on exactly the right topic.

Whom to Interview

Who is an expert? An expert usually is someone who has very precise, in-depth, and up-to-date information. More importantly, the expert probably has first-hand knowledge about a topic. Look at the topics and the list of people in the chart. People like these might have interesting information you could use in an oral report.

People to Interview	
Topic	**Source**
Local government	mayor, city council member, governor, state legislator
Scuba diving	local diving expert or instructor, equipment shop owner
Automobile engines	auto mechanic, auto designer, school shop teacher
The circulatory system	doctor, nurse, medical student, science teacher
Portrait photography	fashion photographer, portrait studio photographer
Caring for infants	parent, day-care worker, nurse, pediatrician

When you have determined that interviewing an expert will add to your report, you must decide on the kind of interview you want to set up. If the person lives far from you, you might arrange a telephone or letter interview. If the subject is nearby, consider an in-person interview. Whichever form you choose, be sure to keep the following things in mind during the early contacts with your subject.

Setting Up the Interview

1. Make sure you clearly state who you are and why you are seeking the interview.

2. Tell the person if you have a deadline, but respect the fact that your interviewee may be very busy.

3. Ask the subject to suggest times for an interview.

4. Give the person the option of an in-person, written, or telephone interview. You can state your preference, but leave the decision to the subject of the interview.

Preparing to Interview

Before you meet with your subject, research your topic thoroughly. Try to learn all you can about the topic before the interview. This preparation will help you to think on your feet during the questioning. You will be able to ask more intelligent questions if you are familiar with the topic. You also will be able to take advantage of interesting information that your subject might reveal. If you know how a new fact fits into the whole picture, you'll be better able to use it or to discard it as irrelevant.

Also try to learn as much as you can about the person you will interview. If the person is a public figure or is in business, you might ask his or her secretary for biographical information. Or you might request it from the person before the interview. You should know about the person to whom you are talking. This information will help you formulate good questions. It also saves you the trouble of asking questions that can be answered in a biographical handout.

Before you conduct the interview, write out the questions you plan to ask. It helps if you have the general outline of the interview in your mind as well as on paper. Try to make your questions open-ended. Don't ask questions that have a yes or no answer. Instead, encourage your subject to talk freely. A *Why?* may bring out important and interesting information. Look at these questions you might ask a marathon runner:

1. How many marathons have you run? Where did you place?
2. How do you prepare for a marathon?
3. What is your weekly running schedule?
4. What types of terrain do you run on when you are in training?
5. What kind of special equipment do you wear?
6. What kind of diet do you eat?
7. What are the three most important aspects of your training?

Conducting the Interview

Your manner during an interview should be serious and respectful, but relaxed. You will put the person you are interviewing at ease if you appear comfortable and confident. This attitude will make the interview flow smoothly. It's much more pleasant to talk in a relaxed atmosphere.

Study the journalist's questions covered in the last lesson. Remember how you used them to evaluate how well a reporter covered a story? See how many *what, who, when, where, how,* and *why* questions you can use in your interview. You'll find that *how* and *why* questions are particularly good for probing deeply into a topic.

Sometimes a person being interviewed will get side-tracked onto something that really doesn't apply to your topic. In this case, it's your job to politely but firmly lead the discussion back to the topic at hand.

Talk as little as possible yourself. Your job as an interviewer is to ask questions clearly and briefly. Then listen to the response. If the interviewee mentions something interesting that you hadn't thought about, ask some follow-up questions. You might bring out an unexpected piece of information— something that might not have been revealed otherwise. That's when an interview can get exciting.

During the interview you have two jobs to perform. You need to keep track of the questions you've prepared, so you don't forget something important. At the same time, you need to listen carefully to what the person is telling you. Be open to new information you didn't think about and that may raise new questions. You can develop this "thinking on your feet" skill by following some tips.

Tips for Interviewing

1. State your topic and the general scope of the discussion you'd like to have. This will give the person you are interviewing an idea of the boundaries that can be expected during the questioning.

2. Look at the person you're interviewing. Nothing cuts the connection between reporter and subject more quickly than the loss of eye contact. If you're conducting a telephone interview, comment briefly after each point the subject makes.

3. Be courteous at all times, even if your subject wanders away from the topic.

4. If you are unclear about anything the person says, ask a question right away. Then you can build on information you understand.

5. Follow up interesting statements quickly by asking another question. Don't wait, or you might forget the importance of the statement.

6. Take notes. At the end of the interview, glance over them. If something is unclear, ask a question.

7. Thank the person for the interview. Ask if you can call back if you have a follow-up question or if something is not clear. Review your notes thoroughly when you are alone. If you need to call the person back, do so as soon as you can.

Exercise 2

Work in pairs, and take turns playing the roles of expert and interviewer. Each interviewer should choose a topic. The interviewer's job is to ask good questions and to lead the expert back gently and politely if he or she wanders from the topic. Use one of the following topics or one of your own choosing:

- Why it's important to do well in mathematics
- How to have a great vacation in your own back yard
- The most important person in your life

26.3 Informal Speech

Someone stops you on the street and asks directions to the nearest grocery store. You talk with your friends on the way to school. You respond to a question the teacher asks in class. All of these situations call for informal speech. They are spontaneous and unrehearsed. They are among the most common speech situations.

There are other kinds of informal speech—discussions and announcements, for example. Four types of informal speech are included on the chart below. The chart describes each type and includes some hints that will help you be an effective participant in that type of speaking.

Tips on Informal Speaking		
Type	**Description**	**Hint**
Conversations	Conversations can occur at almost any time and in almost any place. Each person involved contributes and responds to the others.	Be courteous to the person speaking. Taking turns enables everyone to air his or her thoughts.
Discussions	Discussions can occur in many settings, including classrooms. Usually one person leads the discussion, and all are asked to share their thoughts in an orderly manner.	Stick closely to the topic and follow the directions of the discussion leader. Following these rules will ensure an interesting and productive discussion.
Announcements	Announcements summarize the most important information about an activity or event.	List the information you want to include before you make your announcement. Double-check it for accuracy and completeness.
Demonstrations	Demonstrations explain and show a process—how something works, for example. They are useful in many settings, including classrooms.	Number the steps in the process you will demonstrate to make sure the sequence is clear.

The purpose of all speech should be to communicate clearly. To take part in a discussion, you must be prepared and familiar with the topic the group is going to discuss. For example, to answer a question, you must have the information being asked for. In a conversation, on the other hand, you do not need to prepare in advance. You may cover many topics. Your answer to a question may very well be, "I don't know."

Another factor is attitude. Which of the following words describes how you feel when you talk to friends, family, and teachers?

> shy   enthusiastic   confident   eager   uninterested

Once you've identified your attitude, you can build on your strengths. You can change whatever gets in the way of good communication. It may take practice, but it will benefit you in the end.

Making Introductions

Everyone is a newcomer at one time or another. Entering into a new situation is much easier if someone in the group knows how to make correct introductions. With practice, that someone can be you.

Keep the following points in mind when introducing two people: First, be sure you look at each person. Don't let either party feel left out. You may be introducing one person to a group of people. In this case, make eye contact with the new person and with members of the group. Also, gesture from one person to another as you make the introduction. This will help point out which person you are referring to.

State each person's full name. You might say, "Evan, I'd like to introduce you to Miguel Hernandez. Miguel, this is Evan Schmit." If there are several people in the group, you might mention first names only for people your own age. First and last names are more appropriate when introducing adults. First and last names are also best used when introducing an adult and a younger person.

Tell each person something interesting about the other. If they have something in common, share that. It will become a natural conversation starter.

Participating in a Discussion

Rules of the game exist for discussions as well. A discussion usually has a leader, whose job it is to guide the discussion and keep it on track. The leader may be appointed for the group or chosen by the group. Sometimes a group member just takes over as leader.

As a discussion becomes lively and members of the discussion group get excited about what they are saying, the discussion becomes more difficult to organize. For this reason, it's important that you help the leader by managing your own comments. Be sure they contribute to the topic.

Discussions can focus on any topic. The idea is to come together in an organized group to share ideas and draw conclusions about the subject. A discussion depends totally on the comments of those involved. Before you enter a discussion, have a thorough knowledge of your subject. That way you can be a valuable participant. The following chart has a few more tips about how to act responsibly in a discussion.

Tips for Taking Part in a Discussion

1. Come prepared. Review important information, and bring visual aids or research you can use to illustrate the points you want to make.

2. Be polite. Take turns speaking and listening. You're there to learn as well as to contribute.

3. Go into the discussion willing to modify your opinion. That's the best way to learn.

4. Let the discussion leader take the lead. Concentrate on your part in the discussion—expressing yourself and listening to others.

5. Make your comments brief and concise. People will pay attention to your ideas if they are well thought out and clearly presented.

6. When you state your opinions, back them up with reasons or examples. You'll be much more convincing if you do this.

7. If a member of the group says something you don't understand, ask about it. It's likely that you aren't the only one confused.

Explaining a Process

If you want to explain how to bake a cake, you must do several things. First, you should tell the type of cake the recipe is for. Next, you need to list the ingredients. Then you'll explain the steps to follow.

An explanation of almost any process has the same parts: materials needed, steps to follow, and the result. If the process is long or complicated, you may need to number the steps. Or you might simply use words such as *before, next,* and *finally* to make the sequence of steps clear.

Correct order is all-important. For example, if the steps for building a model airplane are out of sequence, the plane may be incorrectly assembled. To be sure you don't leave out a part of the process, take time to prepare well. Write your explanation in the proper order. Review your instructions to make sure you haven't left out a step or put one in the wrong place.

Making Announcements

When you're asked to make an announcement, think first about what information your listeners need. If you're planning an announcement for an activity, the important facts include the date, the time, the place, and the price of a ticket.

Next, try to determine the briefest way to deliver your information. Announcements should always be short and to-the-point. They are no-fuss pieces of information. You'll want to include just enough information to interest the audience and convey the important facts.

Below are two examples of how the same information might be conveyed. Which is the better announcement?

Example 1

Tryouts for cheerleaders are coming soon. Get in shape now! Don't miss this once-in-a-school-year opportunity!

Example 2

Tryouts for cheerleaders will be this Wednesday afternoon in the gym right after school. Wear loose clothing and plan to stay a few hours. No need to sign up—just show up Wednesday for this once-in-a-school-year opportunity!

Finally, don't forget your audience! Speak so everyone can understand you. That means you must think about who is listening. You might word an announcement one way for preschoolers and another way for their parents.

Exercise 3

Divide into small groups. Let each member of the group select one of the events listed below. Jot down information about the event, including the date, time, and place. Fold the papers and mix them together. Each group member will select a topic at random, then write a short announcement based on the information on the paper. If you need additional pieces of information, invent them. Read your announcements to the group. Discuss how helpful and effective each announcement is.

- Band tryouts
- Countries of the World Festival
- Square-dancing lessons
- Debate Club meeting

26.4 Oral Reports

What image comes to mind when you think about giving an oral report? For some students the image might be exciting; for others, a little scary. However you feel, you can make the experience more enjoyable by preparing well.

You can prepare to give an oral report in three ways. First, you must prepare the content of your report. Make sure you understand everything you will be saying about your topic. Second, you need to prepare your presentation. Practice is the key here. Finally, you need to prepare yourself mentally so that you feel good about your presentation.

Preparing the Report

Think for a few moments about the purpose of your report. Is it to inform, persuade, explain, narrate, or entertain? Perhaps you have more than one purpose. An oral report can inform, persuade, and entertain, but one purpose should be the main one.

Another important consideration is your audience. To whom will you be speaking? Students your own age? Younger people? Older people? A mixed audience? What is the best way to reach your particular audience?

When you've thought about your purpose and audience, think a little further about your topic. Is it sufficiently narrowed down? If not, can you narrow it further? A precisely defined topic is easier to research than one that is unfocused. It is also easier to write about.

Now begin your research. Read articles in newspapers, magazines, encyclopedias, and other sources. You may also want to interview an expert in the field. Take notes. Develop an outline. Check the relationship of your main ideas and supporting details.

When you feel comfortable with the amount of information you've gathered, prepare your notes for the report. You may want to write out the entire report as you'd like to deliver it. Or you may write the key ideas and phrases on note cards. You might want to note the transitions you'll use to get from one main idea to the next. The transitions will jog your memory as you speak and help you move through your report smoothly.

Practicing the Report

Practicing your report is important. Practice will help you understand and remember your main ideas and supporting details. In addition, practice will give you confidence about your presentation. You will know how you want to speak the words, make the gestures, and display any visual materials you've decided to use.

Begin practicing alone. Speak in front of a mirror. Use the voice and gestures you would use if you were in front of a live audience. Time your report as you practice so that you can adjust the length if necessary.

The more you practice, the more natural the report will sound. Practice glancing from your note cards to the audience. You don't want to read your report word for word, but you'll probably want to memorize parts of it.

When you feel comfortable with your report, ask a friend or family member to listen to your delivery. Then try giving it before more than one person.

Ask your practice audience to listen *and* watch you. You'll want feedback about both the content of the report and your presentation. If the audience thinks the content or delivery needs work, make the changes you think are necessary. Then begin your practice sessions over again. If you need work on the delivery of your report, try using the following tips.

Tips on Delivering an Oral Report

1. Make eye contact with the audience. This helps people feel involved in what you are saying.

2. Use your voice to emphasize main points. You can raise or lower it, depending upon the effect you want to achieve.

3. Stop a moment after you've made an important point. This stresses the point and allows people to think about what you've said.

4. Use gestures if you've practiced them.

5. If they relate to your topic, use visual aids to help your audience understand your ideas.

Presenting the Report

When it's time to deliver your report, relax. (You'll find some tips for relaxing on page 679.) Deliver your report just as you've practiced it. Speak in a clear, natural voice, and use gestures when they are appropriate.

As you speak, show that you find your information interesting. Be enthusiastic. Think of your audience as people who are there because they're interested in what you have to say. Speak to them as if they were friends. They'll respond to your positive attitude.

When you conclude your report, ask for questions. Remain in front of the audience until you have answered everyone's questions.

Exercise 4

Select a topic from the following list, or use one of your own choosing. Write how you would narrow the topic. Then write your ideas for researching it.

Share the ideas you've developed with a partner. Ask for comments and suggestions. Then look at your partner's work, and make constructive comments about how he or she narrowed the topic and planned to research it.

- The migration of the monarch butterfly
- How our Constitution provides for the election of a president
- How to navigate by compass
- *Kente* cloth from Ghana

26.5   Formal Speeches

Delivering a formal speech in front of a live audience is the last stage of a five-stage process. You can think of it as the reward for successfully completing the earlier steps in the process. Once you've prepared thoroughly, delivering the speech can be fun and rewarding.

Preparing a Speech

You are familiar with the stages of writing a report: prewriting, drafting, revising, editing, and presenting. Formal speaking depends on a similar five-stage process. In preparing a speech, however, the editing stage becomes practicing. In effect, you edit your speech as you practice giving it. You are preparing for an audience of listeners rather than of readers.

Each step builds on the work done in the previous step. However, you may find it necessary to move back and forth during the drafting, revising, and practicing stages. For example, you might find during the practicing stage that your speech is too short or too long. To shorten it, you can back up to the revising stage or even the drafting stage to prepare a shorter version. The chart shows the process in detail.

Before you move to the practicing stage you'll want to have a speech you feel confident about. Word it in a way that will be easy to deliver.

Prewrite
- Define and narrow your topic.
- Remember your purpose and your audience.
- Complete your research.

Draft
- Make an outline, using main ideas and supporting details.
- Write your speech, or jot down the main points on note cards.

Revise
- Make sure your ideas are in order.
- Mark transitions on cards.
- Change wording until it is the way you want it.

Practice
- Give the speech in front of a mirror.
- Time your speech.
- Deliver it to a practice audience.
- Use the suggestions you receive.

Present
- Relax, and deliver your speech just as you've practiced it.

You don't want words you'll stumble over or phrases that sound awkward. If you aren't sure how to pronounce a term, look it up. If you still aren't comfortable with it, find another term that means the same thing.

Practicing a Speech

Practicing also involves several steps. When you practice your speech out loud, you want to make sure it sounds natural. The first time you practice it, just listen to the words as you speak. Listening to yourself on a tape recorder can be helpful, The rhythm of the speech should feel comfortable to you. If you don't like a phrase, rework it out loud until you come up with another way to express the idea.

The next time through, try looking in a mirror and using a few hand gestures to emphasize main points. Don't force the gestures. Try to think about what you're saying, and let your gestures develop spontaneously. Once you see where you need emphasis, make a point of practicing the gestures while speaking until they feel comfortable to you.

Finally, ask friends or relatives to listen to your delivery. Use their responses to fine-tune your speech. Below are a few more tips for practicing your speech.

Tips for Practicing a Speech

1. Each time you deliver your speech in practice, act just as if you were giving it before a live audience. Try to imagine the audience in front of you. This will help cut down on nervousness when you actually present the speech before a real audience.

2. Practice making eye contact with your imaginary audience. Let your eyes sweep slowly across the room from one side to the other, making contact with each member of the audience. Focus on talking to them, rather than on practicing your speech.

3. Make sure your gestures feel comfortable and fit with the points in the speech. Emphasize main points, or direct attention to visual aids, using gestures that are natural to you.

Delivering a Speech

Formal speaking is like conversation. Although you are the only one talking, your audience is communicating with you. Your success depends in part on how well you can interpret and use the signals they are sending you.

Keep your mind on your speech, and read the audience's response at the same time. A good speaker does both. The best speakers add a third element: They can change what they're doing to accommodate the needs of the audience.

Tips for Relaxing

1. Take a few deep, slow breaths before you begin speaking. When you pause at important points in your speech, you can repeat the process to keep yourself relaxed.

2. When you deliver your speech, talk to people in the audience as individuals rather than to the group as a whole. This will help personalize your message and make you feel comfortable. Some speakers like to pick out and concentrate on a few friendly faces in the audience.

3. Speak in a tone that is normal for you. Speak loudly enough to be heard throughout the room, but don't shout.

4. Let your voice rise and fall naturally at key points in your speech. The idea is to sound comfortable and natural.

5. Keep alert. Don't let your thoughts wander. Focus on the content of your speech and on sharing it with your audience.

Focusing on the audience can help you feel less nervous. The charts on this page can give you some help. The one above contains some tips for relaxing. The chart below offers some suggestions for communicating with your audience.

Communicating with Your Audience

Audience Signals	Speaker Response
People are yawning, stretching, or moving restlessly. They seem not to be paying attention to you.	You may have lost the attention of your audience. Try adding some enthusiasm to what you are saying.
People look confused or seem to want to ask a question.	You may have confused your audience. Try asking if there are questions or if what you've said is clear to them.
People are sitting forward in their chairs, trying to hear you.	People may be having trouble hearing you. Speak more loudly, and note whether or not that eliminates this audience response.
People look pleased with what you are saying. They nod in agreement.	You are doing a great job. Finish your speech in the same manner.

Exercise 5

With a small group, brainstorm ways to become better listeners. Work together to create a list of common listening problems. Then agree on one or two hours of television or radio programming that all of you will watch or listen to in the next few days. Include drama, news, music, comedy, talk shows, and other types of programming.

Listen to the television or radio programs your group selected for you. After each program write comments telling why you found the listening easy or difficult. When you meet again as a group, compare notes, and discuss kinds of programming that are easy to listen to and those that are more challenging. Discuss distractions and ways to listen more carefully to programming with which you had difficulties.

Exercise 6

1. Prepare a two-minute speech on a topic of your choice. Go through each of the steps outlined in this lesson. Then break into small groups, and take turns delivering your speeches within the groups. Discuss each speech. Share ideas you can all use to improve the presentation and content of your speeches. Then make revisions, and deliver the revised speeches to the class.
2. Exchange copies of speeches with someone in your group. If you have notes instead of a complete written speech, exchange the note cards. Try to develop a speech, and practice delivering it. Alter the speech to suit your manner of speaking, but keep the content the same. Join your group, and take turns delivering your new speeches. Discuss how and why they differ from the originals.

Index

Acknowledgments *(continued from page iv)*

Text

Cover: © 1993 ARS, New York/Bild-Kunst, Bonn **4** From the book *The Lost Garden* by Laurence Yep. Copyright © 1991. Used by permission of the publisher, Julian Messner/A division of Silver Burdett Press, Inc. Simon & Schuster, Englewood Cliffs, NJ. **12** Reprinted with the permission of Four Winds Press, an Imprint of Macmillan Publishing Company from *Louisa May: The World and Works of Louisa May Alcott* by Norma Johnston. Copyright © 1991 by Dryden Harris St. John, Inc. **20** Excerpt from *Letters Home by Sylvia Plath* edited by Aurelia Schober Plath. Copyright © 1975 by Aurelia Schober Plath. Reprinted by permission of HarperCollins Publishers. **22** From *The Heart of a Woman* by Maya Angelou. Copyright © 1981 by Maya Angelou. Published by Random House, Inc. **24** Reprinted with permission from *Stone Soup, the magazine by children*, copyright © 1992 (1990 for "The Shellster") by the Children's Art Foundation. **26** "The Clouds Pass" by Richard Garcia. Copyright © 1975 by Richard Garcia. **29** "Jukebox Showdown" by Victor Hernandez Cruz. Copyright © 1976 by Victor Hernandez Cruz. Reprinted by permission. **30** From *Living Up the Street: Narrative Reflections* by Gary Soto. Copyright © 1985 by Gary Soto. Published by Dell Publishing, a division of Bantam, Doubleday Dell Publishing Group, Inc. **50** From *A Writer Teaches Writing: A Practical Method of Teaching Composition* by Donald M. Murray. Copyright © 1968 by Donald M. Murray. Published by Houghton Mifflin Company. **53** The following article is reprinted courtesy of *Sports Illustrated* from the June 12, 1989 issue. Copyright © 1989, Time Inc. "Tigers Burning Bright" by Merrell Noden. All Rights Reserved. **53** The following article is reprinted courtesy of *Sports Illustrated for Kids* from the March, 1991 issue. Copyright © 1991, Time Inc. "Fly, Hollis, Fly!" **54** Reprinted by permission of *Cricket* Magazine, August 1987 Vol. 14, No. 12, © 1987 by Carus Corporation. **73** © 1989. *The Washington Post*. Reprinted with permission. **78** From *Barrio Boy* by Ernesto Galarza. © 1971 by University of Notre Dame Press. Reprinted by permission. **88** "The Game" from *Fast Sam, Cool Clyde, and Stuff* by Walter Dean Myers. Copyright © 1975 by Walter Dean Myers. Published by Viking Penguin, a division of the Penguin Group. **100** From *How the Garcia Girls Lost Their Accents* by Julia Alvarez. Copyright © 1991 by Julia Alvarez. Published by the Penguin Group. **106** From "On Summer" by Lorraine Hansberry. Copyright © 1960 by Robert Nemiroff. All rights reserved. Reprinted by permission of Robert Nemiroff. **107** From *In Nueva York* by Nicholasa Mohr. Copyright © 1977 by Nicholasa Mohr. Published by The Dial Press. **108** From *Merlyn's Pen: The National Magazine of Student Writing*, February/March, 1990. Copyright © 1991. Published by Merlyn's Pen, Inc. **111** Text excerpt from *A Girl From Yamhill* by Beverly Cleary. Copyright © 1988 by Beverly Cleary. By permission of Morrow Junior Books, a division of William Morrow & Co., Inc. **119** From "The Street of the Canon" in *Mexican Village*, by Josephina Niggli. Copyright © 1945 by The University of North Carolina Press. Reprinted by permission of the publisher. **122** From "Teddy" by Amanda Morgan from *Treasures: Stories & Art by Students in Oregon* collected by Chris Weber. Copyright © 1985 by Chris Weber. Published by Oregon Students Writing and Art Foundation. **124** From "Private Property" by Leslie Marmon Silko. Published by Wylie, Aitken & Stone, Inc. Reprinted by permission. **126** Reprinted by permission of Chelsea House Publishers, a division of Main Line Book Co. **130** From *Small Faces* by Gary Soto. Copyright © 1986 by Gary Soto. Published by Arte Publico Press. **149** From *Sojourner Truth: A Self-Made Woman* by Victoria Ortiz. Copyright © 1974 by Victoria Ortiz. Published by J.B. Lippincott Company. **153** From *Homesick* by Jean Fritz. Copyright © 1982 by Jean Fritz. Published by Dell Publishing Company, Inc. **158** From "Revolutionary Tea" from *I Hear America Singing: Great Folk Songs From the Revolution to Rock* by Hazel Arnett. Copyright © 1975 by Hazel Arnett. Published by Praeger Publishers, Inc. **161** From *So Far From the Bamboo Grove* by Yoko Kawashima Watkins. Copyright © 1986 by Yoko Kawashima Watkins. Published by William Morrow & Co. **168** From "Collaborating on Computers" by Theresa A. Martin from *The Boston Sunday Globe*, July 19, 1992. Copyright © 1992. Published by The Globe Newspaper Co. **169** From "A Summer Search" by Mark Ferenchik from *The Repository*. Copyright © 1992. Published by The Repository. **169** From "Runaway Chimp Finds Unwilling Playmate" from *Chicago Tribune,* Wednesday, August 26, 1992, Section 1, Page 3. Copyright © 1992 by National News Service. Published by *Chicago Tribune*. **169** From "Florida Braces for Hurricane Andrew" *Daily Herald*, DuPage County Edition, Monday, August 24, 1992. Copyright © 1992 by Associated Press. Published by *Daily Herald*. **170** From "Best Hopes for the Gold" by Bud Greenspan from *Parade*, July 26, 1992. Copyright © 1992. Published by Parade Publications, Inc. **172** From *Anne Frank: Diary of a Young Girl* by Anne Frank. Copyright © 1952 by Otto H. Frank. Published by Simon & Schuster, Inc. **176** From *Lyddie* by Katherine Paterson. Copyright © 1991 by Katherine Paterson. Published by Lodestar Books. **190** From *Indian America: A Traveler's Companion* by Eagle/Walking Turtle. Copyright © 1989 by Gary McLain. Published by John Muir Publications. **196** Reprinted by permission of Chelsea House Publishers, a division of Main Line Book Co. **200** From *The Minicomputer Simplified: An Executive's Guide to the Basics* by Carol W. Brown. Copyright © 1980 by Carol W. Brown. Reprinted with the permission of The Free Press, A Division of Macmillan, Inc. **206** From "Yo-Yo and Manny" by Michael Shapiro from *World Monitor The Christian Science Monitor Monthly*. Copyright © 1991 by Michael Shapiro. Published by The Christian Science Publishing Society. **209** From *Foods of the World: Latin American Cooking* by Jonathan Norton Leonard and the Editors of Time-Life Books. © 1969 Time-Life Books, Inc. **212** From *Let There Be Light: A Book About Windows* by James Cross Giblin. Copyright © 1988 by James Cross Giblin. Published by Thomas Y. Crowell, HarperCollins Publishers. **236** "Fall" by Sally Andresen from *A New*

Treasury of Children's Poetry: Old Favorites and New Discoveries edited by Joanna Cole. Copyright © 1984 by Joanna Cole. Published by Doubleday & Company. **236** "Something Told the Wild Geese" by Rachel Field from *Reflections on a Gift of Watermelon Pickle . . . And Other Modern Verse* compiled by Stephen Dunning, Edward Lueders and Hugh Smith. Copyright © 1967. Published by Scott, Foresman, and Company. **240** "The Vision of Maya Ying Lin" from *Always to Remember* by Brent Ashabranner. Copyright © 1988. Published by Putnam, Berkley Gorup. **261** "Progress or Plunder " by April Barnes from *Merlyn's Pen: The National Magazine of Student Writing*, Vol. 4, No. 1, October/November 1988. Copyright © 1991. Published by Merlyn's Pen, Inc. **262** From "Save the Prairie Path" by Patrick MacRoy. First appeared in *Call of the Wildcat*, April, 1991. **265** From "Should Animals Be Held In Captivity" by Jacqueline Parks. Copyright © 1992 by Jacqueline Parks. **266** From *What to Do When Your Mom or Dad Says . . . "Don't Overdo with Video Games!"* by Joy Wilt Berry. Copyright © 1983 by Joy Wilt Berry. Published by Children's Press. **266** From *The Second Self: Computers and the Human Spirit* by Sherry Turkle. Copyright © 1984 by Sherry Turkle. Published by Simon & Schuster. **270** From *Jane Brody's Nutrition Book: A Lifetime Guide to Good Eating for Better Health and Weight Control by the Personal Health Columnist of The New York Times* by Jane E. Brody. Copyright © 1981 by Jane E. Brody. Published by W. W. Norton & Company. **273** From "Plastic Bags, Cars and Kids" by Dina Morrison from *Merlyn's Pen: The National Magazine of Student Writing*, Vol. 2, No. 3, February/March, 1987. Copyright © 1987. Published by Merlyn's Pen. **278** From "I'm Outta Here" by David Levine from *Seventeen*, March 1992. Copyright © 1992 by *Seventeen*/David Levine. Published by *Seventeen*. **280** Reprinted by permission of Brookfield Zoo. **285** From *Sports Illustrated for Kids*, September, 1990. Copyright © 1990. Published by Time, Inc. Reprinted by permission of Philip Trevino. **285** From *Sports Illustrated for Kids*, September, 1990. Copyright © 1990. Published by Time, Inc. **286** From "North by Northwest" by Kelinda Peaples from *St. Louis Magazine*, June 1, 1992. Copyright © 1992. Published by St. Louis Magazine. **288** From *The Ways of My Grandmothers* by Beverly Hungry Wolf. Copyright © 1980 by Beverly Hungry Wolf. Published by William Morrow & Company. **290** Reprinted with permission from *Stone Soup, the magazine by children*, copyright © 1992 (1990 for "The Shellster") by the Children's Art Foundation. **292** From *Silent Spring* by Rachel Carson. Copyright © 1978. Published by Houghton Mifflin Company. **338** From *Growing Up* by Russell Baker. Copyright © 1982 by Russell Baker. Published by Congdon & Weed, Inc. **448** From *Morning Girl* by Michael Dorris. Copyright © 1992 by Michael Dorris. Published by Hyperion Books for Children. **558** From *A Small Place* by Jamaica Kincaid. Copyright © 1988 by Jamaica Kincaid. Published by Farrar, Straus, and Giroux. **586** By Permission. From *Webster's New Biographical Dictionary* © 1988 by Merriam-Webster, Inc., publisher of the Merriam-Webster (R) dictionaries. **587** *Readers' Guide to Periodical Literature,* May 1992, Volume 92, No, 5, pages 33 and 83. Copyright © 1992 by the H.W. Wilson Company. Material reproduced with permission of the publisher.

591 "Words" from *Collected Poems* by Edward Thomas. Copyright © 1974 by Edward Thomas. Published by W. W. Norton & Co., Inc. **593** From *Dictionary*. Copyright © 1977. Published by Macmillan Publishing Company. **595** From *Roget's II: The New Thesaurus*. Copyright © 1984 by Houghton Mifflin Company. Published by Berkley Books by arrangement with Houghton Mifflin Company.

Photos

Cover: © 1993 ARS, New York/Bild-Kunst, Bonn. Photo by Sharon Hoogstraten **3** Felix Klee Collection, Berne. **4** Laurence Yep. **5** Allan Landau. **6** Laurence Yep(l); Allan Landau(r). **7** Laurence Yep. **8** Allan Landau. **9** Allan Landau. **10** Allan Landau. **11** David Madison 1991. **12** Allan Landau. **13** Copyright by Leonard Von Matt, photographer, Buochs Switzerland. **14-15** Allan Landau. **18** Art Wise. **20** Art Wise. **21** Edward Owen/Art Resource 1977. **22** UPI/Bettmann (t); UPI/Bettmann (b). **25** Courtesy Bernice Steinbaum Gallery, NYC. **26** Courtesy of Ray Vinella. **28** Allan Landau. **31** Courtesy of Susan Moore. **33** Courtesy of the artist. **35** Art Wise (t)(b). **36** ©Tony Freeman/PhotoEdit. **39** ©Tony Freeman/PhotoEdit. **42** Courtesy Kurtis Productions Ltd. **43** Courtesy Kurtis Productions Ltd.(t)(b). **44** Allan Landau(t); Courtesy Kurtis Productions Ltd.(b). **45** Allan Landau. **46** Courtesy Kurtis Productions Ltd. **47** Allan Landau. **48** Art Wise. **51** Courtesy of Claes Oldenburg Studio(l)(r). **52** Art Wise. **55** Collection of The Grand Rapids Art Museum Gift of Mrs. Cyrus E. Perkins, 1911.1.4. **56** Art Wise. **58** Art Wise. **60** Art Wise. **64** © Jeff Dunn/Stock, Boston. **66** ©Larry Kolvoord/The Image Works. **67** Located in San Francisco at the Pacific Stock Exchange. Dirk Bakker, Photographer. **68** Art Wise. **71** Private Collection. **72** ©Barbara Alper/Stock, Boston(l); © Charle Fell/Stock, Boston(r). **75** The Jamison Galleries, Sante Fe, New Mexico. **76-7** Art Wise. **80** Art Wise. **82** The Far Side cartoon by Gary Larson is reprinted by permission of Chronicle Features, San Francisco, CA. **84** Art Wise. **86** Art Wise. **90** © 1992 Red Grooms/ARS, New York. **93** Art Wise(t)(b). **94** Tom McCarthy/PhotoEdit. **97** Glennon Donahue/Tony Stone Worldwide. **99** © 1992 ARS, New York/ADAGP, Paris; **100** Tad Merrick. **101** © 1992 Martha Cooper/Peter Arnold, Inc. **102** Ralph Brunke. **103** Ralph Brunke. **104** Ralph Brunke. **105** ©Joe Sohm/Chromosohm/The Image Works. **106** ©Larry Kolvoord/The Image Works. **107** Robert Frerck/Odyssey Productions/Chicago. **109** Courtesy American Federation of The Arts. **110** The Saint Louis Art Museum Museum Purchase. **111** Allen Landau. **114** Allan Landau. **115** Cindy Brodie(c); Alex Murdoch(r). **118** © Erich Lessing/Art Resource, NY. **121** Courtesy Nancy Hoffman Gallery. **122** Allan Landau. **126** UPI/Bettmann. **128** Princeton University Library. **129** Courtesy of Frumkin/Adams Gallery, New York. **131** From "Thrashin' Time: Harvest Days in the Dakotas" by David Weitzman © 1991 by David Weitzman. Reprinted by permission of David R. Godine, Publisher, Inc. **133** The Metropolitan Museum of Art, George A. Hearn Fund, 1943 (43.159.1). **135** Art Wise(t)(b). **136** Bob Daemmrich/The Image Works. **139** Willie Hill, Jr./The Image Works. **141** Collection of Donald Kuspit, NYC. © VA Tech Media Services. **142** Tom Green. **144** Tom Green(l)(r); Culver

Pictures(c). **145** Tom Green. **146** Courtesy of The Colonial Williamsburg Foundation. **147** Culver Pictures. **148** Hampton University Museum. **149** The Bettmann Archive. **152** Art Wise. **156** "Rape of the Records" by Les Schrader/Naper Settlement Village Museum. **158** ©1979 Vernon Merritt/Black Star. **159** Focus on Sports. **161** Robert Miller Gallery, New York. **162** Courtesy of the artist. **163** Courtesy June Kelly Gallery, New York. Photo: Manu Sassoonian. **164** Giraudon/Art Resource, NY. **166** Statute of Liberty National Monument, National Park Service. **167** Private Colllection/Laura Platt Winfrey, Inc. **168** Neal Hamburg. **170** Focus on Sports. **172** UPI/Bettmann(t); ©Joe Viesti/Viesti Associates(b). **174** David Young-Wolff/PhotoEdit. **175** Archivo fotográfico, Museo Nacional Centro de Arte Reina Sofia. **177** Erich Lessing/Art Resource, NY. **179** Manchester City Art Galleries. **180** Phillip Evergood. "Lily and the Sparrows" 1939. oil on composition board. 30 x 24 inches. (76.2 cm x 61 cm). Collection of Whitney Museum of American Art. Purchase 41.42. **183** Art Wise(t)(b). **184** Tom Prettyman/PhotoEdit. **187** ©Bob Daemmrich/The Image Works. **189** "Artist and Assistants," Ernie Pepion, 1990, pastel, 22 1/4 x 30 3/16 inches, collection of the artist. Photograph © Courtney Frisse, ©1991 University Art Museum, University at Albany. **190** Courtesy Gary McLain. **191** © 1991 Greg Probst/Allstock. **192-3** Art Wise. **193** Stephen Trimble(l); Courtesy Cherokee Historical Association(r). **194** Allan Landau. **195** David Young-Wolf/PhotoEdit. **196** ©Clark Mishler/Alaska Stock Images. **200** Art Wise. **201** ©Charles Feil/Stock, Boston. **202** The Bettman Archive. **204** Art Wise. **207** The Museum of Fine Arts, Houston; museum purchase with funds provided by Panhandle Eastern Corporation. **208** Art Wise. **210** ©Jon Elliott. **212** Edith G. Haun/Stock, Boston. **213** Culver Pictures. **215** © David Hockney Ref: 67A34. **216-8** ©J. Pickerell/The Image Works. **219** Shelburne Museum, Shelburne, Vermont, Photograph by Ken Burris. **220** William Lishman and Associates. **223** Field Museum of Natural History (Neg# MFA CAT#94902), Chicago. **224** Art Wise. **225** Art Wise. **228** Calvin and Hobbes ©1990 Watterson. Reprinted with permission of Universal Press Syndicate. All rights reserved. **232** Sharon Hoogstraten. **236** © 1992 Roger and Donna Aitkenhead/Animals Animals(t); ©Jack Wilburn/Animals Animals(b). **239** Courtesy Holly Solomon Gallery, New York. **241** Bill Barley/Super Stock, Inc. **245** ©David M. Doody/Uniphoto. **247** Art Wise(t)(b). **248** ©Holt Confer/The Image Works. **251** Tom Wurl/Stock, Boston. **253** ©"John Ahearn, Back to School," 1986 Courtesy: Brooke Alexander Gallery, New York. **254** Art Wise. **255** Courtesy Indira Freitas Johnson. **256** Ralph Brunke. **256,258** Courtesy Indira Freitas Johnson. **257** Courtesy of Indira Freitas Johnson(tc); Ralph Brunke(b). **258** Courtesy Indira Freitas Johnson. **259** Cathlyn Melloan/Tony Stone Worldwide. **260** Historical Pictures/Stock Montage, Inc. **262** ©David Young-Wolf/PhotoEdit. **263** Courtesy Bernice Steinbaum Gallery, NYC. **264** ©Leonard Lee Rue III/Stock, Boston(l); ©Herb Snitzer/Stock, Boston(r). **267** Private Collection. **269** David Young-Wolf/PhotoEdit. **270** Art Wise. **272** Calvin and Hobbes ©1986 Waterson. Reprinted with permission of United Press Syndicate. All rights reserved. **273** Art Wise. **276** ©1992 R. Fukuhara/Westlight. **280** Courtesy Brookfield Zoo. **282** Art Wise. **283** © Faith Ringgold. **284** Art Wise. **285** © Mitchell B. Reibel/Sports Photo Masters, Inc.

286 Art Wise. **288** Art Wise. **290** Alain Le Garsmeur/Tony Stone Worldwide. **291** U.S. Department of The Interior Indian Arts and Crafts Board Southern Plains Indian Museum and Crafts Center. **293** Phyliss Kind Gallery, New York/Chicago. **295** Art Wise(t)(b). **296** Peter Menzel/Stock, Boston. **299** Dean Abramson/Stock, Boston. **325** Giraudon/Art Resource, NY. **326** Gift of W. G. Russell Allen. Courtesy, Museum of Fine Arts, Boston. ©1992. **339** Courtesy Hampton University Museum. **341** Courtesy Nancy Hoffman Gallery, New York. **352** Myrleen Ferguson/PhotoEdit. **359** Henri Matisse, La Negresse, Ailsa Mellon Bruce Fund, © 1992 National Gallery of Art, Washington, 1952. Collage on canvas/paper collage on canvas, 4.539 x 6.233 (178 3/4 x 245 1/2). **361** National Portrait Gallery, Smithsonian Institution, Washington, DC/Art Resource, NY. **362** ©Rhonda Sidney/Stock, Boston. **389** Phyliss Kind Gallery, New York/Chicago. **391** Scala/Art Resource, NY. **409** Phyllis Kind Gallery, Chicago. **411** Scala/Art Resource, NY © 1992 ARS, New York/SPADEM, Paris. **424** ©Dennis Stock/Magnum. **431** The Metropolitan Museum of Art, Fletcher Fund, Rogers Fund, and Bequest of Miss Adelaide Milton de Groot (1876-1967), by exchange, supplemented by gifts from friends of the Museum, 1971. (1971.86) Photograph by Malcolm Varon. **433** © 1992 ARS, New York/ADAGP, Paris. **444** Joan Messerschmidt/Leo de Wys Inc. **446** Julie Houck/TSW. **451** Courtesy of the artist and Deson Saunders Gallery, Chicago. **453** Museum of Art, Rhode Island School of Design; Jesse Metcalf and Walter H. Kimball funds. Photography by Cathy Carver. **459** Gregory Loading His Camera, Kyoto, February, 1983 Photographic Collage 21"x14" © David Hockney. **460** Focus on Sports. **469** National Museum of American Art, Washington D.C./Art Resource, NY. **471** Giraudon/Art Resource © 1992 ARS, New York/ADAGP, Paris. **481** Seattle Art Museum. Photo Credit: Paul Macapia. **483** Courtesy Texas Gallery. **488** Jon Riley/Tony Stone Worldwide(t); David Young-Wolff/PhotoEdit(b). **497** Phyliss Kind Gallery, New York/Chicago. **499** Albright-Knox Art Gallery, Buffalo, New York, Gift of Seymour H. Knox, 1969. **509** Giraudon/Art Resource, NY © 1992 ARS, New York/SPADEM, Paris. **511** Klee, Paul, Twittering Machine. 1922. Watercolor and pen and ink on oil transfer drawing on paper, mounted on cardboard, 25 1/4 x 19 inches. Collection, The Museum of Modern Art, New York. Purchase. **523** Courtesy of Nancy Shutt. **527** The Bettmann Archive. **535** Robert Henri, "Portrait of Po Tse (Water Eagle)" Oil on Canvas, 40 x 32 inches Photograph courtesy of the Gerald Peters Gallery, Santa Fe, New Mexico. **537** Winterthur, Kunstmuseum Winterthur. **549** Ralph Brunke. **561** Henri Matisse, French, 1869-1954, Interior at Nice, oil on canvas, 1921, 132.1 x 88.9 cm, Charles H. and Mary F. S. Worcester Collection, 1956.339. **575** Allan Landau. **576** © 1992 Cathy Ferris. **585** Allan Landau. **588** Allan Landau. **592** © 1992 Frank Oberle/Photo Resource. **597** © 1992 Frank Oberle/Photo Resource. **598** ©Bob Daemmrich/ Stock, Boston. **599** ©Richard Pasley/Stock, Boston. **608** Steve Bentsen/Natural Selection. **609** Lori Adamski Peek/Tony Stone Worldwide. **610** ©George Chan/Tony Stone Worldwide(t); Pete Seaward/Tony Stone Worldwide(b). **614** David Young-Wolf/PhotoEdit. **627** Ralph Brunke. **675** Billy E. Barnes/Stock, Boston. **678** Ralph Brunke(t); Ralph Brunke(c); Ralph Brunke(b).